Understanding Race and Ethnicity in Contemporary Society

A READER

SECOND EDITION

Edited by Clifford L. Broman
Michigan State University

 cognella® | ACADEMIC PUBLISHING

Bassim Hamadeh, CEO and Publisher
Kassie Graves, Director of Acquisitions and Sales
Jamie Giganti, Senior Managing Editor
Jess Estrella, Senior Graphic Designer
Natalie Lakosil, Licensing Manager
Kaela Martin, Associate Editor
Christian Berk, Associate Production Editor

Cover image copyright © Depositphotos/Rawpixel.

Printed in the United States of America

ISBN: 978-1-5165-1571-4 (pbk) / 978-1-5165-1572-1 (br)

Contents

Section IV: Key Issues in Racial and Ethnic Inequality

Introduction

There is inequality in the United States on the basis of race and ethnicity. This basic fact is disputed by some people and misunderstood. It is misunderstood for many reasons. One of these reasons is that it does not fit with the values of equality and opportunity taught to students in their high schools. When teaching classes that concern racial and ethnic inequality, students may resist this basic fact, as it may not fit the worldview that they bring to such a class. Therefore, instructors usually spend some class time convincing students of this basic fact. Another reason that this fact is disputed and misunderstood is that there has been very significant change and improvement in racial and ethnic inequality in the United States in the last fifty years. Before 1964, discrimination and segregation were entirely legal in the United States. This positive change, the change in laws, misleads some to believe that because laws have changed, other aspects of the system of racial and ethnic inequality have changed. The basic facts dispute this view, and a class on racial and ethnic inequality spends much time addressing these facts. At some point in a class, students raise the question of WHY there is racial and ethnic inequality in the United States, and how it came to be. This has been my experience teaching classes on racial and ethnic inequality.

This book, *Understanding Race and Ethnicity in Contemporary Society*, is designed to assist in answering such questions. Why is there racial and ethnic inequality? How did it come to exist? Why are the patterns of racial and ethnic inequality so persistent? And finally, what has to happen for things to change more than they have to this point? The book is proposed as a reader/anthology for a class on racial and ethnic groups, and to supplement a basic text on Racial and Ethnic Inequality. Throughout the book, we use a comparative, socio-historical perspective on race and ethnicity in America. There are several goals of the book. The overarching goal is to assist students in understanding how racial and ethnic relations in the US. developed as they are, and to know and understand the current status of the major racial and ethnic groups in the United States. The second goal is to aid students in understanding the ways in which diverse communities of racial and ethnic minorities became a part of the American racial and ethnic landscape. The third, and major goal, is to expose students to diverse and alternate ways of thinking about majority–minority relations in the contemporary United States.

SECTION I

Introductory Viewpoints

The readings in this section have two goals. The first is for you to consider the construction of what "race" and "ethnicity" mean. What do we think of when we think of "racial group?" Who is it we mean, and what is the basis for that belief? The second goal is to demonstrate the racial and ethnic inequality that exists in the United States. This is done through the use of census data, available from the U.S. Census Bureau at www.census.gov.

Race Is a Slippery Word

By Alain F. Corcos

Editor's Introduction

Corcos discusses the social construction of race. While we tend to view race as a biological construct, Corcos raises the key point that we do not define race through biology, but through social means.

The term "race" is one of the most frequently misused and misunderstood words in the American vernacular.

Peter I. Rose

Peter I. Rose[1] is indeed correct. Race, as applied *to* human beings, is vague and ambiguous. In common speech, it has a whole range of meanings. To focus on the issue, dictionaries offer little help. For example, the *American Heritage Dictionary of the English Language* gives numerous and contradictory definitions of the word "race":

1. A local geographic or global human population distinguished as a more or less distinct group by genetically transmitted physical characteristics.
2. Mankind as a whole [as in the human race].
3. Any group of people united or classified together on the basis of common history, nationality, or geographical distribution.

4. A genealogic line, lineage, family.
5. Any group of people more or less distinct from all others: the race of statesmen.
6. Biologically: (a) plant or animal population that differs from others of the same species in the frequency of hereditary traits: a subspecies; (b) or a breed or a strain of a domestic animal.
7. A distinguishing or characteristic quality, such as the flavor of wine.
8. Sprightliness, style.

These definitions are at variance with one another For instance, definitions 1 and 3 do not agree. One is a biological definition, the other a social definition. Definitions 2, 4, 5, 7 and 8 are taken from literary usage but have no validity in scientific or social science community. Definition 6 comes closest to the one used in this book. But, as we shall see later, much confusion about race has to do with how great the difference in the frequency of hereditary traits must be between two populations before we can label each of them a distinct race.

Race is a slippery word because it is a biological term, but we use it every day as a social term. In the mind of the public at large this leads to great confusion. Social, political, and religious views are added to what are seen as biological differences. All are seen as inheritable and unchangeable defining characteristics of one or another "race" of people.

However, most of the differences between groups are in fact cultural. People are of different national origin; they have different religions; they have different political views; and they speak different languages. These differences can be modified as shown by the fact that every day many of us change nationalities, religions, or political views. Most of us can learn language other than the one our parents taught us.

Race also has been equated with national origin. For example, writers and historians once spoke of the Roman or English races. However, no Roman race conquered much of the Mediterranean world, but rather people sharing Roman ideas of government, law, language, and military discipline. Among the Roman elites, there were many citizens who were not from the city of Rome or even from the Italian Peninsula, for that matter.

Similarly, there is a country called England, but there never was an English race. England was invaded by successive waves of peoples, many of whom differed from other invaders in physical appearance. Hence, no one can point to an English man or an English woman because, among the English, as among other Europeans, there are fair-skinned people, dark-skinned people, tall and short people, long-headed and round-headed people, people with long noses, people with broad noses.

Race also has been equated with religion. For instance, Jews are considered by many as belonging to a separate race. The history of the Jews is well known and reveals that originally they were nomadic people, a grouping of pastoral tribes the members of which spoke a Semitic language. They emigrated from the desert border of southern Mesopotamia to Palestine between the seventeenth and twelfth centuries BCE. On several occasions, they were expelled from the place they took as their homeland: a sojourn in Egypt terminated by the famous Exodus; the Babylonian captivity; the conquest by Rome. Thus, even before they were dispersed throughout the Roman Empire following the destruction of Jerusalem by Titus (70 AD), there were many occasions for breeding with other people of the Near East. Even if the Jews were originally a homogeneous group, which is unlikely, there has been extensive interbreeding with others from antiquity to the present day.

What Jews have preserved and transmitted is a rich body of religious and cultural traditions and modes of conduct. The only valid criterion for determining membership in the group is confessional (adherence to the Jewish faith). Jews are a religious body, not a separate biological human group.

Race has been equated with language, as in the case of "Aryan race." Historically, there was a common Indo-European language, called Aryan, from which Sanskrit, ancient Greek and Latin, and the majority of languages that are spoken today are derived. However, use of derivatives from that common root language does not mean that individuals speaking it look alike or hold similar religious beliefs. People do not speak Chinese, French, or English because of their biological inheritance but because their parents taught them the language, i.e., because of their cultural inheritance. In other words, whatever shape of mouth or vocal cords we have, we learn to speak the language that is spoken around us when we grow up. No matter what the color of our skin, shape of head, or the texture of our hair, we will acquire the language we hear in our homes or schools.

Though it is illogical to use religion, language, or nationality as a basis for inventing races, we continue to do so today. Many still regard Jews, Arabs, Mexicans, French, and Germans as being of different races. It may be more appropriate to consider some or all as ethnic groups, whose members share a common cultural background. Ethnicity is a social term. Race, on the other hand, is a biological term which can be used meaningfully only when applied to plants and animals, but never to human beings.

Even in biology, race is a slippery word. To understand why, we must understand how scientists use it and a related term, "species." Both race and species are used as categories for classification to reduce the vast array of diverse forms of animals and plants to manageable groupings for identification. However, there is a fundamental difference between what scientists mean when they identify a race and when they identify a species. Members of a species can breed with others of the same species but not with individuals belonging to different species. This gives the species a biological continuity and an exclusive membership. Species are real units in nature. Races, which are subdivisions of a species, differ from species in that their boundaries can never be fixed and definite because a member of one race can interbreed with members of an other race.[2] It is, therefore, a capital error to believe that races have the same biological reality as species have. A species is a natural grouping of organisms, while a race is an artificial one whose definition is very vague and has changed with time without becoming clearer or more useful. This is especially true when applied to humans.

Race has been defined anthropologically as

"... a great division of mankind, the members of which show similar or identical combinations of physical features which they owe to their common heredity."

(Seltzer 1939)[3]

or genetically as

"... a population which differs significantly from other human populations in regard to the frequency of one or more of the genes it possesses."[4]

The genetic definition seems at first more precise than the anthropological, because the frequency with which a gene occurs in a population can be calculated. However, it is important to realize that describing races on the basis of such frequency differences between populations presents a serious problem. For example, one wonders how great differences between two populations must be before they can be defined as distinct races. The frequency of a gene can run from 0 to 1, 0 meaning that a given gene is absent from a given population, 1 meaning that every member of the population has that particular gene. If the frequency of a particular gene was 1 in one population and 0 in another, we could argue that we have two distinct races. But in fact we have never been able to find such an example.

Both of the above definitions of a race, the anthropological and the genetic, are vague. They do not tell us how large divisions between populations must be in order to label them races, nor do they tell us how many there are. These things are, of course, all matters of choice for the classifier. It is no wonder that there was so much confusion among scientists when they attempted to classify humanity into distinct races.

Discussion Questions

1. What are some problems with trying to define race biologically?
2. What are the differences between genetic, anthropological, and sociological definitions of race?

Notes

1. Peter I. Rose, *They and We* (New York: Random House, 1964).
2. In a later chapter I will develop in detail the modern biological concepts of race and species. It will then become clear to the reader that, according to such concepts, there are no human races.
3. As quoted by Earl Count in *This is Race* (New York: Henry Schuman, 1950).
4. W. C. Boyd, *Genetics and the Races of Man* (Boston: Little, Brown and Company, 1950).

"One-Drop" to Rule Them All?

Colorism and the Spectrum of Racial Stratification in the Twenty-First Century

By Victor Ray

Editor's Introduction

This reading discusses the phenomenon known as "colorism." Colorism has a long tradition in Western countries where those people of lighter complexions are more favored in societies and receive more status and tangible benefits from their light complexion. Ray makes the important point that colorism operates both between and within racial groups.

The vast majority of empirical studies of racial stratification in sociology conceptualize different races as if they are internally undifferentiated social categories. In this mode of analysis, scholars use "race" as a categorical variable in a regression equation or as a qualitative unit of analysis. This implies that "race" has a similar inferred causal status for all members in a given racial classification (Zuberi 2001).* This style of sociological research tends to assume that races are distinct, "mutually exclusive" social categories, and usually shows that there are substantive and often profound differences in the life chances of Whites and people of color, mostly to the disadvantage of the latter. Much of this work has added greatly to our understanding of racialized social systems and how they divvy up the material and psychological benefits accruing to Whiteness (Mills 1997). However, an exclusive focus on differences *between* races may obscure how racism structures relations *within* minority communities (Collins 2005). As we progress into the 21st

---

* This logic is what allows researchers to claim that the "effect" of race has increased or declined in significance (Wilson 1978).

century, a central question is: in racialized social systems, do psychological and material benefits also accrue to lightness?

Race scholars have long pointed out that the internal differentiations among people of color may have effects just as profound as those between races. For instance, in his classic *Black Bourgeoisie* (1957), E. Franklin Frazier claimed that lighter-skinned Blacks formed the basis of the post-emancipation Black middle class, as they capitalized on privileges afforded them under slavery. Similarly, nearly all of W. E. B. Du Bois' famous "talented tenth" (1903) were of mixed race, a signal some scholars (not un-problematically)[†] have taken to mean they were lighter skinned (Russell et al. 1993). This process of social differentiation based on skin tone is known as colorism. Colorism operates *both* within and across races.[*] Colorism can also serve to clarify theories of racism. While racism is often erroneously perceived as an individual attribute of some Whites (Allport 1954), other scholars argue that racism is structural, implicating us all (Omi and Winant 1994). Colorism offers an alternative theoretical approach to describe how an oppressed minority can become complicit in the hegemony of Whiteness. Further, it confirms the theoretical postulate that most actors in a racialized social system contribute to the maintenance of that system (Bonilla-Silva 2006).

Despite recent claims that racism has ended or that we have somehow "transcended" race in the age of Obama, current research indicates that colorism processes have had some historical continuity, as lighter-skinned Blacks continue to have higher socioeconomic status. While the bulk of this essay will discuss the effects of colorism on Blacks, I will also incorporate some evidence illustrating how the virus of colorism has infected other minority communities, leading to patterns of internal differentiation for Asians and Latino/as. I argue that colorism will continue to internally fracture communities of color in the coming century, and that its effects on stratification may even increase. Further, methodological approaches to the study of race that omit measures of colorism are only telling a small part of the racial story. After a brief overview of the historical and current empirical patterns of colorism in minority communities, I will show how dominant sociological approaches have endorsed a methodological one-drop rule. In conclusion, I will discuss the changing terrain of racial formation (Omi and Winant 1994) and explain why colorism may become a more important factor in understanding the coming racial order.

The Wages of Lightness

In his magisterial *Black Reconstruction in America* (1935), Du Bois claimed Whites received psychological gains beyond the obvious material benefits of racial domination. According to Du Bois these White benefits came in the form of greater public amenities and the ability to define themselves against Blacks (Roediger 1991). While Blacks, due to the one-drop rule, did not have the ability to define themselves racially, it seems that internal differentiation led to a "wages of lightness," through which certain Blacks received social benefits through their proximity to White phenotypic norms. Under slavery, Blacks who were partially descended from Whites (often through rape) were more likely to be manumitted, and had greater educational opportunities

---

[†] The use of mixed-race status as a proxy for light skin may be of some value, but it can also provide misleading results as it provides *no direct measure of skin tone*. This variation in method may explain recent findings that are at odds with each other. For instance, Gullickson (2005) finds that the effects of colorism have decreased using mixed-race designation as a proxy for color. In addition to this, a reanalysis of the same data showed that Gullickson's findings are most likely driven by significant attrition as the final wave of data included less than 15 light-skinned blacks (Goldsmith et al. 2006). Finally, scholars who use a direct measure of skin tone, such as Goldsmith (Goldsmith et al 2007), find that color gradations do indeed matter. More on this below.

[*] It is important to note that factors other than skin tone, such as education level, hair texture, eye color, and facial features, are also often used to make assessments under colorism. This has prompted some scholars to lament the use of the term "colorism" (Bonilla-Silva 2009) as too narrow to encompass the racial calculus that creates stratification.

(Russell et al. 1993). Further, while the one-drop rule characterized much of the United States, categorizing anyone with the slightest bit of African ancestry as Black (Davis 1991), there was some regional variation in classification schemes. This variable application of the "one-drop rule," in addition to producing some logical absurdities, such as being racially reclassified upon crossing state lines (Browning 1951), also had effects for colorism. According to Cedric Herring's (2004) account of the historical course of colorism, the social holes in the application of hypo-descent allowed some mixed-race Blacks to benefit "from the socioeconomic status of their White fathers" (2004: 4). These benefits were particularly clear in Louisiana, where "more than 80% of the free population was of mixed ancestry" (2004, 4). Following abolition, these wages of lightness placed lighter-skinned Blacks in a position to compound these advantages; a number of historical studies have shown that light skin tone was related to better socioeconomic outcomes. Herring's (2004) work also claims that the relationship between light complexion and social advantage that held through the Civil Rights Movement continues to produce a number of social outcomes today.

Similar to Du Bois' (1935) description of Whiteness providing a "public and psychological wage," the wages of lightness are not limited to economic outcomes. Colorism has also historically had effects on beauty norms and personal psychology. Drawing on and extending the insights of Bourdieu (1994), Desmond and Emirbayer (2009) call this internalization of White beauty norms a form of "symbolic violence." This "symbolic violence" involves "the process of people of color unknowingly accepting and supporting the terms of their own domination, thereby acting as agents who collude in the conditions from which they suffer" (2009, 347). Using the example of skin-lightening creams and hair relaxers that have been known to cause severe injury, Desmond and Emirbayer (2009) argue that Blacks who subscribe to White beauty norms are responding to imposed social structural conditions in ways that reinforce the very structure devaluing them. In her essay *Whiteness as Property,* legal scholar Harris (1995) provides a particularly chilling account of how the wages of lightness may also have psychological costs. Harris (1995) claims that the symbolic violence of "passing" as White in order to find work and provide resources for her family haunted her grandmother. This passing put her in daily contact with overtly racist Whites who, unaware of the Black woman in their midst, were candid about their racism. Perfectly aware that the racialized social structure made passing "a logical [economic] choice" in her later life, Harris' grandmother was still enraged that she lived in a society that "made her complicit in her own oppression" and furthered the logic of White supremacy.

This brief historical sketch helps to establish how colorism became instantiated in the Black community, as well as some of the early stratifying processes and psychological costs attributable to skin tone differentiation. More recent research establishes that colorism still stratifies communities. For instance, in an intersectional analysis, several researchers have found that skin color is related to ratings of attractiveness for women (Hill 2002b, Hunter 2004) with light-skinned Black women considered more attractive. Hill (2002a) avoids the "a historical fallacy" (Desmond and Emirbayer 2009) of assuming that the Civil Rights Movement moved us beyond intra-racial stratification by making a direct theoretical connection between the gendered demonization of Black physiology under slavery and current ratings of attractiveness. A number of scholars have found that lighter-skinned Black women are consistently rated as more attractive (Hill 2002b). In this reading, colorism confers a gendered form of social capital (Hunter 2004), as light skin's correlation with socially constructed notions of attractiveness provides advantages for women in dating and marriage markets. Not only are dark-skinned women less likely to be married (Edwards, Carter-Tellison and Herring 2004), but this phenotypic social capital "translates into real material advantages where light-skinned women have access to higher status spouses with more education and presumably higher incomes" (Hunter 2004). Following racial patterns first laid out under slavery, racist patterns of attraction based on notions of colorism continue to affect Black sexuality.

There is also a psychological cost to these patterns of colorism. According to Hunter (2002), light-skinned Mexican-American women and African-American women are subject to questions of ethnic authenticity.

That is, because skin tone is seen as a primary signifier of race, light-skinned members of racial groups are often deemed not "Black" or "Mexican" enough. Further, Hunter (2004) cites evidence that light-skinned Blacks are less likely to be concerned with discrimination and Black pride than are their darker-skinned brothers and sisters. However, as with every sociological assertion, context matters. For instance, Verna Keith (2009) presents data showing that the self-esteem of Black women didn't just vary according to skin tone but also according to whether they are in predominantly White or Black environments. She finds that for Black women at historically Black colleges and universities, darker skin is associated with higher levels of self-esteem, whereas in predominantly White environments, skin tone is unrelated to self-esteem. Keith follows Harvey and colleagues (2005) in explaining this disparity by claiming that in predominantly White environments, Whites are primarily focused on Black-White differences, and treat all Blacks the same (2009). The effects of this similar treatment in all-White environments is perhaps best captured in Hochschild and Weaver's (2007) assertion that colorism does not affect the political attitudes of Blacks across the color spectrum. Despite the vast differences in skin tone within the Black community, these scholars claim that internal cohesion is largely a function of Blacks' continued need to present a united front in the fight against White racism.

Colorism also produces stratification that cuts across gender. Although some scholars claim that the significance of skin color has decreased or disappeared for economic outcomes (Gullickson 2005), or that the effects are exaggerated (Hersch 2005) in the post-Civil Rights era, the bulk of the evidence favors the conclusion that colorism continues to internally stratify minority communities. Some scholars claim that the effect of colorism is more predictive of stratification outcomes than *parental socioeconomic status* (Keith and Herring 1991), a variable classically considered one of the most important for intergenerational stratification (Blau and Duncan 1967). Focusing solely on the economic outcomes of men, Hughes and Hertel (1990) show that colorism creates intra-racial wage differences that are as great as those found between Whites and Blacks when one uses measures that do not include skin tone. Updating this strand of research and advancing a "preference for Whiteness" theory of colorism, Goldsmith and colleagues (Goldsmith et al. 2007) found "significant evidence of a skin-shade wage gradient where wages fall as skin shade darkens" (2007, 729). For men, colorism has also been shown to influence perceptions of criminality and even the length of criminal sentences (Blair et al. 2004). In an innovative research design in which raters coded photos of actual Black male murderers according to how stereotypically Black they looked, Eberhart and colleagues (Eberhardt et al. 2006) found that Blacks who fell into the stereotypical half of the distribution were more than twice as likely to receive the death sentence. Rather than decreasing in significance, convincing evidence suggests that colorism remains a matter of life and death.

Despite the compelling finding that colorism continues to shape the life chances of people of color, the majority of mainstream sociology has largely adopted a methodological one-drop rule (Goldsmith et al. 2007). This is unfortunate because aggregating across race while ignoring intra-racial variation may obscure substantively important findings and over (or under) estimate racial stratification. However, when adopting colorism measures, scholars should be wary. Researchers have shown that over the life course within a single longitudinal data set, racial categorization can change as people gain or lose social class markers (Saperstein and Penner 2008). Further, Hill (2002a) has shown that simple inclusion of reports of skin tone may not solve this problem, as these also vary by race, with Whites and Blacks having very different conceptions of what constitutes light or dark skin tone.

Clearly, colorism stratifies society across a spectrum, paying material and psychological wages according to phenotypical approximations of Whiteness. Evelyn Nakano Glenn's (2009) excellent recent anthology *Shades of Difference* shows that that colorism has gone global. In contrast to Ronald Takaki's (1989) discussion of a pan-ethnic Asian solidarity being born through the murder of the Chinese-American Vincent Chin, Glenn's (2009) anthology shows that Asian Americans are internally differentiated by colorism. For instance, in an analysis of

Asian Indian matrimonial ads in the U.S., Vaid (2009) finds that mention of fair skin in the ads has markedly increased since the 1980's. Similarly, in an analysis of the global trade in skin whitening, Glenn (2009) finds that the consumption of skin whitening products among women from South Africa, India, Latin America, and South East and East Asia, is on the rise. This is despite the severely dangerous nature of skin lightening creams and soaps, which may contain mercury or melanin suppressors. These toxic products can lead to disfiguration and Cushing's syndrome, along with mercury poisoning (Glenn 2009; Thomas 2009).

As a subsystem of White supremacy, colorism has internally stratified communities of color in the U.S. since slavery. Through symbolic violence, communities of color have often participated in their own oppression, valorizing Whiteness by adopting standards of beauty that were intentionally devised to debase them. Colorism has conferred wages of lightness on some people of color while extracting an at times severe psychological cost. However, communities of color have also actively resisted colorism, most notably during the "Black is Beautiful" era of the Civil Rights Movement in the 1960s which embraced Afro-centric styles and undermined White beauty norms. Unfortunately, there is evidence that colorism may become an even more important stratifying factor in the United States, as we are currently undergoing an unprecedented racial transformation.

A Lighter Shade of Hate?: The Future of U.S. Colorism and the Emergence of a Tri-Racial Order

Recently, a number of scholars have contended that in the coming century, the U.S. will experience a fundamental shift in its racial order (Gans 1999, Bonilla-Silva 2006). Similarly, scholars in the assimilation tradition have contended that racial boundaries are increasingly crossed, blurred, and shifted (Alba and Nee 2003). Citing massive immigration from Latin America and Asia coupled with rising intermarriage rates as signs of racial progress, assimilation scholars have adopted a relatively teleological view of race relations. This view sees America in the coming century awakening from its long racial nightmare. For instance, Lee and Bean (2004) argue that rising rates of intermarriage and the growing multiracial population may indicate that boundaries are weakening overall, providing evidence of the declining significance of race for all groups (2004, 203). In contrast, racial pessimists such as Herbert Gans (1999) see a relatively stable structure shifting in the direction of a primarily "Black/non Black" dichotomy. Citing evidence from triracial isolates like the Mississippi Chinese (Loewen 1988) or the historic role of the Creoles in New Orleans, Gans argues that this new racial order will be shaped by social class factors, "deserving" and "undeserving," in his terminology.

Perhaps the most promising model of the future of racial stratification is that of Eduardo Bonilla-Silva (See Bonilla-Silva 2004 in this volume). Bonilla-Silva creates a model that synthesizes the findings of the "new racism" (Bobo 2001, Sears and Henrey 2003, Dovidio 2001) school of post-Civil Rights scholarship (which claims that racism in the post-Civil Rights era has become less overt and harder to detect) with demographic changes to argue that the United States is moving towards a "Latin America like" system of race. Whereas the U.S., for much of its history, has been governed by the "one-drop" racial classification system, Bonilla-Silva contends that Latin-American systems of race function along a continuum, have high levels of racial mixture and an ideology that ties racial mixture to the state (*Mestizaje*), practice Whitening, and are stratified by colorism or "pigmentocracy" (2006, 182). He characterizes this order as "Tri-Racial," composed of Whites at the top, honorary Whites in the middle (serving a buffer function very similar to the middle class in orthodox Marxism), and a collective Black group at the bottom. Like Gans' model, social class factors play a role in which social actors end up in the various racial strata. Bonilla-Silva's model ultimately predicts a racial order that more cunningly hides its abuses.

Despite early, qualified, empirical support for elements of Bonilla-Silva's model (Forman et al. 2004), it is not without its detractors. In a recent exchange in *Ethnic and Racial Studies,* Christina Sue (2009) criticized the Latin Americanization Thesis (LAT) for placing a strong emphasis on colorism, for a lack of specificity about the relative strength of boundaries between racial groups, and for homogenizing racial systems in Latin America. Sue, however, did agree that Latin American racial orders tend to use nationalist rhetoric as a cover for racial exploitation (for an excellent example of this in Brazil, see Twine 1998). Bonilla-Silva's reply covers several major points; however, for this review, two main points are perhaps most important for assessing how colorism will affect the coming U.S. racial stratification order. First, Bonilla-Silva (2009) argues that in Latin America the practice of "Whitening" as a social policy and ideological project did indeed allow for a more fluid system of racial classification that was simultaneously harder to see, as the official ideology denied any internal differentiation. Second, building on his work (Bonilla-Silva and Ray 2009), Bonilla-Silva offers a critique of the Obama phenomenon and the use of "deracialization" in his political career, arguing that Obama's post-racial appeal, his downplaying of his Blackness, his "accommodationist stance on race," and his unwillingness to advocate race-based policies "will exacerbate the existing color-class divide within the Black community" (Bonilla-Silva 2009). Recent social psychological evidence does indeed point to the idea that colorism was a factor in supporting Obama, as his supporters were more likely to claim digitally lightened photographs were more representative of the candidate, while his detractors thought darkened photographs were more representative (Caruso et al. 2009). In the Obama era, it seems colorism may already be having effects on the socio-political order that "one-drop" methodological procedures are unable to uncover.

In conclusion, colorism has had a sordid history in the United States. Despite the longstanding recognition of scholars of color that beyond race, skin tone provides a wage of lightness, the analysis of colorism has not become a standard practice in sociological analyses of race. Recently, several excellent anthologies (Herring et al. 2004; Glenn 2009) have begun to fill this hole in the literature. As the U.S. moves towards a more plural racial system, analyses that refuse to incorporate measures of colorism may miss the racial boat by aggregating across racial categories that are shifting under our feet.

Discussion Questions

1. How does colorism impact life chances of racial and ethnic minorities in the United States?
2. How is colorism gendered? That is, how does it affect women differently than it affects men?

Works Cited

Alba, Richard and Victor Nee. 2003. *Remaking the American Mainstream.* Cambridge: Harvard University Press.

Allport, Gordon W. 1954. *The Nature of Prejudice.* Cambridge: Addison-Wesley.

Blair, Irene V., Charles M. Judd, and Kristine M. Chapleau. 2004. "The Influence of Afrocentric Facial Features in Criminal Sentencing." *Psychological Science* 15(10): 674–679.

Blau, Peter and O.D. Duncan. 1967. *The American Occupational Structure.* New York: Wiley.

Bobo, Lawrence. 2001. "Racial Attitudes and Relations at the Close of the Twentieth Century." In Smelser, Neil J., William Julius Wilson, and Faith Mitchell (Eds). 2001. *America Becoming: Racial Trends and Their Consequences.* Washington, D.C.: National Academy Press.

Bonilla-Silva, Eduardo. 2006. *Racism Without Racists: 2nd Edition.* Oxford: Rowman and Littlefield.

Bonilla-Silva, Eduardo. 2009. "Are the Americas 'sick with racism' or is it a problem at the poles? A reply to Christina A. Sue." *Ethnic and Racial Studies* 32 (6): 1071–1082.

Bonilla-Silva, Eduardo and Victor Ray. 2009. "When Whites Love a Black Leader: Race Matters in Obamerica." *Journal of African American Studies* 13(2): 176–183.

Bourdieu, Pierre. 1994. "Social Space and Symbolic Space." In Calhoun, Craig., Joseph Gerteis, James Moody, Steven Pfaff, and Indermohan Virk (Eds). 2007. *Contemporary Sociological Theory: 2nd Ed.* Malden, Maine: Blackwell Publishing.

Browning, James R. 1951. "Anti-Miscegenation Laws in the United States." *Duke Bar Journal* 1: 27–29.

Caruso, Eugene M., Nicole L. Mead, and Emily Balcetis. 2009. "Political Partisanship Influences Perception of Biracial Candidates' Skin Tone." *Proceeding of the National Academy of Science* 106(48): 20168–20173.

Collins, Patricia Hill. 2005. *Black Sexual Politics: African Americans, Gender, and the New Racism.* New York and London: Routledge.

Davis, James F. 1991. *Who is Black:? One Nation's Definition.* University Park: Penn State University Press.

Desmond, Matthew and Mustafa Emirbayer. 2009. "What is Racial Domination?" *Du Bois Review* 6(2): 335–355.

Dovidio, John F. 2001. "On the Nature of Contemporary Prejudice: The Third Wave." *Journal of Social Issues* 57: 829.

Du Bois. "The Talented Tenth." In Washington, Booker T., (ed.) 1903. *The Negro Problem: a Series of Articles by Representative Negroes of Today.* New York: James Pott and Co.

———. 1935. *Black Reconstruction in America, 1860–1880.* New York: The Free Press.

Eberhardt, J. L., V.J. Purdie-Vaughns, P.G. Davies, & S.L. Johnson. 2006. "Looking Deathworthy: Perceived Stereotypicality of Black Defendants Predicts Capital-sentencing Outcomes." *Psychological Science* 17(5): 383–386.

Edwards, Korie, Katrina Carter-Tellison, and Cedric Herring. "For Richer, For Poorer, Whether Dark or Light: Skin Tone, Marital Status, and Spouse's Earnings." In Herring, Cedric, Verna Keith, and Hayward Derrick Horton (Eds). 2004. *Skin Deep: How Race and Complexion Matter in the "Color-Blind" Era.* Urbana and Chicago: University of Illinois Press.

Forman, Tyrone A., Carla Goar, and Amanda Lewis. 2004. "Neither Black nor White? An Empirical Test of the Latin Americanization Thesis." *Race and Society* 5: 65–84.

Frazier, Franklin. E. 1957. *Black Bourgeoisie.* New York: The Free Press.

Gans, Herbert. "The Possibility of a New Racial Hierarchy in the Twenty-First-Century United States." In Lamont, Michele (Ed). 1999. *The Cultural Territories of Race: Black and White Boundaries.* Chicago and London: The University of Chicago Press and the Russell Sage Foundation.

Glenn, Evelyn Nakano. "Consuming Lightness: Segmented Markets and Global Capital in the Skin Whitening Trade." In Glenn, Evelyn Nakano (Ed). 2009. *Shades of Difference: Why Skin Color Matters.* Stanford: Stanford University Press.

Goldsmith, Arthur., Hamilton, Darrick., and Darity, William. 2006. "Shades of Discrimination: Skin Tone and Wages." *The American Economic Review* 96(2) 242–245.

Goldsmith, Arthur, Darrick Hamilton, and William Darity. 2007. "From Dark to Light: Skin Color and Wages Among African Americans." *Journal of Human Resources* XLII (4): 701–738.

Gullickson, Aaron. 2005. "The Significance of Skin Tone Declines: A Re-Analysis of Skin Tone Differentials in Post-Civil Rights America." *Social Forces* 84(1): 157–180.

Harris, Cheryl. "Whitness as Property." In Crenshaw, K., N. Gotanda, G. Peller, and K. Thomas (Eds). 1995. *Critical Race Theory: Key Writings that Formed the Movement.* New York: The New Press.

Harvey, Richard D., Nicole LaBeach, Ellie Pridgen, and Tammy M. Gocial. 2005. "The Intragroup Stigmatization of Skin Tone Among Black Americans." *Journal of Black Psychology* 31(3): 237–253.

Herring, Cedrick. 2004. *Skin Deep: How Race and Complexion Matter in the "Color-Blind" Era.* Urbana and Chicago: University of Illinois Press.

Hersch, Joni. 2005. "Skin-Tone Effects Among African Americans: Perceptions and Reality." *American Economic Review* 96(2): 251–255.

Hill, Mark. 2002a. "Race of the Interviewer and Perception of Skin Color: Evidence from the Multi-City Study of Urban Inequality." *American Sociological Review* 67: 99–108.

———. 2002b. "Skin Color and the Perception of Attractiveness Among African Americans: Does Gender Make a Difference?" *Social Psychology Quarterly* 65(1): 77–91.

Hochschild, Jennifer L., & Vesla Weaver. 2007. "The Skin Color Paradox and the American Racial Order." *Social Forces* 86: 3–28.

Hughes, Michael, and Bradley Hertel. 1990. "The Significance of Color Remains: A Study of Life Chances, Mate Selection, and Ethnic Consciousness Among Black Americans." *Social Forces* 68(4): 1105–20.

Hunter, Margaret. 2002. "'If You're Light You're Alright': Light Skin Color as Social Capital for Women of Color." *Gender and Society* 16(2): 175–193.

———. "Light, Bright, and Almost White: The Advantages and Disadvantages of Light Skin." In Herring, Cedric., Verna Keith, and Hayward Derrick Horton (Eds). 2004. *Skin Deep: How Race and Complexion Matter in the "Color-Blind" Era*. Urbana and Chicago: University of Illinois Press.

Keith, Verna M., and Cedric Herring. 1991. "Skin Tone and Stratification in the Black Community." *American Journal of Sociology* 97(3): 760–78.

Keith, Verna M. "A Colorstruck World: Skin Tone, Achievement, and Self Esteem Among African American Women." In Glenn, Evelyn Nakano (Ed). 2009. *Shades of Difference: Why Skin Color Matters*. Stanford: Stanford University Press.

Lee, Jennifer and Frank D. Bean. 2004. "America's Changing Color Lines: Immigration, Race/Ethnicity, and Multiracial Identification." *Annual Review of Sociology* 30: 221–242.

Loewen, James. 1988. *The Mississippi Chinese: Between Black and White (2nd Edition)*. Cambridge: Harvard University Press.

Mills, Charles M. 1997. *The Racial Contract*. Ithaca: Cornell University Press.

Omi, Michael and Howard Winant. 1994. *Racial Formation in the United States: From the 1960s to the 1990s*. New York: Routledge.

Penner, Andrew and Saperstein, Aliya. 2008. "How Social Status Shapes Race." *Proceedings of the National Academy of Science* 105 (50): 19628–19630.

Roediger, David. 1991. *The Wages of Whiteness: Race and the Making of the Working Class*. New York: Verso.

Russell, Kathy, Midge Wilson, and Ronald Hall. 1993. *The Color Complex: The Politics of Skin Color Among African Americans*. New York: Doubleday.

Sears, David and P. J. Henry. 2003. "The Origins of Symbolic Racism." *Journal of Personality and Social Psychology* 85: 259–75.

Sue, Christina. 2009. "An Assessment of the Latin Americanization Thesis." *Ethnic and Racial Studies* 32(6): 1058–1070.

Takaki, Ronald. 1989. *Strangers from a Different Shore: A History of Asian-Americans*. Boston: Little, Brown and Company.

Thomas, Lynn M. "Skin Lighteners in South Africa: Transnational Entanglements and Technologies of the Self." In Glenn, Evelyn Nakano (Ed). 2009. *Shades of Difference: Why Skin Color Matters*. Stanford: Stanford University Press.

Twine, France Winddance. 1998. *Racism in a Racial Democracy: The Maintenance of White Supremacy in Brazil*. New Brunswick: Rutgers University Press.

Vaid, Jyotsna. 2009. "Fair Enough?: Color and the Commodification of Self in Indian Matrimonials." In Glenn, Evelyn Nakano (Ed). 2009. *Shades of Difference: Why Skin Color Matters*. Stanford: Stanford University Press.

Wilson, William Julius. 1978. *The Declining Significance of Race: Blacks and Changing American Institutions*. Chicago: The University of Chicago Press.

Zuberi, Tukufu. 2001. *Thicker Than Blood: How Racial Statistics Lie*. Minneapolis: University of Minnesota Press.

Racial and Ethnic Inequality

By John Iceland

Editor's Introduction

This chapter provides a discussion of statistical data on racial and ethnic groups in the United States. A particularly important discussion in the reading is about cumulative disadvantage. Cumulative disadvantage is an important concept in racial and ethnic inequality because it alerts us to the fact that structural inequality in the past leads to disadvantages for racial and ethnic minorities relative to Whites. These disadvantages accumulate over the life course as well.

[...]

Contemporary Patterns of Racial and Ethnic Inequality

U.S. society has become increasingly racially and ethnically diverse. The proportion of the population that was non-Hispanic white decreased substantially from 83 percent in 1970 to 63 percent in 2011. Meanwhile, the relative size of the black population stayed fairly steady (12 percent in 2011), and the representation of Hispanics (5 to 17 percent) and Asians (1 to 5 percent) increased significantly over the period. In this section we examine changes in the educational attainment, income, poverty, and wealth of different groups to shed light on the extent of racial and ethnic socioeconomic inequality in American society.

Figure 3.1 shows that college completion has increased markedly for all racial/ethnic groups over time, but significant disparities remain. In 2012, only about 1 in 7 Hispanics who were 25 years old and over had

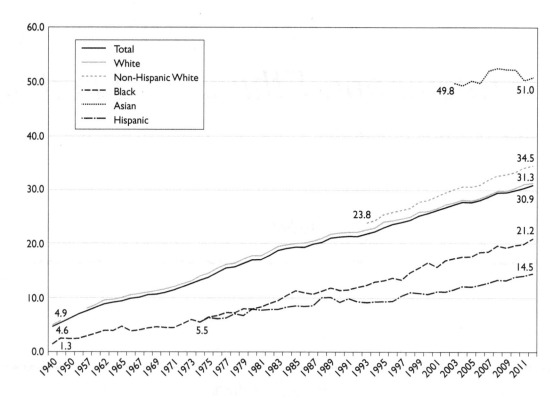

Figure 3.1 Percentage of people age 25 years and older who have completed college, by race and ethnicity, 1940–2012.

Note: Data were collected for different groups at different points in time, which accounts for the various gaps in the graph, including that for whites between ca. 1947 and 1957. Please refer to U.S. Census Bureau 2013d for more information.

Source: U.S. Census Bureau 2013d.

completed college, compared with over a fifth of blacks, over a third of non-Hispanic whites, and over half of Asians. In 1940, only 5 percent of the total population age 25 years and older had a college degree, including 5 percent of whites and just 1 percent of blacks. As one would expect, educational attainment disparities show up in high school graduation rates as well, though the white-black gap is narrower, with 93 percent of non-Hispanic whites and 85 percent of blacks graduating from high school among those age 25 and older in 2012. Hispanics have the lowest levels of high school completion at 65 percent. About 89 percent of Asians had completed high school in 2012.[16]

Racial and ethnic differences persist when looking at median household income (see figure 3.2). All groups experienced real increases in income over time, with all groups also taking a tumble during the Great Recession. Consistent with the educational differences described above, the median household income was highest among Asians at $65,129, followed by non-Hispanic whites ($55,412). However, even though African Americans had higher levels of education than Hispanics, median household income was higher among Hispanics ($38,624) than blacks ($32,229).

Unsurprisingly, racial and ethnic differences also show up in poverty statistics (figure 3.3). In 2011, 10 percent of non-Hispanic whites and 12 percent of Asians were poor, compared with 25 percent Hispanics and 28 percent of African Americans. Notably, the black poverty rate declined significantly over time, from a high of 55 percent in 1959. Nevertheless, the 2000s were a difficult decade for low-income Americans, with blacks experiencing the largest absolute increase in poverty. Finally, racial and ethnic inequality in wealth is even larger than in education, income, or poverty. The mean net worth of white households was $593,000 in 2010, whereas the mean net worth of African American and Hispanic households was only $85,000 and

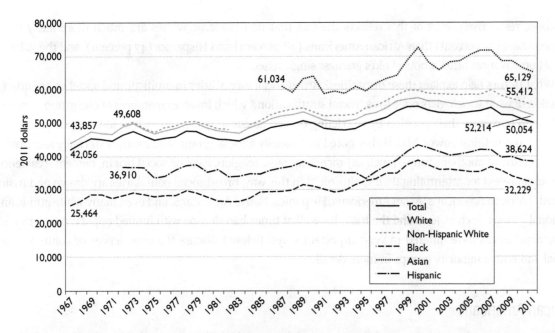

Figure 3.2 Median household income, by race and ethnicity, 1967–2011 (in constant 2011 dollars).

Note: No published data are available for non-Hispanic whites in 1984.

Source: U.S. Census Bureau 2012k.

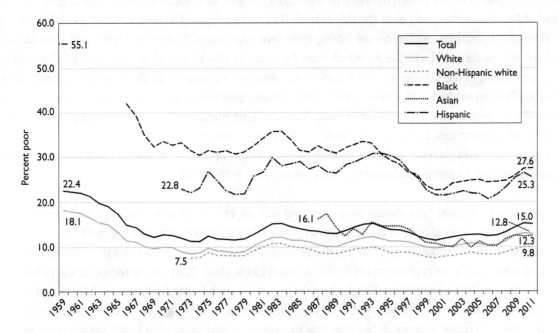

Figure 3.3 Poverty rates, by race and ethnicity, 1959–2011.

Note: No published data are available for blacks between 1959 and 1966.

Source: U.S. Census Bureau 2012g.

$90,000, respectively. Part of this reflects the fact that non-Hispanic whites are much more likely to be homeowners (75 percent) than African Americans (48 percent) and Hispanics (47 percent), and the value of one's home is most often a household's greatest single asset.[17]

What factors help explain these disparities? Broad social inequalities in multicultural societies are often a function of what sociologists refer to as "social stratification," which involves members of one group in power seeking to maximize their position by restricting others' access to resources such as jobs, education, health services, and political power. Max Weber noted that usually a social group "takes some externally identifiable characteristic of another group—[such as] race, language, religion, local or social origin, descent, residence, etc.—as a pretext for attempting their exclusion."[18] In this way, broad social boundaries are drawn and maintained.[19] African Americans, Asian Americans, Hispanics, Native Americans, and even many white ethnic and national groups, such as Jews and the Irish, have all at times had to cope with limited opportunities, though their experiences have differed in very important ways. Below I discuss the experiences of contemporary racial and ethnic minority groups in more detail.

African Americans

African Americans have long struggled against racial oppression. They first arrived in the United States in large numbers as involuntary immigrants during the slave trade and were heavily concentrated in southern states. The Civil War and accompanying constitutional amendments ended slavery and conferred citizenship upon African Americans. Nevertheless, after some hope of equality during Reconstruction, from about 1865 to 1877, when blacks gained the right to vote and a number were elected to state legislatures, the U.S. House of Representatives, and even the U.S. Senate, they were relegated to second-class citizenship by the late 1870s, with southern whites reestablishing their own supremacy. Through violence and intimidation, southern whites denied blacks the power to vote. As many as two thousand to three thousand lynchings were perpetrated in the last decade and a half of the nineteenth century.[20] In the economic sphere, blacks in the South often worked as sharecroppers, mainly because they were barred by law or custom from most other full-time jobs outside the black community. Jim Crow laws mandated segregation in all public facilities, ensuring inferior services, including education, for the black community.[21]

Gunnar Myrdal, in his book *An American Dilemma: The Negro Problem and Modern Democracy,* published in 1944, described the nature and extent of black subjugation in the South:

> Violence, terror, and intimidation have been, and still are, effectively used to disfranchise Negroes in the South. Physical coercion is not so often practiced against the Negro, but the mere fact that it can be used with impunity and that it is devastating in its consequences creates a psychic coercion that exists nearly everywhere in the South. A Negro can seldom claim the protection of the police and the courts if a white man knocks him down, or if a mob burns his house or inflicts bodily injuries on him or on members of his family. If he defends himself against a minor violence, he may expect a major violence. If he once "gets in wrong" he may expect the loss of his job or other economic injury, and constant insult and loss of whatever legal rights he may have had.[22]

During the twentieth century many blacks left the oppressive conditions in the South to look for opportunity in the North, especially in booming industries in many northeastern and midwestern cities such as Chicago, Detroit, and New York. This Great Migration resulted in a striking regional redistribution of the black population in the United States. In 1900, about three-quarters of all African Americans lived in rural southern areas; a century later, that figure had declined to about 12 percent. By 1950, more than 2.5 million southern-born African Americans were living outside the region, a number that increased to more than 4 million by

1980.[23] While economic opportunities were better in the North, and the racial climate was not as oppressive (northern blacks, for example, could for the most part vote), blacks still faced a wide range of discriminatory barriers in the labor and housing market and were segregated in congested northern ghettos.

The civil rights movement in the 1950s and 1960s overturned the legal framework that supported the unequal treatment of blacks. In 1954, for example, in the case *Brown v. Board of Education of Topeka,* the Supreme Court ruled that the separate-but-equal doctrine underlying the Jim Crow system was invalid. In the 1960s several laws were passed in Congress (including the far-reaching Civil Rights Act of 1964) that prohibited racial discrimination in employment practices, public accommodations, and housing market trans-actions. The civil rights movement itself was propelled mainly by nonviolent protest and civil disobedience. The Montgomery Bus Boycott in Alabama in 1955–56, for example, protested racial segregation in the city's public transit system, which relegated blacks to seats in the back of the bus. The campaign began when Rosa Parks, an African American woman active in the movement, refused to give up her seat to a white person. The boycott was a success, and the Supreme Court eventually declared segregation laws to be unconstitutional.

Legal changes have also been accompanied by gradual changes in public opinion. The proportion of whites holding blatantly racist attitudes has dropped considerably over the decades according to national polls. For example, in the 1940s and 1950s, fewer than half of whites surveyed believed that white and black students should attend the same schools or that black and white job applicants should have an equal chance of getting a job. By the 1990s, however, over 90 percent of whites said they believed that schools and employers should treat whites and blacks equally.[24]

The removal of legal barriers and the slowly changing social norms, however, did not translate into im-mediate social and economic equality. Civil rights legislation was being passed during a time of deindustrial-ization—when the share of people employed in manufacturing was declining—and when many northeastern and midwestern cities were losing jobs and people through outmigration to the Sun Belt. (Many jobs also went abroad.) For example, in the twenty-year period between 1967 and 1987, Philadelphia lost 64 percent of its manufacturing jobs, Chicago lost 60 percent, New York City lost 58 percent, and Detroit 51 percent. This hurt blacks as well as whites living in those cities and contributed to the increasing poverty of blacks concentrated in inner cities.[25]

Some commentators, such as William Julius Wilson, have argued that race has become less important in determining the labor market success of African Americans and that class position has become more impor-tant.[26] From colonial times through the first half of the twentieth century, racial oppression was deliberate and overt. By the latter half of the twentieth century, many traditional barriers were dismantled as a result of political, social, and economic changes of the civil rights era. Wilson emphasizes that although discrimination has become less common though not eliminated, economic conditions have come to play an increasingly important role in shaping opportunities available to African Americans. He argues that deindustrialization and class segregation in particular have hampered the economic mobility of less-skilled blacks.[27]

Studies show that the economic "penalty" of being African American has declined since the 1960s, in that occupational mobility has increased, as has wage parity.[28] Racial differences in economic outcomes are significantly reduced when one accounts for educational achievement.[29] Measuring the direct effects of discrimination is difficult, because it is not always clear when a discriminatory action has occurred or if general observed differences between whites and blacks are a result of unmeasured differences (e.g., quality of schooling received) or of discrimination itself. Careful examinations of this issue tend to indicate that discrimination still occurs in labor markets and in other areas. For example, "paired-test studies," in which minority job applicants were paired with white applicants with similar backgrounds and trained to be as similar as possible in behavior, have shown that minorities, particularly African Americans and foreign-sounding Latinos, were less likely to be given job interviews and offers, at least in the low-wage labor market.[30] Economists have estimated that perhaps one-quarter of the black-white wage gap is due to prejudice, suggesting that racism continues to contribute to African American economic disadvantage.[31]

Other factors have also contributed to relatively low levels of socioeconomic attainment among African Americans, some related to race and others more nonracial in origin. One race-related factor is residential and social segregation. Because African Americans often live in segregated and disadvantaged communities, they may have fewer economically useful contacts ("social capital") on which to draw to help achieve success. Many people, for example, find a job via word of mouth through friends and neighbors. Those with affluent friends and neighbors typically have access to more and better opportunities.[32] Residential segregation also affects educational disparities because a significant portion of school funding comes from local taxes. Schools in poor neighborhoods often have inferior resources and fewer enrichment programs. High neighborhood poverty rates are strongly correlated with lower student test scores.[33] Declining levels of black segregation in recent decades, along with rapid black suburbanization, has likely reduced the effects of segregation in contributing to racial inequalities over the past couple of decades. However, many cities—particularly some in the Northeast and Midwest such as Chicago, New York, Detroit, and Milwaukee—still have very high levels of black segregation.[34]

Another factor that contributes to higher poverty rates among African Americans is differentials in human-capital skills. Human capital refers to education attainment and subsequent work experience and skills. The gap in average levels of education has declined over the past few decades. Nevertheless, the quality of schooling received by children in the United States still varies widely, and, as mentioned above, African Americans are more likely to attend inferior schools with fewer resources and have lower test scores. Lower employment levels among young African Americans subsequently contribute to earnings differentials. High black incarceration rates (black men are eight times more likely to be incarcerated than white men) translate to a relatively high proportion of young black men entering the labor force with a criminal record, which further dampens their employability. The rapid growth in the prison population from the late 1970s through the mid-2000s exacerbated this problem. Many contend that high black incarceration rates are in part due to racial profiling by law enforcement and racial biases in the sentencing process.[35]

Differences in family structure affect ethnic socioeconomic differentials as well. While 36 percent of white births were to unmarried women, the figure was double (72 percent) among African Americans.[36] This contributes to socioeconomic inequalities because single-parent families are considerably more likely to be poor: about 4 in 10 (41 percent) female-headed families with children were poor in 2011, compared with fewer than 1 in 10 (9 percent) of married-couple families with children.[37] Single parents often struggle to earn sufficient income for their family while also providing an attentive, nurturing environment for their children.

Thus, some have emphasized that an African American disadvantage has persisted across generations because of *cumulative disadvantages*. Racial gaps show up early in childhood and widen through the life course. As author Michael Wenger puts it:

> On average, African Americans begin life's journey several miles behind their white counterparts as a result of the legacy of our history of racial oppression. This disadvantage is compounded by institutional hurdles they encounter at every stage of the journey: the socioeconomic conditions into which they're born, the system of public education through which they pass, the type of employment they are able to secure, the legacy they are able to leave behind. These hurdles, arduous, relentless, and often withering to the soul, do not confront many white people as they pursue their hopes and dreams.[38]

The importance of cumulative disadvantages suggests that ending inequality has no single easy solution and helps explain why progress has been slow—though some suggest that early childhood interventions revolving around schooling could be the most effective approach to reducing racial disparities.[39] Even as race has become less important in American society, economic inequality and class background have become more important. For example, while the black-white reading gap used to be substantially larger than the rich-poor reading gap in the 1940s, by the 2000s the reverse was true.[40]As a result, while we have seen considerable growth in the black middle class in recent decades, the economic challenges faced by poor African Americans remain daunting.[41]

Hispanics, Asians, and the Role of Immigration

The many racial and ethnic dividing lines in American society have historically reserved privilege for whites. Through much of the twentieth century, some of the factors that impeded African American mobility—discrimination and segregation—also affected Hispanics and Asian Americans. Some of the traditional racial dividing lines have eased, however, mainly since the civil rights era, enabling many members of these groups to achieve socioeconomic mobility and broader incorporation into mainstream society, though people still debate the extent to which racial dividing lines continue to inhibit opportunity.

Hispanics have a long history in the United States, dating at least as far back as the annexation of territory in Florida in the early 1800s. At the request of a growing number of U.S. settlers in what had been Mexican territory, the United States annexed Texas in 1845, precipitating the Mexican-American War. After defeating the Mexican army in 1848, the United States annexed California, New Mexico, Nevada, Arizona, Utah, and Colorado as well. The Mexican-origin population in the American Southwest in 1848 was likely about 80,000 people—roughly one-fifth of the total population of that area.[42] Mexican Americans living in these territories were often treated as second-class citizens. In subsequent decades Mexicans were used as cheap labor in the building of railroads, in mining, and in agriculture. During labor shortages they were often recruited, but at other times they were encouraged to return to Mexico, often with force. Between 1930 and 1960, almost 4 million Mexicans were deported.[43]

The presence of other Hispanic groups is more recent. Puerto Ricans migrated to the U.S. mainland in large numbers in the 1950s and 1960s. Reflecting Puerto Rico's status as a U.S. territory (Spain ceded Puerto Rico to the United States in 1898 as a result of its defeat in the Spanish-American War), Puerto Ricans are U.S. citizens at birth. The Puerto Rican population is generally very mixed, and in the past the darker-skinned Puerto Ricans in particular encountered significant racial barriers.[44] Cubans entered the United States in significant numbers after the Cuban Revolution in 1959. Many of these immigrants were highly educated professionals who had been supporters of the deposed president and dictator, Fulgencio Batista. Another wave entered in 1980 as part of the Mariel Boatlift; this group was decidedly more socioeconomically mixed. Cubans overwhelmingly settled in Miami, and many found success as entrepreneurs and small business owners.[45]

As of 2010, there were 31.8 million Mexican-origin people in the United States (63 percent of the Hispanic population), up from 8.7 million in 1980. The next two traditionally largest groups—Puerto Ricans and Cubans—have been falling as a fraction of the total Hispanic population, from 14 percent and 6 percent, respectively, in 1980 to 9 percent and 4 percent in 2010. In the meantime, the number of Salvadorans, Dominicans, and Guatemalans in the United States has grown rapidly in recent years, though each of these groups still made up no more than about 2 to 3 percent of the Hispanic population nationally in 2010.

Among Asian groups, the Chinese were the first to immigrate in significant numbers around the time of the California gold rush in 1848. In the 1860s, an estimated 12,000 to 16,000 Chinese laborers were employed to build the western leg of the Central Pacific Railroad. Some Chinese also worked in agriculture, and others were entrepreneurs in San Francisco.[46] The Chinese experienced a good deal of discrimination and violence as the community grew; they were viewed as economic competitors who would drive down the wages of native-born Americans. The Naturalization Act of 1870 limited naturalization in the United States to "white persons and persons of African descent"; this meant that the Chinese were aliens ineligible for citizenship and remained so until 1943. The 1882 Chinese Exclusion Act went further, barring the immigration of all Chinese laborers. Because Chinese immigration was so heavily male, the Chinese population in the United States began to gradually decline until about 1920, after which it slowly rebounded as a result of natural increase.[47]

The first group of Japanese arrived in California around 1869 but began to increase more markedly in the 1890s. Initially, most Japanese worked in agriculture, filling a large demand for labor, though many went on to live in larger cities, including San Francisco and Los Angeles, and others became successful farm owners and entrepreneurs. However, white California workingmen and others eventually lobbied for their exclusion. Cognizant of the military might of Japan, which was a considerably more powerful country than China at the time, and not wishing to offend it, the Gentleman's Agreement of 1907 was negotiated between the United States and Japan, ending most kinds of immigration from Japan to the United States, except for family-reunification purposes. In 1913 and 1920 California enacted anti-alien land laws aimed at Japanese farmers, barring "aliens ineligible for citizenship" from purchasing and leasing agricultural land. The resident Japanese population, however, found ways to get around some of these obstacles, and many continued to prosper. Japanese immigration was later completely halted in 1924.[48] Many Japanese on the West Coast were infamously interned in camps during World War II—a fate not suffered by the German American and Italian American communities—indicative of the racism of the time.

Initial migration of Filipinos to the United States came shortly after the American annexation of the Philippines in 1898. In the 1920s and 1930s larger numbers came as farmworkers, filling in the kinds of jobs held by the Chinese and Japanese immigrants in previous years. As Asians, Filipinos were aliens ineligible for citizenship until the 1940s. Filipinos faced a significant amount of prejudice and discrimination. As writer Carlos Bulosan wrote in 1946, "Do you know what a Filipino feels in America? ... He is the loneliest thing on earth. There is much to be appreciated ... beauty, wealth, power, grandeur. But is he part of these luxuries? He looks, poor man, through the fingers of his eyes. He's enchained, damnably to his race, his heritage. His is betrayed, my friend."[49] Another time he wrote, "I feel like a criminal running away from a crime that I did not commit. And that crime is that I am a Filipino in America."[50] Filipinos, like other Asians and other minorities, were excluded from a broad array of economic opportunities and were viewed as unwelcome aliens by the native white majority population.

The second wave of immigration after the elimination of discriminatory national-origin quotas in 1965 included Asians from a variety of other countries, including India, Vietnam, and Korea. In 2010, the largest Asian subgroup was Chinese (24 percent of the Asian population), followed by Asian Indians (19 percent) and Filipinos (17 percent). The fraction of the Asian population that is Chinese has stayed roughly the same over the past three decades, with the percentage of Asian Indians growing substantially (they were 10 percent of the Asian population in 1980) and the percentage of Filipinos declining, but slowly (they were 22 percent of the Asian population in 1980). The percentage of Japanese as a share of the Asian population has fallen considerably, from 20 percent in 1980 to 5 percent in 2010, and Korean and Vietnamese each made up 10 percent of Asians in 2010.[51]

In some respects Latinos and Asian Americans share certain experiences, because both groups have been historically discriminated against, both have experienced substantial increases in their population resulting from immigration since the 1960s, and both are heterogeneous in terms of their national origins (though Mexicans are by far the largest group among Latinos and overall). Nevertheless, as figures 37 through 39 indicate, socioeconomic outcomes of Hispanics and Asians differ substantially. For the most part Asians are on equal socioeconomic footing with native-born whites, and in fact their outcomes exceed those of whites in some respects. Because nearly two-thirds of Asians and about 2 in 5 Hispanics are foreign born and many more of both groups are of just the second generation, we need to investigate the characteristics of immigrants from Latin America and Asia to understand their disparate outcomes.[52]

Chapter 5 described patterns of assimilation among Asians and Hispanics and noted important differences in characteristics of the immigrants from different origins, especially in levels of education. Specifically, immigrants from Asia tend to constitute a more "select" group than immigrants from Latin America. Immigrants from Korea, India, and the Philippines achieve higher average levels of education than both Latinos and native-born whites. For example, about 80 percent of immigrants from India have a bachelor's degree or more, compared with 6 percent from Mexico.[53] One factor explaining these differences is that while many immigrants from Asia become eligible to migrate to the United States because of their work-related skills, a larger proportion of immigrants from Latin America immigrate because they have relatives who are U.S. citizens.[54]

It is important to note of course that poverty among immigrants also varies considerably by country of origin; not all subgroups among Asians and Hispanics are similarly advantaged or disadvantaged. Among foreign-born Hispanics, for example, poverty rates in 2007 were high among Dominicans (28 percent) and Mexicans (22 percent) but more moderate among Cubans (16 percent) and Colombians (11 percent).[55] South Americans have nearly reached parity with non-Hispanic whites in terms of both the proportion having a college education and median household income.[56] Among Asian immigrant groups, poverty rates were a little higher for Koreans (17 percent) than for immigrants from Japan (9 percent), India (7 percent), and the Philippines (4 percent).[57] Many of these differences are explained by the average characteristics of the immigrants themselves (especially educational attainment), though as noted above each group has a unique history of immigration to the United States.

Initial disadvantages tend to persist over time and across generations. Native-born Hispanics obtain on average higher levels of education than immigrant Hispanics, but their educational levels still lag behind those of native-born whites, largely because of the lower initial level of family resources of Hispanics.[58] In contrast, native-born Asian Americans tend to achieve high levels of education, which translate into better jobs, higher incomes, and less poverty. Once family characteristics are taken into account, there is little difference in the poverty rates between native-born Asians and native-born non-Hispanic whites.[59] While Latinos are less likely to have a college degree and tend to work in lower-skill, lower-wage jobs, once human capital differences are accounted for (especially education and English-language proficiency), there is not that much difference between whites and Hispanics in terms of occupational status and earnings.[60]

The research literature does not offer a definitive answer as to the extent of racial/ethnic discrimination faced by Asians and Latinos in the labor market. For Asians, it is probably safe to say that discrimination is not widespread enough to significantly affect average levels of socioeconomic achievement. For Latinos, family background characteristics (such as education and income) are likely to play the most prominent role and ethnicity a more minor one. Race appears to continue to play a significant role in explaining lower wages and higher poverty among blacks and darker-skinned Latinos.[61]

Native Americans

The experience of Native Americans, as the original inhabitants of the North American continent, differs from that of all the other groups. At the time when Jamestown was established in 1607, estimates of the number of Native Americans living in what is now the United States is estimated to have varied from about 1 million to 10 million.[62] The population declined substantially over the course of the seventeenth through the nineteenth century, reaching an estimated low of 250,000 in 1890. The most important factor contributing to the decline in population was the diseases brought by American colonists to which Native Americans had little immunity or resistance, including scarlet fever, whooping cough, bubonic plague, cholera, and typhoid. Other causes for population decline include warfare, displacement, the slaughter of buffalo on which some tribes depended, and alcoholism.[63] The Native American population has grown rapidly since the 1970s, not just from natural increase but also in part because a greater number of Americans have asserted some Indian heritage. The civil rights movement and the decline in negative stereotyping of Native Americans—as well as the increase in positive representations of Native Americans in popular culture, such as the movie *Dances with Wolves*—help explain the increase in self-reported Native American identity.[64] As of 2010, 2.9 million Americans identified as solely Native American (0.9 percent of the total U.S. population), and another 2.3 million (0.7 percent) said they were at least part Native American.[65]

Despite this demographic growth, Native Americans tend to have low levels of educational attainment and income and high levels of poverty. In 2010, among the Native American population age 25 years and older, 13 percent had a college degree or more (compared with 30 percent among the population as a whole). Median household income was $35,000 (the national average was $50,000), and their poverty rate was 28 percent (the national average was 15 percent), placing their level of disadvantage near that of African Americans.[66] Native Americans have long had to overcome a dearth of job opportunities in and around reservations and also poor schooling. Although some evidence indicates a decline in the net negative effect of being Native American on wages over the last half of the twentieth century, Native Americans still have lower levels of educational attainment and earnings than otherwise comparable whites.[67] It is not clear whether these differences are explained by discrimination or by other difficult-to-observe factors correlated with being Native American.[68] Research on Native Americans tends to be more limited than that of other groups, in part because of the relatively small Native American population. Additional research on Native Americans, not to mention the other groups, would help shed further light on the complex interrelationship between race and socioeconomic disparities.

Multiracial America: Are We Postracial?

The number of mixed-race marriages and multiracial individuals has grown considerably in recent years. The multiracial population grew by 50 percent between 2000 and 2010, from 1.8 million to 4.2 million, making it the fastest growing group of children in the country. Despite this growth, the overall proportion of Americans who report two or more races is still small, at 2.9 percent, according to the 2010 census (the races consist of white, black, American Indian, Asian, and Native Hawaiian). The most common multiracial combination is black and white. Nevertheless, only 2.5 percent of non-Hispanic whites reported more than one race (i.e., among those who reported being white either alone or in combination with another racial group), compared with 6.1 percent of blacks, 13.5 percent of Asians, and 44 percent of Native Americans.[69]

The number of Americans identifying as multiracial will likely grow rapidly in the coming years because of recent increases in intermarriage. According to one study, about 15 percent of all new marriages in the 2008–10 period involved spouses of different races or ethnicities—more than double the percentage (6.7 percent) in 1980. (In this same study Hispanic origin was considered as a separate race/ethnicity from white.) The percentage of marriages involving a mix of differing races/ethnicities varies across groups, with a low of 9 percent of newlywed whites who married someone of a different race/ethnicity, compared with 17 percent of blacks, 26 percent of Hispanics, and 28 percent of foreign-born and U.S.-born Asians (see figure 3.4). In fact, nearly half of all U.S.-born Asians marry whites.[70] Overall, about 7 in 10 of mixed-race/ethnicity marriages still involve a white spouse, reflecting the fact that whites constitute the largest racial/ethnic group in the United States. The median household income of mixed-race newlywed couples tends to fall somewhere between the median incomes of couples in the same-race groups.[71]

Americans have become more accepting of intermarriage. In 2011, nearly two-thirds of Americans (63 percent) said they "would be fine" if a family member married someone of a different race. In contrast,

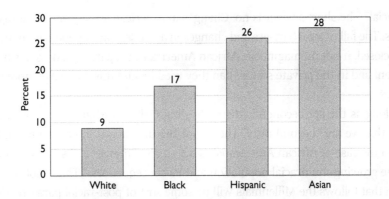

Figure 3.4 Percentage of newlyweds married to someone of a different race/ethnicity, 2010.

Source: Wang 2012, 8.

in 1986 (when the question was asked differently), about a third of the public viewed intermarriage as acceptable for everyone, 37 percent said it was acceptable for others but not themselves, and 28 percent said different races marrying one another was not acceptable for anyone. Younger respondents were more accepting of intermarriage than older ones, suggesting differences in views about race over time and across age cohorts.[72]

One news story reporting on the rise in intermarriage told the story of seventeen-year-old Kayci Baldwin of Middletown, New Jersey, who was the daughter of a mixed-race couple:

> She remembers how her black father and white mother often worried whether she would fit in with the other kids. While she at first struggled with her identity, Baldwin now actively embraces it, sponsoring support groups and a nationwide multiracial teen club of 1,000 that includes both Democrats and Republicans.
>
> "I went to my high school prom last week with my date who is Ecuadoran-Nigerian, a friend who is Chinese-white and another friend who is part Dominican," she said. "While we are a group that was previously ignored in many ways, we now have an opportunity to fully identify and express ourselves."[73]

One blogger, Leighton Woodhouse, describes broader social changes and his own experiences in a similar way:

> My girlfriend and I are both of mixed racial heritage. I'm half Japanese and half Anglo. She's half Salvadoran and half Jewish. If and when we have children, they'll be a quarter Asian, a quarter Latino and half white, with the white side split WASP/Jewish. When our kids become 18 and fill out their first voter registration forms, the only ethnic category that will make any sense for them to check off is "Multiracial." Today, checking off that box feels pretty close to checking off "Other" or "None of the above" on a questionnaire on any given topic; it's a throwaway category for misfits that has little if any analytical value to the researchers who review the data, but that has to be in there to get the respondent to the next section. When enough Americans start checking off that box, however, it's going to be impossible to ignore.[74]

So are we postracial? The short answer is no. Changes in American society since the 1950s and 1960s have been momentous. The fall of legal barriers and changes in attitudes have opened up many opportunities that were previously closed, if not unimaginable. African Americans, Hispanics, and Asians hold more high-level jobs in government and in the private sector than they used to, and this pattern is more pronounced among younger cohorts.[75]

However, as long as the socioeconomic disparities highlighted in figures 37 through 39 persist, it will be hard to claim that we are "beyond race." The disparities are caused in part by factors directly related to race (especially in the case of African Americans), such as discrimination. As Woodhouse goes on to say in his blog about the growing multiracial population and its consequences, "That's not to suggest that the age of the generation that follows the Millennials will be some sort of post-racial paradise. Countries like Brazil have had broad racially mixed populations for generations; that hasn't lessened their citizens' propensity for bigotry."[76]

Racial inequality is also exacerbated by factors that are not specifically racial, and they have disparate impacts. Of note, growing economic inequality in American society is serving to hamper the opportunities of low-income Americans and their children. The soaring cost of college has made it more difficult for poor families to utilize a traditionally important avenue to upward mobility. The overrepresentation of blacks and Hispanics among the poor exacerbates racial inequalities and will serve to lengthen the time until racial and ethnic parity is achieved.

[...]

Conclusion

Despite the decline in racial inequality and overt prejudice in the United States in recent decades, we still see significant differences in socioeconomic outcomes across racial and ethnic groups, such as in educational attainment, income, poverty, and wealth. Some of the continuing differences, particularly among blacks and perhaps Native Americans, can be explained by prejudice, stereotypes, and discrimination. However, the importance of race alone in determining life chances has declined substantially in recent decades, and the importance of socioeconomic background has increased. Unfortunately, the increasing importance of socioeconomic background serves to slow progress in reducing racial disparities, as initial disadvantages among groups often persist across generations because of these economic inequities.

Discussion Questions

1. Why do you think the socioeconomic disparities exist?
2. What, if anything, surprises you when learning about these disparities?

SECTION II

Theoretical Perspectives

The readings in this section are selected to provide perspectives on theoretical ideas of race and ethnic inequality. While students have usually studied theory from other sources, the role of ideology is often not given enough emphasis, despite its obvious importance in maintaining racial and ethnic inequality. Every system of inequality must construct an ideology that serves to justify the inequality. This ideology is self-serving. By this we mean that it serves the interests of those in power in a given society and helps to keep them in power. Johnson and Feagin discuss the importance of what people believe to be true concerning racial and ethnic inequality. Trepagnier also provides an important view of institutional racism—a term poorly understood by many.

The American Dream
of Meritocracy

By Heather Beth Johnson

Editor's Introduction

In this reading, Johnson discusses the deeply held belief that Americans have about meritocracy. Americans believe that their country is a meritocracy, despite acknowledging the advantages granted to people with inherited wealth and the disadvantages faced by those without it. The reading illustrates the power of beliefs that are maintained despite evidence that does not support those beliefs. This shows the importance of ideology in justifying and explaining inequality.

The American Dream has been continually re-invented over time, so that for each generation of Americans it has held different meanings. And since the phrase "the American Dream" could mean different things to every one of us, it might be more accurate to call it "the American Dreams." At its core, however, some aspects of the Dream (or Dreams) are consistently fundamental. Simply, the American Dream explains the logic of our country's social system. *It is a way (or perhaps the way) we are to understand how American society operates.* It is how we make sense of our particular social structure. The American Dream rests on the idea that, with hard work and personal determination anyone, regardless of background, has an equal opportunity to achieve his or her aspirations. The American Dream promises that our system functions as a meritocracy. *Within a meritocracy people get ahead or behind based on what they earn and deserve, rather than what circumstances they were born into.* This notion of [sic] is central to the American Dream, and is the central logic of how our system is supposed to operate. The American Dream, in many ways, defines us and sets our system apart from others.

Given the importance of the American Dream to our national identity, and the enormity of it in shaping our core ideologies, it is curious how little attention the idea has received in academe, especially in the social sciences. Until relatively recently, no one had traced the history of its origins, meanings, or cultural impacts. In the past decade, however, groundbreaking scholarship on the American Dream has yielded important understandings. We know, for example, that the principles of the American Dream were promoted by even the very first settlers to arrive from Britain. Later, the American Dream was central to the charter of the United States when the Declaration of Independence was created. And although the phrase "the American Dream" does not appear to have been coined until around 1931, it has quickly become recognizable the world over. The American Dream is, for better or for worse, the central creed of our nation.

As a creed, the American Dream represents a basic belief in the power and capacity of the individual. Deeply embedded in this belief is a particular notion of individual agency—the idea that over the course of our own lives we are each accountable for whatever position we find ourselves in. Full collective potential for this agency, though, depends on exactly that which the dream promises: A system of opportunity, so that regardless of background each individual has an equal chance to prosper. The American Dream promises that an egalitarian system will allow individuals to advance based on their own merit. This promise resonates throughout contemporary American society telling us—through multiple variations on a theme, through school assignments and television advertisements, through song lyrics and newspaper stories—that in a meritocratic process we rise or fall self-reliantly. So, despite differences across generations and regardless we each have unique hopes and dreams, we share the American Dream of meritocracy in common: That is, we are each subject—in one way or another—to our nationalist ideology of meritocracy.

Meritocracy explains not only how our society works but how inequality exists. The idea is that what we reap—good or bad—is merited; whatever we have, whatever our status, whatever our place in the social world, we earn. A system of meritocracy does not assert equality *per se*—within any social hierarchy some individuals will inevitably be positioned higher and some lower—rather, it justifies inequality of social positioning by the meritocratic process itself. Inequality of outcomes is justified and legitimized by equality of opportunity. This meritocratic idea has roots dating back to the British colonialists' aspirations for a society founded in a "natural aristocracy." In their vision upward mobility and prominence would be merited and achieved, rather than ascribed. For those first families settling from Europe, this vision was a defiant rebellion from other forms of social structure where social rank was inherited based on such distinctions as family lineage, royalty, and caste. Although they never precisely defined how merit should be measured, it was always clear how it should not be: achievement based on individual merit is not unearned advantage; it is not inherited privilege. A meritocratic system is contingent upon a societal commitment to fair competition so that no individual or group is advantaged or disadvantaged by the positions or predicaments of their ancestors.

The American Dream of meritocracy is at once a simple idea and a complex national ethos. For some people the American Dream may simply represent owning a home, while for others it might represent striking it rich. Although those may be part of what the American Dream means for many people, as a foundational ideology it is about more than material abundance or a place with streets-paved-with-gold. It is about opportunity—not just an opportunity, but equal opportunity. It is about not just a chance, but equal chances. In her landmark book, *Facing Up to the American Dream: Race, Class, and the Soul of a Nation*, political scientist Jennifer Hochschild explicates the American Dream and identifies its main tenets. She distinguishes key premises which interlock to form its philosophical foundation. These premises include meritocracy, the notion that in our social system upward and downward mobility is based on personal achievement so that people get ahead or behind based on merit; equal opportunity, the notion that all members of society are given equal opportunity for social mobility; individualism, the notion that each individual makes it on his or her own; and the open society, the notion that the United States is a free country, the melting pot of the world, the land of opportunity for all people. As Hochschild outlines, the American Dream is a set of deeply held beliefs, a particular mindset.

It is a particular way of viewing the world, and it is a particular way in which we want the world to view us. For many Americans, the American Dream is a great source of pride. But even many who question it as an accurate portrayal of social life believe strongly in the egalitarian and inclusive principles for which it stands.

As a dominant ideology the American Dream echoes throughout our nation, it carries on through generations, and can cement in crystal form in our minds. But it can also be easily taken for granted. For as central the American Dream is to our national identity, we don't consciously reflect on it often. As historian Jim Cullen has noted, the American Dream is "an idea that seems to envelop us as unmistakably as the air we breathe." We can be reminded of it, without even being aware, every time we are told that we will achieve if we work hard enough, or that we could have achieved if we had only worked harder. The American Dream can inspire great aspirations and explain great achievements, and it can depress us as we ponder our regrets. It is malleable enough to fit in almost any social situation. We can use it to justify our accomplishments: I earned it on my own. This is the result of my hard work. I deserve this. And we can feel the sting of it as we question ourselves: Should I have worked harder? Could I have gone farther? Why am I not where he is? And, we can use it to question others' social standing: Why doesn't she try harder? Doesn't he want more? Why don't they make better choices? The American Dream is all around us, and, in many ways it is in us.

Ultimately, the American Dream is an explanation for the hierarchical ordering of our class positions in our social world. It explains our relative rank as the result of solely our own doing, not as the result of social forces or the circumstances we find ourselves in. It is not surprising, then, that Americans might genuinely believe that they independently earn and deserve their class positions—the dominant ideology of our culture tells them so. This internalized sense of class positioning has been the subject of scholarly research, especially in regards to working-class and poor families. In Richard Sennett and Jonathan Cobb's pivotal book *The Hidden Injuries of Class*, for example, they discuss the "hidden injury" of the internal class conflict experienced among working-class men. They wrote that "Every question of identity as an image of social place in a hierarchy is also a question of social value. ... This is the context in which all questions of personal and social legitimacy occur." The American Dream helps to sustain these "hidden injuries" by bombarding people with the message that their social place—and their social value, their self-worth—is directly and exclusively the result of their own actions.

In their interviews for this book, people spoke in depth and at length about the American Dream, despite the fact that in the first 182 interviews the families were not even asked about it. Those parents were told that the project was to study assets and inequality, and during the interviews they were asked to speak about the communities they lived in, their children's schools, and their families' financial histories. Over and over, however, the focus of the interviews turned to beliefs in meritocracy as families repeatedly brought up the subject and wove it into the conversations. I must admit that I myself was surprised with the extent to which the interview findings were so ideological in nature. And I was even more surprised when interviews—including those interviews from the second phase which did directly ask people about their thoughts on the American Dream—revealed the depths of people's commitment to, and belief in, meritocracy as a real and valid explanation for how contemporary American society operates. People from all walks of life spoke forthrightly of their belief in meritocracy, not just as rhetoric, but as an accurate explanation of our social system.

Trying to confirm these findings has been frustrating due to the lack of qualitative studies that have asked people in-depth about their perspectives on the American Dream. Curiously, even in terms of quantitative studies, surprisingly few public opinion polls have been conducted on the subject of the American Dream. However, related social survey data that do exist reflect that Americans overwhelmingly believe that their country operates as a meritocracy. Indeed, after his review of the data political scientist Everett Carl Ladd concluded that survey research "shows Americans holding tenaciously and distinctively to the central elements of their founding ideology." He found Americans' belief in the American Dream to be more intense, pervasive, and firmly entrenched than generally recognized. Very recent qualitative research on post-civil rights views also finds that in in-depth interviews people are remarkably insistent in their beliefs that the playing field is level, that meritocracy is real. While these findings are definitely in line with my own, perhaps the most compelling affirmation for me has been to discover that other sociologists doing in-depth interviewing on subjects not explicitly focused on the American Dream are finding, as I have, that respondents consistently evoke the American Dream—specifically the notion of meritocracy—as their own theme in interviews. In the 200 interviews conducted for this study, what families said, their views, their decisions, and their experiences, were explicitly framed by their belief in meritocracy. These families' perspectives give a vivid account of the place and significance of the American Dream in contemporary life.

The reality of wealth in America though—the way it is acquired, distributed, and the way it is used—is a direct contradiction to these fundamental ideas. In interviews with American families we have seen a way how that plays out. Examining school decision-making (just one arena wherein families potentially experience the ramifications of wealth inequality), those parents from backgrounds of even moderate wealth had a significant advantage over parents with family histories of wealth poverty. Disproportionately white, wealth-holding parents used the financial assistance, intergenerational transfers, and security of their family wealth to help access schools for their own children that were viewed as advantageous by all of the parents. Meanwhile, parents without family wealth to rely upon, who were disproportionately black, were navigating the same arena unaided, with relatively limited resources and constrained capacities. *A central incongruity surfaces when families' school decisions are considered in the context of the American Dream: the assets that the wealth-holding families had owned, relied upon, and utilized in choosing schools had most often originated from non-merit sources.* Inherited wealth and the security of family wealth were critical advantages being passed along to the next generation—advantages often unearned by the parents themselves, and always unearned by their children.

A foundational conflict exists between the meritocratic values of the American Dream and the structure of intergenerational wealth inequality. Simply, advantageous resources inherited and passed along in families are not attained through individual achievement. Although wealth can, of course, be earned by an individual entirely independently, in the case of the families we spoke with it had not. This is the aspect of family wealth that concerns us here. Family wealth generates unearned advantages for those who have it. It is a form of privilege. In light of their beliefs in the American Dream, how do those families who present the most transparent contradiction to the idea of meritocracy—families with wealth privilege—understand their positioning and the unearned advantages they pass along to their children?

We could presume that as with other forms of privilege (such as race privilege or gender privilege) wealth privilege would generally appear invisible and be taken for granted by those who have it. However, one of the most striking aspects of the interviews was the acknowledgement of wealth privilege on the part of wealth-holding families. The parents who had benefited from family wealth acknowledged a structure of wealth inequality that grants privilege to some families and disadvantage to others, and they acknowledged the advantages they were passing along to the next generation through the schools that they chose.

Acknowledging Advantage: A Structure of Wealth Inequality

Given the fact that these families had so vehemently expressed their beliefs in the legitimacy of the American Dream, it was startling to hear them so openly discuss the reality of structured wealth inequality in American society. Not only did parents talk openly about this, they expressed specific views concerning the advantages conferred by wealth. Wealth-holding families thought of wealth as a distinctive resource to be used in particular ways, and even asset-poor families had concrete opinions about how they would use wealth—as opposed to income—if they had it. *Regardless of whether a family had a lot, a little, or none, wealth was thought of as a special form of money, different from income.* Wealth was perceived as a vehicle to provide opportunities, experiences, and material things, as well as a source to provide other less tangible advantages that were harder to articulate but no less important (a sense of security, or confidence about the future, for example). *As a whole, families' perspectives on the advantages of family wealth centered around two notions: wealth as a push and wealth as a safety net.* While families across the board alluded to these ideas, they were especially prevalent among the wealthier families, who emphasized them repeatedly. The first notion—a "push"—or an "edge" as some referred to it, was used by parents to explain how family wealth put some people "ahead" of others right from the start and "paved the way" for them over time.

Int: Do you believe that you would have achieved the same social and economic situation that you have today if you weren't given the same financial support from your parents?

James: I would say no, because I feel what it has given me is the edge today. But for us today—for what I am, where I work, my abilities as well as my level of education—I feel without that I don't think I would be where I am today. Because the son would not have been successful without his father doing this—

Pamela: Paving the way for him—

James: [Nods] So, his father paved the way for him to start off and climb up the ladder to be what he is right now. Each kid has the potential, aspiration, a dream. And with wealth you can guide them, you can steer them that way. And you can help them, smooth the way for them, open up doors which they had never seen before.

Pamela and James Gordon, just as the other parents from backgrounds of family wealth, had experienced how that wealth had given them a push and believed it had made a positive difference in the trajectory of their life course. And they believed that this same push they were now giving their own children would make a difference for them too down the road.

Some of the wealth-holding families interviewed were more resistant than others to explicitly conceptualize that "push" they referred to, or those "difference down the road," as concrete "advantage." Joel, for example, asserted right away that wealth passed on to children is "not advantage." He did, however, believe that "it helps." While he described the wealth passed along in families as "a pushing factor," he was careful to not suggest that this translated into actual advantage.

Int: Does the financial help in terms of wealth that some people receive from their families give them certain advantages?

Joel: Not advantage, but it helps. It will help.

Int: Do you think it's significant?

Joel: Depends on what kind of financial help you're talking about.

Int: I'm not talking about billionaires. I'm talking, like, giving a kid after he graduates a $45,000 car. Or giving him, like, $30,000 for his wedding gift. Joel: That helps, yeah, that does help. Yeah, the normal help that the parents give to the children, that is a pushing factor. Just puts you ahead a little bit.

Int: Do you believe those without stable economic situations have a harder time achieving success?

Joel: Yes, I do. That's the rule of life. I mean if you have the money you have peace of mind. So you probably can make better decisions. If you're under pressure for lack of money you could go wrong, you could make wrong decisions, definitely.

Here we see a tension between the ideology of meritocracy and the reality of structured wealth inequality in the nuances of how Joel Conrad talked about, perceived, and made sense of family wealth. While a few other parents expressed similar resistance to acknowledging that the "push" of family wealth was a form of privilege, most families did not. Victoria and Abraham Keenan, for example, conceptualized what they were doing for their own children as "absolutely" giving them advantages. While they were careful to point out that they were not "multi-millionaires" like other people they knew, they did fully believe, and acknowledge, that their family wealth was giving their children "a better chance of becoming successful." Implicit in the way they discussed the passing along of their wealth was their acknowledgement that by doing so they were passing along advantage.

Family wealth was believed to give children a push that, as Abraham said, "gives them a better chance of becoming successful." Some families, of course, can give bigger pushes than others, but even small pushes are clearly advantageous. Children who get the pushes of family wealth benefit from advantages they did nothing to individually earn. The acknowledgement of this on the part of the families who were passing advantages along is an important part of their perspectives on wealth privilege and an important insight to how they think about inequality. The second major way that parents depicted the advantages of family wealth was that it acted as a "safety net" for them in important decisions and throughout their lives. Parents from wealth-holding families repeatedly articulated their sense that family wealth was a "safety net" that gave them tremendous "peace of mind." The Barrys, a white couple whose families on both sides had given them significant financial assets over the years, described their wealth-holdings, and the family wealth they believed they could rely upon in the future, as "a sense of economic security." When asked what that sense of security provides for them, Briggette answered:

Briggette: Sleep at night. It's very non-tangible things. Being able to give my children a sense of peace. Being able to live worry free. It's really non-tangible things. Knowing that I will probably never have the income that my parents had, but still being comfortable with that and being able to provide for my children what they need.

Another parent who explicitly described her family's wealth as a "safety net," went on to explain, "Well, I think just having, um, the assets, just gives us a certain freedom. ... You know? You're more freer and more comfortable." The sense of security parents felt from the safety net of family wealth, their desire to re-establish that safety net for their own children, and their ability to rely on it and expand on it in investing in their children's futures cannot be overemphasized. This was a major way that individuals we interviewed—for example Cynthia and Paul Perkins, a white middle-class couple with three children in Boston—acknowledged the power of wealth and wealth's associated privileges.

When a "safety net" of wealth—or, "a cushion for the future"—could not be relied upon, families without it felt the insecurity of having nothing on which to fall back. This is where the difference between wealth and income is perhaps the clearest. As Lenore Meehan, a young black mother from Boston explained it: "You know, if you look on paper, I make a lot of money, but it doesn't feel like it. ... I mean, I don't feel like I'm economically secure at all." While she was up-front about the fact that she felt she made quite a lot of money working as a dispatcher for the police force, Lenore's income simply could not provide the sense of security that family wealth was granting to other parents who had it. The families interviewed from all race and class backgrounds made a clear distinction between wealth and income and had concrete understandings of the kinds of advantages that family wealth can provide. Their conceptualization of the "push" and the "safety net" that wealth affords for families and children (and that lack-of-wealth prohibits) reveals their intrinsic awareness and understanding of the power of wealth. *Their acknowledgement of the role of wealth in shaping opportunities, life trajectories, and future chances reveals their awareness and understanding of a structure of wealth inequality.*

As Abigail Connor said, "for someone like her" (someone from a wealthy white family with accumulated, historically rooted race and class advantages), intergenerational transfers of wealth along the way had created a real form of contemporary privilege: family wealth advantage that is not earned entirely independently but which make opportunities relatively easier to attain, aspirations relatively more achievable, and life chances relatively more optimistic. When asked to reflect on the way this had played out in their own lives Abigail and others "like her" (others from families of relative wealth privilege) were quite aware of the essential role that their family wealth had played in their lives. Here Emily Mitchel explains:

Int: Do you believe that you would have achieved the same social and economic situation that you have today if you weren't given the same financial support from your parents growing up?

Emily: No.

Int: [silent pause] How essential, if at all, do you believe family wealth is in attaining success?

Emily: I think it certainly helps. I think more people who have money tend to excel than people who have no money. It gives you the education, it gives you the contacts, it gives you the clothes, the way of talking. The things that make life easier. Can you do it without it? Yes. Is it as easy? I don't think so. ... I think early in our history hard work was really important. But I think money— you can work really hard and be the best foreman on a construction job, but it's not gonna get you a villa in France or a villa in Tuscany. It's just gonna get you whatever kind of advance you want, and a place to live. So I really think that wealth or family money is one of the essential ingredients.

Parents who had benefited from the advantages of family wealth consistently expressed their beliefs that they would not have achieved their same level of success without the financial support that they had received. Of the families who had benefited from family wealth, in only two cases did a parent insist without any compromise that they would have ended up in exactly the same position without any of the financial support that they had received from their family. And in the two exceptions it is possible, of course, that they are correct. It is also the case that we have no way to really know.

In addition to talking about how it had impacted them, parents with family wealth also discussed how they were using that wealth to shape their own children's lives. They were consciously aware that their own relatively privileged positions were enabling them to pass advantage along to the next generation. From these parents' perspectives, family wealth provided specific advantages such as educational opportunities that without it their children would not have. Elizabeth Cummings, a white mother from a wealthy St. Louis family, explained her perspective:

Elizabeth: No question about it! I mean, if my parents hadn't had the money to send my kids to *The Hills School*, we couldn't have considered it. We would have had to really do belt tightening, and financial aid, and many more loans, more mortgages. It would have been very difficult and a real strain on us, especially with two. And we probably would have felt like we just couldn't swing it as a family. So, I don't know, I would have had to gone out and gotten a job that would pay enough to justify two kids in private school. With that, it would have meant not being able to mother them as much myself. Or my husband having to change work, and all the soul searching that would have meant for him. It's unimaginable. I can't envision a path that we would have been able to so comfortably just sail on over to *The Hills School*.

The idea that "you have to have wealth to get it" (or, at least, that having wealth makes it relatively easier to get more) and the idea that "wealthier people have better life chances" (or, at least, that wealth confers relatively better chances for success), stood at the heart of the matter in the interviews. And these concepts stand at the heart of the matter here: If family wealth makes the next generation's wealth relatively easier to acquire, and if wealth makes success (however defined) relatively easier to attain, then people born into families with wealth are born with a distinct, unearned advantage. They are born with privilege that others do not have.

Conviction in Meritocracy: Hard Work or Lack Thereof

Carter: The fact of the matter is because you get some assistance from your parents doesn't mean that you haven't primarily achieved anything on your own. The fact of the matter is getting a down payment on a house means you were able to get a house sooner, but you still have to make the payments on the house, you still have to do everything necessary to maintain that house.

So yeah, it's a help, but it's not the overriding factor.

Int: You think the overriding factor is your own—

Carter: Your own psyche. ... At the end of the day, hard work is the most important ingredient—in anybody's success.

Int: Think so?

Carter: Yes. The determination to be successful is like the tide, you know? You can't stop it.

Faith & Carter Martin, Homemaker & Attorney, White, Washington, D.C.

Tracei Diamond, a black single mother from St. Louis, spent much of her interview answering "no" to every question regarding any financial assistance she might have received and explaining the lack of any family financial resources available to her. As a full time banquet waitress at a private country club, Tracei's annual income was $24,000, she had zero net financial assets, and held only a high school degree. Tracei talked about how she sees the members of the country club at functions and events and thinks about how they and their children had advantages that she and her three children simply did not have. She spoke at length, for example, about how the schools "out there" (where the country club was located) were "good schools," how the teachers "really work with them" (the students), and how overall "the education is better." In Tracei's view, for as much as she would like to be able to give her kids those same kinds of opportunities, she simply cannot afford the move to such an area. On top of supporting her three children on her own (she was receiving no child support), Tracei also was doing whatever she could to financially support her younger sister and their mother.

Tracei's interview was typical in that she articulated clear recognition of a structured inequality amongst families that blatantly and categorically translates into unequal educational opportunities for children of different family wealth backgrounds. Yet also typical was Tracei's outright rejection of this inequality and of unequal opportunity. Tracei recognized it and rejected it at the same time. After Tracei had talked about how "wealthy families" get the "better schools," she was asked about how a family's wealth plays a factor in their children's access to quality education. She replied: "It really doesn't have an impact on it. I guess pretty much it depends on you, as far as what kind of life you will have for your child." When she was asked if wealth has any impact, she said "I don't really look at it like that. So, like I say, money definitely doesn't have anything to do with it." When asked to explain further, Tracei did: "It's basically what the parents want or whatever, that's the only thing I really can see. It just depends on how they raise them really." Despite their perspectives that class inequality structures life chances, Tracei and the other families maintained their belief that merit—not money—is what matters; they maintained with conviction their belief in meritocracy.

It was striking to hear disadvantaged parents talk so vehemently about meritocracy, to hear them assert repeatedly that positions in society are earned entirely through hard work and personal achievement, and to hear them deny family wealth inequality as a legitimate explanation. But considering that many of these parents had no direct experience with wealth privilege, that they had no awareness of the extent to which wealthy families are using and extending intergenerational transfers of assets, that they did not know for sure how much others are advantaged by unearned resources, then it makes sense how they clung so resolutely to the dominant ideology. What was most remarkable, however, is that those parents with family wealth who had spoken openly of their unearned advantages, who had so plainly seen and felt and known wealth privilege in motion in their own lives, were, at the same time, insistent that meritocracy is an accurate and realistic explanation for social stratification in America. In an interview in St. Louis, Briggette and Joe Barry spoke in detail of the financial help they had received from their parents. *They openly declared that these resources had allowed for a lifestyle they would not otherwise have had. After listing extensive financial assistance, the security of family wealth, and the many advantages they have had, the Barrys insisted that the way they had earned their assets was through hard work.*

The Barrys were not atypical of the white middle-class families interviewed; on the contrary, they portrayed the sentiments of families like them in the sample. Their socioeconomic positions were due, in large part, to the inheritance and accumulative advantages of family wealth, yet at the same time they were adamant that they single-handedly earned and deserved their places in society. These families' insistence that they had, "worked their butts off" for what they had was astonishing. They listed in detail the help they had received from their families: Financial assistance with major purchases, down payments on houses, school tuition for children, "loans" that were later forgiven, etc. They catalogued the gifts they had received from family members for birthdays, graduations, weddings, and births of children. They discussed the numerous ways their extended families had been financially generous over the years by providing used cars, old furniture, flight tickets home for holidays, family vacations, dining out, kids' back-to-school clothes, and groceries, to name a few. They described the "push" and the "safety net" that comes with family wealth: Feeling that they have had "a head start" or "an edge" over others, knowing they would have something to fall back on in a financial pinch, and the expectation of future inheritances. While they talked about, listed, and described these things when asked, they repeatedly emphasized how hard they had worked for all that they owned and how much they deserved their stations in life.

Regardless of background, families used the American Dream of meritocracy to explain their assertion that anyone can be anything and do anything and get anywhere with hard work. They stressed that hard work or lack thereof was the determinant of each individual's position in society. But for those with family wealth, what was most notable was how they implied, implicitly and explicitly, that their own advantages as well as the advantages they were passing along to their children were earned and deserved autonomously—through hard work, perseverance, and determination alone.

Another example comes from our interview with Chris and Peter Ackerman, a white couple in their early thirties who lived in a white suburb of St. Louis. They had three kids, ages six, three, and two. They had been married for ten years and both worked in management positions on the staff of a local university. Their combined annual income was $83,000, their net worth $210,000, and their net financial assets totaled $91,500. This couple owned savings accounts, savings bonds, small trust funds for each child, and a boat worth $12,500. They had received significant financial assistance from their families, including help with a down payment on their first home, which they bought when they married. The equity from that house was later used as a down payment for an upgraded home when they had their children. Chris and Peter's parents financed their college educations; they never had to take out student loans; their children regularly received cash gifts and savings bonds from their grandparents on holidays and birthdays; Chris's parents had often paid for the family to vacation with them; Peter's parents had bought many of their major household appliances for them, as well as their car; and so on. They talked about how appreciative they were of all this help, about how they would not be in the position that they are without it. Despite this acknowledgement, Chris and Peter continually insisted that their wealth had been achieved single-handedly:

Int: How did you acquire the assets you own?

Chris: By working.

Peter: Saving, working.

Chris: Working and saving, working and saving. That's basically how we do it.

The Ackermans and many of their peers simultaneously acknowledged the power of their wealth privilege and avowed that it does not really matter. They were resolute in their explanation that hard work and determination had gotten them to where they are. For as much as they were upfront about the structure of wealth, they also depicted social positioning as independently earned and deserved. As one young mother from just outside of New York City put it, "You know—and I'm not bragging, I'm not saying anything—but it just comes from setting your priorities straight, and taking care of business!" In discussing hard work and individual achievement people often spoke louder, quicker, and sometimes at a higher pitch. People leaned forward or moved in toward the tape recorder's microphone as if to want to be sure they were heard clearly on this. They spoke with fervor and conviction when crediting themselves with their own success. For example, in talking with Lily and Jonathan Boothe, a white wealthy family from the New York City area, Jonathan had been quite serene throughout the interview. However, when we began talking about the Boothes' perspectives on success and achievement, Jonathan became noticeably more vivacious.

Just as people with wealth credited themselves for their success, conversely, those who lacked family wealth blamed themselves. Conviction in meritocracy worked both ways, and meritocracy could justify both positions. The themes of "sticking to one's ideals," "being focused," "motivated," and "willing to work hard" were as consistent in interviews with working-class and impoverished families as they were in affluent families. People blamed themselves for their inability to attain what they wished for and wanted for themselves and their children, even when they were starting from the most disadvantaged backgrounds. One parent from Boston explained that, compared to others, she comes up short because "I did a lot of fooling around." A mother from St. Louis said, "I would say that I am a little bit limited. But it's nobody's fault but my own. So I can't complain." And still another parent lamented, "If I was to make more, better, wiser decisions along the way, I wouldn't have the debt that I have now."

Most people have regrets in life, and maybe if the families who were struggling to make ends meet had made "more, better, wiser decisions along the way," things would have turned out differently for them. Maybe not. But one of the things that stood out the most about this explanation was that many of these families had in fact done extraordinarily well for themselves. More often than not, however, the fruits of unaided self-achievement simply paled in comparison to the results of self-achievement combined with the advantages of family wealth. Still, throughout the interviews, parents from poor and working-class family backgrounds compared themselves to more "well-off" others, blamed themselves, and legitimized their situations by saying they should have worked harder. While to some extent they understood that a structure of wealth inequality existed, and while they recognized the real advantages for those with family wealth, they simultaneously blamed themselves for not having worked harder and done better than they had.

The interviews also show the power of hope. For these families the American Dream was hope. It held out hope that what is wanted will happen, and that what is wanted can be expected. It held out hope that children's life chances were all equally unconstrained. It held out hope that the world is just. To think otherwise (to think that the world is not just) would be heart-breaking to any parent. And, I believe, many parents fear that to think otherwise (to think that the world is not just) could potentially—if conveyed to children—break the spirit of any child. So they hold on to the American Dream, they hold on to their hope. This hope was reflected in the parents' perspectives regarding themselves, the social system they are acting on and within, and—most importantly—their children.

Discussion Questions

1. What makes the idea of meritocracy so compelling to Americans that people believe in it, even when it is contradicted by evidence all around them?
2. How would the members of your family explain their economic situation to themselves and to others? As the result of hard work and talent alone?
3. Why do you think none of the respondents talked about the role of luck in their own successes and failures?
4. Do you think that the American Dream can survive the increasing economic inequality which is transforming American society? Why or why not?

References

Hochschild, Jennifer. 1995. *Facing Up to the American Dream: Race, Class, and the Soul of a Nation.* Princeton, NJ: Princeton University Press.

———. 1981. *What's Fair? American Beliefs about Distributive Justice.* Cambridge, MA: Harvard University Press.

Schwartz, John E. 1997. *Illusions of Opportunity: the American Dream in Question.* New York: W. W. Norton.

Sennett, Richard & Cobb, Jonathan. 1972. *The Hidden Injuries of Class.* New York: W. W. Norton.

Racist America

Racist Ideology as a Social Force

By Joe R. Feagin

Editor's Introduction

In this reading, Feagin discusses racist ideology. A key point made in the reading is that racist ideology not only exists, but that it is also a social force that drives behaviors and actions of individuals and institutions. This reading is selected to highlight the utility of ideology as it functions to maintain a system of dominance and racial subordination.

Creating a Racist Ideology

The dramatic expansion of Europe from the 1400s to the early 1900s eventually brought colonial exploitation to more than 80 percent of the globe. The resulting savagery, exploitation, and resource inequalities were global, and they stemmed, as W. E. B. Du Bois has noted, from letting a "single tradition of culture suddenly have thrust into its hands the power to bleed the world of its brawn and wealth, and the willingness to do this."[1] However, for the colonizing Europeans it was not enough to bleed the world of its labor and resources. The colonizers were not content to exploit indigenous peoples and view that exploitation simply as "might makes right." Instead, they vigorously justified what they had done for themselves and their descendants. Gradually, a broad racist ideology rationalized the oppression and thereby reduced its apparent moral cost for Europeans.

An ideology is a set of principles and views that embodies the basic interests of a particular social group. Typically, a broad ideology encompasses expressed attitudes and is constantly reflected in the talk and actions of everyday life. One need not know or accept the entire ideology for it to have an impact on thought or action. Thus, each person may participate only in certain fragments of an ideology. Ideologies are usually created by oppressors to cover what they do, and counterideologies are often developed by the oppressed in their struggle against domination. Here we examine a critical aspect of the social reproduction of systemic racism from one generation to the next. The perpetuation of systemic racism requires an intertemporal reproducing not only of racist institutions and structures but also of the ideological apparatus that buttresses them.

The early exploitative relationships that whites developed in regard to African Americans and Native Americans were quickly rationalized, and they became enduring racist relations. From the beginning, racial oppression has been webbed into most arenas of American life, including places of work and residence, and activities as diverse as eating, procreating, and child rearing. Racist practices in these life worlds create, and are in turn shaped by, basic racist categories in the language and minds of Americans, especially white Americans. A racist ideology has overarching principles and beliefs that provide an umbrella for more specific racist attitudes, prejudices, and stereotypes.

Major ideological frameworks, including racist frameworks, are typically created, codified, and maintained by those at the top of a society, although this construction takes place in ongoing interaction with the views and practices of ordinary citizens. Those with the greater power have the greater ability to impose their own ideas on others. As Karl Marx and Friedrich Engels long ago pointed out, "the ideas of the ruling class are in every epoch the ruling ideas: i.e. the class, which is the ruling material force of society, is at the same time its ruling intellectual force."[2] Elites have dominated the creation, discussion, and dissemination of system-rationalizing ideas in business, the media, politics, education, churches, and government. While there is indeed much popularly generated racist imagery and discourse, even this is usually codified and embellished by the elites. As with most important ideas, if the elites had been opposed to the development of the racist ideology, they would have actively combated it, and it would likely have declined in importance. Thus, in his detailed analysis of the racist ideas and actions of presidents from George Washington to Bill Clinton, Kenneth O'Reilly has shown that conventional wisdom about presidents following a racist populace is wrongheaded. The historical evidence shows that most of the men who control U.S. political institutions have worked hard "to nurture and support the nation's racism."[3] Racist thought did not come accidentally to the United States. It was, and still is, actively developed and propagated.

The Emerging Antiblack Ideology: Early Views

For several centuries white ministers, business people, political leaders, academics, scientists, and media executives have developed and disseminated to all Americans a complex and variegated racist ideology that defends the theft of land and labor from Americans of color. The antiblack version of this ideology is the most developed; it has included a variety of religious, scientific, and psychosexual rationalizations for oppression. Although the ideology has been elaborated and changed somewhat over time, in all its variations it has operated to rationalize white power and privilege.

From the 1600s to the 1800s English and other European Protestants dominated the religious scene on the Atlantic coast of North America, and their religious views incorporated notions of European superiority and non-European inferiority. The early English Protestants regarded themselves as Christian and civilized, but those they conquered as unchristian and savage. Religious and cultural imperialism accompanied economic imperialism. Most of the new colonists from Europe saw themselves as Christian people of virtue and civilization. From the first century of American colonization these Europeans frequently portrayed themselves as "virtuous republicans." They did not, or should not, have the instinctual qualities of the "creatures of darkness," the black and red Calibans they saw in their stereotyped images. Europeans were rational, ascetic, self-governing, and sexually controlled, while the African and Native American others were irrational, uncivilized, instinctual, and uncontrolled.[4] The first non-Europeans with whom many European colonists came into contact were Native Americans. Rationalizing the often brutal destruction of Native American societies, European colonists developed early on some negative images of Native Americans. Native Americans were "uncivilized savages" to be killed off or pushed beyond the boundaries of European American society. Moreover, much white thinking about indigenous peoples in the first centuries alternated between great hostility, such as can be seen in the Declaration of Independence's complaint about "merciless Indian savages," and the paternalism seen in the image of a "noble savage" who was independent of the vices of Europeans. Novelists such as James Fenimore Cooper heralded what they saw as the diversity in character of the "native warrior of North America. In war, he is daring, boastful, cunning, ruthless ... in peace, just, generous, hospitable, revengeful, superstitious, modest, and commonly chaste."[5]

Early Color Coding: The Link to Slavery

In the first century of North American slavery the antiblack ideology was becoming ever more developed and comprehensive. The emerging ideology increasingly focused not only on the blackness of the others but also on the whiteness of Europeans. Africans and African Americans were viewed as physically, aesthetically, morally, and mentally inferior to whites—differences that were regarded as more or less permanent. "Whiteness" was created in opposition to "blackness," in comparison to which it was not only different but quite superior. Indeed, from the seventeenth century forward black women, men, and children were "constructed as lazy, ignorant, lascivious, and criminal; Whites as industrious, knowledgeable, virtuous, and law-abiding."[6]

Significantly, the antiblack image was not "out there," but rather in the white mind and emotions. In their thinking and imaging, some whites went so far as to view the dark skin of Africans as a "natural infection" or as "pollution." A leading medical educator of the late 1700s, Dr. Benjamin Rush, thought the dark skin color of African Americans resulted from a type of leprosy that could be cured with medical treatment.[7]

The U.S. Constitution recognized the slave economy and implicitly incorporated an ideology of white supremacy in such provisions as the one that counted an African American as only "three-fifths" of a person. After the new nation was created, the unifying of growing numbers of immigrants from various European countries was done in part through the legal and political doctrines buttressing white privilege and superiority. In the first naturalization law in 1790, the new U.S. Congress made the earliest political statement on citizenship. Naturalization was restricted to "white persons." Whiteness thereby became an official government category; only European immigrants could qualify to become citizens of the new United States. The legal doctrines established by Congress and the courts helped to shape and unify the white consciousness, including that of the nation's leadership.[8]

Emotional Underpinnings

From the seventeenth century to the present the ideology justifying antiblack oppression, while overtly cognitive and legally enshrined, has had a strong emotional base. Antiblack attitudes and actions among whites have long been linked to or supported by such emotions as hate, fear, guilt, and repulsion. W.E.B. Du

Bois suggested that color barriers are created not only out of overt maliciousness but also by "unconscious acts and irrational reactions unpierced by reason."[9]

For instance, many whites have been emotionally obsessed with what they term "racial mixing." Strong and irrational emotions are evident in the taboos and laws against interracial sex and marriage, which have long been considered to be extremely "unnatural" and "abominable" by many whites. In 1662 the colony of Virginia established the first law against interracial sex, and in 1691 a law against interracial marriage was enforced by banishment. White Virginians, scholars have noted, were very "disturbed by the racial intermingling, especially white-Negro mixtures, and introduced laws to prevent what they saw as the 'abominable mixture and spurious issue' by penalizing whites who engaged in interracial sex."[10] Mixed-ancestry Americans were viewed not only as inferior but also as degrading what Benjamin Franklin called a "lovely" whiteness. As Franklin argued, white "amalgamation with the other color produces a degradation to which no lover of his country, no lover of excellence in the human character can innocently consent."[11] Like most whites of the eighteenth century, Franklin seems to have developed a deep fear of black Americans. A slaveholder for several decades, then a leading abolitionist later in life, Franklin openly opposed slavery not because of its inhumanity but because of its negative impact on the whiteness of the American population. Ironically and significantly, for most of American history it was white men who were the most likely to cross the color line and force sex on black women.

Strong emotions are evident in the white violence that has long targeted black Americans. While most of the bloodthirsty lynchings of black Americans took place after the Civil War, they were preceded before that war by barbaric beatings, rape, torture, and mutilation of Africans and African Americans on slave ships, farms, and plantations. The early white notion that African Americans were "dangerous savages" and "degenerate beasts" played a role in rationalizing this violence. To deserve such treatment "the black man presumably had to be as vicious as the racists claimed; otherwise many whites would have had to accept an intolerable burden of guilt for perpetrating or tolerating the most horrendous cruelties and injustices."[12] After slavery, the racist ideology legitimated lynchings, whose sadistic character suggests deep and shared white emotions of guilt, hatred, and fear. Fear is central to the ideology and attitudes woven through the system of antiblack oppression. Significantly, of the three large-scale systems of social oppression—racism, sexism, and classism—only racism involves the dominant group having a deep and often obsessively emotional fear of the subordinate group. This is not generally true for men, who dominate women in the system of sexism, nor is it true for the capitalists who exploit workers in the class-stratified capitalist system.

Developing an Explicit Ideology of "Race"

The ideology rationalizing exploitation did not develop all at once, but was elaborated as colonialism expanded around the globe. First, as we saw above, the "others" were viewed as religiously and culturally inferior. This brought an early accent on a hierarchy of inferior and superior groups. Later on, those oppressed were seen as distinctive "races" that were inferior in physical, biological, and intellectual terms to Europeans. A clearly delineated concept of "race" as a distinctive pseudobiological category was developed by northern Europeans and European Americans about the time of the American Revolution.

By the late 1700s these hierarchical relations were increasingly explained in overtly bioracial terms. This biological determinism read existing European prejudices back into human biology; then it read that biology as rationalizing social hierarchy. Those at the bottom were less than human; they were alleged to have smaller, and thus inferior, brains. Reflecting on European imperialism in the late nineteenth and early twentieth centuries, Frantz Fanon stressed the point that this colonialism was about much more than labor or resource exploitation, for it involved broad social domination constructed in racist terms. European colonialism created the modern idea of "race" across the globe. "In the colonies the economic substructure is also a superstructure. The cause is the consequence; you are rich because you are white, you are white because you are rich."[13] This new racist ideology had three important elements: (1) an accent on physically and biologically distinctive categories called "races"; (2) an emphasis on "race" as the primary determinant of a group's essential personality and cultural traits; and (3) a hierarchy of superior and inferior racial groups.

America's prominent theorist of liberty, Thomas Jefferson, contended that black Americans were an inferior "race." In *Notes on the State of Virginia*, written in the late eighteenth century, Jefferson articulated what were the first developed arguments by an American intellectual for black inferiority. Blacks are said to be inferior to whites in reasoning, imagination, and beauty. Blacks are alleged to favor white beauty "as uniformly as is the preference of the Oranootan [Orangutan] for the black women over those of his own species." Blacks are alleged to be more adventuresome than whites because they have a "want of forethought," to be unreflective, and—perhaps most amazing—to feel life's pain less than whites. Blacks are alleged to have produced no important thinkers, poets, musicians, or intellectuals. Improvement in black minds comes only when there is a "mixture with whites," which Jefferson argues "proves that their inferiority is not the effect merely of their condition of life."[14]

Scientific Racism

As early as the 1730s the Swedish botanist and taxonomist, Carolus Linneaus, distinguished four categories of human beings—black, white, red, and yellow. Though he did not explicitly use the idea of "race," he associated skin color with cultural traits—with whites being superior and blacks inferior. Between the 1770s and the 1790s the prominent German anatomist and anthropologist, Johann Blumenbach, worked out a racial classification that became influential. At the top of his list of "races" were what Blumenbach called the "Caucasians" (Europeans), a term he coined because in his judgment the people of the Caucasus were the most beautiful of the European peoples. Lower on the list were the Mongolians (Asians), the Ethiopians (Africans), the Americans (Native Americans), and the Malays (Polynesians). "White" was viewed as the oldest color of mankind, and white had degenerated into the darker skin colors.[15]

The new scientific racism firmly encompassed the notion of a specific number of races with different physical characteristics, a belief that these characteristics were hereditary, and the notion of a natural hierarchy of inferior and superior races. In their broad sweep these racist ideas were not supported by careful scientific observations of all human societies but rather were buttressed with slanted reports gleaned by European missionaries, travelers, and sea captains from their experiences with selected non-European societies. Most scientists of the late eighteenth and early nineteenth centuries, while presenting themselves as objective observers, tried to marshal evidence for human differences that the white imperialists' perspective had already decided were important to highlight.[16]

Celebrating and Expanding the Racist Ideology

In the United States distinguished lawyers, judges, and political leaders promoted scientific racism and its white-supremacist assumptions. In the first half of the nineteenth century whites with an interest in slavery dominated the political and legal system. This influence was conspicuous in the infamous *Dred Scott v. John*

F. A. Sandford (1857) decision. Replying to the petition of an enslaved black American, a substantial majority of the U.S. Supreme Court ruled that Scott was not a citizen under the Constitution and had no rights. Chief Justice Roger Taney, a slaveholder, argued that African Americans "had for more than a century before [the U.S. Constitution] been regarded as beings of an inferior order, and altogether unfit to associate with the white race, either in social or political relations; and so far inferior, that they had no rights which the white man was bound to respect; and that the negro might justly and lawfully be reduced to slavery for his benefit. He was bought and sold, and treated as an ordinary article of merchandise and traffic, whenever a profit could be made by it. This opinion was at that time fixed and universal in the civilized portion of the white race."[17] The Dred Scott decision showed that the racist ideology was both elaborate and well established.

Senators and presidents played their role in articulating and spreading this ideology. President James Buchanan, a northerner, urged the nation to support the racist thinking of the *Dred Scott* decision. Moreover, several years before he became president, in his debate with Senator Stephen A. Douglas, Abraham Lincoln argued that the physical difference between the races was insuperable, saying, "I am not nor ever have been in favor of the social and political equality of the white and black races: that I am not nor ever have been in favor of making voters of the free negroes, or jurors, or qualifying them to hold office or having them to marry with white people. ... I as much as any other man am in favor of the superior position being assigned to the white man."[18] Lincoln, soon to be the "Great Emancipator," had made his white supremacist views clear, views later cited by southern officials in the 1960s struggle to protect legal segregation and still quoted by white supremacist groups today.

With the end of Reconstruction in 1877 came comprehensive and coercive racial segregation in the South. Distinguished judges, including those on the Supreme Court, played a key role in solidifying the extensive segregation of black Americans and in unifying white defenses of institutionalized racism. In *Plessy v. Ferguson* (1896) a nearly unanimous Supreme Court legitimated the fiction of "separate but equal" for black and white Americans in a case dealing with racially segregated railroad cars. This separate-but-equal fiction was legal for more than half a century, until the 1954 *Brown v. Board of Education of Topeka* decision and until broken down further by the civil rights laws of the 1960s. There was widespread agreement in the elites and in the general white population about the desirability of thorough and compulsory segregation for black men, women, and children.

Social Darwinism

In his influential writings Charles Darwin applied his evolutionary idea of natural selection not only to animal development but also to the development of human "races." He saw natural selection at work in the killing of the indigenous peoples of Australia by the British, wrote of blacks as a category between whites and gorillas, and spoke against social programs for the "weak" because they permitted the least desirable people to survive. The "civilized races" would eventually replace the "savage races throughout the world."[19]

During the late 1800s and early 1900s a perspective called "social Darwinism" developed the ideas of Darwin and argued aggressively that certain "inferior races" were less evolved, less human, and more apelike than the "superior races." Prominent social scientists like Herbert Spencer and William Graham Sumner argued that social life was a life-and-death struggle in which the best individuals would win out over inferior individuals. Sumner argued that wealthy Americans, who were almost entirely white at the time, were products of natural selection and essential to the advance of civilization. Black Americans were seen by many of these openly racist analysts as a "degenerate race" whose alleged "immorality" was a racial trait.[20]

By the late 1800s a eugenics movement was spreading among scientists and other intellectuals in Europe and the United States. Eugenicists accented the importance of breeding the "right" types of human groups. Britain's Sir Francis Galton argued for improving the superior race by human intervention. Like Galton, U.S. eugenicists opposed "racial mixing" (or "miscegenation") because it destroyed racial purity. Allowing "unfit races" to survive would destroy the "superior race" of northern Europeans. Those from the lesser races, it was decided, should be sterilized or excluded from the nation. Such views were not on the fringe, but had the weight of established scientists, leading politicians, and major business leaders. Thus, in 1893 Nathaniel S. Shaler, a prominent scientist and dean at Harvard University, argued that black Americans were inferior, uncivilized, and an "alien folk" with no place in the body politic. In social Darwinist fashion, he spoke of their eventual extinction under the processes of natural law.[21]

Scientific racism was used by white members of Congress to support passage of discriminatory congressional legislation, including the openly racist 1924 immigration law excluding most immigrants other than northern Europeans. In this period overtly racist ideas were advocated by all U.S. presidents. Former president Theodore Roosevelt openly favored scientific racism.[22] President Woodrow Wilson was well-known as an advocate of the superiority of European civilization over all others, including those of Africa. As president, Wilson increased the racial segregation of the federal government. Significantly, no less a racist leader than Adolf Hitler would later report having been influenced by Wilson's writings. (In its contemporary sense, the term *racism* first appeared in a 1933 German book by Magnus Hirschfeld, who sought to counter the Nazi and other European racists' notion of a biologically determined hierarchy of races.)[23]

In 1921 President Warren G. Harding, who had once been linked to the Ku Klux Klan, said he rejected any "suggestion of social equality" between blacks and whites, citing a popular racist book as evidence the "race problem" was a global problem. Not long before he became president, Calvin Coolidge wrote in *Good Housekeeping* magazine, "Biological laws tell us that certain divergent people will not mix or blend. The Nordics propagate themselves successfully. With other races, the outcome shows deterioration on both sides."[24] Ideas of white supremacy and rigid segregation were openly advocated by top political leaders.

Perpetuating the Racist Ideology: Contemporary America

Periodically, the racist ideology framed in the first two centuries of American development has shifted somewhat in its framing or emphases. Those in charge have dressed it up differently for changing social circumstances, though the underlying framework has remained much the same. Some new ideas have been added to deal with pressures for change from those oppressed, particularly ideas about government policy. After World War II, aspects of the dominant racist ideology were altered somewhat to fit the new circumstances of the 1950s and 1960s, during which black Americans increasingly challenged patterns of compulsory racial segregation.

In recent decades white elites have continued to dominate the transmission of new or refurbished ideas and images designed to buttress the system of racial inequality, and they have used ever more powerful means to accomplish their ends. The mass media now include not only the radio, movies, and print media used in the past, but television, music videos, satellite transmissions, and the Internet.

Today, for the most part, the mass media are still controlled by whites. Just under 90 percent of the news reporters, supervisors, and editors at newspapers and magazines across the United States are white. On television whites are overrepresented in managerial jobs, and as on-air reporters; they are greatly overrepresented as "experts" in the mass media. Americans of color have only a token presence in the choice and shaping of news reports and media entertainment. The concentration of media control in a few corporations has increased dramatically in recent decades. In the early twenty-first century, fewer than two dozen corporations control much of the mass media, and that number is likely to decrease further. In addition, the mass media, especially television, are substantially supported by corporate advertisers, and advertisers have significant command over programming. Thus, information about racial matters is usually filtered and whitewashed through a variety of elite-controlled organizations. This filtering is not a coordinated conspiracy, but reflects the choices of many powerful whites socialized to the dominant framing in regard to racial issues.[25]

Looking for data and stories, reporters and journalists typically seek out established government, business, academic, and think-tank reports and experts. The right wing of the U.S. ruling class, a large segment, has historically been the most committed to the racist ideology and has pressed for repression of protests against oppression. The liberal wing of the white elite is much smaller and often more attuned to popular movements; it has been willing to liberalize the society to some degree and to make some concessions to protesters for the sake of preserving the society. (The center of the elite has waffled between the two poles.) In the late 1960s and 1970s many experts consulted by top executives in government and the mass media came from think tanks usually espousing the views of those in the center or on the left of the ruling elite. Becoming very concerned about this, wealthy conservatives began in the 1970s to lavishly fund right-wing think tanks and to press aggressively conservative views of U.S. society on universities, politicians, and media owners. In recent years the right-wing think tanks—including the American Enterprise Institute, the Manhattan Institute, and the Heritage Foundation—have been very successful in getting their experts into mainstream discussions and debates. Working alongside a large group of other conservative intellectuals, media experts, and activists, these right-wing think tanks continue to be successful in an indoctrination campaign aimed at shaping public views on racial and other social issues.[26]

Most Americans now get their news from commercial television and radio programs. The largest single source is local news programming.[27] Using these local and national media, the white elites have the capability to mobilize mass consensus on elite-generated ideas and views; this consensus often provides an illusion of democracy. These elites encourage collective ignorance by allowing little systematic information critical of the existing social and political system to be circulated through the media to the general population.

With the national racial order firmly in place, most white Americans, from childhood on, come to adopt the views, assumptions, and proclivities of previous generations and established white authorities. In this manner the system of racism is reproduced from one generation of whites to the next.

Increased Equality Rhetoric

From the 1960s onward the rhetoric of racial equality, or at least of an equality of opportunity, grew in volume among members of the white elite, including presidents and members of Congress. The black protests and rebellions of the 1950s and 1960s had an important effect in eradicating not only the system of the legal segregation but also most public defense of racial discrimination by the nation's white leadership. Since the late 1960s most leaders have proclaimed the rhetoric of racial and ethnic equality.

The structural dismantling of a large-scale system of compulsory segregation did require a new equality emphasis in the prevailing racial ideology. However, while the structural position of whites and blacks had changed somewhat, at least officially, most whites—in the elites and the general public—did not seem interested in giving up significant white power or privilege. Thus, the racist ideology was altered in some ways but continued to incorporate many of its old features, and it continued to rationalize white privilege—now under conditions of official desegregation. There had long been some fairness language in the prevailing ideology—for example, most whites thought blacks were treated fairly—but now notions of fairness and equality of opportunity were moved to the forefront. The acceptance by the white elite and public of the principles of equal opportunity and desegregation in regard to schools, jobs, and public accommodations did *not* mean that most whites desired for the federal government to implement large-scale integration of these institutions.

A More Conservative Orientation: 1969 to the Present

Beginning around 1969, with the arrival of Richard Nixon's presidential administration, the rhetoric of equality was increasingly accompanied by a federal government backing off from its modest commitment to desegregation and enforcement of the new civil rights laws. At the local level, there was increased police repression of aggressive dissent in the black community, such as the illegal attacks on Black Panthers and other militant black groups by local police and FBI agents. The old racist images of dangerous black men and black welfare mothers were dusted off and emphasized by prominent white leaders who often spouted the rhetoric of equality at the same time. Moreover, the liberal wing of the white elite, which had provided some funding for the civil rights movement and other social movements of the 1960s, significantly reduced its support for these movements.[28]

By the mid-1970s the right wing of the ruling elite was accelerating its attack on the liberal thinking associated with the new civil rights laws. Since the 1970s a growing number of conservative organizations have worked aggressively in pressing Congress, the federal courts, and the private sector to eviscerate or eliminate antidiscrimination programs such as affirmative action efforts, as well as an array of other government social programs. This signaled the increasing influence on national policy of a more conservative Republican Party that represented, almost exclusively, the interests of white Americans. Moreover, even at the top of the Democratic Party there was also some shift to the right, which could be seen in the relatively modest antidiscrimination policies of the Jimmy Carter and Bill Clinton administrations.

The shift away from government action to remedy discrimination was associated with a reinvigoration of notions about inferior black intelligence and culture. In the 1970s, and increasingly in the 1980s and 1990s, numerous white journalists, politicians, and academics were critical of what they saw as too-liberal views in regard to black Americans and remedies for discrimination and defended arguments about black intellectual or cultural inferiority. In public policy discussions, increasingly led by white conservatives, there was a renewed emphasis on the view that only the individual, not the group, is protected from discrimination under U.S. law.

The federal courts provide an important example of this conservative shift. In the decades since the 1970s these courts have often ruled that group-remedy programs against racial discrimination violate the U.S. Constitution, which they assert only recognizes the rights of individuals, not groups. For instance, in 1989 a conservative Supreme Court handed down a major decision, *City of Richmond, Virginia v. J. A. Croson Co.*, which knocked down a local program designed to remedy past discrimination against black and other minority businesses.[29] The high court ruled in favor of a white-run construction company, the plaintiff, which argued that the municipal government had unconstitutionally set aside business for minority companies. The court ruled that the city of Richmond had not made a compelling case for racial discrimination, even though the defendant's statistics showed that in a city whose population was one-half black, *less than 1 percent of the city government's business* went to black-owned firms.

Still Arguing for Biological "Races"

In recent years some social and behavioral scientists have joined with certain physical scientists to continue to press for the idea of biological races and to connect that idea to concerns over government social policies. Since the late 1960s several social scientists at leading universities, including Arthur Jensen and Richard Herrnstein, have continued to argue that racial-group differences in average scores on the so-called IQ tests reveal genetic differences in intelligence between black and white Americans. Their views have been influential, especially on white politicians and the white public. In 1969 the *Harvard Educational Review* lent its prestige to a long article by Jensen, a University of California professor. The arguments presented there and Jensen's later arguments in the next two decades have received much national attention, including major stories in *Time, Newsweek, U.S. News and World Report, Life,* and major newspapers. Jensen has argued that on the average blacks are born with less intelligence than whites, and that the "IQ" test data support this contention. In addition, he has suggested that high birth rates for black Americans could result in a lowering of the nation's overall intelligence level.[30]

Perhaps the most widely read example of biological determinism is a 1990s book, *The Bell Curve,* which sold more than a half million copies. Into the twenty-first century it is still being cited and read. Like Jensen, the authors of *The Bell Curve*—the late Harvard University professor Richard Herrnstein and prominent author Charles Murray—argue that IQ test data show that black (and Latino) Americans are inferior in intelligence to whites. Though the authors have no training in genetics, they suggest that this supposed inferiority in intelligence results substantially from genetic differences. Thus, biological differences account to a substantial degree for racial inequalities. The fact that the book has sold many copies and has been widely debated in the media—in spite of the overwhelming evidence against its arguments—strongly suggests that biologically oriented racist thinking is still espoused by a large number of white Americans, including those who are well-educated. Indeed, Herrnstein and Murray explicitly suggest that their views are *privately shared* by many well-educated whites, including those in the elite, who are unwilling to speak out publicly. This book was launched during a major press conference at the conservative American Enterprise Institute. This publicity insured that the book would get much national attention, while antiracist books have generally gotten far less media play.[31]

Racist arguments about contemporary intelligence levels are grounded in nearly four hundred years of viewing blacks as having an intelligence inferior to that of whites. Today, such views are much more than an academic matter. They have periodically been used by members of Congress and presidential advisors in the White House to argue against antidiscrimination and other government programs that benefit Americans of color. Given this elite activity, it is not surprising to find these views in the white public.

Another aspect of older racist views that can be found in new dress is the idea of what one might call "cultural racism"—the view that blacks have done less well than whites because of their allegedly deficient culture with its weak work ethic and family values. As early as the seventeenth century, black Americans were seen as inferior in civilization and morality to white colonists. These blaming-the-victim views have regularly been resuscitated among the white elites and passed along to ordinary Americans as a way of explaining the difficult socioeconomic conditions faced by black Americans.

Since the 1970s leading magazines have published articles accenting some version of this perspective on what came to be called the black "underclass"; the perspective accents the allegedly deficient morality and lifestyle of many black Americans. Prominent author Ken Auletta wrote an influential set of *New Yorker* articles, later expanded in his book *The Underclass.* He accented the black underclass and its supposed immorality, family disorganization, and substandard work ethic.[32] A later article in the *Chronicle of Higher Education* surveyed the growing research on the underclass, noting that "the lives of the ghetto poor are marked by a dense fabric of what experts call 'social pathologies'—teenage pregnancies, out-of-wedlock births, single-parent families, poor educational achievement, chronic unemployment, welfare dependency, drug abuse, and crime—that, taken separately or together, seem impervious to change."[33] To the present day, similar stories designed to explain black problems in cultural terms regularly appear in the local and national media across the nation.

A Whitewashed Worldview

This antiblack ideology links in so many ways to so much of white thought and behavior that we might speak of it as a broad worldview. Seen comprehensively, all the mental images, prejudiced attitudes, stereotypes, fictions, racist explanations, and rationalizations that link to systemic racism make up a white racist worldview, one deeply imbedded in the dominant culture and institutions. The U.S. system of racism is not just something that affects black Americans and other Americans of color, for it is central to the lives of white Americans as well. It determines how whites think about themselves, about their ideals, and about their nation.

In the early 1900s European immigrants to the United States came to accept this worldview and its implicit assumption that being "American" means being white. This has not changed much in the intervening years. Today the term "American" still means "white"—at least for the majority of white Americans, and probably for most people across the globe. One can pick up most newspapers or newsmagazines and find "American" or "Americans" used in a way that clearly accents *white* Americans. Take this sentence from a news writer in a Florida newspaper: "The American Public isn't giving government or police officers the blind trust it once did."[34] Clearly, "American" here means "white American," for the majority of blacks have never blindly trusted the police.

One research analysis examined all the articles in sixty-five major English-language newspapers for a six-month period and estimated that there were thousands of references to "black Americans" or "African Americans" in the articles. However, in the same newspapers there were *only forty-six* mentions of "white Americans."[35] In almost every case these mentions by newspaper writers occurred in connection with "black Americans," "blacks," or "African Americans." (The exceptions were three cases in which "white Americans" was used in connection with "Native Americans" or "Korean Americans.") A similar pattern was found for major magazines. Not once was the term "white Americans" used alone in an article; if used, it was always used in relation to another racial category. The same study examined how congressional candidates were described in news articles in the two weeks prior to the November 1998 elections. In every case white congressional candidates were *not* described as "white," but black congressional candidates were always noted as being "black."[36] In the United States blackness is usually salient and noted, while whiteness generally goes unmentioned, except when reference is specifically made to white connections to other racial groups.

Being "American" still means, in the minds of many people, including editors and writers in the media, being white. This need not be a conscious process. For several centuries most whites have probably not seen the routines of their everyday lives as framed in white. "Race" is often not visible when one is at the top of the social hierarchy. Today, major social institutions, those originally created by whites centuries ago, are still dominated by whites. Yet from the white standpoint they are not white, just normal and customary. They are not seen for what they actually are—whitewashed institutions reflecting in many of their aspects the history, privileges, norms, values, and interests of white Americans. When whites live in these customary arrangements, they need not think in overtly racist terms. Nonetheless, when whites move into settings where they must confront people of color in the United States or elsewhere, they usually foreground their whiteness, whether consciously or unconsciously.

Fear of a Multiracial, Multicultural Future

Today, many white analysts still see Western civilization as under threat from groups that are not white or European. Racist thinking is more than rationalizing oppression, for it also represents a defensive response, a fear of losing power to Americans of color. In recent years many advocates of white superiority have directed their attacks at the values or cultures of new immigrants of color coming to the United States, as well as at black Americans. In one recent interview study elite numerous white men openly expressed some fear of the growth of Americans of color in the United States, seeing Western civilization as under threat.[37]

We observe examples of this fear among U.S. politicians and intellectuals. For example, in several speeches and articles Patrick Buchanan, media pundit and once a candidate for the Republican presidential nomination, has argued that "our Judeo-Christian values are going to be preserved and our Western heritage is going to be handed down to future generations and not dumped on some landfill called multiculturalism."[38] Once again, we see the linkage between religion and a strong sense of European supremacy. We also see a concern for the reproduction of the white-dominated system from current to future generations. In addition, Buchanan told one interviewer that "if we had to take a million immigrants in, say, Zulus next year or Englishmen, and put them in Virginia, what group would be easier to assimilate and would cause less problems for the people of Virginia? There is nothing wrong with us sitting down and arguing that issue that we are a European country, [an] English-speaking country."[39] The Zulus, who are Africans, seem to represent in his mind the specter of strange or savage hordes who would not assimilate well into the nation. Ironically, Africans have been in the nation longer than Buchanan's Irish ancestors, and Virginia has been home to African Americans for nearly four centuries.

Conclusion

The systemic racism that is still part of the base of U.S. society is interwoven with a strong racist ideology that has been partially reframed at various points in U.S. history, but which has remained a well-institutionalized set of beliefs, attitudes, and concepts defending white-on-black oppression. Until the late 1940s commitment to a white supremacist view of the world was proud, openly held, and aggressive. Most whites in the United States and Europe, led by elites, took pride in forthrightly professing their racist perspectives on other peoples and their racist rationalizations for Western imperialistic adventures. Brutal discrimination and overt exploitation were routinely advocated. Indeed, white domination of the globe was "seen as proof of white racial superiority."[40]

Beginning in the late 1940s, however, the open expression of a white supremacist ideology was made more difficult by a growing American awareness of actions of the racist regime in Nazi Germany. In addition, by the 1950s and 1960s growing black civil rights protests against U.S. racism—with their counterideology of black liberation—and the U.S. struggle with the Soviet Union made the open expression of a white supremacist ideology less acceptable. The dominant racist ideology changed slowly to reflect these new conditions, with a new accent on equality of opportunity and some support for moderate programs to break down the nation's segregated institutions. Still, as we have seen, many aspects of the old racist ideology were dressed up in a new guise, and they persist, with some barnacle-like additions, to the present day. From the beginning, the age-old idea of the superiority of white (Western) culture and institutions has been the most basic idea in the dominant ideology rationalizing oppression.

For some time now, most whites have viewed the last few centuries of societal development in terms of a broad imagery equating "human progress" with Western civilization. We hear or see phrases like "Western civilization is an engine generating great progress for the world" or "Africans have only seen real advancement because of their contacts with Western civilization." Western imperialism's bringing of "civilization" or "democracy" to other peoples is made to appear as an engine of great progress, with mostly good results. However, this equating of "progress" with European civilization conceals the devastating consequences of imperialism and colonialism. The actual reality was—and often still is—brutal, bloody, oppressive, or genocidal in consequence for those colonized. When whites speak of Western civilization as equivalent to great human progress, they are talking about the creation of social systems that do not take into serious consideration the interests and views of the indigenous or enslaved peoples whose resources were ripped from them, whose societies were destroyed, and whose lives were cut short. Images of Western civilization, like the racist ideologies of which they are often part, are too often used to paper over the sordid realities of Western colonialism and imperialism.

Discussion Questions

1. What is a racist ideology, and when did it first develop in North America?
2. Are elites or the rank-and-file population most responsible for the growth and importance of the racist ideology?
3. Is the racist ideology still important today? How and where?
4. Have prominent presidents and scientists played any important role in the development of racist ideas and notions? If so, how and when?
5. What is social Darwinism, and is it still important in U.S. society today?

Notes

1. W.E.B. Du Bois, *Dusk of Dawn: An Essay Toward an Autobiography of a Race Concept* (New Brunswick, NJ: Transaction Books, 1984 [1940]), p. 144.
2. Karl Marx and Friederich Engels, *The German Ideology*, ed. R. Pascal (New York: International Publishers, 1947), p. 39.
3. Kenneth O'Reilly, *Nixon's Piano: Presidents and Racial Politics from Washington to Clinton* (New York: Free Press, 1995), p. 11.
4. Ronald T. Takaki, *Iron Cages: Race and Culture in 19th Century America* (Oxford: Oxford University Press, 1990), pp. 11–14.
5. James Fenimore Cooper, *The Last of the Mohicans* (1826), as quoted in Emily Morison Beck, ed., John Bartlett's Familiar Quotations, 15th ed. (Boston: Little Brown, 1980), p. 463.
6. Tomas Almaguer, *Racial Fault Lines* (Berkeley and Los Angeles: University of California Press, 1994), p. 28.
7. Takaki, *Iron Cages*, pp. 30–34.
8. See Frances Lee Ansley, "Stirring the Ashes: Race, Class and the Future of Civil Rights Scholarship," *Cornell Law Review* 74 (September, 1989): 993.
9. W.E.B. Du Bois, *Dusk of Dawn: An Essay Toward an Autobiography of a Race Concept* (New Brunswick, NJ: Transaction Books, 1984 [1940]), p. 6.
10. A. Leon Higginbotham, Jr., and Barbara K. Kopytoff, "Racial Purity and Interracial Sex in the Law of Colonial and Antebellum Virginia," *Georgetown Law Journal* 77 (August 1989): 1671.

11. Benjamin Franklin, quoted in Takaki, *Iron Cages*, p. 50; Claude-Anne Lopez and Eugenia W. Herbert, *The Private Franklin: The Man and His Family* (New York: Norton, 1975), pp. 194–95.

12. George Frederickson, *The Black Image in the White Mind* (Hanover, NH: Wesleyan University Press, 1971), p. 282.

13. Frantz Fanon, *The Wretched of the Earth* (New York: Grove Press, 1963), p. 32.

14. Thomas Jefferson, *Notes on the State of Virginia*, ed. Frank Shuffelton (New York: Penguin, 1999 [1785]), pp. 145, 147–48.

15. William H. Tucker, *The Science and Politics of Racial Research* (Urbana: University of Illinois Press, 1994), pp. 8–9; Ivan Hannaford, *Race: The History of an Idea in the West* (Baltimore: Johns Hopkins University Press, 1996), pp. 205–207.

16. Audrey Smedley, *Race in North America* (Boulder, CO: Westview Press, 1993), p. 26.

17. *Dred Scott v. John F. A. Sandford*, 60 U.S. 393, 407–408 (1857).

18. Abraham Lincoln, "The Sixth Joint Debate at Quincy, October 13, 1858," in *The Lincoln-Douglas Debates: The First Complete, Unexpurgated Text*, ed. Harold Holzer (New York: HarperCollins, 1993), p. 283.

19. Charles Darwin, quoted in Frederickson, *The Black Image in the White Mind*, p. 230.

20. See Joe R. Feagin, *Subordinating the Poor: Welfare and American Beliefs* (Englewood Cliffs, NJ: Prentice-Hall, 1975), pp. 35–36; and Frederick L. Hoffman, "Vital Statistics of the Negro," *Arena* 5 (April 1892): 542, cited in Frederickson, *The Black Image in the White Mind*, pp. 250–51.

21. John Higham, *Strangers in the Land* (New York: Atheneum, 1963), pp. 96–152; Tucker, *The Science and Politics of Racial Research*, p. 35.

22. Tucker, *The Science and Politics of Racial Research*, p. 93.

23. See Theodore Cross, *Black Power Imperative: Racial Inequality and the Politics of Nonviolence* (New York: Faulkner, 1984), p. 157; Magnus Hirschfeld, *Racism*, trans. and ed. by Eden and Cedar Paul (London: V. Gollancz, 1938). The book was published in German in 1933.

24. Warren G. Harding and Calvin Coolidge, each quoted in Tucker, *The Science and Politics of Racial Research*, p. 93.

25. David K. Shipler, "Blacks in the Newsroom," *Columbia Journalism Review*, May/June 1998, pp. 81 26–29; Robert M. Entman *et al.*, *Mass Media and Reconciliation: A Report to the Advisory Board and Staff, The President's Initiative on Race* (Washington, DC, 1998); Edward Herman, "The Propaganda Model Revisited," *Monthly Review* 48 (July 1996): 115.

26. Sidney Blumenthal, *The Rise of the Counter-Establishment* (New York: Times Books, 1986), pp. 4–11, 133–70; Peter Steinfels, *The Neoconservatives: The Men Who Are Changing America's Politics* (New York: Touchstone, 1979), pp. 214–77.

27. Franklin D. Gilliam Jr., and Shanto Iyengar, "Prime Suspects: the Effects of Local News on the Viewing Public," University of California at Los Angeles, unpublished paper.

28. Thomas Ferguson and Joel Rodgers, *Right Turn: The Decline of the Democrats and the Future of American Politics* (New York: Hill and Wang, 1986), pp. 65–66.

29. *City of Richmond, Virginia v. J.A. Croson Co*, 488 U.S. 469 (1989).

30. Arthur R. Jensen, "How Much Can We Boost IQ and Scholastic Achievement?" *Harvard 99 Educational Review* 39 (1969): 1–123.

31. Jean Stefancic and Richard Delgado, *No Mercy: How Conservative Think Tanks and 100 Foundations Changed America's Social Agenda* (Philadelphia: Temple University Press, 1996), p. 34.

32. Ken Auletta, *The Underclass* (New York: Random House, 1982).

33. Ellen K. Coughlin, "Worsening Plight of the Underclass Catches Attention," *Chronicle of Higher Education,* March 1988, A5.

34. I draw here on Nick Mrozinske, "Derivational Thinking and Racism," unpublished research paper, University of Florida, fall, 1998.

35. The search algorithm did not allow searches for the word "whites" alone, because this picks up the surnames of individuals in the Lexis/Nexis database.

36. Mrozinske, "Derivational Thinking and Racism."

37. Rhonda Levine, "The Souls of Elite White Men: White Racial Identity and the Logic of Thinking on Race," paper presented at annual meeting, Hawaiian Sociological Association, February 14, 1998.

38. Patrick Buchanan, quoted in Clarence Page, "U.S. Media Should Stop Abetting Intolerance," *Toronto Star*, December 27, 1991, A27.

39. Patrick Buchanan, quoted in John Dillin, "Immigration Joins List of '92 Issues," *Christian Science Monitor*, December 17, 1991, 6.

40. Frank Furedi, *The Silent War: Imperialism and the Changing Perception of Race* (New Brunswick, NJ: Rutgers University Press, 1998), p. 1.

Selected Bibliography

Cross, Theodore. *Black Power Imperative: Racial Inequality and the Politics of Nonviolence* (New York: Faulkner, 1984).

Du Bois, W. E. B. *Dusk of Dawn: An Essay Toward an Autobiography of a Race Concept* (New Brunswick, NJ: Transaction Books, 1984 [1940]).

Furedi, Frank. *The Silent War: Imperialism and the Changing Perception of Race* (New Brunswick, NJ: Rutgers University Press, 1998).

O'Reilly, Kenneth. *Nixon's Piano: Presidents and Racial Politics from Washington to Clinton* (New York: Free Press, 1995).

Smedley, Audrey. *Race in North America* (Boulder, CO: Westview Press, 1993).

Takaki, Ronald T. *Iron Cages: Race and Culture in 19th Century America* (Oxford: Oxford University Press, 1990).

Tucker, William H. *The Science and Politics of Racial Research* (Urbana: University of Illinois Press, 1994).

The Production of Institutional Racism

By Barbara Trepagnier

Editor's Introduction

In this reading, Trepagnier discusses the production and maintenance of institutional racism. Institutional racism has been a key factor in impeding change in racial-ethnic relations since the 1970s. The author shows some important effects of institutional racism. A key issue raised in the reading is how institutional racism is produced and the role of silent racism, passivity, and everyday racism in this process. This reading is also selected to highlight some of the important theoretical insights that help us to understand racial and ethnic inequality.

Chapters 2 and 3 described the concepts of silent racism and passivity, both of which are instrumental in the production of institutional racism. And because silent racism and passivity are found in well-meaning white people, institutional racism is frequently produced by whites who do not intend to produce it but do so nonetheless.

This chapter begins with the sociological concept of institutional racism, including the effects it produces and the theories that have developed around it. Several of the theories imply the role of actors (people who take action); however, none bridges the micro/macro gap satisfactorily. In other words, none of the theories explains how the action of individuals produces societal patterns of racial inequality. I will present a theory of institutional racism that forges a link between social institutions and the actors who sustain them. The theory also explains how institutional racism is carried out largely by people who have no intention to produce it. Grounded primarily in the work of Pierre Bourdieu ([1994] 1998), the theory demonstrates how silent racism produces both racist practice and everyday racism in organizations and institutions. Social network theory (Whitmeyer 1994) is also utilized to argue that passivity regarding others' racist practices contributes to institutional racism. The ideas gleaned from these theorists and others illustrate that silent racism and passivity are essential in the production of institutional racism, an insight that shifts the focus from individuals' intentions onto what they do and what they do not do, regardless of intention.

Institutional Racism

Sociologists have recognized institutional racism—a form of oppression structured into the fabric of society—since the mid-1960s, when civil rights activists Stokely Carmichael—later known as Kwame Ture—and Charles Hamilton (1967) introduced the term. Since then, institutional racism as a concept has been expanded to include the role of cultural beliefs as integral to the process (Blauner 1972; Bonacich 1972, 1976; Kovel 1970; Omi and Winant 1986, 1994; Turner and Singleton 1978; Van der Berghe 1967). Despite these changes, sociology has been slow to explain the role of actors involved in the production and maintenance of institutional racism.

A breakthrough in sociological race theory, institutional racism has remained a compelling macrolevel concept primarily because it demonstrates the important idea that racism permeates society through its institutions; that is, the concept reveals that racism is systemic. In accomplishing this, institutional racism illustrates that racism is more than the prejudice of individuals. The difficulty, however, is that the concept implicitly disconnects individuals from institutions. This false separation results in institutional racism being undertheorized in terms of the mechanism through which institutions produce racial inequality.

Institutions, as defined by sociologists, are the set of ideas or expectations about how to accomplish the various goals of society, such as the socializing of a society's young, meeting the economic needs of society's citizens, and protecting members of society from outside threat (McIntyre 2002). The norms and expectations surrounding families, religion, education, the economy, and the government differ somewhat from one society to another, making each society distinctive from other societies. When the ideas and expectations that constitute any institution in a given society has racist undercurrents due to past and present social relations, institutional racism occurs in the organizations associated with that sector of society. Patterns that result from following the expectations surrounding institutions eventually become habitual, making behavior somewhat predictable, although not determined. These behavioral rules provide a measure of social control, mediated through the institutions mentioned above. Through the socialization process, children are taught to act within the institutions of their parents. In this way, institutions become legitimate (Berger and Luckmann 1966) and influence people's behavior.

Although the idea is historically rooted in the ideas of Frederick Douglass, W. E. B. Du Bois, and Frantz Fanon, the term *institutional racism* first emerged toward the end of the civil rights movement in the writings of Carmichael and Hamilton (1967). These authors posit that more damaging effects for blacks as a group come from U.S. institutions than from bigoted white individuals. This occurs because institutions favor the dominant group—white Americans—over black Americans and other minorities. Racial inequality results when U.S. social institutions such as the criminal justice system, education, and the economy put people of color at a disadvantage while simultaneously giving white people an unwarranted advantage.

Carmichael and Hamilton maintain that much institutional racism is invisible, especially to those benefiting from it. They also argue that institutional racism does not necessarily reflect any deliberate or malicious intent on the part of members of the dominant group. In reference to "respectable" white people who would never bomb a church or burn a cross, the authors point out that "they continue to support political officials and institutions that would and do perpetuate institutionally racist policies. Thus *acts* of overt, individual racism may not typify the society, but institutional racism does—with the support of covert individual *attitudes* of racism" (Carmichael and Hamilton 1967:5, emphasis in original). At the time it was introduced, institutional racism offered an alternative view to the narrow psychological assertion that prejudice explains racism. Moreover, since the late 1960s, sociological theories have leaned heavily toward the structural concept of institutional racism and away from the role of individuals as an explanation of racial inequality.

Effects of Institutional Racism

The legacy of slavery as well as the Reconstruction and Jim Crow eras was not eliminated by the Civil Rights Act of 1964 and the Voting Rights Act of 1965. Vestiges of racism produced by white Americans of all stripes—the far right, the new right, neoconservatives, neoliberals, and new abolitionists—is carried out daily, producing harmful effects for black Americans. A few of the negative effects are listed here, some of which are linked to well-meaning white people like the ones in this study. The forms of institutional racism mentioned in this section do not come close to covering all of the ways institutions produce racist effects. For a more comprehensive record, see Brown et al. (2003) and Feagin and Sikes (1994). However, the negative effects produced by well-meaning white people are important because they are produced unintentionally by people who, if their race awareness were increased, would produce fewer negative effects themselves and would interrupt others' racist acts.

The negative effects of institutional racism begin before blacks and other minorities enter the labor force. People of color face scarcity in terms of contacts with white people already in workplaces where they may wish to be employed. Many well-meaning whites avoid initiating relationships with blacks, some because of fear, others because of apprehension about whether blacks would welcome them as acquaintances. And, not only are ties important in learning about better jobs, but people who get jobs through social ties also tend to experience morejob satisfaction as well (Breaugh 1981; Lin, Vaughn, and Ensel 1981).

Once in the labor force, blacks continue to experience institutional racism in the social relations they experience. The social relational approach relates individuals' social relations—that is, how individuals inter-act—to job satisfaction and indirectly to promotion opportunities (Baron and Pfeffer 1994). Feeling comfort-able with coworkers eases tension and the stress that often occurs in the workplace. In addition, information sharing, especially for newcomers in the workplace, is important for achievement on the job (Hackman 1976; Ibarra and Andrews 1993; Jacobs 1981).

Social categorization in terms of in-group and out-group characteristics could be a pivotal issue when administrators consider prospective candidates for new positions within the organization (Baron and Pfeffer 1994). Not only would white administrators see white candidates as more differentiated than black candidates, but silent racism would influence their decisions as well. Take, for example, Vanessa's view that blacks are inherently different from whites and that difference in language skills is due to biological factors. If someone with Vanessa's white perspective were an administrator, her inflammatory viewpoint would undoubtedly influence decisions about any position requiring good language skills. Even Ruth, who is relatively race aware, inadvertently referred to a black student as bright as if it were remarkable. Views like these produce everyday racism and racist practice that result in institutional racism.

Institutional racism is even more evident in the criminal justice system, as it is especially hard on young black males (Brown et al. 2003). Sentencing differentials for drug offenses, for example, are striking: Whites go to federal prison half the number of times blacks go and spend less time in federal prison once they are sent. This trend holds for Latinos as well as blacks. Institutional racism is also evident regarding penalties for property crimes. Controlling for the facts that the rate of crime is higher in poor black neighborhoods and that crime in these neighborhoods is routinely performed by young blacks, practices that favor whites account for a disproportionate conviction rate of blacks over whites (Brown et al. 2003). Furthermore, controlling for prior offenses and seriousness of a given crime, black offenders are twice as likely as their white counterparts to be committed to a juvenile institution or sent to an adult court for adjudication (Bishop and Frazier 1996). The decisions that underlie this pattern could very well be acerbated by a view of the black family—especially poor, single-parent black families—that is influenced by silent racism. Remember Kelly, who viewed the black mother she saw on TV as "ignorant" and "somehow or another implicated in the violence within the ghetto." A person with Kelly's view is likely to see putting young blacks who get in trouble with the law into a facility where professional assistance is available as a better alternative to leaving them in families that might encourage criminal behavior. Misguided notions such as Kelly's result in a self-perpetuating cycle as the young people are pushed further into a system that labels them "delinquent" and treats them as adult criminals.

The death penalty, which is under scrutiny in some states due to the number of inmates proven by DNA evidence to be innocent of the crime that condemned them, is the ultimate form of discrimination in the criminal justice system. The most striking distinction, again, concerns sentencing, which operates on two fronts. First, defendants accused of killing a white victim are four times more likely to receive the death sentence as those accused of killing a black victim. And second, black defendants are more likely than white ones to receive the death penalty, regardless of the race of the victim. Lack of adequate legal representation accounts for some of this pattern. However, silent racism makes conviction more likely when circumstantial evidence is all the prosecution has to offer.

One study of middle-class blacks found that racism has a cumulative effect on the blacks and other people of color that are its targets (Feagin and Sikes 1994). Racism is experienced as blacks go about their daily lives, not in extraordinary circumstances. In addition to racial strain at work, it is experienced when shopping at the grocery store and when driving in the "wrong" neighborhood. Because racism is routine, it occurs throughout society, which gives blacks few safe havens where they are not exposed to it.

Finally, institutional racism is not limited to disadvantages that accrue to blacks and other minorities. It also includes the "miseducation of white children" (Knowles and Pruitt 1969:46), which teaches that racial equality has been achieved despite gross evidence to the contrary. As white children grow up, they rarely discover the truth about racial inequality. This is evident in the women in this study, including myself. Even in college, where exposure to new ideas is expected, students can proceed from matriculation to graduation without ever having their assumptions about race being challenged.

Theories of Institutional Racism

Race theorists have utilized the concept of institutional racism first articulated by Carmichael and Hamilton in various ways. Examples include the following: White Europeans founded American institutions, and the guiding principles of the institutions reflect the whiteness of their creators, with members expected to "think and act in white ways" (Hacker 1992:23). The result is that institutional racism constrains racial or ethnic minorities much the way a birdcage constrains the bird inside (Frye 1992). Looking solely at a single wire of the cage cannot reveal the network of wires that constrict the imprisoned bird. The term *systemic racism* portrays racism as permeating all of society, including but not limited to its institutions (Feagin 2001). *Racialization* suggests the idea that racism is a process that binds people and the institutions of society, both of which utilize race as an organizing principle (Omi and Winant 1986, 1994). And since institutional racism is an ideology that permeates organizations and institutions, to escape it one would have to escape society itself, an impossible feat (Dworkin and Dworkin 1999). All of these aspects of institutional racism are compatible with the theory constructed in this chapter. The difference between these portrayals of institutional racism and the theory to be outlined here is that, in this chapter, the focus shifts from the institutions and their effects on people of color to the role of well-meaning white people in the process. A few race theorists dismiss the concept of institutional racism, arguing, for example, that racism as portrayed by the "institutionalist perspective" is a "mysterious" notion, and that the approach does not explain the origin of racism or how it operates (Bonilla-Silva 2001: 26–27).

Several of the race theories mentioned in Chapter 3 are pertinent here in that they are the foundation for a theory that highlights the role of individuals in the production of institutional racism. For example, the historical theory of racism, which captures dominative racism, aversive racism, and metaracism, illustrates how individuals' racism evolves as institutions in society change over time (Kovel 1970). That psychological and emotional aspects of aversive racism continued to manifest even though aversive racism was transformed into metaracism is useful when thinking about the irrational fear of black men evident in a number of the participants in this study. This point is pivotal when considering how racism within police departments operates, especially in terms of white police officers' actions toward black suspects (Bolton and Feagin 2004).

The cultural approach illustrates that structures of oppression are linked in significant ways to cultural beliefs, and that progressive beliefs are important to social change (Turner and Singleton 1978). This insight informs the claim that beliefs held by progressives and the action following from those beliefs are important in changing the racial status quo.[1] The theory of racial formation is also important to the theory presented here because it highlights the importance of ideology on the process of racial formation (Omi and Winant 1986, 1994). The idea that race is an organizing principle of social structures and that individuals carry out the "rules of racial etiquette" (1986: 62) is borne out by both silent racism and passivity.

Two forms of institutional racism interest us here: *direct* institutional racism refers to actions within an organization that intentionally harm a member of a minority group and that are known about and supported by the organization (Feagin and Feagin 1994). The harm that results from direct institutional racism is intended by the organization and by the members who carry it out. Indirect institutional racism, in contrast, "is carried out with no intent to harm" the members of the subordinate group affected (Feagin and Feagin 1994:122). The theory outlined in this chapter is related to indirect institutional racism in two ways: indirect institutional racism has become more prominent as overt forms of racism have diminished since the civil rights movement, and indirect institutional racism concerns the population of interest in this study—well-meaning white people. This is also the group that is most likely to change its thinking regarding racism.

The Production of Institutional Racism

The proposed theory does not presume to explain all institutional racism. However, like silent racism itself, which has long been overlooked, the theory focuses on the population that is thought to be the least likely to produce institutional racism. The production of institutional racism described here, then, involves persons who are well-meaning white people, not those who are overtly racist or even those who are color-blind racists. This does not imply that overt racists and color-blind racists do not produce institutional racism but that they are not the focus here. In addition, the production of institutional racism refers to *action* that is not intended to do harm to blacks or other people of color; that is, action that is not chosen by the actor for that purpose.

In forging a theory of institutional racism, I must first broach the topic of combining the concept of actors and the idea of social structure. The once-divided camps of micro and macro sociologists have been under scrutiny by sociologists interested in forging a link between the two (Alexander 1987; Collins 1988; Ritzer 1990). An example is "methodological relationism," which refers to studying how individuals and structures interact (Ritzer and Gindoff 1994:163). Although much race theory has been written about the micro approach (the racism of individuals) and the macro approach (institutional racism), the focus here is on both: the role of individuals in the production of institutional racism, a relational approach.

The debate in the United States over the micro/macro link is cast in Europe as the *agency-structure* debate (Ritzer and Gindoff 1994). Although "micro and agency" do not correspond perfectly, just as "macro and structure" do not, the distinction is largely philosophical rather than empirical (Ritzer and Gindoff 1994). Because our concern is the mechanism that explains how individuals produce institutional racism, the debate is not a primary concern here. The point is important, however, because the theoretical foundation for the theory begins with the theory of structuration developed by British sociologist Anthony Giddens (1984) and borrows liberally from the work of European sociologist Pierre Bourdieu ([1972] 1978).The theory of structuration closes the gap between actor and structure that gives us a map showing how the actions of individuals and the functioning of institutions fit together. Because race theorists have largely fallen either into the micro or the macro camp, their theories have exhibited the theoretical artifact that Giddens seeks to expose. Giddens's work is especially important for race theory because the dichotomy between institutional racism and individual actors has reinforced the false notion that white people *as individuals* are not implicated in the phenomenon of institutional racism and racial inequality. The title of Bonilla-Silva's book, *Racism Without Racists* (2003), captures this paradox. The theory of structuration illustrates that racism must be and is instituted by individuals.

Giddens (1979) proposes that neither structure nor agency occurs in isolation. Structuration is a process that occurs *between* social structure and individual actors; it is "the mutual dependence of structure and agency" (p. 69). For Giddens, individuals have the *capability* to make choices (1981), although they do so rarely and only when routines are breached. Therefore, in Giddens's theory of structuration, everyday acts are not thought through and decided upon beforehand; action generally takes place without thoughtful awareness on the part of the actor. This use of the concept of agency differs from what many North American theorists propose: that *agency* not only refers to individuals' ability to make meaningful choices but that virtually all decisions are thought through and made deliberately.

For Giddens, actors' knowledge of the system within which action occurs—as well as knowledge about expectations in the system—make structuration possible. When the theory of structuration is applied to institutional racism, we can see that white actors within the institutions of society take action based on their knowledge (white understanding) of the norms and expectations associated with the institution. Because action goes largely unexamined by the actor, it reproduces the white institution. Bourdieu offers several concepts that further implicate the role of well-meaning white people in the production of institutional racism.

Bourdieu's Theory of Practice

Bourdieu's ([1972] 1978) theory of practice—another word for *action*—helps explain the mechanism for how well-meaning white people produce institutional racism. Since the 1980s, numerous disciplines, including sociology, have developed theories of practice that seek to explain how the action of individuals affects social structures and institutions (Ortner 1994). The goal of these various theorists has been to "understand where 'the system' comes from—how it is produced and reproduced, and how it may have changed in the past or be changed in the future" (Ortner 1994: 390). This is precisely our goal: to understand where institutional racism comes from, how it is produced and reproduced, and especially, how it might be changed. Bourdieu modestly refers to his theory of practice as a "thinking tool" (Jenkins 1992: 67), which is also useful for our purposes—a tool that will help us think about and understand how well-meaning white people's silent racism produces (and reproduces) institutional racism.

For Bourdieu, practice is what people *do* and is not tied to an actor's intention. In other words, "practice happens" (Jenkins 1992: 70).[2] This does not imply that practice occurs accidentally or randomly. Practice is structured, but it happens, nevertheless, without being entirely in the awareness of the actor. Like Giddens,

Bourdieu sees practice as the result of actors' understanding of things—what Bourdieu calls *practical logic* and Giddens calls *practical knowledge*. This means that well-meaning white people who produce institutional racism do so without intention. I do not make this point so that well-meaning whites are excused for their part in the production of institutional racism; rather, I make it in order to expose the fact that well-meaning white people contribute to the problem of institutional racism and to racial inequality.

Bourdieu's depiction of practice is contingent on the concepts of *habitus* and *field*. Simply put, *habitus* refers to people's conception of reality. More specifically, it is a set of dispositions that does not cause a given action but does "incline" an actor to take certain action (Butler 1999: 114). The word *habitus* is Latin for "habit," the notion that ideas are taken for granted, not necessarily thought through. For Bourdieu, speech illustrates how habitus works. People generally do not think through the precise words they will use in a given conversation; they improvise. Most people take part in conversations effortlessly, using speech spontaneously and often automatically. This is because speech is taken for granted, just as habits are taken for granted. Bourdieu says that people carry out most social interactions in a similar fashion—automatically, and without thinking.

Sociologically, acting from habit was apparent in the writing of both Emile Durkheim and Max Weber (Camic 2000). Only later was the concept eschewed by American functionalists striving to set sociology apart from psychology. Talcott Parsons (1949) in particular avoided Weber's use of *habit* as traditional action—action taken without thinking—and focused instead on action determined by the norms of society. Parsons's effort to frame sociological theory as a structural explanation for action in contrast to psychological theory—especially the behaviorist claim that action is an automatic response to stimuli—had the effect of casting all action as voluntaristic, and therefore deliberate (Camic 2000). The symbolic interactionist counterclaim that action is not always determined by the norms of society but often relies on human agency sets up an either/or dichotomy. The result is that *action* came to be viewed by American sociologists as either determined by norms of society or the result of human agency, both of which avoid action as habit. The resulting micro/macro divide is evident in race theory, and my goal is to bridge that divide by introducing actors—in this case, well-meaning whites—into the production of institutional racism.

Bonilla-Silva (2003) borrows the term *habitus* when he speaks of a "white habitus that creates and conditions [white people's] views, cognitions, and even sense of beauty" (p. 123). This quote implies that the white habitus, which embodies white people's view of the world as well as their view of themselves in relation to others, is central to white people's actions. If the white habitus is filled with silent racism that is taken for granted, the action following from it will necessarily reflect that silent racism. This action is what I call *racist practice*.

Field, a concept related to habitus, refers to a network of social positions, which themselves are embedded within dominant, subordinate, and equivalent power relations (Bourdieu [1980] 1990). A social field becomes embued by race in any situation where race or racism is invoked, regardless of who is present in the field. For example, everyday racism does not necessarily occur between black and white individuals. To the contrary, much everyday racism is carried out among white people (Feagin 2001). This occurs often in casual conversation or with jokes that would not be stated in the presence of a person of color but are performed "in private" (Bonilla-Silva 2003:56). Because of our collective history, all U.S. organizations have a racial component. This means that the field embodies race and that the possibility for racist practice is likely. Moreover, as if the white habitus were not enough to produce racist practice, the social field contributes as well. The field puts "demands" on the habitus (Butler 1999:117), altering it at a given moment; put differently, the habitus adapts to the field. For example, the social field in a bank where red-lining is an accepted practice has a field in which racist practice would be the path of least resistance (see Johnson 1997). Not to take the path of least resistance would require a deliberate act because it would entail departing from existing expectations.

It is safe to say that practice not only happens but that practice matters. In this regard, it is useful to delineate what practice is not. *Practice* does not refer to individuals' enactment of societal norms and values, so practice is not determined. Neither does *practice* imply agency, the idea that action is chosen. Rather, *practice* refers to action that occurs without thought. Through practice, people produce effects that reinforce social institutions. Much of institutional racism, clearly that which is not intentional, results from racist practice made up of thoughtless actions based on silent racism that was learned unawarely and is acted upon unawarely.

The view that racist practice produces institutional racism is pertinent to a debate among social psychologists, described herewith.

Social Psychology and Practice

Stereotyping is closely related to differential categorization, the process described in Chapter 3. Differences among members of the out-group are minimized in the sorting process, whereas differences between members of the in-group are recognized, making out-group members appear to be more similar to each other than they really are (Fiske and Taylor 1984). The frames for organizing information of out-groups are less complex than those for organizing information of in-groups. More differentiation therefore occurs in in-groups (Jussim, Coleman, and Lerch 1987).

Some studies within the social psychology literature support the idea that the spontaneous activation of well-learned responses may cause whites who reject negative stereotypes about blacks to inadvertently act in accordance with the stereotypes due to an automatic response (Devine 1989). Others in the field refute this finding, arguing that people are not "wired to categorize" (Fiske 1989:251) and that stereotyping need not be a given, that people can individuate out-group members instead of stereotyping them if they try. The concern is related to discrimination cases, which rely heavily on intent in order for discrimination to be proven, a very difficult barrier to overcome.[3] If a plaintiff cannot prove that discrimination was intended, he or she has little chance of winning a discrimination case. This view favors human agency in that it assumes that people who stereotype are making a choice to do so because other options are available for them. By stereotyping, then, people exhibit intent. The remedy is for people to concentrate and make the hard choice by "valiantly" choosing to individuate instead of choosing to stereotype (Fiske 1989:267).

However, John Bargh (1999), also a social psychologist, disagrees with the claim that stereotyping can be interrupted by will, arguing that successful attempts to interrupt stereotypical thoughts had been accomplished in the laboratory and would be impossible to replicate in the real world. Bargh lists four conditions, all of which must be met if an attempt to interrupt stereotyping in people's lives is to succeed. First, people must be aware of particular stereotypes they hold in order to interrupt them; second, they must be aware of how a given stereotype impacts their thinking and action if they expect to interrupt it; third, they must be overly vigilant in noticing when a stereotype is triggered; and fourth, they must have the goal of interrupting a given stereotype in mind at the moment it is triggered (Bargh 1999). These conditions place an impossible burden on people in their everyday lives, making interrupting stereotypes highly unlikely. I am in agreement with Bargh: compliance with the conditions he identifies would entail an inordinate reliance on human agency, an assumption underlying Fiske's remedy. Some even say that trying to suppress stereotypes may have an opposite, ironic effect by activating the very stereotypes one is trying to suppress (Bodenhausen and Macrae 1996; Wegner 1994).

Although I agree that interrupting automatic stereotyping is not feasible, I am more optimistic than Bargh, who says that little can be done realistically to lessen stereotypical thinking. If we think of stereotypes as being embedded in the white habitus, and if we assume that racist practice proceeds from the white habitus, then we see why racist practice is not likely to be disrupted by being vigilant. However, suppressing stereotypes may not be the only way to lessen them; increasing race awareness by increasing the number of close ties with blacks may be another, better way. The challenge is to change the white habitus.

Critique of Bourdieu

The critique of Bourdieu ironically does not diminish the utility of his ideas for explaining the production of institutional racism. Criticisms of Bourdieu's theories include their being overly structural, especially for blurring the line between the structural and the cultural (Apple 1982; Giroux 1983; MacLeod 1987)—a critique that Bourdieu rejects (1989)—and for his disregard of human agency (Margolis 1999; also see Mehan 1992). The criticism that Bourdieu blurs the line between structure and culture may be what is needed regarding race theory. The misleading separation of structure and culture lessens the explanatory power of theories regarding institutional racism, forcing theories into either a macro- or a microlevel analysis. Explaining how institutional racism operates as a process entails the inclusion of culture. Structure without culture is static and cannot produce anything, including racism. Taking the relational view adopted here, culture and structure are inextricably linked. Sociologists agree that a change in structure produces a change in culture; however, a more interesting question is: If large enough, would a change in culture also produce a change in structure?

In terms of the criticism that Bourdieu disregards human agency, I would argue that the inclination of some social psychologists to stress the role of human agency in racist behavior obscures the racism of well-meaning white people, setting them apart from overt racists, just as the oppositional categories do. Bourdieu's focus on unintended action offers important insights that are useful to race theory in explaining the important role of well-meaning white people in the production of institutional racism.

In arguing that racist practice happens without thought, I do not claim that racist practice is inevitable because of cognitive processes. Nor do I suggest that racist practice is unavoidable because silent racism exists in the white habitus. However, to say that racist practice is not inevitable or unavoidable is different from saying that it is not predictable. And because practice results from actors' understanding of things, racist practice appears to be strongly linked to people's level of race awareness. Practice is not intended to accomplish particular ends; therefore, it is plausible that the lower one's race awareness, the higher the likelihood of practice having unintended racist consequences. If that is correct, then the converse is true as well: the higher one's race awareness, the lower the likelihood of practice having unintended racist consequences. Moreover, the higher one's race awareness, the higher the likelihood of antiracist practice, action that interrupts others' racist practice. Notice that agency is not part of this equation. Rather, when the white habitus contains a clearer understanding of race matters, the practice that emerges from it is not as likely to produce institutional racism and may in fact decrease it.

Not all racist action taken by well-meaning white people is taken through habit, even though much of it is. Everyday racism, which is performed with more intention than racist practice, also contributes to institutional racism. Symbolic interactionism helps to explain how the purposeful action of well-meaning whites also contributes to the production of institutional racism.

Symbolic Interaction and Everyday Racism

The difference between racist practice and everyday racism concerns intention. Racist practice is action that is not intended; everyday racism is intended action although there may be no intention that the action have racist effects. The emphasis on human agency sets symbolic interactionist theory apart from Bourdieu's theory of practice.

Everyday racism is similar to racist practice in that both arise from the silent racism in people's minds. However, everyday racism, unlike racist practice, is intended behavior. This is made clear through the symbolic interactionist concept of definition of the situation. W. I. Thomas argued in 1923 that the definition of the situation is a "stage of examination and deliberation" that precedes any "self-determined act of behavior" (p. 42). Actors interpret a situation through self-communication, using what is noticed in the present and drawing on relevant information from the past. According to symbolic interactionist theory, the deliberation process entails human agency. It is important to note that although everyday racism occurs through deliberate acts, the actor may be unaware that a particular act would be racist. This point contradicts the commonsense (and false) notion that people's intention regarding an act determines whether the act is racist. Ignorance of what is racist is not a safegaurd against performing everyday racism.

An individual's definition of a situation precedes any action he or she may take. The Thomas theorem captures this point: "If [people] define situations as real, they are real in their consequences" (Thomas and Thomas 1928:572). In the Thomas theorem, "consequences" refers to whatever action results from the actor's definition of a given situation (see Ball 1972). Thus, unless what is noticed is problematic—in some way at odds with people's expectations—they are likely to use their definitions as a reliable guide to action, including those definitions embued with racist thoughts and beliefs. Definitions contaminated with silent racism, then, will necessarily produce racist actions, including when those actions are deliberate. The definition of the situation consists of the total of all recognized information from one's point of view (Ball 1972). Individuals both rely on the information they have in devising their definitions *and* interpret the information through their particular point of view. As data from this study illustrate, the white point of view is consistently represented by misconceptions, negative emotions, and white assumptions regarding race matters. Because one's definition of the situation is precisely what is regarded (by the actor) as relevant in determining behavior, individuals without awareness of their own silent racism cannot see that any behavior following from it, deliberate or otherwise, will be racist.

Symbolic interactionism is helpful in illustrating that what people think (that is, their definitions) determines what they do intentionally. This line of thinking is useful when well-meaning white people take action purposefully that inadvertently produces racist effects. For example, in Thomas and Thomas's preceding statement, "examination" and "deliberation" as well as "self-determined act of behavior" all imply that people choose their behavior based on their thoughts and images. Consider Karen's patronizing attitude toward her black friend in the ice cream parlor. Karen believed that Belle could not negotiate ordering her own ice cream, a paternalistic assumption. This belief is why Karen ordered Belle's ice cream for her. Karen's deliberate act suggested that Belle was her inferior. Belle sensed Karen's patronizing attitude and rebuffed it. It does not matter that Karen did not intend, or even know, that the effect of her act would be racist.

If a patronizing incident similar to the one above occurred in the workplace, it would be problematic for Belle, who might be seen as difficult or even a troublemaker by her white coworkers if she rebuffed what they would likely see as a generous gesture. The only other response for Belle—not reacting to a coworker's patronizing attitude—would produce stress of a different sort. She would then be putting up with white people's everyday racism, a type of stress that may account for why turnover is greater in more diverse work groups (O'Reilly, Caldwell, and Barnett 1989; Wagner, Pheffer, and O'Reilly 1984).

The role of silent racism in the minds of well-meaning white people produces institutional racism in two ways: through racist practice that is taken routinely without thought, and through everyday racism, which is action that is intended even though the racist effects it causes may not be intended or even known to the actor. Because silent racism is protected by the oppositional categories of racism, changing how we think about racism is an important goal. Another reason to change the oppositional categories is the passivity of some well-meaning white people. Some of the passivity is a result of the "not racist" category, indicating that evidence for eliminating the categories is mounting.

Passivity and the Production of Institutional Racism

A central question must be answered in this section on the production of institutional racism: is passivity in the presence of everyday racism and racist practice, itself, racist practice? I turn to social network theory for insight into this question. Network analysts avoid explaining individuals' motives for behavior, relying solely on action and its effects (Wellman 1983). In explaining social phenomena, network analysts therefore ignore both attitude—a central component of macrosociologists—and human agency—an underlying assumption of many microsociologists. Network analysts instead focus on the "social distribution of possibilities: the unequal availability of resources such as information, wealth, and influence as well as the structures through which people may have access to these resources" (Wellman 1977:163). This makes network theory especially compatible with Bourdieu's theory of practice and the concept of racist practice. Social network theory also ignores categorical variables such as race and class, focusing solely on relational data such as number of social ties and strength of ties (Wellman 1983). This relational method allows network analysts to describe structure in terms of its inhabitants' connectivity rather than in terms of group attitudes or other normative characteristics.

A modeling approach demonstrates that theories of social structure should not only consider what actors do but also what they do *not* do. "Social causation is a process" that entails action and/or inaction (Whitmeyer 1994:156). Because neither action nor inaction can be performed by a structure, human actors—or groups of actors—are a necessary component of the model. This means that in order for institutional racism to cause racial inequality, individuals' action (everyday racism and racist practice) and inaction (passivity) will be involved in the process. Passivity, then, is a significant feature in the production of institutional racism. Patterns develop through the action and inaction of actors, producing a given effect, called structure; therefore, an individual actor's performance is not the focus of the modeling approach. Patterns within an organization are what count.

There are three components of the network model: action, inaction, and effect. *Action* refers to what people do, *inaction* refers to what people do not do, and *effect* refers to the outcome of the other two components of the model. Regarding the production of institutional racism, action is the everyday racism and racist practice that results from silent racism in the habitus; inaction is the passivity found in well-meaning whites, those who are either detached from race matters, who experience apprehension about being racist, or who are

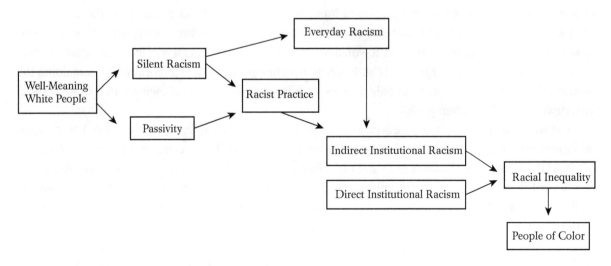

Figure 6.1. Map of Production of Institutional Racism

confused about race issues; and the effect of these—everyday racism, racist practice, and passivity—within a given social system is indirect institutional racism. See Figure 6.1 for a map of the production of institutional racism by well-meaning whites.

If passivity, or inaction, matters, then it produces some effect. Social network theory answers the question posed earlier in the affirmative: passivity in the presence of everyday racism and racist practice is, itself, racist practice. If we recall the literature on the bystander role, we will remember that passive bystanders have a significant effect on the people involved in an incident of wrongdoing, especially on the transgressor, who is empowered (Staub 2003). In the case of institutional racism, passivity, then, has an empowering effect on others' racism, and this effect alone qualifies it as racist practice. Passivity, whether it is caused by detachment from race matters or from the latent effects of the "not racist" category, is a noteworthy component in the production of institutional racism.

Conclusion

In this chapter, I have offered a theory that explains how well-meaning white people—in contrast to overt racists and to color-blind racists—perpetuate racism. Silent racism and the racist practice and everyday racism that follow from it are forces behind much of the institutional racism that perpetuates the racial divide. Furthermore, the passivity of well-meaning white people encourages institutional racism. In addition to direct institutional racism produced intentionally by whites who harbor ill will toward blacks, indirect racism performed daily by well-meaning white people who intend no harm deserves theoretical attention. As it stands, most sociological race theory ignores this less obvious form of racism in favor of "a phenomenon anchored in whites' rational defense of their collective ... advantages" (Bonilla-Silva 2003:193). Racist practice, everyday racism, and passivity are significant and should not be ignored or misinterpreted as a defense of white privilege. This is the racism of racial progressives—the neoliberals and new abolitionists—who are the putative allies of blacks and other people of color today, just as abolitionists and antisegregationists were their allies in the past.

The existence of the "not racist" category produces in the minds of well-meaning white people the illusion that they bear no responsibility for institutional racism or for racial inequality. Yet, silent racism cannot be isolated from the racist practice and everyday racism of white people who produce indirect institutional racism daily, regardless of their recognition of it or their intention to do so. In this way, the illusion that most white people are "not racist" virtually ensures the perpetuation of institutional racism. Although silent racism by definition is not spoken aloud, it would be a mistake to assume that it is of little importance or that the behavior following from it is not racist. Passivity by white people is also important in maintaining the process of institutional racism. It not only colludes with institutional racism, allowing it to operate without interruption, but also encourages it.

Most white people believe that race is no longer a problem in the United States (Blauner 1994), that racism disappeared when slavery ended and legal segregation was abolished. To the contrary, the ravages of slavery persisted throughout the Jim Crow era,[4] and racial inequality supported in the past by law continues to this day. Nevertheless, some conservative writers (e.g., Thernstrom and Thernstrom 1997) argue that racism has declined precipitously since the mid-1960s, a claim that has a strong hold on the white American psyche. But the conservative claim ignores subtle forms of racism, focusing instead on overt racism. Given that the oppositional categories "racist/not racist" uphold this false claim, racial conservatives have a stake in keeping the categories as they are. Nevertheless, the truth that everyone is somewhat racist and that the silent racism hidden by the "not racist" category perpetuates the racial divide—a truth that most blacks already know—could cause a cultural/political shift if recognition of the truth occurs at the "less racist" end of the racism continuum. It is not imperative or probable that all whites would recognize the truth of these ideas. Neither would all whites consider that they might be racist. However, if racial progressives—the least likely whites to be racist—recognize their own racism and act on that acknowledgment, the category "not racist" would not hold.

I point out in the next chapter that race awareness should receive at least as much attention from race theorists as white people's racism. Whites, including those who are well meaning, are woefully ignorant of race matters. Many well-meaning white people know little of the history of racism in the United States, and most are not aware of institutional racism. Fewer still are aware that their own silent racism shapes what they do, often without their knowing, and that racist practice, silent and everyday racism, and passivity hold the racial formation in place.

Discussion Questions

1. How is symbolic interaction theory used in the reading to help us to understand the production of institutional racism?
2. Explain how institutional racism develops and is maintained in our society.
3. How does silent racism contribute to institutional racism?

Notes

1. It is interesting to note that Turner and Singleton claim that the working class is less likely to hold progressive beliefs regarding racism, a claim that is contradicted by Bonilla-Silva's finding that working-class females are the most likely whites to hold antiracist beliefs. This disjunction may be the result of gender difference rather than class difference. Turner and Singleton's claim is based on Bonacich's study (1972), which was done in the early 1970s and was based primarily on working-class men, not women.

2. Practice being outside an actor's awareness is related to Hall's (1959) observation that what people learn informally has an impact on action even if the impact is not in the person's awareness.

3. In many cases, the plaintiff must prove intent to discriminate through a burden-shifting formula: one, the plaintiff's case must show that a discriminatory action occurred; two, the employer must articulate a nondiscriminatory reason for the action taken; and three, the plaintiff must prove that the employer's stated reason is fabricated in order to hide discrimination.

4. I encourage you to visit the Jim Crow Museum on-line at www.Ferris.edu/jimcrow/ for an informative glimpse into many artifacts from the era of segregation.

SECTION III

Historical Perspectives on Racial and Ethnic Groups in America

T he readings in this section are selected to provide historical insights on the various racial and ethnic groups. A goal of the readings in this section is to provide an illustration of how the past, through structural disadvantages and/or racial and ethnic labeling, carries over into racial and ethnic relations that exist today. The readings for this section are selected to make the important point that a fuller understanding of racial and ethnic inequality today requires a better understanding of the past.

SECTION III

Historical Perspectives on Racial and Ethnic Groups in America

Introduction: Exterminate Them

By Clifford E. Trafzer and Joel R. Hyer

Editor's Introduction

Many Americans romanticize Native Americans as the "first environmentalists," "noble savages," and "fierce warriors." The fierce warrior idea is so popular that a number of sports teams have named themselves after Natives. However, few truly know the brutal and genocidal history of White-Native relations from the first coming of Whites. This set in motion a pattern whereby today, Natives are dispossessed of their lands and their well-being. In this reading, the author discusses California Indians and White relationships, beginning with the Gold Rush of 1849. The reading is an example of the harsh, brutal treatment that Whites perpetrated against the Natives for the purpose of conquering them.

Holocaust is an excellent word to use to describe the terror, death, and destruction brought to Native Americans in California during the era of the Gold Rush. One might also use the words "extermination," "debasement," or "genocide" to depict Indian-white relations from 1848–1868. The *Chico Courant* of July 28, 1866 offered the position that "It is a mercy to the red devils to exterminate them, and a saving of many white lives Treaties are played out—there is one kind of treaty that is effective—cold lead."[1] This was a point of view expressed by other editors in California, one that resonates throughout California's dark and hidden past—one that does not appear in popular literature of the Gold Rush era. This was not the view of all non-Indians of California, but one that helped stir a bloody killing field in California and cost the native population thousands of lives.

It had not started out that way. In 1848 a group of Maidu, Nissinan, and other California Indians joined James Marshall in his task to build a saw mill on the American River for John Sutter. Indians led Marshall to a Maidu village called Coloma where the white man decided to build the mill. In order for the mill to operate, Marshall ordered his Indian employees to dig a mill race. Native California Indians dug the mill race and found gold nuggets in the process, showing them to whites, including James Marshall. The Indians had lived in the foothills of the Sierra Nevada Mountains for generations, and they had seen gold before. However, they placed no value on the metal. But the gold found on January 24, 1848 had great meaning to the white men working at Coloma, and the gold discovery would have significant meaning to thousands of California Indians and peoples throughout the world.[2]

When the Gold Rush began in 1848, Californios who ran extensive ranches in California packed up their Indian cowboys and Indian families and took them to the streams rushing through the Foothills of the Sierra Nevada Mountains. Approximately 4,000 Indian miners worked in the gold fields by 1850, and in 1848, Acting Governor Richard B. Mason reported that over half the miners in California were Indians.[3] However, this quickly changed after white miners from Oregon began murdering Indian miners, and it became unhealthy for most Indians to remain the in the gold fields. White men coming to California resented the Californios, in part because some of them were of Spanish and Mexican ancestry, but more importantly because white miners felt that the Californios had an unfair advantage by using large numbers of Indian miners. Many whites hated Indians, and some of them organized vigilante or militia groups to prevent Californios and Indians from taking too much gold. Their solution was to harass Indian miners, burn their villages, or kill them outright. This had been a successful technique in dealing with Indians used by the Spanish, English, French, Russian, and other European invaders, and it was employed successfully by white miners in California.

In his account, *An Excursion to California*, British Forty-Niner William Kelly wrote in 1851 that a store-keeper in the gold fields told him that "no Christian man is bound to give full value to those infernal red-skins" since California's Indians were "vagabones and have no more bissness with money than a mule or a wolf." The storekeeper added that Indians have "no religion, and tharfore no consciences:'[4] Like the storekeepers, other whites did not consider California Indians to be human, calling them "Diggers," a pejorative term related to the better-known term, "Nigger." In addition to cheating Indians, white miners began raping and murdering Indians in March 1849 when Oregon miners raped Maidu Indian women at a village along the American River. When Maidu men tried to rescue their daughters, sisters, and wives, the Oregonians shot them to death. Oregonians countered with an attack on an Indian village on Weber's Creek, killing twelve or more Indians and capturing many more. The Oregonians took seven or eight of these Indian captives to Coloma where the whites told them to run. When they did, the white men shot them to death. The great killings of California's first people had begun.[5]

Bloodshed along the American River was not the first spilled in California, but the event foreshadowed future events of greater severity and magnitude. A year after Indians had found gold at Coloma, roving bands of armed men murdered men, women, and children in a war to destroy all obstacles in the way of native land, water, and mineral resources. White men murdered Indians in a defensive war in order to kill native peoples before Indians could kill them. Miners literally drove Indians from their native lands, stealing their resources and claiming land that had been the homes of native peoples for generations. Many miners were young men raised in the United States during the 1820s and 1830s, and they had lived through the forced removal of thousands of Indians from every corner of the eastern United States. White farmers, merchants, and militia forces had driven Wyandots, Shawnees, Lenape, Ottawa, Anishinaabe, and others from Ohio, Cherokees from Tennessee and Georgia, Choctaws from Mississippi, and Muscogees from Alabama. White miners recreated the violence of their fathers and grandfathers, making Native Californians "strangers in a stolen land."[6]

Native California Indians

Circumstances surrounding the California Indian holocaust did not begin in a vacuum. By 1848 and the birth of the Gold Rush era, California's Indians had witnessed many changes as a result of their contact with Spaniards, Russians, Mexicans, and other Euro-Americans. Prior to European contact, Native Americans had dwelled for centuries in what is now California. The relatively mild climate, coupled with abundant resources, enabled the diverse, indigenous populations to flourish. In California, native peoples resided in arid deserts, rich valleys, rolling foothills, rugged mountains, and along the Pacific coast. Depending on their location, Native Californians subsisted on an abundance of food resources, including fish, deer, rabbit, and shellfish.[7]

Most California Indians relied on acorns as a staple food, and the entire region was rich in natural foods. Women typically ground acorn meal into a flour, drenched it with water to remove the unpalatable tannic acid, and baked it into flat bread or used it to make mush or pudding. They ate a diet rich in natural fruits, vegetables, seeds, and nuts as well as meat, fowl, and fish. All of these foods contributed greatly to the well-being of California's first people, for over the centuries they had developed a biological reliance on them. Beginning with the Spanish period and continuing through the American period, natural habitats for fish, game, and plants foods declined due to ranching, agriculture, and other economic development. The Gold Rush brought white miners who summarily destroyed natural habitats, killing plants and animals while introducing more livestock and alien plants that destroyed the natural landscape of California. In addition to the outright murder of Indians during the era of the Gold Rush, Indians lost their native foods for which they had a biological and spiritual relationship. The destruction of this relationship further jeopardized the lives of native peoples.

By 1769, at least 300,000 Indians lived in California, although this number provided by Alfred Kroeber is believed by contemporary scholars to have been a low estimate. California's Indians speaking over one hundred distinct languages. Instead of belonging to "tribes," these Native Americans dwelled in smaller groups, including bands and villages that were often autonomous but culturally and linguistically related to their neighbors. Frequent contact among these native peoples resulted in extensive trade networks. Coastal and interior groups conducted trade with each other, often traveling great distances to exchange baskets, beads, shells, herbs, and seeds. Many tribes also traded with peoples living in Mexico, the Southwest, Great Basin, Northwest Coast, and Northwest Plateau. Indeed, oral traditions among Native Californians indicate that they had a relationship with Native Hawai'ians and other peoples of the Pacific Islands.[8]

While some Indians forged relatively peaceful relations with each other, others were more inclined to warfare. The contemporary image of California's Indians—created by the Catholic Church and its historians—is one of native peoples always being "docile and domesticated." This is an unfounded image born of the mission system where Indians were and are depicted as kneeling neophytes accepting of the Christian dogma brought by the Franciscans without question or intelligence. Violent confrontations often erupted among Native Californians, stemming from competition over natural resources as well as hunting grounds. Other conflicts arose between old enemies or competing leaders, and some of these animosities continued for generations. Despite this, boundaries between "tribes" appear to have remained fairly stable, although it is clear that some groups expanded onto lands previously controlled by a former group.

In spite of conflicts, American Indians in California developed rich cultures that have endured for generations. Because of the mild climate and abundance of foods, native peoples developed complex religions, social systems, laws, literature, economies, and arts. Dance, music and song flourished in California and continues to grow today. Many Native Californians were known for their beautiful basketry, an art form that has been revitalized by native weavers and is growing rapidly today. Numerous peoples of California excelled in the art of basket weaving and developed elaborate religious ceremonies, festivals, and oral traditions that required the use and remembrance of basketry. Ajumawe and Atsugewe scholar Darryl Babe Wilson has pointed out that the people of the Pit River country believe that at the time of creation, a basket was placed into the peak of Mount Shasta where it remains today sending out its contents of peace and good will. Baskets are more than material culture and art objects. They are spiritual elements of the communities woven into the history, culture, and religion of the peoples.[9]

Spain's Invasion

Spanish invasions into the region eventually altered the world of many California Indians. During the first half of the sixteenth century, Spaniards explored vast regions of the Americas in search of gold and other precious metals. In 1540, Francisco Vasquez de Coronado penetrated what is now the American Southwest, while his associates Hernan de Alarcon and Melchior Diaz briefly entered Alta and Baja California. Two years later, Juan Rodriguez Cabrillo and his men sailed up the California coast, making contact with Kumeyaays living near the shores of San Diego Bay and Tongva-Chumash of Catalina Island. Subsequent voyages up the coast by Sir Francis Drake and Sebastian Vizcaíno also resulted in minor interaction between Europeans and Indians. By right of discovery, these Europeans' nations claimed California, and Spain proclaimed that California's native peoples were subjects of the crown. Spain claimed Alta California but did not resettle the region until 1769.[10]

Despite these encounters, the Spanish did not invade and conquer California until they had heard rumors of Russian vessels sailing along the California coast during the 1760s. Jose de Gálvez, the *visitador-general* of New Spain, feared the Russian presence on the northern frontier of the Spanish Empire. In order to fortify that region from Russian control, Gálvez dispatched a major expedition in 1769 led by Gaspar de Portolá and Father Junípero Serra. The priest set out to establish Catholic missions throughout upper California and convert the Indians to Christianity. He brought religious materials to achieve those ends as well as seeds and vegetables to instruct the Native Americans regarding European agricultural methods. Although Serra and other priests may have possessed what they considered to be honorable intentions in converting the Indians to Christianity, their presence introduced devastating diseases, widespread despair, and genocide among California's native peoples.[11]

Experiences prior to the conquest of California profoundly influenced Spanish attitudes toward non-Europeans. In 711, Muslims from North Africa crossed the Strait of Gibraltar and seized much of the Iberian Peninsula. Between 718 and 1492, the people who would become the Spanish and Portuguese gradually reconquered the Iberian Peninsula. During these centuries—in what Spaniards regarded to be a series of holy wars—Spain regained lost territories, became increasingly militant, and developed a vicious form of racism. According to the Spanish, Europeans were Christian, white, upright, civilized, and crusaders for God's holy causes. They contended that their victories against the Muslims confirmed their superiority. In contrast, they considered non-Europeans to be savage, dark, idolatrous, and uncivilized. Spaniards carried these notions to the Americas and treated indigenous inhabitants with deadly severity.

In California, as well as in other parts of the Spanish Empire, Spaniards endeavored to make Native Americans into productive Spanish citizens and Christians. However, Spaniards never intended for California's Indian people to be equals to Spaniards born in Spain or Mexico. They were not even to be equals with mestizos. California's Indians were seen as a labor force within and outside of the mission system. They were to be the laborers who would allow Spain to reshape California into a bulwark against intrusion by other European powers. Spain sought to accomplish this by founding missions, presidios, and pueblos. These three institutions set in motion Indian cultural decline and resulted in the physical demise of at least one hundred thousand California Native Americans—perhaps more.

Beginning in 1769 when Father Serra began Mission San Diego, the system ultimately included twenty-one missions. The missions stretched from San Diego to Sonoma, stretching along El Camino Real—the King's Highway—which ran along or near the west coast of California. Serra and his missionaries created reducciones or reductions where Catholic priests worked to destroy native culture and religion, replacing it with Christianity. Some priests sincerely desired to save the souls of native peoples and win their allegiance. Clearly, some missionaries viewed proselytization of California's native inhabitants as a labor of love, but many—including Father Serra—employed brutality and intimidation to achieve their goals. They attempted to entice Indians with food and European goods in order to lure them into the missions. When this failed, the padres solicited the aid of Spanish soldiers, who captured Native Americans and forced them to remain within the Catholic missions.[12]

Forced concentration and imprisonment of Native Californians within the mission system is an element of the mission's history that the Church fails to share in its contemporary presentations of these historic sites. The Church also denies whipping men, women, and children, actually characterizing the beatings as "spankings." Spanish soldiers and Christian neophytes ran down Indians who escaped imprisonment at the missions, forcing families to remain within the mission system in violation of the teachings of Jesus. The missions served as reduction centers where Spanish priests, with military support, attempted to reduce Native American peoples and cultures and rebuild them through Catholic discipline. Spanish soldiers concentrated various indigenous peoples into one village in an attempt to destroy the link of the people to each other and their villages. The Catholic fathers then commenced the so-called "civilization" process. They baptized entire villages en mass, forced Spanish law and Christian dogma on the people, and diligently tried to destroy their native languages by requiring Spanish to be spoken.

The Church also forced California's Indians to do nearly all of the work in the missions and labor as slaves of Christ. Native men, women, and children mixed mud for adobes, built forms for adobe blocks, hauled the mud and bricks, laid the bricks, cut timbers for vigas, and made tiles for the structures. Native Californians became cobblers, carpenters, masons. Indians cleared fields for orchards and crops. They planted, harvested, and preserved foods in the missions. They learned to ride horses so they could herd the longhorn cattle brought by the Spaniards, and they slaughtered cattle so they could make tallow to help finance the missions. Christian missionaries exploited Indian labor, and as the missions became economic institutions, priests demanded that their laborers remain within the mission system so they could work, become civilized, and be converted fully to the one true religion. Native religious leaders and their doctrines were obstacles to the missionaries who sought to root out and destroy these elements of California Indian culture. Native Americans encountered miserable conditions in the missions. Perceiving Indians to be children, priests humiliated, flogged, and incarcerated them for various offenses.[13]

Some missionaries reportedly wanted to turn the missions over to the Indians within ten years, yet this never happened. Instead, Catholic fathers subjected Indians to forced labor, poor living conditions, and rampant diseases that mercilessly took the lives of tens of thousands of Native Americans. For the indigenous peoples of California, the mission system was a living nightmare, and memories of native life within the missions remains a haunting memory to many California Indians—Christians and non-Christians. However, the mission was not the only institution of the Spanish Empire that affected Indians. Presidios and pueblos also constituted vital elements of Spain's plans to make the Indians of California loyal subjects.

Most presidios or Spanish forts served to support the missions, although they were separate institutions under a different bureaucracy than the Church. The four military installations in California—located in San Francisco, Monterey, Santa Barbara, and San Diego—housed soldiers who searched for runaway Indians and protected the missions from attack. Spanish and Indian accounts both attest to the fact that soldiers frequently raped native women and indiscriminately murdered native men for protesting the rape of their daughters, wives, mothers, and grandmothers. Soldiers summarily murdered Indians for protecting their families. Sexual abuses were so grave at Mission San Diego that Father Luis Jayme asked Serra to permit him to move Mission San Diego up the San Diego River, a request that Serra granted.[14]

Pueblos built by Spaniards from New Spain provided village communities for Spaniards, including the families of soldiers. Officials in New Spain encouraged Spaniards to move to California by promising them "free" land, real estate that rightfully was controlled by Indians but claimed by the Spaniards by right of discovery and right of conquest. Spanish farmers at the pueblos sold surplus crops to presidios and fought Indians in emergencies. In other words, Spaniards living at the pueblos upheld and strengthened the presidios and missions which sought to alter the lives and destroy the cultures of California's native peoples. In addition, pueblos served as examples for Indians so that they could witness a "civilized" life. The increasing presence of Spanish immigrants had disastrous consequences for the Indians and their environment.

Spaniards who resettled California, displacing the native population, introduced sheep, horses, mules, and cattle which overgrazed lands. Alien livestock consumed vast quantities of grasses and other plants, driving away native game and making hunting for traditional game more difficult. Livestock also destroyed plant habitats of natural foods that were critical to Native Californians. Thus, the Spanish incursion into California disrupted the delicate balance which existed between Indian peoples and the earth, plants, and animals. However, as dramatic as these changes were to native peoples, they could not compare to those that emerged with the invasion of the United States and discovery of gold at Coloma.[15]

California Indian Agency and Resistance

Despite the Spanish systems of coercion, Indians resisted foreign domination, sometimes subtly, other times violently. In the missions, Native Americans occasionally disregarded orders or instructions given by the priests. Although Indians learned the Spanish language and various tenets of Catholicism, they frequently retained their native languages, religious beliefs, rituals, ceremonies, songs, and oral narratives. Young Native American men defied the strict gender-segregated living conditions at the missions slipping into the monjarios or dormitories of young Indian women. Sometimes women escaped their nightly imprisonment to be with friends and families they loved. Native women defied the Church by aborting babies conceived by being raped by soldiers, civil officials, or priests.

Hundreds of Native California Indians expressed their disdain for the missions by fleeing into the interior of California. Patriots among the native people who fled the missions often confiscated Spanish weapons and horses. When they returned to their people or joined other groups of Indians, they often gave riding lessons and taught military tactics to those Indians not under Spanish control. These Indians became raiders and forces that harassed the Spanish throughout the mission period. Thousands of Native Americans abhorred the Spanish presence and struggled to expel them from the region. For instance, approximately eight hundred Kumeyaay Indians (also known as Ipai and Tipai), representing perhaps three dozen villages or more, stormed the San Diego Mission and burned it to the ground in 1775. Father Jayme had built the new mission in the heart of Nipaguay, a Kumeyaay village that was unearthed in 1989–1990 when the Diocese attempted to build a fellowship hall and bingo parlor on top of the mission, village, and Indian cemetery.[16]

Kumeyaay leaders—particularly religious leaders—who encouraged, planned, organized, and executed the action against Mission San Diego viewed Christianity as a threat to their traditional culture. This was no less true of other California Indians. In 1781, Quechans living along the Colorado River attacked two nearby pueblos at Mission La Purisima de la Concepcíon and Mission San Pablo y San Pedro de Bicuity as a threat to their traditional culture. This was no less true of other California Indians. In 1781, a Spanish army under

Pedro Fages rescued the captives, the Spanish never returned to resettle the region or challenge Quechan rule of their homelands. In fact, Quechans successfully harassed Spanish and Mexican herders and immigrants traveling to California, thereby curtailing further settlement.[17]

Other less successful uprisings occurred at numerous locations, including Mission San Gabriel in 1785–86, Missions Santa Clara and San Juan Bautista between 1790 and 1800, and the Mission Santa Cruz in 1812. The most spectacular example of resistance among the Native Americans of California occurred in 1824, three years after Mexico's independence from Spain. Between 1772 and 1804, Spanish overlords forced Chumash Indians inhabiting the coast between Los Angeles and San Luis Obispo to participate in the construction of five missions and one presidio on native lands. Many of this people had suffered ill treatment by local Spanish soldiers and priests. In February 1824, the Spanish had an Indian at San Ynez Mission flogged, and the event resulted in a massive native revolt. Indians living at the mission rose up and attacked their oppressors and destroyed several structures. The next day, almost two thousand Native Americans seized and fortified the nearby La Purísima Concepcíon Mission. Chumash Indians from the missions at San Ynez and San Fernando soon traveled to La Purísima to reinforce that mission against the Spanish.[18]

News regarding these events reached the Santa Barbara Mission not long afterward. Tensions rose there. Fearing that the Indians might rebel, Spanish soldiers—without provocation from local native people—attacked Indian laborers at Santa Barbara. After fighting several hours, the Spanish withdrew from the mission. The Native American victors then destroyed the mission and retired to safer territory. One month after these initial takeovers, Spanish soldiers mounted an attack on Mission de la Purísima. Padres eventually negotiated a cease-fire between the two parties. While most of the Chumash Indians received little or no punishment for participating in these events, the Spanish condemned and executed seven of their leaders for their involvement in the uprisings. The Spanish viewed the conflict as a revolution against their regime, but contemporary Chumash argue that they acted as patriots against foreign invaders who had stolen their lands, oppressed their people, and forced many cultural changes.

Mexico's Rule

The years between 1821 and 1846 marked the period of Mexican rule in California. The new nation of Mexico inherited a massive, overextended empire from Spain. Mexicans assumed control over the missions, presidios, and pueblos of Baja and Alta California. As demonstrated by the Chumash fight for freedom, Native Americans at the missions resisted the priests throughout the Spanish colonial era in a variety of ways. In 1821, over twenty-one thousand Indians resided and worked at the missions. Widespread disease, death, and the escaping of Indians reduced that number to sixteen thousand by 1834. Missionaries hoped to force additional laborers from outlying native villages and establish a series of new missions into the interior. Yet the dearth of money and personnel prevented the fruition of these plans. Instead of growing, the mission system declined rapidly during the Mexican era of California's native past.

In 1833, the government of Mexico passed legislation secularizing the missions of California. The new laws stipulated that local officials were to distribute mission lands to native peoples who had converted to Catholicism. These Indians were to receive half of the missions' livestock, seeds, and tools. Instead of complying with the statutes, civil authorities confiscated most of the mission lands for themselves, forcefully pushing California's Indians aside and denying them lands that had belonged to them since the time of their creation. On extensive, prime, mission lands, Mexican officials and wealthy landowners established large, private ranchos, stealing former mission lands that had been intended—under law—to be returned to the native population. Rather than regaining their traditional lands, California's native population became the labor force for the ranchos. Many of California's Indians became vaqueros, cooks, wranglers, and general employees—the labor force—for Californio rancheros.[19]

These changing conditions offered new choices for indigenous inhabitants of California. They could work on the ranchos or in one of the developing Mexican towns, doing wage labor. They could apply for their own land grants, although this was an avenue rarely pursued by First Nation's people in California. Or, native people in California could move away from the Mexican population and join their friends and relatives, forming new and dynamic social, political, and economic units. Some Indians worked in towns such as Los Angeles, San Diego, San Jose, San Francisco, and Santa Cruz. Many of these communities became completely dependent upon native labor, as Indians and non-Indians interacted with each other on a constant and daily level in such occupations as smiths, cobblers, wheelwrights, whalers, and teamsters. Indians labored in fields near Los Angeles and San Jose, harvesting grapes and other crops. Native Americans worked on ranchos, performing numerous tasks, including shearing sheep, raising crops, herding and slaughtering cattle, dressing hides, and building houses. Californio rancheros did not generally regulate the noneconomic affairs of native laborers, but largely ignored native religious ceremonies, music, art, and festivals. Throughout the Spanish and Mexican periods, native peoples nurtured and preserved various aspects of their diverse cultures, and Californios made no concerted effort to destroy native religions, rituals, or ceremonies.

A few Indians filed for Mexican land grants in California, but most did not, and their "legal" title to their homes has been a major issue ever since the eighteenth century. The process of filing a land grant included written documents, legal processes, and paper work. Indians who succeeded in this endeavor tended to be literate and knowledgeable about Mexican law. Through these means, a few Native Americans eventually possessed ranchos two thousand acres in size. Such men appear to have led lifestyles more like local Mexican rancheros than their indigenous predecessors. Indian women also asserted themselves in this manner. In 1838, one native woman named Victoria obtained a rancho in the San Gabriel Valley. By 1852, at least fifty Native Americans had secured "legal" land titles in southern California alone.[20]

Other Indians carried out a more traditional existence, living with kin in indigenous villages. The seventy-five-year presence of the Spanish invaders had sufficiently damaged the environment and diminished local game that these native societies had to adapt. For example, the acquisition of horses enabled Indians to travel long distances quickly. Deteriorating food supplies forced previously peaceful Indians to become expert raiders. Such peoples became increasingly nomadic and warlike. Native groups frequently descended on Mexican settlements to raid for horses, cattle, and mules. However, they usually preferred to seize horses because of their value as a means of transportation, trade commodity, and food item. Ranchos near Los Angeles, Monterey, San Diego, and Santa Barbara were particularly susceptible to attack. One Plains MeWuk named Yozcolo conducted successful raids against the Mexican Californios for almost ten years. Native Americans outside of California also pillaged ranchos. Walkara, identified as a Ute but one who may have been Paiute or Chemehuevi, seized livestock annually from ranchos near San Bernardino, driving them north to Utah. Other Indian raiders carried on a brisk trade with Indians and non-Indians from New Mexico.[21]

Indian raids resulted in increased violence between Californios and native societies. Californios gained prominence by conducting military campaigns against indigenous peoples in the interior. Mariano Guadalupe Vallejo emerged both wealthy and powerful after he and his followers attacked and murdered over two hundred Wappos in 1834. By 1846, Mexico's Assembly passed resolutions calling for funds to pay Mexican citizens to locate and destroy Indian villages. Californio rancheros also employed Native Americans to crack down on livestock theft. For instance, the Lugo family of Rancho San Bernardino recruited Cahuilla Chief Juan Antonio and his people in the mid-1840s to guard the rancho's cattle and horses against Indian, Mexican, and white thieves. The alliance between the Lugo family and the Cahuillas was so strong that both groups joined forces on one occasion to kill approximately forty Luiseños and Cupeños.[22]

Rampant disease continued to be an acute problem for indigenous inhabitants of California during the Mexican period. Like other peoples throughout North America, the Indians of California had little or no immunity to European pathogens. Prior to 1827, diphtheria, measles, and pneumonia ravaged Indians living at the missions. In 1833, other maladies—such as cholera, smallpox, and syphilis—spread like wildfire. Approximately forty-five hundred Maidus, MeWuks, Wintuns, and Yokuts perished from various illnesses in that year alone. Some Mexican and white American immigrants to the region deliberately infected native peoples with these ailments, but other diseases spread unabated through the air and water as a result of non-Native contact. Native Americans struggled to comprehend the ferocity and mercilessness of these invisible killers. Between 1830 and 1848, almost 11,500 Native Americans died of "white man's diseases." By 1848, the population of Native California Indians was roughly 120,000, but it would decline radically during the era of the Gold Rush.[23]

California Indians and the United States

In the fifteen years prior to the war between the United States and Mexico, non-Spanish immigration to California accelerated. While most of the newcomers were Americans, John Sutter was a native of Switzerland who established a rancho at the confluence of the American and Sacramento rivers. Sutter built Rancho New Helvetia near several native villages, and the Swiss immigrant "contracted" local Indian peoples, treating them like serfs and offering them gifts for their labor. Native response to the Swiss immigrant varied. While some Indians expressed their disapproval of Sutter's presence by seizing his stock, others willingly worked for him. He and two MeWuk leaders, José Jesús and Polo, solidified an alliance in which Sutter provided the MeWuks with goods in exchange for their assistance against Indian raiders. José Jesús and Polo also regularly brought laborers to Sutter. This relationship appears to have benefited some people but caused resentment among some Indians living in the Sacramento Valley.[24]

While Sutter strengthened his ties with MeWuks, Mexican officials became concerned over the rising power of foreign rancheros who had no allegiance to Mexico. In the spring of 1846, General José Castro convinced the Muqueleme Indians to attack Sutter's rancho. Castro also hired a Muqueleme named Eusebio to murder Sutter. However, for one hundred dollars in assorted goods, MeWuks killed Eusebio before he could assassinate the Swiss ranchero. Such conflicts reflect the increasing tension between Californios and non-Spanish immigrants. This also demonstrates the complex relations between native societies and non-Indians.[25]

In May 1846, the United States declared war on Mexico. American civilians captured Sonoma one month later. Americans and Californios fought each other for control of southern California that fall. Native Americans reacted to these new circumstances in various ways, recalling their long history of oppression by the Spanish in California, some decided to side with the Americans. For instance, forty Tulare Indians joined John C. Frémont's battalion. Known as Company H, these Native Americans conducted numerous raids against Mexican ranchos. They successfully seized hundreds of Mexican cattle and horses. Others fought courageously beside Americans near Los Angeles in January 1847, forcing the Californios to surrender. Still others chose to take advantage of unprotected ranchos by stealing livestock for their own gain.[26]

With California claimed by Americans, military governor Stephen Watts Kearny dispatched soldiers to end Indian raids on livestock belonging to Californios. Carlos, a Yokuts chief, agreed to take Captain Henry Naglee and his troops to the accused raiders. Instead, he purposely led them in circles. On another occasion, Naglee's forces indiscriminately murdered two chiefs. The Americans hoped that Native Americans would discontinue their campaigns against ranchos, but Indians continued to steal livestock. Within months, animosity grew between Americans and some of the local native peoples.[27]

The year 1848 altered the lives of California's First Nations forever. The United States invaded California, wresting it from Native Americans and Mexicans who claimed it. Without the permission of Native Americans who held original title to their conquered lands, the United States formally "acquired" California under the Treaty of Guadalupe Hidalgo. Native Americans in California have contested the treaty since its ratification, arguing that they never surrendered their lands or their sovereignty. Indians argue that Spain and Mexico never "owned" California and the region did not belong to Mexico and thus could not be transferred to the United States. Americans seeking land and economic opportunity, have always ignored the native reality about the land and native sovereignty. Immigrants from the United States assumed ownership of California and began to trickle into the region after 1848.[28]

White immigrants brought with them hostile attitudes toward Indians which white Americans had developed from over 200 years of interaction with native peoples in the Eastern part of the country. Previously in California, the Spanish converted native peoples to Catholicism and tried to incorporate some Native Americans into Spanish and Mexican society. In addition, the Spanish and Mexicans had exploited native laborers, a well-worn tradition throughout Latin America. The incoming Americans surpassed Spaniards and Mexicans in their brutal treatment of Native Americans. For years, white Americans and their colonial forbears conquered and exterminated indigenous peoples of North America. Native Americans in the East did not remain idle but fought back and resisted white domination. However, most of the Eastern Woodland tribes lost their lands and peoples, resulting in a displacement of many peoples and forced removal of some Indians into the Indian Territory—present-day Kansas and Oklahoma. Most American immigrants to California viewed California's Indians in a manner comparable to the way they had viewed Indians in the East, obstacles that had to be relocated or annihilated. Yet through all this, Native Americans of California openly defied the American invaders and fought to defend their lands, cultures, and families.

California's Gold Rush

Another major event in 1848 caused thousands of Americans and people from all over the world to move to California. John Sutter decided to erect a sawmill in the late 1840s. He placed James Marshall in charge of selecting a site for the mill and to oversee its construction. In May 1847, an Indian guide led Marshall up the American River to a heavily-timbered area and a Maidu village called Coloma. As Marshall and the Maidus were on congenial terms, these Native Americans assisted in building the sawmill. While Maidus were digging a mill race along the American River on January 24, 1848, one of them uncovered gold. Maidus were already aware of the existence of gold, but they did not value it as a precious substance. Maidus, Nissenans, and other Native Americans of the Sierra Foothills working at Coloma had no idea of the significance of their discovery. They had no conception of its meaning in terms of their homes, families, and future. For Indians in California, the gold discovery at Coloma was an infamous event, one that would become a watershed in their history and that of many peoples of the world.[29]

The impact of the Gold Rush on Indians was tremendous. Some Native Americans living in or near the California foothills secured employment as miners. Rancheros hastened to the mining region, bringing with them Indian vaqueros and other native workers. Native laborers, as a result, quickly transformed from cowboys on the ranchos to gold miners in the Sierra Foothills. This was true in the case of Charles M. Weber, a rancher living near Stockton, who took his native employees into the foothills to pan for gold. During the early months of 1848, Weber and his Indian laborers journeyed to the mining camps, arriving at a mountainous area known as Dry Diggings (modern-day Placerville). Weber employed approximately one thousand Native Americans in hope of unearthing a bonanza of mineral wealth, and it was American Indian miners who found the first gold at Placerville. William Daylor from the Sacramento Valley soon joined Weber, and within a short time, the two men reportedly earned fifty thousand dollars off their Indian miners.[30]

Weber's optimism led him to hire Yokuts in the summer of 1848 to search for gold. Some of them worked at Dry Diggings, while others traveled south to what are now Calaveras and Stanislaus counties. Soon after, Yokuts discovered gold along Carson's Creek and Wood's Creek. This area eventually became known as the Southern Mines. The *Monterey Californian* reported that there were about three thousand Indians labored in the gold fields by August. Besides working on behalf of employers, some Native Americans staked out their own claims and labored for their own benefit, not for Californios. An estimated four thousand Native Americans worked as miners by the end of 1848, including men, women, and children.[31]

Like most prospectors, Indians who participated in the first few years of the Gold Rush panned for placer gold. This method was probably the cheapest way to obtain gold, but it was back-breaking work. People also employed other methods to obtain the coveted mineral. Native American miners and others used a common instrument known as a "rocker." This contraption somewhat resembled an infant's cradle and typically required three people to operate it. Workers placed it on an incline. One miner shoveled dirt into the hopper at the upper end, and another poured water on the dirt. The third person then rocked the apparatus, thereby forcing the mud through the rocker and out its lower end. Gold particles settled in the device's cleats. Yet the rocker was not totally effective or efficient, as small gold flakes often slid out with the tailings. By the fall of 1849, Indian miners used another contraption known as a "long tom." Functioning much like a rocker, this instrument enabled gold seekers to quickly wash large quantities of earth. It was usually about twelve feet in length. Prospectors channeled a stream of water through the long tom, thereby employing water to separate and sort through dirt and gravel. Long toms, some hundreds of feet long, were called sluices.[32]

White employers and merchants often cheated Native American laborers. For instance, Charles Weber and William Daylor paid native workers in goods, including blankets, coffee, clothing, meat, and sugar. These men and white traders greatly inflated the value of the goods, particularly in light of the value of the gold they unearthed. As a result, indigenous miners received meager compensation. Traders also cheated Indians, setting up stores near the gold fields and successfully swindling Indians and non-Indians alike. Self-employed Indians usually traded their gold at trading posts for rope, handkerchiefs, and cloth. As Native Americans could typically speak no English and only a little Spanish, merchants charged Indian miners exorbitant prices for goods. Several traders offered two prices for an item, the lower price for white miners and a higher price for Native Americans. Merchants commonly referred to the steeper rates as "Indian prices": When Indians insisted that they receive goods based on the weight of their gold, retailers used a two ounce weight, known as a "Digger Ounce," in order to secure gold from Native Americans at half its value. However, Indians soon realized the white man's love of gold and increasingly sought more equitable exchanges for this coveted mineral.[33]

Killing Indians

Indian miners underwent dramatic changes during and after 1849. That year, people from all over the globe flooded into California. Thousands of Americans, French, Germans, Italians, Chinese, Chileans, Englishmen, Australians, and Mexicans converged on the mines hoping to obtain wealth beyond their wildest dreams. Even other Indians, including Cherokees and Wyandots, hurried to California to stake a claim. The influx of people brought a sharp increase in disease to the region, devastating indigenous peoples of California. Expanded mining activity disrupted the lives of thousands of Indians who had chosen not to participate in the Gold Rush but continued to lead traditional lifestyles. For these native men, women, and children of

California's interior, their traditional food supplies sharply decreased and their streams became polluted. Lawless foreign adventurers appropriated Indian lands in order to uncover new gold deposits. The recent arrivals also considered native miners a menace, human obstacles to their own prosperity. Soon many newcomers viewed all Indians negatively and sought to exterminate them. Open conflict between the two groups resulted.[34]

In March 1849, a party of prospectors from Oregon attacked a Maidu village on the American River. These White invaders sexually assaulted many Maidu women and shot some of the Maidu men who attempted to intervene. Soon thereafter, Maidu warriors descended on a party of Oregon miners on the middle fork of the American River and killed five of them. About twenty white men from Oregon retaliated by forming a mob. This group of ruffians stormed an Indian village on Weber's Creek, killing at least twelve Native Americans and taking several prisoners. The Oregonians later brutally murdered eight of the Indian hostages. One visitor to California named William McCollum contended that whites from Oregon generally "hunt [Indians] as they would wild beasts."[35] James Marshall, who ascertained that many of the prisoners were his employees, was furious. The men from Oregon threatened Marshall's life and he retreated. George Parsons, a contemporary biographer of Marshall, asserted that the Native Americans butchered by the Oregon mob "belonged to a different tribe" of Indians than those who killed the five miners from Oregon. This mattered little to the whites from Oregon who blamed all Indians for the killings and indiscriminately retaliated against native people.[36]

Bayard Taylor, who visited the mining camps during the Gold Rush, wrote of another confrontation between whites and Native Americans in his book, *Eldorado*. California Indians unearthed gold near what is now Grinding Rock State Historical Park. After whites arrived, native congenial relations prevailed for several days until a white prospector accused Indians of stealing his pick. A local chief agreed to visit the Indian mining camp to inquire about the missing tool. According to Taylor, as the indigenous leader hurried to the native encampment, "one of the whites raised his rifle and shot him."[37] The white miners gathered together, spread a false report that Native Americans had murdered an innocent white man, and decided to drive the Indians out of the rich region. California Indians retaliated by wounding a white man named Aldrich with three arrows and then retreated into the nearby mountains.

These events had considerable impact on Native Americans in the mining camps. California Indians recognized that the newcomers—jealous of their lands, resources, and claims—wanted to annihilate them. The hostilities committed by whites forced Native American miners to withdraw en mass from the gold fields. Indigenous societies not involved in mining also had to protect themselves from future incursion, as many whites began murdering, burning, and raping Indians. They also started kidnapping women and children, selling them into slavery. White miners, no longer viewing the indigenous inhabitants of California as productive employees, considered them a collective threat to their prosperity or a commodity to be sold to the highest bidders.

Between 1849 and 1850, violence against California Indians escalated. An incident known as the Clear Lake Massacre is a case in point. Two white men, Andrew Kelsey and Charles Stone, established a ranch in the vicinity of Clear Lake. They coerced several Pomo Indians to work for them. Kelsey and Stone exploited, abused, and murdered some of their native laborers. In 1849, the Pomos rose up and killed their oppressors. Whites blamed the entire affair on the Indians, but the Pomos knew better and remember the incident well in their own oral histories. American military forces, after hearing about Pomo defiance, proceeded to the area to retaliate. The soldiers soon surrounded about three hundred Native Americans on an island and began their assault. Troops fired at any Indian in sight, killing dozens of non-combatants, including women, children, and elders. Captain Nathaniel Lyon—who led the massacre—described the island to which the Indians fled as "a perfect slaughter pen."[38] Some American military officers and men in California, as in other parts of the United States, felt that the only good Indian was a dead Indian, and they put their beliefs into actions against the Pomos.

"Protecting" Native Californians

Americans in the area as well as throughout the United States demanded statehood for California. Under the Compromise of 1850, California entered the union. The new California state legislature, dominated by whites from the United States, passed statutes limiting the rights of "foreigners," which of course did not include white Americans. Whites in the Golden State wanted only white Americans to work in the gold fields. Under state law, miners who did not possess American citizenship had to pay a monthly fee of twenty dollars. This caused thousands of Mexicans to leave the mines. Many Chinese miners, however, initially paid the tax and continued to work, while other Chinese miners returned to San Francisco to begin anew. Angry at the recalcitrance of many Chinese miners to pay the tax and continue mining, xenophobic Americans taunted, beat, and murdered several Chinese miners. White miners and government officials clamored to rid the region of so-called foreigners as well as native people who competed with whites for limited gold.[39]

This general antipathy toward all non-whites, coupled by intensified white-Indian relations, resulted in the legal discrimination of California Indians. On April 22, 1850, the state legislature passed California Statute Chapter 133, known as "An Act for the Government and Protection of Indians." This series of twenty laws, similar to the Black Codes of the post-Civil War South, reflected the anti-Indian attitudes of whites during the mid-nineteenth century. For years, Americans had legislated against Native Americans at the state level. Generally speaking, Chapter 133 "legally" curtailed the rights of Native Americans in the Golden State and placed California Indians in a subordinate legal, political, social, and economic position within California's new society. The state laws significantly affected the lives of thousands of Indians for years, and the racist attitudes that initiated and executed these laws remain a part of the state's treatment of Native California Indians in contemporary society.[40]

Some of the statutes within this act influenced the course of Native Americans' history. Section 1, for instance, granted justices of the peace authority in all legal cases involving Native Americans. This ensured a dangerous amount of power at the municipal and county levels of government. White magistrates often despised Indians and deliberately favored local white citizens in cases involving land, resources, personal property, criminal offenses, and custody of children. Section 2 allowed the state to determine the residence of California's Native Americans, stating that Indians could continue to reside on indigenous lands. However, the provision stipulated that a justice of the peace could determine how much land Indians needed to survive and offer excess land—not deemed necessary for Native Americans—to be obtained by whites. Clearly, local judges possessed sufficient power to dispossess Native Americans of most of their homelands, including prime land in San Diego, Los Angeles, Santa Cruz, San Francisco, and other towns that emerged as major cities. Section 6 prohibited the native peoples of California from testifying against whites in a court of law. Indians, therefore, could not assist in convicting a white person through their own testimony. In civil cases, Native Americans could not testify against whites for burglary, land theft, cattle rustling, assault, battery, or other crimes. Whites simply stole land, livestock, and property from Native California Indians who had no legal recourse against white thieves. Worse yet, whites kidnapped Indian women and children, raping and committing other indignities for which Indians had no recourse under a legal system that denied them access.[41]

Other elements of this legislation sought to force Indians to work for whites. For example, Section 5 permitted white employers and Native American employees to enter into labor contracts. Indians, however, frequently did not understand the details of these agreements and remained in a state of perpetual servitude. According to Section 20, Native Americans who appeared to be "loitering and strolling about" would be arrested and incarcerated.[42] The definition of vagrancy under this law was highly subjective, depending on the interpretations of white justices of the peace who often incarcerated Indians. Virtually any white person could call on sheriffs, deputies, or marshals within cities or counties to arrest Indians who were unemployed or who had upset or inconvenienced a white person. Once the Indian was arrested and convicted, he or she was assessed a fine. When Indians could not pay their fines, officials allowed whites to pay the fine in return for the Indian's labor for a proscribed period of time. Section 14 allowed this transaction, permitting non-natives to post bond on Indian prisoners and legally force them to work for them, usually for four months. Under this legislation, abuse abounded. Whites were able to enjoy cheap and constant labor as well as dominate and frighten California's first people. American citizens and the California legislature worked together to compel Native Americans into oppressive labor relationships with whites.[43]

Chapter 133 was also a direct attack on native societies, and it was intended to establish and maintain white domination of native peoples. According to Section 10, Indians could not "set the prairie on fire, or refuse to use proper exertions to extinguish the fire when the prairies are burning." For years, indigenous inhabitants of California had set fire to their grasslands in order to draw game into canyons and other areas where Native American hunters could kill them. Burning the grass encouraged plant growth as well and was a form of range management. Without the ability to start range fires, the food supply for native peoples declined rapidly causing starvation. The invasion of thousands of non-Indians into California diminished local game and plant life, compelling some Native Americans to confiscate horses and livestock belonging to the newcomers for food. American Indians in California had been raiders for generations, but the destruction of the natural environment encouraged other Indians to steal and develop an economy based on livestock raiding. Indians were forced to steal or they would starve which was exactly what California's politicians and many citizens had in mind.[44]

Indian raids were a direct violation of Section 16 which prohibited Indians from stealing animals from whites. The state laws attempted to constrain the native peoples of California to completely abandon traditional practices while at the same time punishing them from stealing so that they could survive. This presented Indians with few options and justified white suppression and destruction of California's native population. Indians had no legal alternatives and were often dominated by whites or killed outright like animals. Section 13 of the law required indigenous leaders to turn over suspected Indian criminals to white officials. This section clashed with traditional Indian law which permitted local native leader to adjudicate wrongdoings. Moreover, Indian leaders well understood that there was no "justice" for native people through the courts. The law was also an assault on tribal and village authority and sovereignty that had rested with native peoples since the beginning of time. But Chapter 133 was intended by whites to destroy tribalism and place Native Americans into a subservient, dependent condition within California's racist society.[45]

Treaties with California's Indians

Besides California state officials, the United States government also altered the lives of California Indians. During the 1840s and 1850s, the United States Army had men stationed in California, but the Army generally did nothing to protect the rights and lives of Native Americans in California. Instead, the Army allowed state officials, city fathers, county officers, and militia groups to murder, rape, and kidnap Indians. In addition, the national government, which had claimed primacy in Indian affairs since the Federalist period, did not exert itself in California. The newly formed Department of Interior and Office of Indian Affairs did not present a strong agenda in California, in spite of the fact that three officials negotiated eighteen treaties.

In 1850, the federal government dispatched three commissioners—George Barbour, Redick McKee, and O. M. Wozencraft—to the Golden State to negotiate treaties with indigenous peoples. Considerable confusion surrounded the activities and instructions of these three officials, but they were the first federal officials to deal directly with the tribes in terms of treaties and reservations.[46]

Between 1851 and 1852, the three men concluded eighteen treaties with over one hundred native societies throughout the state. The negotiations were between sovereign governments or sovereign peoples—government to government relations. Indians did not passively submit to the demands of the United States. Instead, they negotiated doggedly with the Indian agents, thereby securing a portion of their aboriginal lands and some decent lands for their peoples. However, they lost vast acres of beautiful, productive, and bountiful land along the coast, in the valleys, throughout the mountains, and into the deserts—all land they once had controlled before the Spanish, Mexican, and American invasions. The agreements of the 1850s were significant in that they stipulated that Native Americans remove to reservations within California rather than relocate out of state. Under the accords, California's indigenous inhabitants were to retain approximately one-seventh of the state, but in the process, they lost millions of acres of their native estates.[47]

Most whites opposed the treaties because they asserted that the commissioners set aside lands too valuable for Indian occupation. Redick McKee attempted to pacify such objections by maintaining that "once the Indians adopted the food, clothing, and working habits of whites ... they would provide [whites] with vital labor for their mines and farms."[48] The governor of California, John Bigler, feared that establishing Indian reservations near American communities would result in violence. Other local officials regarded federal negotiations a violation of states' rights. Public pressure encouraged California's United States Senators to oppose ratification of all the treaties. In June 1852, the Senate formally rejected the eighteen treaties. Whites in California wanted all of the land and resources in the new state, and without federal recognition through the treaties, Indians had no legal relationship with the United States or federal protection of their lands. Without treaties, Indians in California were under the thumb of state laws that discriminated against them. Still, during the 1850s, some of the reservations created by the federal agreements functioned briefly. Other reservations emerged through acts of the Office of Indian Affairs operating within the state.

Prior to the arrival of Barbour, McKee, and Wozencraft in 1851, native societies in the Southern Mines challenged the invasion of miners into their territories. In December 1850, Yokuts raided James Savage's trading post on the Fresno River, stealing furniture, horses, mules, tents, and other items reportedly worth $25,000.[49] One week later, over one hundred Native Americans attacked a ferry crossing, killing one white person and stealing several horses and cattle. Yokut Indian leaders, José Rey and José Juarez, united native peoples in the region and conducted numerous campaigns against miners working the Southern Mines. Native California Indians killed at least twenty miners and wounded many others in an attempt to drive whites off their land. Between December 1850 and April 1851, Indians reportedly seized as much as $500,000 worth of livestock and goods, although this amount may have been inflated to encourage immediate and harsh reprisals against California's native population.[50]

State officials responded to the successful Indian raids by authorizing the creation of a volunteer military force known as the Mariposa Battalion. This unit of militia soldiers soon arrived in the Southern Mines and harassed native peoples, whether or not they had been involved in the recent raids. As a result of these attacks, several Indian leaders negotiated with the three federal Indian commissioners because native leaders believed it in their best interest to do so. Yosemite MeWuk and Chowchilla Indians refused to speak with the agents, while at the same time, they evaded the Mariposa Battalion. Tenaya, one prominent Yosemite leader, never signed a treaty with the Americans. Many Indians who entered into such agreements frequently bolted the temporary reservations, preferring to live in their mountain homelands. As a result, the California state legislature appropriated over $1.5 million during the 1850s for local troops to fight indigenous peoples who were unwilling to remove to the reservations and live under federal domination.[51]

California Indian Resistance

While whites typically sought to exploit, harass, or exterminate indigenous peoples of the Golden State, the newspapers on a few occasions offered an honest assessment of the plight of California's Indians. The *Alta California* printed one such article—one which likely fell on deaf ears. The anonymous journalist began the essay by defining the relationship of California's native peoples to their lands. The Indians "are the original possessors of the soil," an editor pointed out, for the earth holds "all the associations of their lives" and "their traditions." Afterward, the author blamed avaricious miners for driving out local game, desecrating indigenous grave sites in search of "the glittering gold which lay beneath," and mercilessly robbing and murdering native peoples. The writer also related how whites "pushed [Indians] from the valleys where their arrows procured their meat, from the rivers where they caught their fish, ... [and from] their oak orchards."[52] Despite this eloquent plea for whites to end hostilities against Native Americans, white Americans—as previously mentioned—organized the Mariposa Battalion to destroy native men, women, and children.

Native Americans answered white depredations by raiding Americans whenever possible. In February 1853, Indian peoples attacked a pack train bound for Yreka. They killed a white man named Dick Owen, but another man, one Mr. Archer, managed to escape. The Indians seized a horse and thirteen mules, including the supplies each animal carried. Before withdrawing, these Indians also attacked another train, wounding a number of mules.[53] Such campaigns, though completely justified, enraged whites. According to the *Alta California,* "Indians have committed so many depredations in the North, of late, that ... [whites] are ready to knife them, shoot them, or inoculate them with small pox—all of which have been done."[54]

In addition to indigenous peoples near the gold fields, other Indians in the Golden State opposed the ever-increasing presence of American citizens. Native Americans retaliated against the numerous white invaders who seemed to engage in hostilities and stir up trouble wherever they went. John Glanton, a Texan of questionable character, stole a ferry business from Able Lincoln on the Colorado River. He and his associates charged exorbitant fees for passage across that desert waterway and wanted to eliminate all competition. In April 1850, some Americans passing through the region disapproved of Glanton's inflated prices and decided to construct their own ferry. These American travelers crossed the Colorado on their vessel and then offered the boat to local Quechan Indians. The Native Americans began their own ferry operation in direct competition with Glanton.[55]

According to the *Alta California,* Glanton and his men "marched down to the Indian[s'] ferry, seized their boat and destroyed it." They also grabbed "an Irishman [one Callahan], whom the Indians had enlisted in their service, tied his hands and heels together, and threw him into the Colorado." The Quechans assembled and "determined that the Americans must die."[56] Waiting for an opportune moment, the Indians struck Glanton's camp while he and his men slept off a drunk. Historian Donald Jackson states that Glanton and ten Americans died in the attack, and Harvey Johnson, the most celebrated historian of the lower Colorado River confirmed that while the Quechans killed the Texans, two ferrymen watched in horror and walked from the river to San Diego to announce the "massacre."[57] A militia group led by Major Joseph G. Morehead organized to punish the Quechans, but the Quechans counterattacked these irregular forces, surrounding them in a small stockade previously built by new ferry operators. If it had not been for the stockade and the new ferrymen working at the Yuma Crossing, Quechans likely would have annihilated Morehead and his makeshift troops.[58]

White migration to California not only affected Indian-white relations, but also influenced the formation of alliances between indigenous groups. For example, a pan-Indian resistance movement developed in southern California in 1851. Antonio Garra, a primary leader of the Cupeños, intended to drive the Americans from the area. He solicited the support of various Cahillas, Kumeyaays, Luiseños, and Quechans. His plans centered on attacking Camp Independance (just west of Fort Yuma on the Colorado River at the base of Pilot Knob), Los Angeles, San Diego, and Santa Barbara. Garra's warriors burned the Rancho of Juan José Warner, an American who exploited Cupeño workers, but the war did not develop beyond Warner's ranch. Although many Indians were outraged by the growing American presence, few joined the armed resistance. The prominent Cahuilla leader Juan Antonio opposed Garra, most likely because the two men—both powerful within the native communities of the desert—were at odds with each other.[59] Juan Antonio ultimately captured Garra, presenting him to local authorities. A military tribunal convicted and executed Garra. His multi-tribal alliance broke down, and Native Americans sought other ways to resist.[60]

Images of California's Indians

Most foreign immigrants arriving in California blamed Native Americans for most murders and other crimes. Americans and their newspapers portrayed the image that Indians were responsible for most acts of violence in the state. For instance, the *Alta California* reported that one "murder of an atrocious character was perpetrated by some persons, probably Indians," in San Diego on the night of January 13, 1853. The newspaper graphically described how the body of George Warren "was found stripped nearly naked, ... and his brains literally beaten out." People at the crime scene discovered a "jaw bone of an ox ... near [the white person's corpse] covered with blood, brains and mangled masses of flesh and hair." After providing this gory depiction, the author of this article cast swift judgments. "Suspicion points to certain Indians last seen in his company, who undoubtedly murdered the poor wretch for the sake of the miserable clothing he wore." The report concluded that San Diego "is infested with a gang of Indian thieves and murderers, who should be driven out."[61] Thus, a mysterious murder instantly became a rallying cry to expel all American Indians from this part of southern California.

Americans also attributed murders in and near the gold fields to Indians. One Mr. Slater, a rancher, disappeared for a number of days. According to the *Alta California,* an anonymous person found Slater's body "much eaten by wolves." The paper recalled that the white man's "head, arms and legs had been carried away, and not enough left to identify him, had he not been previously missed." Again, the *Alta California* "supposed that the deed was done by the Indians." The American press in California recounted such scenes in gruesome detail in hope of casting Native Americans as savage brutes who killed whites for no reason. This image of native California Indians justified the theft of Indian land and resources. It also encouraged the destruction of Indian people and their cultures, depicting native peoples as barbaric savages who deserved to be extinguished from the earth in order to make way for superior, civilized people. Such appalling reports as that presented above horrified whites and significantly influenced their attitudes toward California Indians.[62]

California's Reservation System

While whites continued to view the Native Americans of California as scapegoats, the federal government attempted to deal with the state's so-called "Indian problem." However, federal control of Indians affairs in California was poorly orchestrated in the 1850s and 1860s as state and local officials assumed superiority in Indian affairs. In March 1852—three months before the United States Senate turned down the treaties of Barbour, McKee, and Wozencraft—Congress created the office of superintendent of Indian affairs of California. The president appointed Edward F. Beale to that position, and in September 1852, Beale arrived in the Golden State to assume his duties. He eventually established an Indian reservation system that in many respects resembled the efforts of Barbour, McKee, and Wozencraft. He hired Indian agents to reside near reservation Indians and ideally wanted a military post to be located adjacent the reservation. However, in contrast to the three commissioners, Beale organized smaller reservations in areas not heavily populated by whites which were each approximately seventy-five thousand acres in size. After Congress appropriated a total of $350,000 during 1852 and 1853, the superintendent commenced his operation.[63]

In 1853, Beale created California's first official reservation near Tejon Pass at the southern end of the San Joaquin Valley. Beale created the first reservation system in the United States, the prototype for future "modern" reservations designed to "civilize" Indians through agriculture and ranching regulated by agents of the Office of Indian Affairs. The next year he proudly reported that Tulare first reservation system in the United States, the prototype for future "modern" reservations designed to "civilir or complaint, but with the most cheerful alacrity." He further stated that "as the fruits of their labor begin to show itself [sic] in the immense field ..., [the Indians] look at it in amazement, and with delight."[64] If Beale is reporting accurately, these California Indians were enjoying the reservation life as farmers, but Beale took the credit for the initial success at Tejon, failing to mention that the Tulareños did all the work involved in raising crops. Soon soldiers forced nonagricultural Indians to relocate to the Tejon Reservation.[65]

The drastic change in lifestyle for California's native peoples from freedom to confinement onto reservations where they faced strict discipline and foreign domination caused several Native Americans to flee the reservation for sanctuary in their traditional homelands. The reservation at Fort Tejon eventually failed, closing in 1864, but the concept of Beale's reservation system lived on into the twentieth century. Out of the 1850s and after the Civil War, the United States embarked on a national reservation policy of forcing Indians onto confined areas where agents of the Office of Indian Affairs could control them. The government isolated Indians onto reservations, diminishing their freedoms, and concentrating diverse peoples onto small land bases where agents could "civilize" them through farming and Christianization. Once corralled and confined, the government permitted non-Indians to resettle former Indian lands, legally securing title to it and prohibiting Indians from living on or using their traditional homelands or resources. This became the national model for reservations from the mid-nineteenth century to the twentieth century, and this national policy, with traditions in the American past, emerged full-bloom in California.[66]

One year after the creation of the reserve at Fort Tejon, Beale's successor—Thomas J. Henley—established the Nome Lackee and Fresno reservations. Henley later founded the Klamath and Mendicino reservations in 1855. In addition, he created two "Indian farms." On these farms and reservations, agents taught Native Americans how to cultivate vast tracts of land. Almost ten thousand of the state's fifty thousand Indians lived under this paternalistic system in 1857. Echoing the events at Fort Tejon, Indians loathed the conditions at the other reservations and escaped in droves during the late 1850s and early 1860s. California newspapers initially printed rave reviews of the reservations and the grand harvests there, but the newspapers soon began writing alarming critiques as the "truth" of the failures became apparent. One by one, the Office of Indian Affairs closed reservations. By the end of the 1860s, all of the five original reservations created in the mid-1850s were no longer in operation. Only three others—the Tule River, Round Valley, and Hoopa Valley reservations—remained.[67]

Dismal conditions prevailed on the reservations in California. Through the patronage system, corrupt and incompetent men often became Indian agents. These men received cash appropriations from the federal government to purchase decent rations for reservation Indians. Instead of fulfilling this obligation, Indian agents frequently acquired blankets, cattle, food, and supplies of inferior quality and then pocketed the remaining funds. Meat was often rancid by the time Indians on the reserves obtained it. For these native peoples, they could either remain on the reservations and starve to death or leave and live as their ancestors or raid non-native communities and ranches for horses, cattle, and other livestock. They often chose the latter.[68]

California Indian Holocaust and Survival

Whites, however, failed to recognize that Indians really had no choice but to flee the reservations. It was a question of survival. American citizens forgot that whites had polluted the streams and rivers, drove off or killed local game, and disrupted traditional societies. In essence, the actions of whites compelled many of California's Indians to steal cattle and horses. Whites viewed reservations as a place to concentrate, confine, and control Indians so that non-native peoples could develop the state in a manner they saw fit. When Indians left the reservations to raid local ranches, whites retaliated swiftly—even without legal authority. For instance, a volunteer militia group in Fresno and Tulare counties forcibly assembled approximately two hundred Yokuts during the fall of 1858. The militia destroyed native villages and forced the men, women, and children onto the Fresno Reservation. This vigilante group carried out this action, because these Indians had reportedly stolen pigs and cattle from local ranchers. At least this was their justification for forcing them off their traditional homelands and onto the government reservation. In this way, the militia force could open Indian lands for white to resettle, claiming choice lands near water resources while at the same time corralling their native enemies.[69]

Military campaigns against native societies typically involved the indiscriminate murders of several Indians and forcing survivors onto reservations. One Captain Jarboe, for example, proudly proclaimed that within four months he and his cohorts had killed 283 Indians and escorted 292 others to Mendocino Reservation.[70] There are no records regarding how many native women and children were raped, kidnapped, or sold into slavery. Some white Americans openly committed genocide, killing many Indians to drive them from the land and exterminate them. This was their intention, and racism mixed with economic gain combined to cause a deadly mixture for native men, women, and children. In order to encourage the extermination of California's First Nations, white individuals and communities offered monetary rewards for the heads and scalps of Indian people.

Indeed, Shasta City awarded five dollars for each Indian head presented to municipal officials. Residents of Honey Lake paid twenty-five cents per Indian scalp in 1863. Volunteer militia groups of cut throats murdered Indians indiscriminately and turned their body parts into cash money while at the same time, cleared the land of its original inhabitants. Concentration of Indians on reservations posed problems for native people other than starvation, for they were easy targets for white vigilantes and scalp hunters. As a result, the bloody and vicious cycle continued in California, as Indians jumped the reservations, stole livestock to survive, and fought disgruntled whites. Native California Indians either died in their fight for survival off the reservations or returned to the reservations to await attack or death by starvation.[71]

During the 1860s, California Indians did not willingly submit to white power or vigilantism but fought for their families and people against the foreign invaders and murderers. In 1862, Native Americans in the Coso Mining District in Owens Valley forced whites to abandon the area for a year. In the same year, Indians in Humboldt County conducted successful raids on white communities that caused non-natives to desert many farms and ranches. Native peoples burned American homes and farms, and such campaigns effectively hampered the economic development of the region by whites. Indians also captured whites during raids. In the summer of 1862, Yahis kidnapped three white children. Likely retaliating for the murder of Yahi infants, these Indians killed two of the young hostages. Whites eventually discovered one of the slain children with seventeen arrows in him, his throat slit, and his head scalped. Innocent children—Indian and non-Indian— were truly the victims in these wars initiated and conducted by adults. Clearly, both Native Americans and whites committed heinous acts against helpless youngsters, and both justified their actions within their own communities. However, whites generally had the upper hand, killing and kidnapping far more people and selling them into slavery.[72]

White militia groups during the 1860s continued to hunt down and destroy native peoples. In 1860, whites living in Humboldt County attacked a number of the local Indian villages. The Americans endeavored to annihilate indigenous peoples in retaliation for cattle and other items taken in raids. Native men often were not in the villages at the time of these attacks, owing to the fact that whites preferred to wait for them to leave the villages before commencing hostilities. According to the San Francisco *Bulletin,* "bands of white men, armed with hatchets ...[,] fell on the women and children, and deliberately slaughtered them, one and all." One witness to these atrocities counted twenty-six bodies of women and children in one camp. The *Bulletin* discussed the victims of this mindless assault. "Some of them were infants at the breast," one editor wrote, "whose skulls had been cleft again and again." The writer of this newspaper account was highly critical of the whites who participated in this carnage, referring to these cowards as "the lowest and most brutal of the border population." The anonymous journalist asserted that the whites who precipitated the attack "possess nothing of humanity but the form and the bestial instincts."[73]

Nadir and Survival

By 1870, the native population had declined to 20,000 from 40,000 people. The killing and kidnapping of California's first peoples had been great. Some Indians that died during the era of the Gold Rush California succumbed to bacteria and viruses brought by foreigners who invaded the region, as diseases spread throughout the gold fields and onto the reservations. Yet volunteer militia units murdered thousands of Native Americans, and enslaved thousands more. Non-native immigrants to California from many parts of the world brought their racist attitudes with them to California, mixing their racism with their greed to produce bloody violence against a people the outsiders generically labeled "Diggers." The foreigners denigrated California's Indians in their writings, depicting native people much as they would wild animals who aimlessly "roamed" the land like herds with no social organizations, governments, laws, or religions. This was the biased image that whites intended to portray of a people they wanted removed from the land or exterminated completely.

Despite the efforts of some whites to exterminate the native peoples of California, American Indians in California survived the holocaust. They have survived in spite of one hundred and fifty years of racial hatred and discrimination which forced them off their lands and marginalized them throughout the state. They have survived civilization programs, Christianity, forced removals to reservations, and rape of their lands and resources. In spite of obscene death rates during the twentieth century caused by tuberculosis, pneumonia, sudden infant death syndrome, and numerous other health problems, they have survived. And California's Indians continue to survive in spite of a state government that has discriminated against them since 1850 and continues to deny them educational opportunities and a measure of economic prosperity through the gaming industry.[74]

At the end of the twentieth century, there are roughly 200,000 Native Americans living in the Golden State, and many of them are watching with interest as the state launches its sesquicentennial of the California Gold Rush. While the governor, legislators, representatives, and senators make much political hay of the Gold Rush, California's Indian people are not celebrating. They are remembering the genocide of their people, the rape of their women and children, and the enslavement of their family members who helped build the Golden State. For California's First Nations, the era of the Gold Rush was truly a holocaust, a watershed in their history that they remember through their oral histories and numerous written accounts left by non-natives who watched and recorded the horror.

Editing Written Accounts

The editors have made every effort to reproduce the accounts found herein as accurately as possible. However, several editorial problems have emerged that readers should be cognizant of before analyzing the documents below. Spelling, punctuation, use of nouns and verbs, and use of the English language is not always consistent with contemporary dictionaries or grammar. For example, some writers use semicolons-colons instead of commas, or they use hyphens instead of periods. Sometimes writers broke words that are not broken today such as any thing or hyphens in between such words as anything. Sometimes writers italicized the names of other newspapers and sometimes they do not. Rarely do editors italicize the names of ships in accordance with rules of grammar today. The documents emerged out of the mid-nineteenth century when newspaper reporters and editors as well as military and civilian writers had varying degrees of education. Often the articles are written in an awkward fashion or by writers who use colloquial phases that are difficult to understand today. In addition, many of the articles have been taken from microfilm that is extremely difficult to read due to missing words, smudges, and dark dots that obscure the text. None of this diminishes the significance of the accounts or their importance as historical sources.

The original and classic works of Robert F. Heizer and Alan Almquist—published by Ballena Press, Peregrine Smith, and the University of California—have been out of print for over twenty years. One of the objectives of this work was to introduce them again to the general public and a new generation with the sincere hope that they may alter the way in which the history of California during the Gold Rush era is presented in schools and colleges. The work may also encourage scholars to rethink genocide among California's native peoples.

Discussion Questions

1. How were Native women treated differently from Native men? Why?
2. What ideology did Whites use to justify their treatment of the Natives?
3. How did Natives resist White incursions? Why wasn't Native resistance ultimately successful?

Notes

1. *Chico Courant,* July 28, 1866.
2. James J. Rawls, "Gold Diggers: Indian Miners in the California Gold Rush," *California Historical Quarterly* 55 (Spring 1976): 29–30; James J. Rawls, *Indians of California: The Changing Image* (Norman: University of Oklahoma Press, 1984): 116–17. Rawls has conducted the most recent and comprehensive research on the Gold Rush era. For a work intended for young readers, see Clifford E. Trafzer, *California Indians and the Gold Rush* (Newcastle, California: Sierra Oaks Publishing Company, 1989): 1–6.
3. See Mason's report in House Executive Document 1, 30th Congress, 2nd Session, 60.
4. William Kelly, *An Excursion to California over the Prairie, Rocky Mountains, and Great Sierra Nevada* ... 2 (London: Chapman and Hall, 1851): 45.
5. The best discussion of the developing conflict between California's Indians and Oregonians is Rawls, "Gold Diggers," 36–39.

6. For a general discussion of Eastern Indians, see Clifford E. Trafzer, *As Long as the Grass Shall Grow: Native American History, 1400-2000* (New York: Harcourt Brace, 1999). For the quote, see Richard L. Carrico, *Strangers in a Stolen Land: American Indians in San Diego, 1850-1880* (Newcastle, California: Sierra Oaks Publishing Company, 1987): 18-36.

7. For general information about the cultures of California's Indians, see Alfred L. Kroeber, *Elements of Culture in Native California* (Berkeley: University of California Press, 1922); Alfred L. Kroeber, *Handbook of the Indians of California* (Washington, D.C.: Smithsonian Institution Press, 1925); Robert F. Heizer, editor, *California: Handbook of North American Indians* 8 (Washington, D.C.: Smithsonian Institution Press, 1978); Rupert Costo and Jeannette Henry *Costo, Natives of the Golden State: The California Indians* (San Francisco: The Indian Historian Press, 1995).

8. Ibid.

9. Oral interview, Clifford E. Trafzer with Darryl Babe Wilson, 1992.

10. Hubert Howe Bancroft, *History of California,* 7 vols. (San Francisco: The History Company, 1886): 1-64.

11. Ibid., 110-25.

12. Ibid.; Edward D. Castillo, "The Impact of Euro-American Exploration and Settlement," in Heizer, ed., *California,* 99-104. Hereafter cited as Castillo, "The Impact."

13. For a general study of the missions, see Edith B. Webb, *Indian Life at the Old Missions* (Lincoln: University of Nebraska Press, 1952). Also see this volume intended for young audiences, Clifford E. Trafzer, *American Indians as Cowboys* (Newcastle, California: Sierra Oaks Publishing Company): 11-17.

14. Jayme to Serra, October 17, 1772 in Maynard Geiger, ed., *Baja Travel Series* (Los Angeles: Dawson's Book Shop, 1970): 43-44.

15. Rawls, *Indians of California,* 25-43.

16. Bancroft, *History of California,* 251-53; Castillo, "The Impact." 102-4.

17. Clifford E. Trafzer, *Yuma: Frontier Crossing of the Far Southwest* (Wichita, Kansas: Western Heritage Books, 1980): 15-21.

18. Castillo, "The Impact," 103.

19. Ibid., 105-6.

20. George Harwood Phillips, *Chiefs and Challengers* (Berkeley: University of California Press, 1975): 37-39.

21. Ibid., 43; Paul Bailey, *Walkara* (Los Angeles: Westernlore Press, 1954).

22. Castillo, "The Impact." 105-6; Phillips, *Chiefs and Challengers,* 45-62.

23. Castillo, "The Impact," 106.

24. Rawls, *Indians of California,* 77-79.

25. Bancroft, *History of California,* 6: 12-17.

26. Ibid., 5: 1-29.

27. Ibid.

28. Castillo, "The Impact." 107.

29. Bancroft suggests that a California Indian named Jim may have discovered the gold, while Rawls points out that Marshall first claimed that he had found it and later acknowledged that whites and Indians found the gold. Rawls, "Gold Diggers," 29-30; William McCollum, *California As I Saw It,* edited by Dale E. Morgan (Los Gatos, California: The Talisman Press, 1960): 147.

30. Bancroft, *History of California,* 6: 67-81.

31. Ibid., 82-109, 351-80.

32. Ibid., 409-28.

33. Rawls, "Indian Diggers," 34-36; Trafzer, *California Indians and the Gold Rush,* 28-34.

34. Trafzer, *California Indians and the Gold Rush,* 34-39.

35. McCollum, *California As I Saw It,* 147.

36. George Frederic Parsons, *The Life and Adventures of James W. Marshall* (Sacramento, California: James W. Marshall and W. Burke, 1870): 113.

37. Bayard Taylor, *Eldorado* (New York: Alfred A. Knopf, 1949): 185.

38. Nathaniel Lyon to E. R. S. Canby, May 22, 1850, National Archives, Records of the War Department, Document 329a, Record Group 98, Letters Received, 1850, as found in Robert F. Heizer, ed., *The Destruction of California Indians* (Santa Barbara: Peregrine Smith, Inc., 1974): 245.

39. Robert F. Heizer and Alan F. Almquist, *The Other Californians* (Berkeley: University of California Press, 1971): 121, 145–46, 151, 154, 156.

40. Ibid., 39–40; California Statute 133, "An Act for the Government and Protection of Indians, Statutes of California, April 22, 1850. Hereafter cited as California Statute 133. See S. Garfielde and F. A. Snyder, compilers, *Compiled Laws of California* (Benicia, California: S. Garfielde, 1853): 825. In this compilation, the law is known as Chapter 150. Also see, Carrico, *Strangers in a Stolen Land,* 38–40.

41. California Statute 133.

42. Ibid.

43. Ibid.

44. Ibid.

45. Ibid.

46. Heizer and Almquist, *The Other Californians,* 68–81.

47. Ibid.

48. George Harwood Phillips, *Indians and Indian Agents* (Norman: University of Oklahoma Press, 1997): 164–65.

49. Savage was an Anglo American who immigrated to California in 1846. With the discovery of gold, he used Indians to get rich. Then he made greater wealth by establishing three trading posts at the Southern Mines.

50. Phillips, *Indians and Indian Agents,* 37–56, 78–91; Rawls, *Indians of California,* 185; Costillo, "The Impact of Euro-American Exploration and Settlement," 108.

51. Heizer and Almquist, *The Other Californians,* 67–85.

52. *Alta California,* January 15, 1851.

53. Ibid., March 2, 1853.

54. Ibid., March 6, 1853.

55. Trafzer, *Yuma,* 52, 74–77.

56. Ibid.; *Alta California,* January 8,1851.

57. Donald Dale Jackson, *Gold Dust* (New York: Alfred A. Knopf, 1980): 268. Harvey Johnson was the foremost scholar on the history of the Colorado River and worked for years as a volunteer for the Yuma County Historical Society. His work on the Glanton gang and Quechan attack are represented in Trafzer, *Yuma,* 74–77.

58. Trafzer, *Yuma,* 52, 76. See also the Johnson Collection, Yuma County Historical Society, Yuma, Arizona.

59. Oral interview, Clifford E. Trafzer with Katherine Saubel, 1997.

60. Phillips, *Chiefs and Challengers,* 170.

61. *Alta California,* February 21, 1853.

62. Ibid., April 1, 1853.

63. Rawls, *Indians of California,* 148–50.

64. As quoted in Rawls, *Indians of California,* 151.

65. Ibid., 148–50.

66. Clifford E. Trafzer, *The Kit Carson Campaign: The Last Great Navajo War* (Norman: University of Oklahoma Press, 1982): 224–37.

67. Rawls, *Indians of California,* 152.

68. Ibid.

69. Ibid.

70. Ibid., 164.

71. Ibid., 185.

72. Ibid., 182.

73. *San Francisco Bulletin,* June 18, 1860, as quoted from Heizer, ed., *The Destruction of California Indians,* 254.

74. Clifford E. Trafzer, Luke Madrigal, and Anthony Madrigal, Chemehuevi People of the Coachella Valley (Coachella, California: Chemehuevi Press, 1997): 117–24.

Racial Formation

Spain's Racial Order

By Martha Menchaca

Editor's Introduction

In this reading, Menchaca discusses race mixture and the creation of the Mexican population. She discusses the racial order of Spain, and how the Spanish treated and used the Indians and African slaves and ultimately had children with them. This created a group of people we know today as Mexicans. A key point raised in the reading is the commonality of interracial liaisons. This reading also illustrates how classification of the offspring of interracial liaisons has always been a social product based on elaborate rules.

I n the aftermath of the conquest, the Spanish military strategy of "divide and conquer" effectively created disunity among the Indians of central Mexico and opened the path to a new social order. At first, the Spanish left the indigenous economy and lifestyle relatively undisturbed, allowing elites who pledged allegiance to the crown of Spain to continue governing their peoples (Diaz del Castillo 1963). About twenty-five million Indians inhabited central Mexico at that time (Borah 1983:26; Meyer and Sherman 1995:212; Miller 1985:141). Within fifty years of the conquest, Spanish-Indian relations were redefined and race became a principal factor in the social and economic organization of Spanish colonial society. Exemptions were made for the Indian nobility, and this tokenism effectively served to entrench a racial order that solely benefited White people. Interracial political and marital alliances commenced the restructuring process (Gibson 1964; Liss 1975). My focus here is on central Mexico, because during the sixteenth century Spaniards concentrated their efforts on populating and stabilizing this zone before launching their assault upon the present southwestern United States. Most of central Mexico constituted the former Aztec Empire.

Shifting Political Alliances

After the conquest, the Spanish chose present Mexico City as their principal administrative center and placed their Tlaxcalan allies in positions of power throughout Mexico (Frye 1996). Tlaxcalans were given land formerly belonging to the Aztec Empire as well as the right to govern the people living in those regions. To further undermine the political confederacy established by the Aztec, the emperor was killed and the regional kings were replaced when they did not accept Spanish rule (Liss 1975; Lockhart 1991). These kings were called *tlatoques* (singular *tlatoani)* and under their command was a *cacique* cadre that directly governed the villages. The *cacique* was in charge of overseeing one or more villages, depending on his relation with his *tlatoani*. The *tlatoques* resided in the *cabeceras,* the regional capitals. After the conquest, the *tlatoques* who were loyal to Spain were allowed to continue governing and collecting tribute from the villages and towns they controlled (Gibson 1964). If their *caciques* were also loyal, they in turn were allowed to continue to oversee the communities they supervised (Aguirre Beltrán 1991; Vigil 1984). When a *tlatoani* rebelled, it was common for the royal government to replace him and reconfigure the political boundaries of that region. Often the governance of a region was broken apart and distributed among several lower-ranking *caciques.* In this way the Spanish crown rewarded its most faithful Indian subjects.

To demonstrate their loyalty *tlatoques* and *caciques* often repressed anti-Spanish political revolts (Gibson 1964; Powell 1952,). Through this process of repression, the Spanish were able to create a "middleman" political infrastructure to govern the masses. Though it was sometimes necessary to replace *tlatoques* with *caciques,* the Spanish knew that it was more effective to co-opt rulers, as this generated a semblance of legitimate rule and political continuity. Spaniards rewarded their allies and outfitted the *tlatoques'* armies with weapons and horses (Powell 1952).

The Spanish also retained the *tlatoques'* families—the indigenous nobility—in power as a means of averting regional revolts (Vigil 1984). By retaining the Aztec nobility in positions of power they placated the masses. Political continuity created a facade, hiding from the people the fact that the ruling families were under the control of Spain (Aguirre Beltran 1991; Lafaye 1974). In most places the nobility accepted the lifestyle introduced by the Spanish and the political transition. For them, accommodation became a survival strategy and a safety net to maintain the privileges their families had enjoyed for centuries. In return for their postconquest complicity members of the indigenous nobility were allowed to retain control of their property and were awarded additional land (Gibson 1964). They were also exempt from paying tribute to the Spanish crown and were given gifts including clothing, furniture, literature, utensils, and other European commodities.[1]

After the defeat of the Aztec, the royal crown rewarded the *conquistadores* by giving them *encomiendas* (Meyer and Sherman 1995), agricultural estates carved out of land occupied by Indians. As part of their reward, Spaniards also received tribute from the Indians living in the *encomiendas* in the form of free labor and material goods such as money, crops, farm animals, textiles, ceramics, and beverages. Of most importance to the *conquistadores* was Indian labor, since land was useless unless it had people to farm, construct buildings, and work as domestic servants. The *encomienda* system was clearly an abuse of the Indians' property rights, but was rationalized under the pretense that it was the most effective method of acculturating them. Such a rationalization was necessary because in 1512 the Spanish crown passed the Laws of Burgos, establishing the procedures and laws to govern Indians (Hanke 1949:24). These laws decreed that Indians, like orphans, widows, and the wretched, would be protected and Christianized.[2] Indians were legally declared wards of the crown and church. The laws also contained additional stipulations with respect to Indian laborers and the acculturation process they would be subjected to.[3] Though the *encomiendas* were beneficial to the *conquistadores,* many clergy opposed them and charged that in effect they were a legal method of enslaving Indians and dispossessing them of property. The Catholic Church, after hearing many complaints from New World clergy, launched a campaign to limit the growth of the *encomiendas* and to delineate the legal rights of the Indians. Such a legal battle was necessary to avoid their enslavement, for unless Indians were legally declared human Spaniards could treat them as beasts of burden.

Ginés de Sepúlveda, a juridical scholar, became the most influential spokesman in Spain arguing in favor of enslaving Indians. Sepúlveda wrote several inflammatory books demonizing Indians; his most famous text, *Democrates Alter,* received a favorable reception throughout Spain (Hanke 1949). He asserted that Indians were savages without souls—a view that countered the Catholic Church's interpretation of Indians as descendants of the lost tribe of Israel (Lafaye 1974). The divergent positions of the church and Sepúlveda came to be known as the Noble Savage debate (Stocking 1968). Although Sepúlveda and his followers concurred that Indians probably were from the "promised land," he argued that on their exodus from Israel they came in contact with the devil and entered a stage of demonic savagery, citing the iconography found in hieroglyphic texts and on buildings as proof of his assertions. He claimed that Spaniards in the New World therefore had the right to enslave these savages.

On the other side of the debate was Father Francisco de Vitoria, who challenged Sepúlveda's demonization of Indians. Vitoria has been credited with having been the most influential legal philosopher to persuade the Catholic Church and crown to classify Indians as humans and thus to bestow on them the legal rights of human beings (Borah 1983; Hanke 1949). These rights included not being enslaved, being able to marry anyone they chose, being Christianized, being allowed to own property, and being allowed to live in towns and villages. Essentially, Vitoria argued that Indians had the right to pursue happiness. His philosophy was reflected in the political activism of other clergy, such as Father Bartolomé de Las Casas, who moved from theory to activism by obtaining field evidence to support the position that Indians were rational beings with souls.

In 1502, Las Casas arrived in the New World in Hispaniola (present-day Haiti and Dominican Republic) and later observed the mistreatment of the Indians throughout Latin America (Haring 1963:10–11). In his travels he observed the colonists overworking the Indians and treating them as animals. In essence, the colonists were breaking the religious and labor laws by denying Indians time to rest and to learn Christian doctrines (see *Recopilación de leyes de los reynos de las Indias* 1774, Book 1, Title 1, Laws 3, 5, 9, 10, and 12). Most of the atrocities were committed by *encomenderos.*

Although in theory the *encomiendas* were acculturation sites to civilize and Christianize Indians, they became unofficial slave institutions (Vigil 1984). Many missionaries who were concerned about the suffering of the Indians intervened. They sent countless complaints to the Spanish king and began to lobby to end the *encomienda* system (Borah 1983). The king sent investigators to the New World to determine whether Indians were indeed being mistreated. Las Casas became the most outspoken critic of the *encomiendas* and launched an attack on them. Knowing that he needed evidence to prove the Indians' humanity if Sepúlveda's claims were to be discredited, he refined the hypothesis that the Indians had migrated from Israel to the New World by adding a cognition argument. Las Casas's main argument centered on the Indians' capacity to learn Christian doctrine. He asserted that since Indians were able to learn Christian doctrines and many were able to read Spanish, they had the capacity to think abstractly, thus proving they were human (Wagner and Parish 1967).[4] As a consequence of the Las Casas research, Vitoria successfully obtained the legal classification of the Indians as human beings.

The enslavement of Indians became illegal in 1537, when Pope Paul III, in the papal bull *Sublimis Deus,* proclaimed Indians to be human, with the rights to be Christianized and to own property (Hanke 1949:72–73). The Spanish crown endorsed the proclamation and over time imposed additional protectionist legislation. The liberal position taken by the Catholic Church and crown was not shared by the entire Spanish population or by most of the countries of Europe (Menchaca 1997). Not until 1859 did most European countries accept that Indians and other people of color were not animals (Menchaca 1997:30).[5]

Although the church succeeded in obtaining the legal status of human being for the Indians, it also endorsed the crown's position that they must be governed and protected. The crown therefore named the church the Indians' legal protector and gave it the responsibility of Christianizing and converting them into loyal tax-paying subjects (Cutter 1986; Polzer 1976; *Recopilación de leyes de los reynos de las Indias* 1774: Book 1, Title 1, Laws 1, 3, and 9).[6] These legal rights, which came to be known as Vitoria's Natural Laws, in theory became standard practice in Mexico by 1550 (Hanke 1949:150–154; Liss 1975:38–43). As long as Vitoria's Natural Laws did not conflict with the crown's colonization plans, officials were instructed to extend Indians their legal rights; if Indians resisted colonization, however, they were not to be given any legal rights and could be enslaved (*Recopilación de leyes de los reynos de las Indias* 1774: Book 1, Title 1, Law 1).

Changing Intermarriage Laws: The Eve of a Racial Hierarchy

Though forming political alliances with the *tlatoques* became the primary manner in which Spaniards maintained control of the masses in central Mexico, intermarriage was also an effective and peaceful approach to accomplish a similar goal. It was an important practice used to solidify alliances, serving as a public testimonial of the Spaniards' trustworthiness (Liss 1975). In many societies where intermarriage served a utilitarian function, as in Mexico, this practice became a symbolic gesture to attest that Indians and Spaniards had good intentions toward each other. Claude Lévi-Strauss (1982) proposes that in pre-capitalist societies intermarriage has traditionally been used to form enduring alliances between political groups. The ritual of marriage becomes a public testimonial to assure communities that they are safe during a period of political transitions when mistrust between allies is common. Intermarriage becomes a stabilizing factor. Lévi-Strauss also suggests that members of the dominant group will accept wives as a symbol of peace, but will not exchange their own women. Apparently, this practice was replicated in Mexico: the Indians offered their women kin, but the Spanish did not return this symbolic gesture (Meyer and Sherman 1995).

To encourage intermarriage between Spaniards and Indians in central Mexico, the Spanish crown awarded military officers and soldiers more acreage than was commonly assigned (Meyer and Sherman 1995:209). In 1524 the crown publicly demonstrated its support of intermarriage by officially decreeing such unions to be legally valid (*Recopilación de leyes de los reynos de las Indias* 1774: Book 6, Title 1, Law 8). Moreover, the crown increased its pressures on Spanish men to marry Indian women by penalizing those who had concubines and refused to wed. A soldier who had a concubine was required to marry within three years of receiving his *encomienda* or risk losing the property (ibid.). To support the legal penalty placed on the soldiers, the church ardently professed that concubinage was a sin and temporarily refused to baptize *mestizo* children born out of wedlock (Seed 1988). These pressures were necessary if the colony was to be stabilized and the children of these unions were to be raised to identify with Spain. By having the father live with his family, Spanish culture and the Catholic faith could be transmitted to his children and to his wife's kinfolk.

Fray Bernal Diaz del Castillo offered a glimpse of the widespread practice of concubinage in his account of the conquest of Mexico. Concubinage potentially posed a danger to the stability of the colony because Indian *caciques* did not welcome this behavior. Diaz del Castillo informs us that after Tenochtitlan fell

Indian *caciques* visited Hernán Cortés and complained that his soldiers had forcibly taken many Indian women:

> *Guatemoc* and his captains complained to Cortés that many of our men had carried off the daughters and wives of chieftains, and begged him as a favor that they should be sent back. Cortés answered that it would be difficult to take them from their present masters. ... So he gave the Mexicans permission to search in all three camps, and issued an order that any soldier who had an Indian woman should surrender her at once if she of her own free will wished to return home. (Díaz del Castillo 1963:408–409)

Encouraging intermarriage also had an economic function for the church, since under the Laws of Burgos it was responsible for taking care of orphaned children (Haring 1963; Miller 1985). By 1527 the Catholic Church concluded that its efforts were succeeding: many *encomenderos* in central Mexico were marrying their concubines (Liss 1975; Meyer and Sherman 1995). Orphaned children, however, continued to be a problem because most *encomenderos* had more than one concubine and many children were not provided for (Bonifaz de Novello 1975). This forced the church to open orphanages throughout central Mexico.

In southern Mexico, nearly two decades later, the Maya peoples of the Yucatán Peninsula, who had remained independent after the Aztec Empire fell, also surrendered to representatives of the Spanish crown. All regional revolts had been suppressed in the Yucatán Peninsula by 1542, and Spain expanded its empire (Perry and Perry 1988:20). The process of restructuring Maya society replicated the colonial policies of central Mexico. Disloyal Indian chiefs were replaced and loyal Mayan nobles allowed to continue overseeing their communities. Unlike the situation in central Mexico, however, where Spaniards established residences, few *conquistadores* chose to settle permanently in the Yucatán Peninsula. Only in Mérida, Campeche, and Valladolid were *encomiendas* established at this time. The Maya masses were governed via the Maya nobility, the Spanish military, and a few Catholic missionaries. The process of *mestizaje* among the Maya was gradual and occurred much later than it did in central Mexico because few Spaniards lived there.

Throughout the colonial period the Catholic Church continued to encourage Spaniards to marry their Indian concubines. In 1575, however, the royal government reversed its liberal position on intermarriage and began to institute antimiscegenation laws (*Recopilación de leyes de los reynos de las Indias* 1774: Book 2, Title 16, Law 32). The royal crown passed a decree penalizing Spaniards of high social standing who wished to marry Indians. Viceroys, presidents, mayors, and all fiscal officers and their families were prohibited from marrying Indians. If any section of the decree was disobeyed, the crown required immediate dismissal of the official. Within a few years, the government expanded the decree to include all its employees; only military personnel were exempt. This exemption may have been necessary because the crown was in the process of conquering lands in northern Mexico and stabilizing its colony in the Yucatán Peninsula; thus intermarriage was still a useful military strategy.

Interestingly, the enactment of the first marriage prohibition law coincided with the growth of an elite Spanish class that was of noble birth and economically prosperous in comparison to the soldiers and first Spanish immigrants. By 1560 there were 20,211 Spaniards in Mexico, and a large number of them were recent immigrants (Meyer and Sherman 1995:208). Unlike most of the *conquistadores,* who had commoner origins, the new colonists were well educated, and many were from distinguished noble families. A large number of these colonists came at the request of the royal crown, because they were needed to administer the government, while other Spanish elites came to oversee the agricultural estates granted to their families. These two groups became the crown's favorite subjects and were given political, economic, and social advantages not available to other colonists. These special privileges, however, were dependent upon their loyalty, including obeying the marriage prohibitions. The passage of the marriage prohibition laws also coincided with another event in Mexico City. All political movements to overthrow the Spanish had been repressed by the allies of the Spanish crown, and the rebels from Tenochtitlán, Texcoco, and Tacuba had finally been placated (Gibson 1964). These regions had previously constituted the political center of the Aztec Triple Alliance and had been zones of periodic political outbreaks.

In 1592 the crown added a harsher amendment requiring government employees to marry spouses born in Europe (*Recopilación de leyes de los reynos de las Indias* 1774: Book 7, Title 3, Law 5). Once again, breaking the decree meant immediate dismissal. By this time, the crown was not solely interested in creating a White elite class; it had become necessary to form a loyal class with limited social commitment to the inhabitants of Mexico. For this purpose, the crown needed to extend privileges to those Whites who were born in Spain (Miller 1985). Ironically, while the royal government was forming an elite ruling class and passing laws to ensure their racial purity, it had to continue encouraging low-ranking soldiers to marry Indian women in order to entrench Spanish culture via intermarriage. In 1627, with the approval of the Catholic Church, the crown facilitated the marriage of its lower-ranking military personnel by allowing married men with wives in Spain who did not have any children to annul their marriages and remarry in Mexico (*Recopilación de leyes de los reynos de las Indias* 1774: Book 3, Title 10 Law 2,8). By 1646 sexual relations between Spaniards and Indians had produced a *mestizo* population estimated at 109,042 (Aguirre Beltrán 1946:221), and approximately half of the children were born in legitimate marriages (Coupe 1994:68; Seed 1988:25).

In retrospect, the marriage laws passed in Mexico signify the initial formation of a racial order where race and nativity became the basis of ascribing and denying social and economic privileges. The crown had begun to use the legal system to entrench a hierarchical racial order and place Whites as the gatekeepers.

Factionalism among the Indian Nobility and the Epidemics of Central Mexico

By 1570 the political restructuring implemented by the administrators of the Spanish government in central Mexico had fueled political and territorial disputes between many *tlatoques* and *caciques* (Vigil 1984). To reward the most faithful *tlatoques* Spanish administrators expanded their political regional control and likewise reduced the regions overseen by disfavored *tlatoques*. This caused factionalism among the Indian nobility and spurred a sense of distrust among the masses. When a *tlatoani* was demoted, the local people did not recognize his replacement as their legitimate governor. Factionalism among the nobility was further exacerbated when the judicial function was stripped from the *tlatoques* and assigned to other administrators. To decentralize the power of the *tlatoques,* the role of *juez gobernador* (judge) was assigned to influential *caciques* (Gibson 1964:166–167). Though *tlatoques* were not dispossessed of their lands, this led to their political downfall and to the political ascent of many *caciques*. *Caciques* now had the power to adjudicate civil and property manners, a very important political function that for centuries had been solely the domain of the *tlatoques* (Aguirre Beltrán 1991).

Throughout central Mexico the *tlatoques'* political influence further eroded during the disastrous epidemics of 1576 to 1581 (Gibson 1964:6, 138). Due to these widespread epidemic outbreaks, the Indian population of central Mexico radically declined. By 1581 the Valley of Mexico's population had been reduced to approximately 70,000 (Gibson 1964:6, 138);[7] as the epidemics spread, central Mexico's population was reduced to 1,075,000 by 1605 (Meyer and Sherman 1995:2, 12). During this time the epidemics did not affect the Yucatán Peninsula; yet within four decades disastrous diseases also broke out there, generating similar devastations. As villages were depopulated in central Mexico, those who survived moved. Many villages were abandoned as

Indians recongregated and new communities were formed. As a result of these changing settlement patterns, the new communities refused to pay tribute to the regional *tlatoques* because they did not consider them to be their legitimate governors. In contrast, the *jueces gobernadores* became more powerful politically; only in places where a *tlatoani* held both titles did his power remain intact.

To respond to the depopulation crisis the crown instituted a reorganization of Indian tribute and land. The *tlatoques, encomenderos,* and *caciques* lost the right to obtain tribute from the Indians (Gibson 1964; Liss 1975). Only the crown and church retained that right. Part of the land that had been depopulated was reserved for the Indians under the *corregimiento* system. Sadly, a large part of the abandoned land was retained by the crown or given to influential Spaniards. In this way, many Indians in Mexico lost the land they had inhabited for centuries.[8]

Under the *corregimiento* system, the crown retained legal title to the Indian lands, yet it recognized their occupational use rights (e.g., farming, pasture) and ability to transfer land use rights from one generation to the next. Families were not given alienation rights to sell their land, however, unless they obtained permission from the crown or church. The crown also reserved communal land for the Indians (Borah 1983). Part of this communal land was to be used to erect civic buildings, the rest for communal agriculture or pasture.[9] Although it was a liberal practice to reserve a large part of the depopulated land for the Indians, the crown nonetheless sold or granted most of the acreage to Spaniards (Gibson 1964). Many wealthy *caciques* also took advantage of the crisis and purchased large tracts of land.

Once the land was reallocated, the new landowners needed workers to farm their estates. In response to this demand, the royal administrators allowed influential Spaniards to tap into the *repartimiento* system, which was a rationed and rotational labor system instituted to construct buildings for the church and crown (Gibson 1964). Since 1555 Indian communities had been required to organize crews able to work on any project commanded by the crown (Gibson 1964:224–235). Because Indian labor became scarce after the epidemics, the *repartimiento* system was increasingly exploited, as Indian labor was virtually monopolized for private use. Because Indian labor was insufficient to fulfill labor demands, many landowners also turned to slave labor (Aguirre Beltrán 1944, 1946; Pi-Sunyer 1957). Mexico's slave traffic grew dramatically, and the large-scale importation of Black slaves began. Nearly half of the slaves who entered Mexico during its entire history came between 1599 and 1637, totaling approximately 88,383 (Aguirre Beltrán 1946:220).

During this labor crisis, the church did not stand by idly as Indian labor was increasingly used for private purposes. When New World missionaries complained to the royal crown of the abuses, agents were sent to investigate matters. On 1 January 1633, after reviewing the evidence presented by the church, the crown concurred that the *repartimiento* system was corrupt and ordered its termination (Gibson 1964:235). This forced landowners to hire workers, and many supplemented their labor needs with slaves. Spaniards who had entirely relied on the *repartimiento* system went into bankruptcy shortly after its termination. They were unable to bear the costs of switching to a different type of agricultural production. The Spanish landowners, *caciques,* and *tlatoques* who had previously hired wage workers or purchased slaves were able to make the transition, however (Liss 1975). Many of these successful landowners supplemented their labor needs with tenant farming, allowing people to live on their estates and farm a tract of land in return for a percentage of the harvest. Because the amount to be turned over was set by the landowners, the tenant farmers' profits were often minimal, providing only a subsistence income. By the mid-seventeenth century the majority of the Indian population in central Mexico worked for Spaniards or *caciques* (Gibson 1964:255). Only those Indians who owned land or remained in the *corregimientos* were not under the control of the landed elite.

Malinké Slaves

The importation of Black slaves to Mexico from Africa began in 1527 (Aguirre Beltrán 1946:8). It started as a trickle, became a torrent during the epidemics in central Mexico, and dwindled by the mid-1600s (Aguirre Beltrán 1944:42, 6, 1946:10). After the turn of the seventeenth century only a few thousand slaves entered Mexico. The last large shipments of slaves arrived between 1715 and 1738 (Palmer 1981:104). During that time, 3,816 Bantu slaves were sold in Veracruz and were then transferred throughout Guatemala and Mexico. Scholars estimate that 150,000 to 200,000 Black slaves were imported to Mexico during its entire history (Aguirre Beltrán 1944:431; cf. Meyer and Sherman 1995:215). Most slaves shipped to Mexico came from West Africa, and the vast majority of them were registered as Malinké (see Chapter 1). Dispersed among the Malinkés were other West African peoples, including Soninkés, Sosos, and Wolofs. Though slaves were sold throughout Mexico, they were shipped to four main areas: Mexico City, Tlaxcala-Puebla, Michoacán, and Zacatecas (Aguirre Beltrán 1946:209; Love 1971:79, 80; Roncal 1944:534). Mexico City received more than 50 percent of the slaves imported throughout the country's history (Aguirre Beltrán 1946:209, 212, 220, 221,224). Slaves were used for varied tasks, including farm labor, mining, and household domestic work.

By the mid-1600s Mexican residents had nearly ceased importing slaves, largely due to the political activism of the Catholic Church. Since 1573 New World missionaries had condemned the slave trade and urged the crown to prohibit the sale of slaves in the New World (Palacios 1988:9). The crown and the royal administrators in Mexico initially refused to comply. After Mexico recovered from the epidemics and Indian labor was once again plentiful, however, the administrators in Mexico began to pay attention to the church's views on the immorality of the slave trade. Many royal administrators discouraged people from purchasing slaves and enforced the labor codes prohibiting the physical abuse of slaves. Feeling the pressure from the Catholic Church, the crown reluctantly followed suit and discouraged Spanish entrepreneurs from investing in slave trade expeditions. It did not, however, issue a proclamation discouraging people from purchasing slaves—quite the contrary. The crown was not prepared to end the slave trade and instead circumvented its agreement with the church by contracting with Portuguese and British businesses to export slaves to Mexico. In this way Spaniards were not directly involved in capturing slaves. The crown was not about to end the slave trade in Mexico, because the profits from the sale of licenses to slave traders as well as the tax revenues collected from ships docking in the Americas went directly to the royal family.

Though the Catholic Church clearly was influential in decreasing the importation of slaves to Mexico, it was prompted by political self-interest. If the slave trade did not end, the church would alienate a large number of its wealthy patrons (Aguirre Beltrán 1946; Palacios 1988; Palmer 1981). During the depopulation crisis in central Mexico, the importation of a massive number of slaves altered the traditional Indian-Spanish racial composition of the country. Mexico's national census in 1646 indicates that there were 130,000 people of Black descent and only 114,000 to 125,000 Spaniards, most of whom were *criollos* born in Mexico (Meyer and Sherman 1995:208).[10] Though both racial populations were relatively small in comparison to the 1,269,607 Indians in 1646, Blacks as a group were sizable enough to influence the racial composition of Mexico (Aguirre Beltrán 1946:221).[11] Continuation of the slave trade would place the church in a politically precarious position because it had obtained the reluctant support of the crown and of many influential Spaniards to free the children of slaves and allow them to marry whomever they wanted. If more slaves were imported, their children could one day convert Mexico into a nation of *mulattos* (half Black and half Spanish) or *lobos* (half Black and half Indian).

Why the Children of Black Male Slaves Were Born Free

When Mexico was first colonized, the Catholic Church supported the royal crown's position on slavery (Blackburn 1998). Enslaving people imported from Africa was considered a necessity if the colonies in the New World were to prosper. It was a popular belief that a Black person could equal the labor output of four Indians (Aguirre Beltrán 1946; Palacios 1988). Spaniards, however, acknowledged they were enslaving human beings and chose to accord them some legal rights (see Cortes 1964). For example, people who were one-sixteenth Black were legally classified as Spaniards (Aguirre Beltrán 1946:174; Love 1971:79–80). Furthermore, under the *Siete Partidas* law code slaves were granted the right to select their spouse and slave masters were prohibited from intervening (Aguirre Beltrán 1946:261–262; Love 1976:135). This legislation was of monumental importance because it became the gateway for the children of slaves to gain their freedom. Due to the lobbying efforts of the Catholic Church the children of Black male slaves and Indian women were declared free and given the right to live with their mother. Unfortunately, the children of Black women were not given a similar privilege and were not emancipated.

Throughout Mexico's colonial history, slave owners attempted to convince the royal crown to annul the slave marriage code, arguing that their investments were lost within one generation, as most male slaves married Indian women. Indeed that was the case: marriage registries between 1646 and 1746 in Mexico City and Veracruz indicate that 52 percent of the Black population married Indians (Love 1971:85). The slave masters' zeal to enslave the children of Black males heightened during the depopulation crisis of central Mexico. In 1585 masters launched a lobbying campaign to change the law and convert such children into chattel (Aguirre Beltrán 1946:257).The church protested and overwhelmingly triumphed in its counter-lobbying efforts. The crown failed to annul the slave marriage code and instead issued a warning to slave masters. If a priest could demonstrate that a master had tried to prevent his slave from selecting a marriage partner, that master would be penalized financially. Slave masters were also prohibited from separating married couples (Aguirre Beltrán 1946; Love 1971).

For the church it was important to protect the rights of Black slaves, because this also affected the Indians and *mestizos*. Throughout Mexico Black slaves, Indians, and *mestizos* met while working as household domestics, and many subsequently married. In particular, this was the case in Mexico City, where a major part of the slave population worked as servants and produced a large *afromestizo* population (Coupe 1994; Roncal 1944; Seed 1982, 1988). By 1742 the national census indicates that there was a population of 266,196 free *afromestizos,* a general term used to indicate a racially mixed person of partially Black descent (Aguirre Beltrán 1946:225).

The Racial Order and the Move North

Spain instituted a racial order called the *casta* system through which Mexico's population came to be legally distinguished based on race. This system was used to deny and prescribe legal rights to individuals and to assign them social prestige. In particular, distinguishing the population on the basis of parental origin became an adequate legal method of according economic privilege and social prestige to Spaniards (Lafaye 1974; Mörner 1967; Vigil 1984).[12] The Spaniards included both *peninsulares,* individuals of full European descent who had been born in Spain, and *criollos,* who were also of full European descent but had been born in the New World. As miscegenation increased among the Spanish elite, the *criollo* category eventually came to be redefined. The *castas* were *mestizos* and other persons of mixed blood. The Indian category included only people of full indigenous descent.

Of the various racial groups, the Spaniards enjoyed the highest social prestige and were accorded the most extensive legal and economic privileges. The legal system did not make distinctions between *peninsulares* and *criollos*. Nevertheless, the Spanish crown instituted policies requiring that high-level positions in the government and Catholic Church be assigned to *peninsulares,* with the rationale that only *peninsulares* were fervently loyal (Haring 1963). If the crown could not find *peninsulares* willing to accept appointments in the colonies established along the frontier, it made exceptions to the decree for those areas and appointed *criollos,* although they had to be the sons of *peninsulares*. As a rule, *peninsulares* were appointed to positions such as viceroy, governor, captain-general, archbishop, and bishop, whereas *criollos* were appointed to less prestigious positions, such as comptroller of the royal exchequer, judge, university professor, and mid-level administrative positions in the church (e.g., priests or directors of schools) (Haring 1963). Furthermore, only *peninsulares* could obtain commercial licenses for direct trade between Spain and Mexico. *Criollos* were limited to the domestic commercial market.

The social and economic mobility of the rest of the population was seriously limited by the legal statuses ascribed to their ancestral groups. In theory, many Indians were economically more privileged than *mestizos* because they held title to large parcels of communal land protected by the crown and the Catholic Church (Haring 1963; Mörner 1967). Despite their claim to property, however, the Indians were accorded little social prestige in Mexican society and were legally confined to subservient social and economic roles regulated by the Spanish elite. Most Indians were forced to live in a perpetual state of tutelage controlled by the church, state, or Spanish landowners.

Mestizos enjoyed a higher social prestige than the Indians, but were considered inferior to the Spaniards. They were also often ostracized by the Indians and Spaniards and did not enjoy certain legal privileges accorded to either group. For example, most *mestizos* were barred by royal decree from obtaining high and mid-level positions in the royal and ecclesiastical governments (Haring 1963; Mörner 1967). Throughout the colonial period they were prohibited from becoming priests, except in the frontier zones, where Indians and *mestizos* would be their parishioners (Haring 1963:2,01). Moreover, the Spanish crown did not reserve land for the *mestizos* under the *corregimiento* system as it did for the Indians. The best economic recourse for most *mestizos* was to enter the labor market or migrate toward Mexico's northern and southern frontiers. Each migrant who was the head of a household was awarded land and exempted from taxation for a period of approximately ten years (León-Portilla 1972; Rubel 1966; Weber 1982). If they chose to move to the frontier, they were prohibited from being members of the town councils or generals of presidios or garrisons; these privileges were reserved solely for Spaniards (Poyo 1991a; *Recopilación de leyes de los reynos de las Indias* 1774: Book 3, Title 10, Law 12).

Free *afromestizos* were accorded the same legal privileges as the *mestizos*. Because they were of partially African descent, however, they were stigmatized and considered socially inferior to Indians and *mestizos* (Love; 1970, 1971; Pi-Sunyer 1957; Seed 1988). For example, *afromestizos* were subjected to racist laws designed to distinguish them from *mestizos* and to impose financial and social penalties upon them. An *afromestiza* who was married to a Spaniard or was of noble birth was forbidden to use the traditional clothing of a Spanish woman or person of high social standing (*Recopilación de leyes de los reynos de las Indias* 1774: Book 7, Title 5, Law 28). She could not wear gold jewelry, a pearl necklace with more than one strand, or silk clothes, and her *mantilla* (veil) could not pass her waist. If she broke any part of this decree, it was lawful to humiliate her in public and confiscate the items.

Furthermore, free *afromestizos* were forced to pay special taxes because they were part Black (McAlister 1957; Pi-Sunyer 1957; *Recopilación de leyes de los reynos de las Indias* 1774: Book 7, Title 4, Law 3; Roncal 1944). To levy taxes local authorities kept registries of the *afromestizos*. When they traveled or lived outside of their communities for extended periods they were required to reregister and pay additional taxes. *Afromestizos* were also legally prohibited from walking on roads at night (*Recopilación de reyes de los reynos de las Indias* 1774: Book 7, Title 5, Law 14) and from carrying weapons, unless they were a *peninsular's* private guard (*Recopilación de leyes de los reynos de las Indias* 1774: Book 7, Title 5, Law 15). Most heinous of all, if free *afromestizos* in Mexico City were unable to pay their bills or became paupers they could be placed in indentured servitude (Coupe 1994).

Although the racially mixed populations increased in number throughout Mexico's colonial era, the governing class in Mexico remained exclusively White, or at least its members professed that they were White (Meyer and Sherman 1995).[13] Notwithstanding this fact, there were economic and prestige differences among the *mestizo* and *afromestizo* populations. Their social positions varied and were highly dependent upon the father's social position and whether a child was born in a legitimate marriage (Seed 1988). Children whose Spaniard fathers were of high social standing but whose mothers were women of color were often fictively referred to as *criollos* and included as part of the White population. A similar exemption, however, was seldom available to the commoner classes. Though by law the *criollo* racial category was reserved for Whites, it was common for parish priests to register *mestizo* children of means as *criollo* by including in the baptismal registry only the race of the father (Meyer and Sherman 1995; Seed 1988). In this way no record was left of the mother's race. This also applied to *afromestizo* children who did not appear to be Black. If children's baptismal records indicated they were *criollo,* they were granted the legal privileges of Spaniards. Furthermore, it was also possible to register a child of means who was born out of wedlock as a *criollo.*

The case of the children of Hernán Cortés illustrates this scenario. Don Martin Cortés and Doña Isabel Moctezuma Cortés were born outside of a sanctioned marriage. Martin was the son of Doña Marina, Hernán Cortés's Indian translator and concubine throughout the conquest of Mexico, while Isabel was the daughter of Isabel Moctezuma and the granddaughter of Emperor Moctezuma Xocoyotzin (Chipman 1977; Meyer and Sherman 1995). Both were treated as *criollos* and were considered noble. Martin was taken as a young boy to Spain's royal court and treated as part of the noble class. After completing his education, he returned to Mexico and was granted an estate and a royal endowment to lead the lifestyle he was accustomed to.

Though not all *mestizos* were as fortunate as Martin, racially mixed women who were fair-complexioned were highly valued as marriage partners. Such fair-skinned women were called *castizas* because they were the daughters of Spaniards and *mestizas* (Chapman 1916; Liss 1975; Weber 1992). By the late 1600s there were sufficient *castizas* for *peninsulares* and *criollos* to marry, and it was no longer necessary for them to marry darker-toned women (Meyer and Sherman 1995:210). Although some *criollos* and *castizas* were incorporated into the social circles of Whites, similar privileges were unavailable to the rest of the non-White population. Most *mestizos, afromestizos,* and Indians continued to experience racial discrimination (Menchaca 1993). Blatant racial disparities became painfully intolerable to the non-White population and generated the conditions for their movement toward the northern frontier, where the racial order was relaxed and people of color had the opportunity to own land and enter most occupations.

Discussion Questions

1. Discuss some rules of classification used by the Spanish in deciding who was of what racial group.
2. Why were the rules of classification important to the Spanish?
3. Do you think the Spanish treatment of the Natives significantly differed from the treatment received by Natives from the English? Why or why not?

The Second Great Migration

A Historical Overview

By James N. Gregory

Editor's Introduction

The formation of Black ghettos in the North is a very poorly understood phenomenon in the sociology of race and ethnicity. In this reading, Gregory discusses the migration of African Americans from the South and rural areas to the urban North and South. This led to Black ghettos in the North and South. Key points raised in the reading are how migration and settlement differed by gender and socioeconomic status. Education also played a key role in the conditions faced by migrants to the cities.

With a four-year-old boy and a ten-week-old girl I boarded a train bound for Oakland. Thus begins Dona Irvin's account of leaving Houston in September 1942. Her husband, Frank, was already in California and had taken a job in one of the shipyards that had recently started to hire African Americans. Full of anticipation, hoping for a better standard of living and freedom from southern Jim Crow restrictions, the young family instead found Oakland very difficult. Housing was a nightmare. Initially, they squeezed into an aunt's already crowded flat in West Oakland, which before the war had been the site of Oakland's small black community. Dona felt lost in the frenzied wartime city, where black people were finding certain kinds of jobs but struggled for living space. She appreciated the new freedoms. She could sit in the same seats on streetcars and shop in the same stores as white people. But Oakland crackled with racial tension. "I seriously considered returning to Houston," Dona recalls. Then things got much worse. Four-year-old

James N. Gregory, "The Second Great Migration: A Historical Overview," *African American Urban History since World War II*; ed. Kenneth L. Kusmer & Joe W. Trotter, pp. 19-38. Copyright © 2009 by University of Chicago Press. Reprinted with permission.

Frank Jr. died during a routine tonsillectomy. The devastated couple had many reasons to think that they had made a mistake in leaving Texas.[1]

Dona and Frank Irvin, their daughter Nell, and their son Frank Jr. were part of the Second Great Migration, a term historians use to distinguish between two eras of massive African American migration out of the South. The exodus began in the early part of the twentieth century, especially during World War I and the 1920s, and that first phase has long been called the Great Migration. The label may have been premature. By some measures, a greater migration was still to come. Beginning during World War II and lasting through the Vietnam era, African Americans left home in unprecedented numbers, and in doing so, they reshaped their own lives and much more. Close to five million people left the South between 1941 and the late 1970s. More millions left farms and villages and moved into the South's big cities. Within one generation, a people who had been mostly rural became mostly urban. A people mostly southern spread to all regions of the United States. A people mostly accustomed to poverty and equipped with farm skills now pushed their way into the core of the American economy. And other changes followed. A people who had lacked access to political rights and political influence now gained both.[2]

This essay explores key dimensions of the Second Great Migration. Less is known about the second than about the first sequence of black migration from the South, and even the basic numbers appearing in encyclopedias and textbooks are often incorrect. New statistical data and new research by historians and sociologists enable us to clear up some of the confusion. Much of what I will report is based on the Integrated Public Use Microdata Series (IPUMS) that have been developed by the Minnesota Population Center in cooperation with the Census Bureau.[3] The pages that follow assess several issues: where people went and in what numbers; who moved and why; their impact on the cities they went to and on the South they left behind. And I also assess their experiences. Did most benefit from relocation?

The Second Great Migration is usually defined as migration from the South to other regions of the country. But the same forty years saw a massive intraregional shift from farms to cities within the South, and I will discuss some aspects of internal southern migration as well as migration away from the South. When I refer to the South or southern-born, I am following the Census Bureau's definition of the District of Columbia and sixteen states (Alabama, Arkansas, Delaware, Florida, Georgia, Kentucky, Louisiana, Maryland, Mississippi, North Carolina, Oklahoma, South Carolina, Tennessee, Texas, Virginia, and West Virginia).

How Many?

Historians and demographers have typically underestimated the number of African Americans who left the South during the four decades associated with the Second Great Migration. Figure 9.1 provides an updated look at the volume of migration during each decade of the twentieth century. It uses IPUMS data and a more sophisticated formula than earlier studies, taking into account estimates of mortality and return migration in calculating how many new migrants left the South each decade. The volumes are low-side estimates. We can be confident that the actual numbers were higher.[4]

Over the course of the twentieth century, approximately eight million African Americans left the South. Figure 9.1 shows the relative size of the Second Great Migration. From 1940 to 1980, roughly five million blacks moved north and west, more than twice the volume of the earlier sequence that is most readily associated with the label "Great Migration." The war years and the rest of the 1940s saw both the start and the peak volumes of the Second Great Migration, as close to 1.5 million southerners left home. Migration rates declined a bit in the 1950s. This chart may underestimate somewhat the volume of the 1960s and overestimate the 1970s by the same margin. A badly worded question in the 1970 census seems to have generated

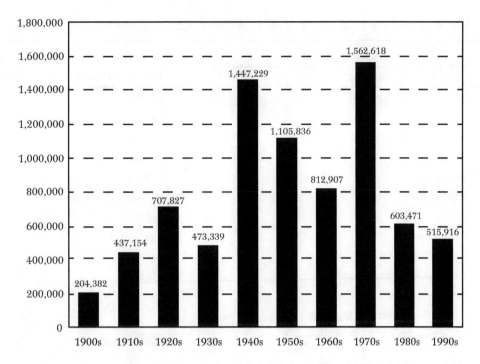

Figure 9.1 Volume of black migration out of the South, by decade. (Data from 1900–2000 IPUMS samples; see note 3.)

some erroneous birthplace information. Most likely, volumes of migration were steadier across the 1950s, 1960s, and 1970s than they appear to be in the census data. On average, 1.2 million black southerners left that region during each of these decades. Those numbers fell off dramatically in the 1980s and 1990s, when a booming Sunbelt and a devastated northern Rust Belt reversed regional patterns of economic opportunity that had prevailed for more than a century.

Destinations

The five million southerners who participated in the Second Great Migration mostly followed pathways that had been established by the generation of southerners who moved north during World War I and the 1920s. The key geographic fact about both migration sequences is that they were tightly focused on big cities. This was a critical part of what made the great migrations "great." The concentration of large numbers of African Americans in cities that were centers of the American economy and centers of political and cultural influence would give black Americans opportunities that would have been lost if migration patterns had been more dispersed.

Table 9.1 shows the major destinations of both waves. In 1930, almost 72 percent of all southern black migrants were living in just ten metropolitan areas: New York, Chicago, Philadelphia, St. Louis, Detroit, Pittsburgh, Cleveland, Indianapolis, Kansas City, and Cincinnati. Only 11 percent of migrants had settled in rural areas and small cities. Another 17 percent were scattered in other metropolitan areas. The Second Great Migration added some new destinations while maintaining the basic pattern. New York and Chicago remained the top two destinations, and Detroit, Philadelphia, St. Louis, and Cleveland continued to attract large numbers of newcomers. Those six cities in 1980 housed more than two million former southerners,

Table 9.1 Ten Most Important Destinations for First Great Migration and Second Great Migration

Rank	Metropolitan area	Southern-born black residents	% of city's black pop.
	1930		
1	New York–Northeastern NJ	260,952	56.8
2	Chicago, IL	198,061	72.7
3	Philadelphia, PA-NJ	152,329	63.1
4	St. Louis, MO-IL	88,459	56.6
5	Detroit, MI	68,101	72.2
6	Pittsburgh, PA	64,083	65.2
7	Cleveland, OH	59,454	74.1
8	Indianapolis, IN	42,125	69.4
9	Kansas City, MO-KS	39,904	50.5
10	Cincinnati-Hamilton, OH-KY-IN	34,264	71.4
	Total, top 10 cities	1,007,732	
	% of all southern-born migrants		71.8
	All southern-born in North and West	1,403,889	
	1980		
1	New York–Northeastern NJ	750,157	28.1
2	Chicago, IL	532,861	34.0
3	Los Angeles–Long Beach, CA	386,290	39.5
4	Detroit, MI	328,161	36.8
5	Philadelphia, PA-NJ	244,311	27.4
6	San Francisco-Oakland-Vallejo, CA	172,344	41.0
7	Cleveland, OH	123,403	35.5
8	St. Louis, MO-IL	119,643	29.3
9	Milwaukee, WI	60,444	39.6
10	Cincinnati-Hamilton, OH-KY-IN	51,601	30.2
	Total, top 10 cities	2,769,215	
	% of all southern-born migrants		67.4
	All southern-born in North and West	4,106,945	

Source: 1930 IPUMS 0.5% sample; 1980 IPUMS 1% Metro sample.

over half the migrant population. Some cities that had been primary destinations ceased to be so in the second wave. Pittsburgh had 64,000 southerners in 1930, but fewer than 40,000 in 1980. Pittsburgh's black population had continued to grow, but mostly not as a result of new migration. Indianapolis and Kansas City also experienced only modest new migration after 1940. But the second wave added new cities to the list of black metropolises. The West Coast had benefited very little from the early migration. With World War II, families like the Irvins turned west, creating, almost overnight, major populations in Los Angeles and the San Francisco Bay Area, as well as significant concentrations in San Diego, Seattle, and Portland. [5]

The westward turn was not the only geographic change of the Second Great Migration. Migrants now settled in more cities. The earlier migration had been tightly focused on the major cities of the mid-Atlantic and Great Lakes states, the nation's traditional industrial belt. The new phase deepened the impact on those cities while adding others. By 1980, there were eighteen metropolitan areas outside the South claiming a black population of more than 100,000, and another eleven above 50,000.

These patterns set up the history-making potential of the two great migrations. Had black people dispersed as widely as white interstate migrants generally do (including white southerners), their impact would have been much more modest. The concentration in cities in numbers large enough to make a substantial impact on their social and political institutions was key to the transformations that would be set in motion by the great relocation. [6]

Reorganizing the South

The Second Great Migration decisively transformed the South. The earlier exodus had begun the shift from farms to cities. The second phase completed the process, all but eliminating black farm life in the South—indeed, in America. The southern agricultural economy had been losing acreage and shedding people since the mid-1920s, as marginal lands were taken out of production and farming techniques were modernized and mechanized. This process had accelerated when prices in the cotton belt collapsed during the 1930s, but the major changes belonged to the era of the Second Great Migration. As late as 1940, the South's rural population was still growing, and that year 6,288,501 African Americans made their homes in the South's rural areas, most of them living and working on farms, typically as sharecroppers. These rural dwellers accounted for 63 percent of the South's black population in 1940.[7] Forty years later, the black rural South existed in a much-reduced and very different form. The farm population was gone. Whereas 45 percent of blacks in the South had lived on farms in 1940, only 1 percent did so in 1980. Those who remained in areas classified as rural usually had little to do with agriculture. These declining numbers, dramatic as they are, understate the change. Villages and towns disappeared. Indeed, a whole subregion—the great cotton belt, also known as the "Black Belt"—changed composition. Whites also left, but not at the same rate. The rural South became whiter as a result of the Second Great Migration. By 1980, 85 percent of rural residents were white, as were 94 percent of all those living on farms. The "Black Belt" had pretty much disappeared. [8]

Mississippi, Alabama, and Arkansas had included the most productive section of the cotton kingdom and the demographic heart of black America. Each of these states experienced a dramatic diaspora, sending much of its African American population elsewhere. In 1970, 52 percent of all black adults who had been born in Alabama lived outside that state; 62 percent of adult black Mississippians and 63 percent of black Arkansans had left home. Figure 9.2 reveals more about the state-by-state nature of the diaspora. Blacks born in border states such as Maryland and Delaware rarely moved away. That was true also of Florida and Texas; fewer than 30 percent of their natives had left. Louisiana had lost 38 percent of its natives, but in other states at least 40 percent of adults had moved away by 1970, with West Virginians topping the list at 70 percent.

Figure 9.2 also shows the preference for nonsouthern destinations. In almost every case, far more migrants settled in northern or western states than in southern states. This defies a long-standing assumption in migration theory. The rule of thumb is that people are more likely to move short distances than long distances and to choose the familiar over the unfamiliar. But not during the Second Great Migration. Even as southern cities grew dramatically, northern and western cities were much more attractive. Some black Mississippians, for example, moved to neighboring Tennessee, especially Memphis, and to New Orleans; but most left the South. In 1970, there were more Mississippians living in Illinois (155,259) than in all of the states of the South beyond their birth state (127,963). Some Alabamans moved east to Georgia and Florida, but they headed north in much greater numbers, to the Great Lakes states or to New York or California. [9]

So who was moving to southern cities?[10] As people left the farms and villages, they seemed to have made a choice: either go to a very nearby city or leave the South. Rarely did they choose a more distant southern city. The growth patterns of the southern metropolises reveal this tendency. Black populations of major

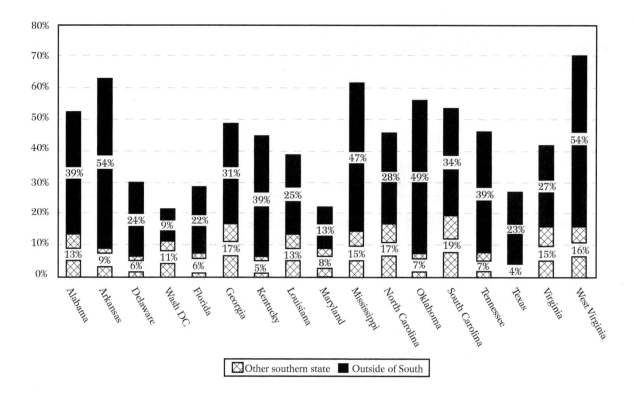

Figure 9.2 Percentage of black adults born in a southern state who were living in either a different southern state or outside the South in 1970. (Data from 1970 IPUMS 1% Form 1 State sample; see note 3.)

southern cities expanded dramatically in the decades between 1940 and 1980, with growth rates comparable to those of the northern black metropolises. But the composition of these cities was very different. Table 9.2 shows the birthplaces of African American adults living in six key cities as of 1970, dividing those birthplaces into "same state" as the city, "contiguous states," and "distant states." Atlanta shows the pattern common throughout the South. Seventy-nine percent of its black adult residents had Georgia birthplaces; another

Table 9.2 Birthplaces of Black Adults Living in Key Southern and Northern Cities, 1970

	Southern Cities		
	Atlanta	Houston	New Orleans
Same State	79%	69%	80%
Contiguous States	9%	19%	11%
Distant States and Abroad	13%	13%	9%

	Northern Cities		
	Chicago	Detroit	New York–NJ
Same State	33%	29%	35%
Contiguous States	3%	2%	1%
Distant States and Abroad	64%	69%	63%

Source: 1970 IPUMS 1% Form 2 Metro sample.

9 percent were from neighboring South Carolina, North Carolina, Alabama, Tennessee, or Florida. A mere 13 percent were from more distant states. Compare that to Chicago, where in 1970 only 33 percent of adults claimed Illinois birthplaces and 64 percent came from distant states, mostly in the South. These patterns had all sorts of implications. More homogeneous than the northern black metropolises, southern urban communities experienced less of the population circulation that promoted black cosmopolitanism elsewhere. They also, of course, dealt with different political systems and regimes of racial hierarchy.

Rural southerners made a choice between the nearby and the North, and they often did so in a particular sequence. It was common for farm people to first try out a southern city and then at a later date head north. Historians and demographers have argued over whether the Great Migration consisted mostly of rural people or of people with urban skills. [11] The data are mixed. A spot survey of the Detroit area conducted by the Census Bureau in March 1944 found that close to 30,000 newcomers had arrived from the South since 1940. Only 15 percent of them reported having lived on a farm four years earlier. Had they been a representative sample of black southerners, 45 percent would have said they had lived on a farm. [12] These early war migrants almost certainly were more urban than those who followed. Data from later censuses show that rural people made up a large segment of the migrant population. In 1960, 52 percent of southerners living in the North or West who had moved between states within the past five years had come from nonmetropolitan settings. Among those who left the South between 1965 and 1970, at least 46 percent had lived in nonmetropolitan areas. [13]

But these numbers may hide a more complicated migration story. Many former migrants talk about their relocation history as a series of tests and steps that began with an initial move to a nearby city, perhaps followed by a return home. Experiences of that sort made it easier to contemplate more distant relocations, and urban experiences in the South helped formerly rural people gain access to both skills and contacts that facilitated migration to northern and western places. Ultimately, it is hard to disentangle the rural-urban chain. What is clear is that the vast majority of migrants had grown up on the farms and in the villages of the South and that many had spent time in southern cities before leaving the region.

Who Moved?

There has been a great deal of research in recent years on the demography of the two great migrations, most of it enabled by the IPUMS data. We have a better sense than ever before of the selectivity of the migrants: how they compared in terms of age, sex, education, and family composition to southerners who did not leave. [14]

Dona Irvin was twenty-five years old when she left Houston. In that sense, she was a very typical migrant: cross-country relocation was for young people. Figure 9.3 shows the age distributions of migrants during the two intervals for which we have adequate data. The 20–24 age group led all others, and a large portion of each migration cohort consisted of people between the ages of 15 and 29. That cohort accounted for 45 percent of those who moved between 1955 and 1960, and 54 percent of the 1965–70 movers. Some of the migrants were in their thirties, but willingness to relocate trailed off dramatically with age. Just 18 percent of movers were 40 or older in 1955–60, and only 12 percent in 1965–70. This age distribution doubled the demographic effect of the exodus. It meant that the South was losing—and the other regions were gaining—not just the migrant generation, but also their unborn children and grandchildren.

The Irvins' experience also represented a fairly typical family migration configuration. Frank had gone west first to check things out, following aunts and cousins who had moved to Oakland before the war. Dona and the children joined him soon after. Intact young families of this sort were very common. A spot census conducted in Detroit in April 1944 found that among new migrants over the age of fifteen, 63 percent of

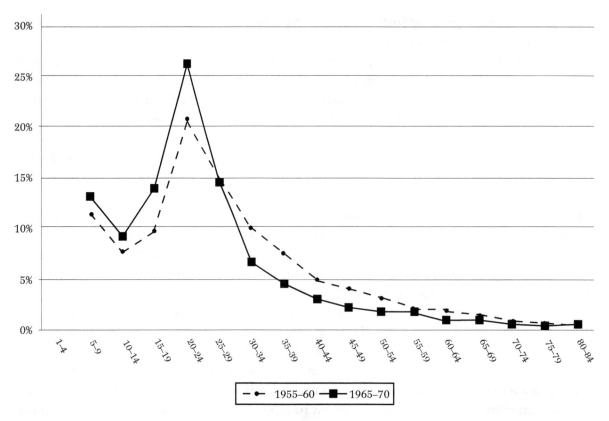

Figure 9.3 Age distributions of new migrants, 1955–60 and 1965–70. (Data from 1960 IPUMS 1% sample and 1970 IPUMS 1% Form 1 State sample; see note 3.)

females and 71 percent of males were married, and more than three-quarters of the married segment had a spouse present. Those percentages came down in later decades, but it is safe to assume that the majority of migrants either traveled as families or reconstituted family life in short order. [15]

Belle Alexander was not married, and in that sense she was not a typical migrant. In 1943, the twenty-three-year-old Georgian signed up for a training program conducted by the National Youth Administration to prepare young people for jobs in defense plants. She had been living in Atlanta for some time, having left her Georgia farm village—like so many other young women—because there were few opportunities. Now she was about to join a second migration. After several months of training in sheet-metal work, she and her classmates learned that jobs awaited them in a place called Seattle, where the Boeing Airplane Company had finally agreed to hire African Americans. "I don't know nothing about Seattle," she told her supervisor, "but I will take it." She recalled, "There must have been fifty or seventy-five of us got on that train, and five days later we ended up at Union Station in Seattle." [16]

Belle Alexander may not have been statistically typical, but she represents one of the surprising dimensions of the Second Great Migration: the important role played by unaccompanied females. Demographers often assume that men are more likely than women to undertake long-distance relocations. In the early phase of the black exodus, during World War I, that was indeed the case. But women outnumbered men during the 1920s and throughout the Second Great Migration. In late March 1944, the Census Bureau conducted spot censuses of Detroit, Los Angeles, the San Francisco Bay Area, San Diego, Seattle-Tacoma, and Portland, all of which had been designated "Congested Production Areas." Except for the last two, females were in the majority in each of these black communities, and the female population had grown at least as fast as the male population since 1940. [17] The trend continued after the war. During 1955–60, there were only 88 migrating men for every 100 women; in 1965–70, 91 men accompanied each 100 women. [18] Females especially outnumbered males in the young adult age range.

The gender distribution had something to do with unequal job opportunities in the rural South. Farmwork privileged young males, especially as agriculture contracted and family-oriented production through tenant farming and sharecropping gave way to employment on consolidated and mechanized farms. Because this was usually seasonal and undependable work, it put pressure on family incomes. Female incomes became increasingly important but also increasingly difficult as women in the rural South competed for scarce positions, mostly in domestic service. Belle Alexander thus had more reason than the young men in her village to head for a city. [19]

On another dimension, neither Belle Alexander nor Dona Irvin was a typical migrant. Both were better educated than the norm. Belle had graduated from high school. Dona had graduated from Prairie View College, an all-black institution in Texas. As college graduates, she and Frank were part of a tiny minority. As of 1950, only 5.7 percent of adult former southerners living in the North or West had any sort of college experience. Only 17.8 percent had graduated from high school. The majority had stopped school at the eighth grade or before. [20]

Even though they were much better educated than most who left the South, the Irvins and Belle Alexander illustrate something important about the Second Great Migration: the exodus represented a brain drain from the black South. In 1970, 38 percent of all southerners who had ever been to college lived outside that region. [21] Moreover, migrants were, on average, better educated than southerners who remained behind. Like many mass migrations, this one shows evidence of self-selection on the basis of education and ambition. The best study was conducted by Stewart Tolnay, who compared the schooling levels of blacks who left the South with those of blacks who remained and found that migrants enjoyed a significant educational advantage that shows up consistently across the decades. He also reported that the migrants were educationally disadvantaged in comparison with African Americans born in the North or the West, and also in comparison with whites. Compounding that, northerners assumed that southern schools were inferior in quality. Even blacks with educational credentials had trouble using them in their new homes. [22]

One other selection criterion looms large in the Second Great Migration: military service. The South has long contributed disproportionately to the armed forces. During World War II, close to one million African Americans served, mostly southerners. And military service took them to other regions and overseas. After discharge, many chose to settle outside the South. That was true also for the servicemen and women who followed in the 1950s and 1960s. Military service proved an important pipeline out of the South. In 1970, 41 percent of southern-born black veterans lived outside their birth region. [23]

Transforming Cities

Apart from the introduction of automobiles, it would be hard to think of anything that more dramatically reshaped America's big cities in the twentieth century than the relocation of the nation's black population. This began with the first era of migration, but the most dramatic changes occurred as a result of the second phase. In 1940, blacks were just beginning to become a political force in New York, Chicago, Philadelphia, and a few other cities. Nowhere outside of the South did they account for more than 13 percent of a city's population. By 1980, African Americans were a majority in several cities and above 40 percent in many others. And they had developed political influence proportional to those numbers. What's more, the growing concentration in major cities had keyed dramatic reorganizations of metropolitan space, accelerating the development of suburbs and shifting tax resources, government functions, private-sector jobs, and a great many white people out of core cities. [24]

A new online tool allows us to quickly map the spatial expansion of black communities in the major cities. SocialExplorer.com provides a mapping system using census-tract data for every decade since 1940. With these maps, we can illustrate the expansion of ghettos in, for example, Chicago, one of the cities dramatically transformed by the Second Great Migration. In 1940, virtually all African Americans in Chicago were crammed into a narrow corridor of census tracts on the city's South Side. In 1960, whites were still fiercely contesting black residential needs, but the ghetto had expanded, covering an area at least three times as large as twenty years earlier. The expansion accelerated in the next two decades. Chicago was still a sharply segregated city in 1980, but African Americans now had much more living space (see map 1.1). [25]

Success and Failure

Much of what has been written about the Second Great Migration emphasizes difficulties and disappointments. Nicholas Lemann's *The Promised Land* is the best-known book on the subject, and it is decidedly pessimistic about the experience of southerners in the North. Lemann focuses on an extended family led by Ruby Haynes, who moved to Chicago in 1946 from Clarksville, Mississippi; he describes lives notched with more failures than successes. He ends the book with Haynes returning to Clarksville in 1979, grateful to be back home after thirty-three complicated years in a northern city that proved to be something less than the "promised land." Lemann's book is valuable in many ways, including his attention to the policy failures that by the 1970s had left northern ghettos with shrinking job access and escalating poverty. But the impression that the Great Migration lived up to few of its promises is misleading. [26]

Belle Alexander and Dona Irvin, like many veterans of the migration, speak in very different terms about their experiences. Belle faced enormous challenges in Seattle. At Boeing she became a "Rosie," she says, but not a "Rosie the Riveter": "I cut the parts" that other women riveted. She liked the work, and within a year she was also happily married. But as the war ended, fortunes shifted. She lost her Boeing job when the company laid off much of the workforce, especially females. Her husband, who had been serving in the Navy, came home with a fatal medical condition. By 1946, Belle was a widow with small children. The Veterans Administration helped her buy a house, and she went back to work at the local VA hospital in food service. She spent most of the next thirty years working in that hospital and today is as proud of that as she is of her now celebrated status as one of Boeing's pioneer "Rosies." She is also proud of her children and their education and careers. As she talks about her life, there is not a hint of the broken-dreams tone that infuses much of the academic writing and journalism about the Second Great Migration. [27]

Dona Irvin has spent years thinking about and writing about the meanings of her life and migration experience. Author of two books—a memoir and a history of the Oakland church that she and fellow migrants from Texas and Arkansas turned into a center of community life and political activism in the 1950s and 1960s—she knows that migration experiences varied dramatically, and she avoids clichéd concepts such as "the promised land" that invite monolithic assessments. Her own story encompasses a full range of experiences, beginning with the unimaginable tragedy of losing her eldest child. And there were other disappointments. For years, her college education counted for almost nothing in the racialized labor market of California. She was even rejected when she applied to a training program to become a physical therapist: "Your training would be useless. No one would hire you, a Negro woman." It was only after years of low-skill jobs, and only after civil rights activism began to open doors, that she "started to climb the ladder of inner and outward progress, milestone by milestone." She became a medical technician, an education specialist, an administrator with the

Map 9.1 1980 Chicago census tract, percent black (non-Hispanic). (Courtesy SocialExplorer.com)

Oakland Public Schools, and finally a writer. There were other triumphs. Her husband, after a time, found a rewarding career as a technician in the Chemistry Department at the University of California, Berkeley. Her daughter, ten weeks old when the family set out for California, grew up to become the eminent historian Nell Painter. "Time has been generous in the magnificence of its gifts to me, from childhood into the ninth decade," Irvin writes at the end of her memoir. [28]

Like most who have contributed memoirs or oral histories, Dona Irvin and Belle Alexander are proud of their experiences. That is predictable: people who feel differently are less likely to volunteer their life stories. So we do not want to rely too heavily on such sources in trying to evaluate the overall pattern of migrant experiences.

But census data suggest that most migrants benefited economically from migration and lend support to the kind of evaluations found in so many oral histories. Table 9.3 compares the average incomes of black southerners living in the North and West in 1950 and again in 1970 with the incomes of those remaining in the South. The table focuses on men and women in the prime earning years (ages 35–49) and separates them by educational level. The benefits of migration are clear in these comparisons. In 1950, men who had left the South reported incomes from the previous year that averaged 68 percent higher than for their counterparts who had remained in the South; for women, incomes were 67 percent higher. [29]

There were important variations based on education. Poorly educated southerners gained more from migration than better-educated southerners; indeed, college-educated women on average earned 11 percent less in the North or West in 1949 than their counterparts in the South. Like Dona Irvin, most discovered that their education held little value in their new homes. The teaching jobs that were a mainstay for educated females in the Jim Crow South were usually not available in the school systems of the other regions. Well-educated men also struggled, both because race discrimination closed off most white-collar positions to African Americans until the late 1960s and because degrees from the historically black colleges of the South were considered inferior. Men with college experience did earn 25 percent more than their southern

Table 9.3 Average Income at Prime Earning Age (35–49) for Southerners Who Left and Those Who Stayed Behind, by Sex and Education, 1949 and 1969

	1949			1969		
	Migrants	Remained in South	% gain/(loss) for migrants	Migrants	Remained in South	% gain/(loss) for migrants
	Males, age 35–49					
0–8th grade	$2,253	$1,318	71	$6,681	$4,111	63
9th–12th grade	$2,604	$1,858	40	$7,376	$5,389	37
Some college	$2,940	$2,351	25	$10,206	$8,238	24
All	$2,375	$1,415	68	$7,548	$5,036	50
N	1,109	2,325		3,584	5,967	
	Females, age 35–49					
0–8th grade	$1,167	$640	82	$3,512	$2,032	73
9th–12th grade	$1,379	$884	56	$4,063	$2,932	39
Some college	$1,737	$1,950	(11)	$6,499	$6,024	8
All	$1,273	$761	67	$4,342	$3,066	42
N	713	1,726		2,563	5,119	

Source: 1950 IPUMS 1% sample; 1970 IPUMS 1% Form 2 State sample.

counterparts in 1949, but compare that to the 71 percent premium earned by a grammar-school-educated male who had left the South or the 82 percent income advantage of poorly educated females.

Migration continued to pay off in substantial income benefits twenty years later, but the differential had been reduced. In 1969, men in the prime earning years improved their incomes by 50 percent, women by 42 percent. And the educational differences continued. Migration remained more financially beneficial for those with less education than for those who had been to college.

These income comparisons need to be put in context. The same data also show that migrants struggled with labor markets that offered only limited opportunities to African Americans. If anyone had headed north expecting to escape severe racial discrimination, they would indeed have been disappointed. The clearest way to demonstrate the powerful effects of race in the labor markets of the North and West is to compare the jobs and incomes of black southern migrants with those of white southern migrants, who shared many of the background factors (mostly rural southern origins, mostly poorly educated) and who were participating in their own great migration out of the South. I have demonstrated this skin-color effect elsewhere and will summarize it here.[30] Table 9.4 shows the wage gap between the two groups of southerners living in the metropolitan areas of the Great Lakes region (Illinois, Indiana, Michigan, Ohio, and Wisconsin). It controls for sex, age, and education. In 1949, black male southerners in their prime earning years earned on average 79 percent of what white southern migrants earned, while black females earned 78 percent of their counterparts' income. These ratios had become worse by 1959, when black male southerners in the Great Lakes region earned only 69 percent of white southern-born incomes; this figure improved slightly, to 73 percent,

Table 9.4 Average Income for Black and White Southerners Living in Metropolitan Areas of the Great Lakes States, by Sex and Education, 1949–69

	Males, age 35–49			Females, age 35–49		
	Black	White	Ratio B/W (%)	Black	White	Ratio B/W (%)
1949						
0–8th grade	$2,481	$3,035	82	$1,109	$1,369	81
9th–12th grade	$2,740	$3,805	72	$1,354	$1,720	79
Some college	$3,271	$5,271	62	$1,850	$2,011	92
All	$2,583	$3,250	79	$1,251	$1,606	78
N	455	423		256	192	
1959						
0–8th grade	$3,845	$5,021	77	$1,711	$2,252	76
9th–12th grade	$4,365	$6,063	72	$1,958	$2,518	78
Some college	$5,178	$9,311	56	$3,134	$3,456	91
All	$4,137	$6,028	69	$1,956	$2,531	77
N	1,742	2,099		1,255	1,145	
1969						
0–8th grade	$6,659	$8,399	79	$2,770	$3,394	82
9th–12th grade	$7,583	$10,401	73	$3,714	$3,931	94
Some college	$10,739	$14,998	72	$6,411	$6,048	106
All	$7,628	$10,478	73	$3,851	$4,106	94
N	1,483	2,519		1,300	1,554	

Source: 1950 IPUMS 1% sample; 1960 IPUMS; 1970 IPUMS 1% Form 2 State sample.

in 1969. Notice again the strange effects of education. The worst ratios were endured by college-educated black men, especially before 1969. College-educated black women earned incomes that were closer to those of white southern women in 1949 and 1959 and actually exceeded their 1969 earnings. The female comparison, however, is a bit misleading. Black southern women logged slightly longer workweeks on average than their white counterparts, and their jobs did not carry the same status as those of the white migrants.

A third framework of comparison is also revealing. Most of the scholarship on the Second Great Migration explores the question of success and failure through a comparison of the accomplishments of southern migrants with those of blacks born in the North and West. For decades, it was assumed that southern migration imposed social and economic costs on northern black communities, that migrants came north with educational and other social disadvantages that would hurt their chances and drag down their new communities. This was the impression developed in fiction as well as scholarship. Richard Wright's *Native Son*, James Baldwin's *Go Tell It on the Mountain*, E. Franklin Frazier's *The Negro Family in Chicago*, and *Black Metropolis* by St. Clair Drake and Horace Cayton—these classics all emphasized the idea that southerners were poorly prepared for life in the big cities and likely to suffer for it.

But recent scholarship has shown just the opposite. Compared to northern-born African Americans, southern migrants did reasonably well during the era of the Second Great Migration, earning slightly higher incomes, maintaining more two-parent families, relying less on welfare services, and contributing less to prison populations than the old settlers. Larry Long, Stewart Tolnay, Kyle Crowder, Stanley Lieberson, and others have conducted the detailed analyses of census and other data that show these modest but meaningful differences. [31] Table 9.5 displays some of what can be found in 1970 census data for residents of the metropolitan areas of the Great Lakes states. Here we broaden the age range to the main working years: ages 25–54. Southern-born men were more likely to be employed than men born in the North or West (85.7 percent versus 80.6 percent). Southern-born women had slightly lower rates of welfare use (12.7 percent versus 13.2 percent). Southern-born black men enjoyed significant income advantages, earning on average between 6 and 12 percent more than their counterparts, depending upon educational level. Among women, the income patterns were less consistent. Northern-born black women with high school or college experience earned somewhat more than southerners. At lower educational levels, southerners averaged 10 percent more than their northern-born counterparts.

There are a number of theories about why black southerners enjoyed this advantage: selective migration by more ambitious individuals; selection that favored stable and helpful family systems; selective return migration by those who had trouble in their new homes; hard work and ambition as a self-fulfilling mythology among the migrant generation; and the possibility that northern young people grew up with less

Table 9.5

	Males, age 25–54			Females, age 25–54	
	Southern-born	Other U.S.-born		Southern-born	Other U.S.-born
% employed	85.7	80.6		51.4	52
% receiving welfare	3.2	3.6		12.7	13.2
Average income, 1969					
0–8th grade	$6,337	$5,672		$2,944	$2,666
9th–12th grade	$7,317	$6,712		$3,582	$3,714
Some college	$9,481	$8,941		$5,971	$5,991
All	$7,273	$6,842		$3,742	$3,938
N	2,908	2,522		2,546	2,421

advantageous value systems in ghettos that after midcentury became zones of distress and discouragement. All of these factors may have been involved. [32]

Five million people participated in the Second Great Migration, and each of their stories was unique. Some suffered the kinds of disappointments that Lemann chronicles. A few knew the sort of triumphs that Dona Irvin celebrates. Most led lives marked by the dignity of smaller accomplishments, lives that took some of their meaning from the sense of having done something important by leaving the South.

They had indeed done something important, and not just in the way they remade their own lives. The Second Great Migration proved to be one of the great engines of change for late-twentieth-century America, resulting in major transformations in where and how African Americans lived and setting up stunning developments in politics and culture. The urbanization of black America, which had begun during the first great migration, reached its apex during the second, as cities in the North, the West, and the South became increasingly African Americanized. The proletarianization of black America followed the same trajectory. Breaking both the spatial and racial barriers that had long kept African Americans trapped in agricultural and service sectors, blacks fought their way into key industries and core jobs. Deindustrialization would soon threaten these gains, but census data from the end of the 1970s show that African Americans held a disproportionate number of industrial and blue-collar jobs. [33]

Urbanization and proletarianization in turn enabled new cultural and political formations. As southerners moved in force into the cities, they provided the expanded consumer power and often the leadership that made the postwar black metropolises centers of innovation in music, literature, journalism, sports, and religion. They also helped supply the energy and ideas that turned the black metropolises into epicenters of political change, fueling first the northern civil rights struggles of the 1940s and 1950s, then the southern civil rights breakthroughs of the 1960s, and then the electoral mobilizations that brought African Americans into urban political leadership in the 1970s and 1980s. [34] The millions who had left their homes to participate in the Second Great Migration indeed had much to be proud of. Without their collective and individual efforts, the late-twentieth-century history of the United States would have been very different.

Discussion Questions

1. How did the Second Great Migration transform cities? Think about three ways this transformation happened.
2. Did migration to the cities in the North differ from migration to Southern cities? Why or why not?
3. What do you think was the impact of the Second Great Migration on the Whites in those cities that received the migrants?

The Reality of Asian American Oppression

By Rosalind S. Chou and Joe R. Feagin

Editor's Introduction

In this reading, Chou and Feagin discuss the disadvantage of racial and ethnic inequality suffered by Asian Americans. The authors critique the viewpoint that Asian Americans, as "model minorities," do not suffer from systemic and cultural racism. The reading demonstrates that Asian American populations do indeed suffer the disadvantages of racial and ethnic inequality.

[...]

The Reality of Systemic Racism

Traditional analytical approaches to immigrants and immigration to the United States mostly emphasize various assimilation orientations and processes. Some assimilation analysts have argued that all incoming immigrant groups will eventually be fully integrated into U.S. society, including the more distinctive ethnic and racial groups. Many social science researchers view the adaptation of Asian immigrants and their children to U.S. society since the 1960s through an assimilation lens, one similar to that used for assessing the adaptations of past and present European immigrants. Numerous assimilation analysts have argued that Asian American groups are on their way to full integration into the "core society," by which they mean white middle-class society. For example, Paul Spickard has argued that by the 1980s whites no longer viewed Japanese Americans "as very different from themselves, and that fact is remarkable."[5] To make this case, these analysts usually focus

Rosalind S. Chou and Joe R. Feagin, "The Reality of Asian American Oppression," *The Reality of Asian American Oppression*, pp. 4-20. Copyright © 2014 by Taylor & Francis Group. Reprinted with permission.

on Asian American socioeconomic progress in areas such as educational and income achievements. However, this limited definition of success in adaptation in the United States is mostly white-generated and ignores other important areas of Asian American lives.

Indeed, the fact that Asian immigrants and their children are heavily pressured to conform to a white-imposed culture, racial frame, and racial hierarchy—and suffer from much racial hostility and discrimination—is usually left out of most assessments of Asian immigrants and their children and grandchildren. Here we go beyond the typical assimilation approach and accent a systemic racism perspective. Since at least the seventeenth century, European Americans have created a complex North American society with a foundation of racial oppression, one whose nooks and crannies are generally pervaded with racial discrimination and inequality. Near their beginning, the new European colonies in North America institutionalized white-on-Indian oppression (land theft and genocide) and white-on-black oppression (centuries of slavery), and by the mid-nineteenth century the Mexicans and the Chinese were incorporated as dispossessed landholders or exploited workers into the racial hierarchy and political-economic institutions of a relatively new United States. Our systemic approach views racial oppression as a foundational and persisting underpinning of this society. From the beginning, powerful whites have designed and maintained the country's economic, political, and social institutions to benefit, disproportionately and substantially, their racial group. For centuries, *unjust* impoverishment of Americans of color has been linked to *unjust* enrichment of whites, thereby creating a central racial hierarchy and status continuum in which whites are generally the dominant and privileged group.[6]

Since the earliest period of colonization, moreover, European Americans have buttressed this hierarchical and entrenched system of unjust material enrichment and unjust material impoverishment with legal institutions and a strong white racial *framing* of this society. In the past and in the present, whites have combined within this pervasive white frame a good many racist stereotypes (the cognitive aspect), racist concepts (the deeper cognitive aspect), racist images (the visual aspect), racialized emotions (feelings), racist narratives (e.g., "manifest destiny"), and inclinations to take discriminatory action. This white racial frame is old, enduring, and oriented to assessing and relating to Americans of color in everyday situations. Operating with this racial frame firmly in mind, the dominant white group has used its power to place new non-European groups, such as Asian immigrants and their children, somewhere in the racial hierarchy whites firmly control—that is, on a white-to-black continuum of status and privilege with whites at the highly privileged end, blacks at the unprivileged end, and other racial groups typically placed by whites somewhere in between. This white racist framing of society is now a centuries-old rationalizing of the racism systemic in this society.

Our concept of *systemic* racism thus encompasses a broad range of racialized realities in this society: the all-encompassing white racial frame, extensive discriminatory habits and exploitative actions, and numerous racist institutions. This white-generated and white-maintained system entails much more than racial bigotry, for it has been from the beginning a material, structural, and ideological reality.

The Exploitation and Oppression of Asian Immigrants

In the classroom, our non-Asian students, regardless of their backgrounds, are often shocked to hear about Asian American oppression. These students have never been taught Asian American history, or been privy to significant events that have shaped these communities in the United States. Students often ask us why these things have been "left out" of their regular curriculum. Additionally, they start to make the important societal connections that Asian Americans do have with other groups—with African Americans, Native Americans, Latinos, working-class whites, and the list goes on. We encourage our students to relearn an accurate U.S. history—and to recognize that our common bonds may keep us from making the same mistakes of the past. Knowing our racial past is imperative to help us with our racial future.

While some Asian Americans today trace family histories back to nineteenth-century immigrants, most have a more recent immigration background. Older members of the families of R. W. and Cho are relatively recent immigrants, and thus these families are typical. Changes in U.S. immigration laws since 1965 have allowed a substantial increase in immigration from Asian and Pacific countries, and thus Asian/Pacific Islander Americans have become the fastest growing U.S. racial group. In 1940 they made up less than 1 percent of the population, but by 2012 their numbers had grown to more than 17.5 million, about 5.6 percent of the U.S. population. The largest Asian/Pacific Islander group is Chinese American. In numbers, Filipino Americans are not far behind, and Japanese, Korean, Asian Indian, and Vietnamese Americans constitute other large Asian-origin groups.

Much scholarship on Asians in North America has addressed Asian experiences with racial hostility and discrimination over a long history of immigration. Scholars have examined more than 150 years of Asian immigration and shown, to take one example, that Asian workers have regularly been pitted against white workers. The first major immigrant group was Chinese. Between the 1850s and 1880s, Chinese contract laborers migrated in large numbers to the West Coast to do low-wage work in construction and other economic sectors. The preference that white employers had for Chinese workers fueled tensions in the racial hierarchy, often pitting white workers against Asian workers. After whites' racist agitation and exclusionary legislation stopped most Chinese immigration, Japanese immigrants were recruited by employers to fill the labor demand on white-run farms and construction projects. (By the late nineteenth century the Chinese were viewed by whites as the stereotyped "yellow peril.") The racially motivated termination of Japanese immigration in 1907–1908 spurred white employers to recruit other Asians and Pacific Islanders (such as Filipinos) to fill labor needs on the U.S. mainland and in Hawaii. This employers' strategy of using immigrant workers from Asia and the Pacific Islands to replace white and other native-born workers has continued in some U.S. workplaces to the present.[7]

In the nineteenth and early twentieth centuries, Asian and Pacific Islander immigrants and their children—mostly Chinese, Japanese, and Filipino—suffered extremely blatant and institutionalized racism. They were negatively positioned, and imaged, by whites as "black" or "near black" on the dominant sociocial continuum. Powerful whites imposed a strong racial framing on these subordinated immigrants, with barbed racist stereotypes and images. Reviewing the history, Robert Lee has commented on white constructions of hated "Orientals": "Six images—the pollutant, the coolie, the deviant, the yellow peril, the model minority, and the gook—portray the Oriental as an alien body and a threat to the American national family."[8] For example, from the 1850s onward the first Asian Americans, the Chinese, were stereotyped by white officials and commentators as "alien," "dangerous," "docile," and "dirty." At that time, such negative images were not new to the white racist framing of Americans of color. They had precedents in earlier white views of African Americans and Native Americans.[9]

In 1896, even as he defended some rights for black Americans as the dissenter in the *Plessy v. Ferguson* Supreme Court decision upholding legal segregation, Justice John Marshall Harlan included this racial argument: "There is a race so different from our own that we do not permit those belonging to it to become citizens of the United States. Persons belonging to it are, with few exceptions, absolutely excluded from our country. I allude to the Chinese race."[10] In the first decades of the 1900s, this negative view was applied to other Asian Americans as well. U.S. government agencies have played a central role in defining racial groups. Thus, in the important 1922 *Ozawa* case, the U.S. Supreme Court ruled that Asian immigrants were *not white* and thus could not become citizens. The "not white," "alien race," and related racist notions had been generated by elite whites in earlier centuries to stereotype and name Native Americans and African Americans as an early part of white racist framing for a "civilized" Eurocentric society. These ideas have persisted for four centuries, with at least 160 years now of application to Americans of Asian descent.[11]

Racist Framing and Large-Scale Discrimination

New ways of circulating the racist framing of Americans of color were developed by innovative white entrepreneurs in the early decades of the twentieth century. These included a burgeoning advertising industry making use of many magazines and radio stations, as well as the developing movie industry. White advertisers, cartoonists, and moviemakers commonly portrayed Chinese, Japanese, and other Asian/Pacific Islanders as outsiders or villains, who were often crudely stereotyped as "inscrutable," poor at English, criminal, and dangerous.

For example, between the early 1900s and the 1940s, hostile visual images and stereotypes of "buck-toothed Japs" were prominent in U.S. media, contributing to anti-Japanese and other anti-Asian hostility in the United States. With extensive media support and facilitation, white commentators and political leaders spoke of an alleged alien character and the immorality of Japanese Americans, sometimes using vicious apelike images.[12] These very negative images and other white racist framing of the Japanese and Japanese Americans contributed greatly to the international tensions leading to World War II, especially the recurring conflicts between the growing U.S. empire and the expanding Japanese empire, both in and around the rim of the Pacific Ocean.[13] This racist framing of the Japanese also contributed to extreme discriminatory actions undertaken by the U.S. government: the imprisonment of Japanese Americans in U.S. concentration camps during World War II. The government's rationale for the camps was openly racist. In 1943 West Coast military commander General John DeWitt articulated what most whites then believed when he argued that "a Jap's a Jap. The Japanese race is an enemy race, and while many second- and third-generation Japanese born on U.S. soil, possessed of U.S. citizenship, have become 'Americanized,' the *racial strains* are undiluted."[14] With no evidence, mainstream commentators and leading politicians, all white, asserted there were enemy agents in this "alien" Asian population. Significantly, one main reason for the existence of this "alien" population was the discriminatory U.S. law prohibiting Asian immigrants from becoming citizens.

Negative framing of Asian Americans during that era can be observed in a 1940s *Time* magazine article on "How to Tell Your Friends from the Japs." Here the white author offered a biologized and blatantly racist explanation of supposed differences between the Japanese and the Chinese—a task taken on because China and the United States had become allies against Japan in World War II:

> Virtually all Japanese are short. Japanese are likely to be stockier and broader-hipped than short Chinese. Although both have the typical epicanthic fold on the upper eyelid, Japanese eyes are usually set closer together. The Chinese expression is likely to be more placid, kindly, open; the Japanese more positive, dogmatic, arrogant. Japanese are hesitant, nervous in conversation, laugh loudly at the wrong time. Japanese walk stiffly erect, hard heeled. Chinese, more relaxed, have an easy gait, sometimes shuffle.[15]

The *Time* editors who published this wildly stereotyped statement probably thought they were saying something positive about the Chinese. Yet, this is a clear example of the arrogant power of *group definition* that has long been part of the dominant white group's historical framing of Americans of color.

However, the white view of the Chinese and of Koreans became more negative with the new conflicts that developed after World War II. With the rise of state communism in China in the late 1940s, Cold War stereotyping again positioned the Chinese, and by implication Chinese Americans, as "dangerous Orientals" in many white minds. Moreover, the U.S. intervention in Korea in 1950 was accompanied by emergency congressional legislation that gave the U.S. attorney general the authority to set up new concentration camps for Koreans, Chinese, and other Asians who might be perceived to be a domestic threat. The U.S. intervention in Korea, and later in Vietnam, further perpetuated an intensive racist stereotyping and framing of Asians and Asian Americans in the minds of many white and other non–Asian Americans.[16]

Even in this crude stereotyping we see a certain ambiguity in white views. Over the past century whites have sometimes positioned Asian Americans at the bottom end of the dominant racial hierarchy, while at other times they have positioned at least some Asian groups in a more intermediate status. From the late 1940s to the end of legal segregation in the 1960s, whites were sometimes perplexed as to where to place Asian Americans in the racial hierarchy, as we observe in this account from a Japanese American speaking about experiences during the legal segregation era:

> I stopped at a McDonald's in Mississippi and there were two lines, one for whites and the other for blacks, well, "coloreds." I stood there confused about which line to join. I stood there and decided to go in the colored line because there was nobody in it and I could get my food faster. When I got up to the counter the guy told me "hey you can't use this line, get in that other line." The line for whites was long and I had gone about halfway up when this guy says, "Hey, you can't be in this line, get in the other line." I just stood there and thought, "Ah, what am I!?"[17]

This recollection indicates not only the stereotyping and subordination of Asian Americans but also a white confusion about Asian Americans' being closer to whiteness or blackness in the dominant racial hierarchy. This placement has become ever more problematic for white Americans with the dramatic growth in the Asian American population since the 1960s.

White Racial Framing: Anti-Asian Imagery Today

Today whites and others still apply numerous elements of an old anti-Asian framing to Asian Americans. As we will see throughout this book, many whites hold inconsistent views of Asian Americans. They commonly view Asian Americans as high achievers and "model minorities," but will often discount the meaning of those achievements as being done by exotic "foreigners," "nerds," or social misfits. For example, some research studies show that Asian American students are often viewed positively by whites, but mainly in regard to educational or income achievements. A recent summary of research concludes that most stereotypes of Asian American students "are negative, such as non-Asians' notions that Asians 'don't speak English well,' 'have accents,' and are 'submissive,' 'sneaky,' 'stingy,' 'greedy,' etc."[18] To complicate matters, racial stereotyping is gendered and sexualized. Asian American men feel the brunt of emasculating white stereotypes that place them at the bottom of a U.S. masculinity hierarchy, while many Asian American women are exoticized as sexual objects.[19] Racism is often perpetuated through different systems of oppression in an intersectional way—thus, these differences in white-imposed constructions of Asian American men and women.

Subtle and blatant stereotyping of Asians and Asian Americans still predominates in many areas of U.S. society. Consider just a few recent examples. In November 2013, comedian and talk show host Jimmy Kimmel aired a skit on his late night show in which he led a roundtable discussion with children. The discussion topic in the roundtable was the U.S. debt to China and the punch line was delivered by one of the children suggesting that we "*kill* all the Chinese." The broadcasting of the skit demonstrates how Kimmel, and the writers and producers of the show, consider mass genocide of the Chinese as acceptable comedic content. Moreover, in February 2013, Asian American basketball player Jeremy Lin burst onto the NBA scene with "surprising" athletic prowess for the New York Knicks team. During the months of "Linsanity" where media outlets dedicated extensive coverage to the exceptionalism of Lin's play, he was also met with numerous racial taunts and slurs by fans and other athletes. Two ESPN cable channel writers used a racial slur in their headlines about Lin: a "Chink in the Armor" was used on their journalistic website. Floyd Mayweather insisted Lin was not worthy of this attention and was made a celebrity only because of his Asian heritage, not in spite of it.[20] In fall of 2013, a documentary on Jeremy Lin's journey to the NBA was released, and in an interview in the film he noted that racism has played a part in his entire athletic career.

In spring of 2011, a UCLA student, Alexandra Wallace, created an anti-Asian YouTube video titled "Asians in the Library" that went viral.[21] In it, Wallace complains of "hordes of Asians" at UCLA, of their not having "American" manners, and about their parents for "not teaching their kids to fend for themselves." She also makes a mockery of Asians who speak their native languages and minimizes the Fukushima nuclear tragedy in Japan. The university failed to address the racist rant, although Wallace did apologize and resign from the school for personal reasons.[22] She received some notoriety from the racist incident and was asked to appear on MTV. This is one of very few examples of institutional consequences for whites who engage in anti-Asian racism, and of the apparent acceptance of Wallace as a humorous figure in pop culture.

The Adidas company was challenged by civil rights groups for making shoes that had a negative caricature of a buck-toothed, slant-eyed Asian as a logo. In another case, a large pictorial cartoon concerning fund-raising investigations of Democratic Party leaders appeared on the cover of an issue of the prominent magazine *National Review*. The cover showed caricatures of then president Bill Clinton and his wife, Hillary Clinton, as slant-eyed, buck-toothed Chinese in Mao suits and Chinese hats—images suggesting old stereotyped images of Asian Americans' characteristics. Since the nineteenth century, white cartoonists, political leaders, and media commentators have portrayed Chinese and other Asian Americans in such stereotyped terms, often to express a fear of the "yellow peril." When confronted, the *National Review's* white editor admitted these were negative Asian caricatures but refused to apologize. Such reactions, and the fact that there was little public protest of the cover other than from Asian American groups, suggest that such crude images and other associated stereotypes remain significant in a dominant racial framing of people of Asian descent.[23]

In addition, a U.S. animation company made a cartoon (*Mr. Wong*) and placed at its center an extreme caricature of a Chinese "hunchbacked, yellow-skinned, squinty-eyed character who spoke with a thick accent and starred in an interactive music video titled *Saturday Night Yellow Fever*."[24] Again Asian American and other civil rights groups protested this anti-Asian mocking, but many whites and a few Asian Americans inside and outside the entertainment industry defended such racist cartoons as "only good humor." Similarly, the makers of a puppet movie, *Team America: World Police,* portrayed a Korean political leader speaking gibberish in a mock Asian accent. One Asian American commentator noted the movie was "an hour and a half of racial mockery with an 'if you are offended, you obviously can't take a joke' tacked on at the end."[25] Moreover, in an episode of the popular television series *Desperate Housewives* a main character, played by actor Teri Hatcher, visits a physician for a medical checkup. Shocked that the doctor suggests she may be going through menopause, she replies, "Okay, before we go any further, can I check these diplomas? Just to make sure they aren't, like, from some med school in the Philippines." This racialized stereotyping was protested by many in the Asian and Pacific Islander communities.

Although sometimes played out in supposedly humorous presentations, continuing media-reproduced stereotypes of Asians and Pacific Islanders include old white-framed notions of them as odd, foreign, un-American, relatively unassimilated, or culturally inferior. Noteworthy in these accounts is the connection of more recent anti-Asian stereotyping, mostly by whites, to the old anti-Asian stereotyping of the nineteenth and early twentieth centuries. For the majority of non–Asian Americans, particularly those who control the media, certain negative images of Asians and of Asian Americans (especially Asian immigrants and their children) blend together in a common anti-Asian racial framing. The strong protests of Asian American civil rights and other organizations to all such racialized stereotyping and mocking underscore this important point.

Anti-Asian stereotypes are still frequently encountered in everyday discourse. Asian Americans, including children, often note that they face mocking language and other racially hostile words, such as these: "Ching chong Chinaman sitting on a rail, along came a white man and snipped off his tail"; "Ah so. No tickee, no washee. So sorry, so sollee"; and "Chinkee, Chink, Jap, Nip, zero, Dothead, Flip, Hindoo."[26] A disc jockey at a Toledo, Ohio, radio station called Asian restaurants and made mock Asian commentaries, such as "ching, chong, chung" and "me speakee no English." Similarly, a CBS talk show host mocked an Asian Excellence Awards ceremony by playing a fake excerpt with "Asian men" saying things like "Ching chong, ching chong, ching chong." Comedian Rosie O'Donnell also used a repeated "ching chong" to mock Chinese speech on her ABC talk show. One striking reaction to the O'Donnell comment was hundreds of blogger entries on Internet websites that defended her comments and (erroneously) asserted the comments were *not* racist.[27]

To modern ears such language mocking and other Asian mocking may seem novel, but it is actually an old part of the white racist framing of Asian Americans. White English speakers on the West Coast developed this mocking in the mid- to late nineteenth century as their way of making fun of the English-Chinese speech of Chinese workers, as well as of racializing them. An early 1900s ragtime song goes, "Ching, Chong, Oh Mister Ching Chong, You are the king of Chinatown. Ching Chong, I love your sing-song."[28]

Anthropologist Jane Hill has shown how in the United States such mocking of language links to systemic racism. In particular Hill has studied the extensive mocking of Spanish, such as the making up of fake Spanish words and phrases. Mock Spanish—common on birthday cards, on items in gift shops, and in commentaries from board rooms to the mass media—is mostly created by college-educated Americans, especially white Americans. Similar language mocking has long been directed at African Americans and Asian Americans. "Through this process, such people are endowed with gross sexual appetites, political corruption, laziness, disorders of language, and mental incapacity."[29] Language mocking is not just lighthearted commentary of no social importance, because such mocking usually is linked to racial framing and societal discrimination against the racialized "others." While native speakers of languages such as French or German do not face serious discrimination because of their accents when they speak English, Asian Americans, Latinos, and other Americans of color do often face such discrimination. As one scholar has underscored, "It is crucial to remember that it is not all foreign accents, but only accent linked to skin that isn't white, or which signals a third-world homeland, evokes such negative reactions."[30]

Model Minority Imagery: An Apparent Contradiction?

Today, frequent anti-Asian mocking and caricaturing signal the continuing presence of a strong racist framing of Asians and Americans of Asian descent. Some people, especially whites, may play down the significance of such racist framing and instead argue that a strong positive image of Asian Americans has often been asserted by whites. They note that whites, especially in the mainstream media and in politics, regularly broadcast positive reports on achievements of Asian Americans in schools and workplaces. From this point of view, one should note, an Asian American group has "succeeded" in U.S. society when its attainments on a limited number of quantitative indicators of occupation, education, and income are at least comparable to those of white Americans. A superficial reading of these indicators leads many to view virtually all Asian Americans as successful and thus as not facing significant racial barriers in this society. Such analyses may be correct in regard to a certain type of success measured by particular socioeconomic indicators for Asian American groups as a whole, but not in regard to the socioeconomic problems faced by large segments within these groups or in regard to the various forms of racial discrimination that most Asian Americans still face in their daily lives.

Take Japanese Americans, for example. Recent data indicate that Japanese Americans are more likely to hold managerial or professional jobs than their white counterparts, and their unemployment rate is less than that for whites. Median income for their families is more than for white families nationally, and a smaller percentage falls below the federal poverty line than for whites. However, Japanese American workers mostly live in the West, where there is a relatively high cost of living. We should note too that in California the difference in median incomes between Japanese American families and white families is reversed. Per capita income for Asian American groups is also generally lower than that for whites, who average smaller families. In addition, many Asian immigrants and their children, especially those from Southeast Asia and rural backgrounds, have experienced much poverty and other serious economic difficulties over the past few decades.[31]

Moreover, although Japanese Americans and certain other Asian American groups have achieved significant socioeconomic success, they still face a substantial array of subtle and overt acts of discrimination, as we demonstrate fully in later chapters. Research studies reveal some of this picture. For example, when researchers have examined Japanese and other Asian American workers in comparison with white workers with similar jobs, educational credentials, and years of job experience, the Asian American workers are found to be paid less on average and are less likely to be promoted to managerial positions.[32] In addition, Asian American workers often face exclusion from numerous positions in business, entertainment, political, and civil service areas, regardless of their qualifications and abilities. Japanese and other Asian Americans periodically report a "glass ceiling" in corporations or exclusion from business networks. About 5 percent of the population, Asian Americans are far less than 1 percent of the members of the boards of Fortune 500 firms; one tabulation revealed that just *one* Asian American headed up a Fortune 500 firm not founded by an Asian American. White executives periodically assert that in their firms Asian Americans are best as technical workers and not as executives. Given this stereotyped view, Asian Americans are often hired as engineers, computer experts, and technicians, but no matter what their qualifications are they are rarely considered for top management positions. Moreover, given this discrimination, many younger Asian Americans have pursued scientific and technical educations and rejected the fine arts, humanities, and social sciences, areas they might have preferred. Career choices are thus influenced by both past and present discrimination. In addition, many business opportunities in corporate America remain limited by persisting anti-Asian sentiment.[33]

The "great recession" of 2008–2009 disproportionately affected Asian Americans, further challenging the "model minority" myth. According to the National Coalition for Asian-Pacific American Community Development, Asian Americans have seen a 38 percent increase in their poverty population while the general poverty population grew by 27 percent during the same time period, with the African American poverty population growing by 20 percent.[34] This poverty rate is not just affecting the newer immigrant population, for 60 percent of the net increase in Asian American/Pacific Islander poverty was in the native-born segment of that population.[35] In 2010, compared to whites, blacks, and Latinos, Asian American workers had the highest share of unemployed workers who were unemployed long term (more than half a year). Additionally, when compared to their similarly educated white counterparts, highly educated Asian Americans suffer from disproportionately higher unemployment rates. Asian Americans with bachelor's degrees are more likely to be unemployed than whites. This is especially significant because 57 percent of the Asian American labor force is in this category.[36] Oftentimes, education is seen as the "great equalizer," but we see that Asian Americans obtaining advanced degrees still face economic disadvantages. In spite of much data contradicting their commonplace view, numerous social scientists and media commentators have regularly cited the educational and economic "success" of a particular Asian American group, one typically described as the "model minority," as an indication that whites no longer create significant racial barriers for them.[37] For example, a 2012 research report of the prestigious Pew Research Center cites this socioeconomic success and asks unreflectively, "Are Asian Americans a 'Model Minority'?" The report also compares, again uncritically, the supposedly successful achievements of Asian Americans with the lesser achievements of Hispanic Americans.[38]

This continuing use of a white-named and white-framed perspective on Asian Americans is highly problematical. We can pinpoint when this model myth was likely first constructed. In the mid-1960s, largely in response to African American and Latino (especially Mexican American) protests against discrimination, white scholars, political leaders, and journalists developed the model minority myth in order to allege that all Americans of color could achieve the American dream—and not by protesting discrimination in the stores and streets as African Americans and Mexican Americans were doing, but by working as "hard and quietly" as Japanese and Chinese Americans supposedly did. This model image was created *not* by Asian Americans but by influential whites for their public ideological use.[39] One example is a 1960s *U.S. News & World Report* article entitled "Success Story of One Minority Group in U.S." This major media article praised the hard work and morality of Chinese Americans, and its analysis strongly implied that if black Americans possessed such virtues, it would not be necessary to spend "hundreds of billions to uplift" them.[40]

For decades now, prominent commentators and politicians have cited the educational or economic success of Asian Americans as proof that they are fully melded into the U.S. "melting pot," with many "ascending above exclusion" by "pulling themselves up by their bootstraps."[41] Today, variations of this model stereotype remain pervasive, and leading politicians, judges, journalists, and corporate executives assert them regularly.[42] Even other Americans of color have sometimes been conned by this model minority view and declared it to be so true that governments do not need to be concerned with the discrimination against Asian Americans. For example, black Supreme Court nominee Clarence Thomas, at his Senate confirmation hearings, asserted that Asian Americans have "transcended the ravages caused even by harsh legal and social discrimination" and should not be the beneficiaries of affirmative action because they are "overrepresented in key institutions."[43]

One of the contemporary ironies of such uninformed views is that private and government reports in recent years have shown that today educational success varies among the Asian American groups and, indeed, that many Asian Americans in numerous groups still face significant obstacles to academic success, in some cases more than in the past.[44] For example, one savvy higher education journalist noted that numerous articles in college newspapers have used Asian Americans as a point of humor, but their portrayals usually feed the "model minority" myth. Asian American students are still often seen as an "invasion" and their demeanors as "inscrutable." On these college campuses lies a "continued pattern of Asian American students being (a) the butt of such jokes, basically the punch line; (b) that the jokes are heavily laden with racial stereotypes; and (c) that these ... essays reveal volumes about racial relationships, tensions, and perceptions of Asian American students as all being, in some way, the same—foreigners, math and science nerds, and all around different from the regular average college student."[45]

Assimilation and the "Model Minority" Imagery

Several researchers—mostly Asian American—have challenged the rosy view of Asian American success in the complex assimilation process forced on them in the United States. These researchers have shown that Asian immigrants and their children have long faced discrimination and other serious difficulties in adapting to U.S. society. Some have also explored how the societal conditions of Asian Americans are racialized.[46]

Several social scientists have focused on Asian American adaptation to the dominant culture and society using traditional assimilation theories. For example, drawing on interviews with young Asian American professionals, Pyong Gap Min and Rose Kim report that these young professionals have highly assimilated socially and culturally, and have significant friendship ties to middle-class whites and significant assimilation to white folkways. They found that these Asian American professionals are bicultural, with strong assimilation to "American culture," but express a strong national-origin or pan-Asian identity as well. An earlier study of Korean immigrants by Won Moo Hurh and Kwang Chung Kim reported similar findings, in that their respondents demonstrated what they term "additive" or "adhesive" adaptation—that is, assimilating substantially to the new economy and society, yet maintaining a strong sense of their ethnic and racial identities. While both research studies discuss difficult identity choices of their respondents, like most contemporary researchers looking at immigrant assimilation, they do not examine in depth the harsh racial realities surrounding these choices. In this still-racist society, personal or group identity "choices" by Asian immigrants and their children are severely limited by the racial identity typically *imposed* on them by white outsiders.[47]

In a study of second-generation Chinese and Korean Americans, social scientist Nazli Kibria has also explored the formation of identities. Assessing the adaptation of Asian immigrants and their children, she distinguishes between an "ethnic American" model and a "racial minority" model of assimilation. The old ethnic assimilation model, asserted by scholars and others, has set the framework for Asian assimilation into the core society, yet creates significant problems because it assumes that an ethnic immigrant group is white. In Kibria's view, as Asian immigrants and their children accent a new umbrella identity of "Asian American," they are updating the old ethnic assimilation model to include their racial minority experience. While Kibria recognizes that her respondents are set apart, discriminated against, and stereotyped as foreigners or model minorities, she keeps her analysis of the perpetrators of this stereotyping and discrimination rather vague and provides no in-depth analysis of the systemic racism context in which these Asian Americans are forced to adapt. Her Chinese and Korean respondents report on some "lessons about race," "race socialization," and not being accepted "by others," yet in her analysis Kibria does not assess the central role of white discriminators or the white-imposed framing and hierarchy in forcing such hard lessons.[48]

One of the few analysts of Asian Americans to explicitly name white discriminators as central is sociologist Mia Tuan. Interviewing nearly 100 third- and later-generation Chinese and Japanese Americans, she found that although most were well assimilated into the dominant culture, most also had a strong sense of a racialized identity because whites constantly imposed the identity of "Asian foreigner" on them. They reported being caught between feeling perpetually outside, as "forever foreigners," and sometimes being given greater privileges by whites than other people of color. They spoke too of the difficulty they had in viewing themselves in terms of their national origin when they were constantly being defined in "generically racial terms" as "Asian Americans" or as "Orientals." Though offering a probing analysis that assesses well racial-ethnic identity struggles and recognizes whites as having a privileged status, Tuan also does not, in our view, provide enough in-depth analysis of the anti-Asian racism that surrounds, and imposes oppressive predicaments on, Asian Americans.[49]

Several researchers have specifically targeted the model minority stereotype. One early analysis was that of the innovative legal scholar Mari Matsuda, who suggested that Asian Americans might be positioned as a "racial bourgeoisie," a racial middle status between whites and other people of color. This protects the white position at the top by diffusing hostility toward them and sets up Asian Americans to be a "scapegoat during times of crisis."[50] In a more recent analysis, Vijay Prashad has shown how Asian Americans are termed model minorities and thus come "to be the perpetual solution to what is seen as the crisis of black America." Prashad does not specifically identify and assess the white agents who have created this crisis for black America. He does note a certain "Orientalism" among white Americans—the view that many have of Asia as being "static and unfree" in contrast to a "dynamic and free" Western civilization. Holding to this framing, whites frequently stereotype Asian Americans negatively as alien, exotic, barbaric, or primitive. Prashad adds that for Asian Americans "it is easier to be seen as a solution than as a problem. We don't suffer genocidal poverty and incarceration rates in the United States, nor do we walk in fear and a fog of invisibility."[51] Ironically, he here evokes part of the model minority stereotype yet does not note that this hoary stereotype often creates an invisibility cloak hiding severe problems of racism faced regularly by Asian Americans.

The pioneering legal scholar Frank Wu has done much to dispel model minority stereotyping. In his work he has explained the benefits that whites enjoy because of that labeling. Reviewing the long history of anti-Asian discrimination, he notes that "non–Asian Americans can discriminate against Asian Americans by turning us into noncitizens, either officially by prohibiting even legal long-term residents from naturalizing or informally by casting doubt on our status. The alien land laws, passed to drive Japanese immigrants out of farming, are the prime example." While he accents well the many decades of anti-Asian discrimination, Wu regularly uses vague terms such as "non–Asian Americans" and thereby skirts around using the word "whites" for those doing such intense discriminating. While in many of his analyses Wu recognizes how anti-Asian racism is institutionalized, at times he seems to play down certain aspects of white racism: "Other than among a few idealists, as a nation we accept discrimination on the basis of citizenship as necessary. But except among a few extremists, as a society we reject discrimination on the basis of race as immoral."[52] Wu here seems to neglect the societal reality that *many* whites still do find it acceptable to engage in racial discrimination against Americans of color, yet may find it no longer fashionable to discriminate openly or assert racist views publicly.

Clearly, these often-pioneering Asian American scholars have moved social science analysis of the adaptive barriers faced by Asian Americans in very important directions. Still, some of them tend to avoid explicitly naming and analyzing fully the role of whites (especially elite whites) as central protagonists in creating anti-Asian racism today—often preferring instead to name vague social agents such as "non-Asians," "the law," "the government," or "the larger society" as generators of contemporary racism. Such analytical practices can be found as well among many scholars researching the racialized situations of other Americans of color. They too are often reluctant to name whites *specifically* as the key actors in past or present dramas of U.S. racism.[53]

One of the few researchers to examine in critical detail the contemporary impact of *systemic racism* on Asian American communities is sociologist Claire Jean Kim. Examining periodic conflicts between Korean American merchants and African American patrons in a few cities, Kim shows that these conflicts should be understood in the context of whites' long-term discriminatory actions against both groups. She illustrates how Asian immigrants have come to be positioned, mainly by *white* actions, between white urbanites and black urbanites, and how these Asian Americans are given a negative evaluation by whites on both the axis of superior/inferior racial groups and the axis of insiders/foreigners. Such intergroup conflict involves more than just stereotyping by African Americans or Korean Americans of the other group, but instead reflects the white-imposed racial hierarchy and its effects on both racially subordinated groups. Like other Americans of color, Asian Americans serve as pawns in the racially oppressive system maintained at the top by whites.[54] White Americans may prize Asian Americans relative to African Americans in certain limited ways so as to ensure white dominance over both. Whites may sometimes place or consider Asians "nearer to whites," a relative valorization, because of Asian American achievements in certain educational and economic areas. Yet this middling status is possible only because other Americans of color, such as African Americans or Mexican Americans, have been allowed fewer opportunities by whites. Whites' use of Asian Americans as a measuring stick for other Americans of color is highly divisive, for it pits groups of color against each other, as well as isolates Asian Americans from white Americans.

Kim underscores well the price paid for becoming the white-proclaimed model of a successful minority: "By lumping all Asian descent groups together and attributing certain distinctively 'Asian' cultural values to them (including, importantly, political passivity or docility), the model minority myth sets Asian Americans apart as a distinct racial-cultural 'other.' Asian Americans are making it, the myth tells us, but they remain exotically different from Whites. Beneath the veneer of praise, the model minority myth subtly ostracizes Asian Americans."[55] In this process of exoticizing and of civic ostracism, whites treat Asian Americans as foreigners not fully assimilable to white culture and society. Exoticized and celebrated for docility, Asian Americans have relatively little political clout and as yet are less involved in the U.S. political process. As Kim's data demonstrate, this lack of political involvement at the local level is often *not* a voluntary choice but results from active discrimination and exclusion in the political realm by whites.

Discrimination persists in many institutional areas. The astute scholar Gary Okihiro sums up the contemporary Asian American situation this way: Whites have "upheld Asians as 'near-whites' or 'whiter than whites' in the model minority stereotype, and yet Asians have experienced and continue to face white racism 'like blacks' in educational and occupational barriers and ceilings and in anti-Asian abuse and physical violence. This marginalization of Asians, in fact, within a black and white racial formation, 'disciplines' both Africans and Asians and constitutes the essential site of Asian American oppression."[56]

The Many Costs of Anti-Asian Racism

Conforming to the Hierarchy and Racial Frame

The omnipresent racial hierarchy and its rationalizing racial frame directly or indirectly affect most areas of the lives of those who live in U.S. society. Whites are collectively so powerful that they pressure all immigrant groups, including those of color, to collude in the white racist system by adopting not only many white ways of doing and speaking, but also numerous stereotyped views and notions from the old white racial frame. The white frame is all-encompassing and has infiltrated the minds both of native-born Americans and of European and other immigrants. By adopting the perspective of the dominant racial frame, earlier European immigrant groups, such as the Irish and the Italians, eventually secured a high position on the U.S. racial ladder and are now considered "white," but this has not been the case for darker-skinned groups such as those of African, Latin American, and Asian descent. Asian immigrants often have a chance at some socioeconomic mobility, but they, their children, and their grandchildren have not been awarded full acceptance by whites. Most whites expect the intermediate positions offered to many Asian Americans on the old racial status ladder to be valued by them, but, as later chapters will demonstrate, this middling position has typically come at the high price of conformity, stress, and pain—and often of abandoning much of a person's home culture and national-origin identity.

Generally, new immigrants quickly begin to conform to the dominant hierarchy and frame or else face significant emotional or economic punishment. On the one hand, they often try to conform well, which they generally view as a method to prevent discrimination targeting them. On the other, conforming is pressed hard on them as the targets of white-generated racism. The dominant white racial frame ensures that those at the bottom of the racial order are repeatedly denigrated. In this situation fighting for one's dignity will sometimes mean that another individual or group will be pushed down and set up for failure. Vying for position in a preexisting racial order creates volatility and conflict. Groups of color are frequently pitted against each other for the title of "top subordinate," while whites as a group remain at the top.

The dominant white group and its elite stand in a position of such power that they can rate groups of color socially and assign them "grades" on a type of "minority report card." Whites thus give certain Asian American groups a "model minority" rating while other groups of color receive lower marks as "problem minorities." However, the hierarchical positions that whites are willing to give any group of color are always significantly below them on the racial ladder. Today, some media and scholarly discussions suggest that Asian Americans are now viewed as white or "honorary white" by most white Americans, yet this is not likely the case. In one research study, we gave 151 white college students a questionnaire asking them to place numerous racial and ethnic groups into "white" or "not white" categories. An overwhelming majority classified all the listed Asian American groups, including Japanese and Chinese Americans, as clearly *not white*. These well-educated, mostly younger whites still operate with the old racial hierarchy and racial status continuum in mind when they place individuals and groups of color into racialized categories.[57]

[...]

Discussion Questions

1. Why are Asian Americans thought of as "model minorities?"
2. Is the discrimination suffered by Asians structurally based, individually based, or a combination of the two? How would you explain your answer?
3. How is the idea of panethnicity relevant to this discussion?

Whiteness as Contingent Hierarchies

Who Counts as White and Why

By Steve Garner

Editor's Introduction

In this reading, Garner discusses the evolution of the racial term "White" and how various people came to be considered "White." As discussed in the reading, this is a global phenomenon. Garner uses examples from the United States, Australia, and the United Kingdom. Garner makes the key point that power is always an element in racial naming and categorization. This reading illustrates the principle that race is socially defined by those with the power to name and categorize.

What Is the Point of Using 'Whiteness' as an Analytical Tool?

So far we have observed that whiteness has been conceptualized in a number of complementary ways. In this chapter I will focus on the idea that in addition to a set of borders between people categorized as 'white' and 'non white', there is another set of internal borders produced by racialization. In other words, there are socially observable degrees of whiteness between the groups that seem to be unproblematically white. Examples here include Southern, Central and Eastern European immigrant groups, Jews, Gypsy-Travellers/Roma, as well as the numerous and important divisions based on class, gender, sexuality, region, etc., identified in the literature on both America and Britain (Hartigan 2005, Nayak 2003, Daniels 1997). The reader may well be experiencing trepidation about the extent to which we are encroaching onto other areas of work. We already have concepts like 'anti-semitism', 'sexism' and 'homophobia'. Class divisions are already covered in other literatures. Considering that European migrants are white anyway, how is this to do with 'race'? Isn't it ethnicity, another area abundantly, if not excessively, analyzed already? I do not want to be proscriptive. There are plenty of perspectives that can bring fruitful analyses to bear on these identities and social hierarchies, and using the whiteness problematic is one of them. However, I hope to convince you of its utility through the use of three of the broad areas of study dealt with in the literature: immigration into America in the nineteenth and early twentieth century (the 'inbetween peoples' thesis); the 'White Australia' policy (1901–1972); and the related ideas of 'white trash' in America, and the working class in the UK.

Before we look at those case studies, I want to provide a brief outline of the history of 'white' as a racial identity, in order to put them into perspective. We have to keep in mind that we are dealing with social interpretations of physical and cultural phenomena, and these interpretations can change over time and place, reflecting the political, economic and cultural distinctiveness of the context.

Where Did Whiteness Come From?

Primarily we have looked so far at the intersection of whiteness and its Others, those racialized identities created by white world's military, commercial and ideological domination of the globe since the sixteenth century. That is the story of how Europeans simultaneously created whiteness and otherness as collective identities. Although from the vantage point of the twenty-first century, the terms 'white' and 'black' seem to go without saying, these words have not always been used to identify human beings. Indeed use of the term 'white' to describe people dates back only to the sixteenth century. At that time however it was one of a range of labels, and not the one most frequently used. Religion, nation, and social class were all deployed more than color. The literature on the period from 1500 to the end of the seventeenth century arrives at a rough consensus: the co-existence of religious labels of identity; 'Christian' and 'heathen' in the American colonies (Jordan 1968, Frederickson 1988) rendered color distinctions redundant until slaves began to convert to Christianity. Elsewhere in the New World, V.S. Naipaul (1969) notes that after the slave revolt in Berbice (then in Dutch Guiana, South America) in 1764, the dead were divided up in official reports neither as 'black' and 'white', nor even as 'slave' and 'free', but as 'Christians' and 'heathens'.

Slavery is now irrevocably linked in popular understandings of history to the transatlantic slave trade and its institutions in the Americas, with Africans as its principal population. However, vital to the development of whiteness is the acknowledgement that in the Anglophone colonies, it was the end of the seventeenth century before the status of 'free' and 'unfree' labor corresponded perfectly to European and African workers respectively. This is because in the earlier days of colonization, white indentured laborers (1) were employed before, and then alongside Africans. When these indentured laborers became numerically inferior due to their access to landownership after indentureship, then the numbers of enslaved Africans started to rapidly over take them. So it was around the last decade of the seventeenth century that the only unfree laborers were Africans. There were free Blacks as well as free white laborers, and it is at this point that we see the emergence of colony-level legislation against voting rights for Blacks; 'race' mixing; and the introduction of restrictions on property ownership for Black people. We can thus start the clock of 'whiteness' as an explicit legitimized collective identity in North America and the Anglophone Caribbean from around that point. This was clearly not a historical coincidence. The sixteenth and seventeenth centuries was the period when Europeans were beginning to encounter people from Africa, the Americas and Asia on an ongoing basis, and notice the obvious if cosmetic physical differences between groups alongside the cultural ones.

In the period between then and the mid nineteenth century, the idea that some people's identities were 'white' came to be attached to the new ways of understanding mankind that developed out of the Enlightenment (Eze 1997). These understandings were enshrined in elite scientific discourse as empirically provable racial differences explaining cultural, political and technological inequalities. While earlier eras had noted that physical appearance, climate and culture differed from place to place, there was no sustained intellectual effort to link these in a coherent philosophy of difference. This changed during the Enlightenment. Climate, it was argued, determined physical appearance, and in turn these determined the capacity of different people to evolve, that is, toward the goal of European norms. However, the mainstream discourse fixed the relationship of climate to civilizational capacity: only those living in temperate climates, that is, white Europeans, could properly attain the heights of civilization, and the others trailed behind. Versions of this logic appeared throughout the eighteenth and early nineteenth centuries. By the mid nineteenth century, this was no longer up for discussion, but was itself the basis for further discussion.

Indeed, as racial science and philosophy garnered credence, increasingly complex schemas were produced, in which there were subdivisions of whiteness. Notions of Anglo-Saxon supremacy (within the multi-layered 'white race') began to gain intellectual support, bolstered by an amalgam of the press, a network of scientists engaged in somatic measurements (Horsman 1981) and internationally read work. Robert Knox and Joseph Arthur Comte de Gobineau developed the notion that within the white 'race', Anglo-Saxons were particularly capable of civilization in comparison to Celts, Slavs and Latins (2). This hierarchy within a hierarchy is the basis of the thesis developed by US labor historians David Roediger and James Barrett, whose work we shall look at next.

Case Study 1: 'Inbetween People'?

In a set of influential publications (Roediger 1991, Barrett and Roediger 1997, 2004, 2005), Roediger and Barrett argue that in the period from the 1850s to the 1910s, incoming migrant Europeans were exposed to a situation where the American mainstream racialized values exerted forces that pushed Europeans to claim whiteness for themselves, in order to gain privileged access to resources, and psychological and social capital (Du Bois's 'wages of whiteness')(3). Barrett and Roediger (1997, 2004) maintain two principal and connected points. Firstly, 'Whiteness' is to do with cultural and political power and, secondly, not all those who appear phenotypically white are incorporated equally into the dominant group.

Catholic and Jewish migrants from the various Southern, Eastern and Central European countries, they argue, were not immediately accepted socially and culturally as white. Differential access to this resource was sought by successive waves of migrants learning the rules of the game, or 'this racial thing', as one of Barrett and Roediger's respondents puts it (1997: 6). They label these groups of less dominant Europeans, who were temporarily disadvantaged in the US context by class and culture, 'inbetween people': not white, but not black either.

Scholarship in dialogue with the writers above has debated the extent to which various ethnic groups such as Jewish- (Brodkin 1994, 1998) and Italian-Americans (Guglielmo and Salerno 2003) can be considered 'white'. These arguments posit some parallels between the Irish and the Italians in America, suggesting that over time they 'became' white. However, there is a counter-argument developed by some historians such as Eric Arnesen (2001) and Tom Guglielmo (2003) that European immigrants did not actually have to 'become' white, relative to Blacks and Mexicans, for example, and that the 'inbetween people' theory does not withstand scrutiny. I think the keys to unravelling this knot are reasonably straightforward. They are to do with understanding the priorities and assumptions of the protagonists. The first thing to realize is that the 'inbetween people' thesis does not claim that Irish, Italian and other European immigrants were really 'black', but that they were literally 'denigrated', that is, likened to black Americans (in terms of civilization and social status), and they temporarily occupied the lowest positions on the economic and social ladder of free labor. This social, occupational and often geographical proximity to Free Blacks gave rise to the imperative for these migrant groups to distance themselves from them. The further they moved from blackness, the closer they got to whiteness. This strategy was executed in some cases through the urban equivalent of ethnic cleansing (Bernstein, 1990; Ignatiev, 1996).

So the point is not to suggest that certain groups of immigrants were not phenotypically white, which is why Tom Guglielmo (2003) correctly identifies 'race' and color as often separate but overlapping criteria in late nineteenth- and early twentieth-century American institutional definitions, but that ideologically and culturally they were indeed considered different and lesser 'white races'. The corollaries of this categorization were not a set of life chances equivalent to those of Blacks, Native Americans or Hispanics, rather the obligation to define themselves as 'white' in a society where that mattered a great deal, whereas in their countries of origin, it had mattered scarcely at all. European immigrants thus 'became' white on arrival in the New World, runs the argument, because they disembarked into a new set of social identities that articulated with those they had brought with them, and one overarching identity was whiteness.

I think this conclusion needs qualification. Not being white, and being black, are two very different things: the Catholic Irish were always salvageable for whiteness in a way that African, Mexican, Asian and Native Americans were not (Garner 2003). This is because legally they were definitely white, in as far as they could become naturalized citizens, and were not treated as imports (Haney-Lopez 1996, Jacobson 1998). The second problem is an interesting one that illustrates a divergence of interpretations of identical material. The protagonists in this debate prioritize different arenas as the source of their claims. On one side, Barrett and Roediger see the cultural domain as the one in which perceptions of 'inbetweenness' are made explicit, while Arnesen and Guglielmo pragmatically see the legal domain as predominant. Whatever people said or did, argue the latter, in law all white people were white. However, this reasoning is open to the criticism that in sociological terms, the law can just as easily be deconstructed as can popular culture: it is not a superior level of discourse. The legal domain, argues Cheryl Harris (1993), was utilized from the nineteenth century to inject scientific rationality into decisions about who belonged to which race: and these decisions had material impacts. Yet the basis of the law was spurious, reliant as it was on unfeasibly accurate records about people's ancestry, and understandings of definitions of 'race' that were not empirically provable. The result of this was that the legal concept of 'blood' was no more objective than that which the law dismissed as subjective and unreliable (Harris 1993: 1740). Guglielmo (2003), for example, refers to material suggesting that Italians (especially from the South) were subject to the same kind of racializing discourses, placing them at a lower level of civilization vis-a-vis Anglo-Saxons, as were the Irish. Yet it is worth reiterating that 'not white' does not mean 'black'. Even if it did, how can we explain the court ruling referred to by Jacobson (1998: 4) in which an Alabama court found that the State had not proved beyond doubt that a Sicilian woman was white?

Used sociologically, the term 'white' can be interpreted as encompassing non-material and fluid dominant norms and boundaries. Within the white racialized hierarchy were, as Guglielmo rightly points out, a number of 'races'. Indeed, using the distinction between 'white' and 'non white' as a starting point is a legitimate historical argument. In the USA, white migrants were people with rights, while Blacks were property without rights, for example. Yet this approach regards the terms 'white' and 'black' themselves as natural entities or givens, whose existence is then transposed into law. A sociologist however, ought to view these terms and the social relations they cover as part of the puzzle itself, that is, as products of the processes of racialization.

What emerges from this is that there are various contexts: economic, social, legal, cultural, for example, in which meaning is attributed to types of difference. In practice, it is impossible to completely separate these dimensions, but it is useful to start from this basis as a way of thinking through these issues. Moreover, the period covered, around 70 years from the mid nineteenth century to the First World War, enables us to see that understandings of who fits where in the social hierarchies can change. Why this happens when it happens can only be answered by reference to the historical record. We might put forward a few important structural items here, such as the Irish Famine, which altered the complexion of Irish migration to America; the Civil War, Reconstruction and after, which provided the framework both for black/white relations and for the formation of a 'white vote' in American politics; the development of the US economy to a stage which required so many manual workers that the labor supply was exhausted within the country and meant that there was plentiful work available for migrants; the consequent slump at the end of the nineteenth century experienced by Western Europe, which meant that the availability of employment that had absorbed some of the workers from Southern and Eastern Europe was diminished. Place all these together with the framework for understanding difference established by racial science in the nineteenth century, and outlines of the problem we have seen conceptualized, using the shorthand 'inbetween peoples', or the process of 'becoming white', emerge more clearly. Bear in mind that being white was not just about a certain range of phenotypes, but also about claims on culture and values.

Case Study 2: 'White Australia'

The Australian colonies were founded, much like the American colonies, as separate entities. Their foundation at the end of the eighteenth century, under the British Crown, proceeded on the legal principle that Australia was empty, uninhabited and unsettled land (*terra nullius*). Thus the white European settlers founded the colonies on the contradictory basis that the Aboriginal populations (now referred to as 'First Australians') did not exist, yet their collective relations with them were, as for the European settlers in North America, frequent and necessary. By the mid nineteenth century, the Australian colonies were absorbing migrant labor from the Pacific Islands, China and India. Between 1901 (when the Commonwealth of Australia became a dominion, with its own federal government) until 1972, Australia's immigration policy was based on the objectives of:

1. Protecting indigenous (i.e. white) labor from competition with Asian and Pacific Island labor, and
2. Preserving an Anglo-Celtic majority in the country.

The term 'White Australia' was coined in 1906, as an assertion of these twin objectives. The point of looking at this policy and the problems it ran into later in the twentieth century is firstly, to highlight both the haziness around who is considered white at a given moment and why; and secondly, to give an idea of some of the contextual, structural considerations that frame such changes within a hierarchy.

'White Australia' then was not a single piece of legislation, but a doctrine underlying an accumulation of laws and practices that restricted immigration from outside the country (except Europe) and excluded foreign nationals within Australia from various benefits and elements of citizenship. The 1901 Commonwealth Immigration Restriction Act (I.R.A) was the first piece of legislation passed by the new Federal Government. Its most well-known features were its provision for a written test in any European language, at the discretion of an immigration officer, to determine a prospective immigrant's fitness for approval; and the categories of person whose entry was prohibited. These were: the physically or mentally ill, categories of criminal other than political prisoner, prostitutes, those living on prostitutes' earnings, and those likely to be a charge on the communal purse (Tavan 2005: 7–8). In addition, various other laws provided for the repatriation of foreigners (Pacific Island Labourers Act 1901), excluded foreigners from voting (Commonwealth Franchise

Act 1902; Naturalization Act 1903) and from benefits like pensions (Old-Age and Invalid Pensions Act 1908) and the Commonwealth maternity bonus (1912).

However, to properly understand the compound anxieties about being usurped by foreign labor and facing 'racial contamination', as Labor Party leader John Christian Watson put it during parliamentary debate in 1901, it should be noted that blueprints of White Australia were already embodied in the legislation of the various Australian colonies before they combined to form the Commonwealth of Australia in 1900. Asian and Pacific Islanders had been working in Australia since the first half of the nineteenth century, primarily in the mining and sugar industries respectively. Hostile political agitation as a response to the migration of Indian, Chinese and Pacific Islanders into various parts of the country had led to state governments passing restrictions in a number of waves during the second half of the century. This became particularly intense in the late 1880s. By the end of the century, a model of indirectly discriminatory policies had been introduced. The 1901 I.R.A was therefore the endorsement, on a national level, of a set of practices ongoing across Australia. What was at stake was a conception of Australia as a unique civilization of Europeans encountering and overcoming a natural environment that other Europeans did not have to tame. The combination of whiteness, Britishness and embryonic Australianness that this embodied was most clearly defined in its dealings with First Australians and with the Chinese, not only through the physical differences shorthanded as racial, but the underlying values that Australians saw themselves as having and the other groups as lacking: vitality, industriousness, purity, cleanliness. The idea of geographical vulnerability added urgency to turn-of-the-century Australians' view of themselves as the pioneers of civilization surrounded by potential adversaries. In the prevailing social Darwinist ideological context, they were the spearhead of the white race forced into proximity with lesser races. In the ensuing struggle, they would prevail as the stronger, fitter race (4). This is why although non-Europeans had their uses, mixing with them and allowing them citizenship was seen as counter-productive. Governments did not attempt the mass deportations provided for in the IRA, and particular industries such as pearl diving enjoyed, de facto, special dispensation to employ Pacific Islanders and Chinese, who were seen as 'naturally' more suited to this work. Gwenda Tavan (2005: 15) interprets White Australia as a populist and popular device for generating nationalism in a fledgling society. It garnered support from all interest groups despite tensions of gender, class and religion. She goes on to contextualize it as central to the specific form of social liberalism that was the national ideology of the emergent State. This required state intervention to mitigate the excesses of the market, ensure fairer distribution of wealth, and provide minimum living conditions. The cultural homogeneity putatively anchoring this set of values was seen as essential to successfully building a civilization geographically remote from the epicenter of world civilization (Europe). Within this, the labor movement's opposition to the conditions of Kanaka (Pacific Island) workers in the sugar industry, on the grounds of their virtual slavery, was not viewed as contradictory to its support for repatriation of the foreign element of the workforce.

Indeed, it was the tropical part of Australia, the Northern Territories, that most exercised elite Australians' minds in the first half of the twentieth century. While the baseline for Australian immigration was to build on British and, to a lesser extent, Irish stock, the idea of 'race' and its relationship to climate and space proved problematic. Simply put, the association of different 'races' with particular types of climate, and with innate characteristics militated against Northern Europeans flourishing in this tropical environment (Anderson 2006). Yet with the departure of the Pacific Islanders in the first decades of the twentieth century, the North required a substitute labor force. The settlement of the North needed not just white supervisors, as had been the case in other tropical areas of colonial expansion, but a tropical white male laboring workforce. Was this a contradiction in terms? Alison Bashford (2000: 255) argues that tropical medicine debated the question, 'Is White Australia possible?' between 1900 and the 1930s. The problem revolved not around white men colonizing other people in the tropics, but 'as colonizers of a difficult and resilient space' (2000: 258). In this debate, First Australians had again been made invisible. The focus was on how whiteness could be adapted to overcome the tropical environment. Indeed, suggestions of how to accomplish this contributed, maintains Bashford, to producing 'an idea that whiteness was not only a characteristic of skin and color, but was also about how one lived, how one arranged one's moment by moment existence in space and time [...] the capacity to live in the tropics had to be learnt in minute, detailed and constant ways' (2000: 266).

At least for those engaged in the public health discourse, the solution was to apply science and rationality to impose order on the environment (Anderson 2006). A more pressing problem for employers in the Queensland and Northern Territories sugar plantations was to remain economically viable. Here, the niceties of the public health debate were ignored by workers intent on retaining a standard of living promised by the dismissal of competition in the form of Pacific Island labor. Yet in the mid 1920s, migrants from Italy began arriving in their thousands to work on the estates. This triggered a hostile campaign led by the Brisbane-based *Worker* newspaper against Italian immigration (Sheills 2006). The Italians occupied a position straddling the lines of whiteness. Officially categorized as 'white aliens', they became the object of a discourse aimed at presenting them as a threat not just to jobs, but to living standards (being willing to work for lower wages) and the cultural future of Australia (due to their clannishness, corruption, backward civilization and unfitness for vigorous pioneer activity required to settle and develop empty land). By 1925, the Queensland government had set up a Royal Commission to investigate the impact of the increased number of aliens in North Queensland. The Commissioner charged with producing a report made a sharp distinction between Northern and Southern Italians, castigating the latter *vis-à-vis* their Northern counterparts, for their clannishness, resistance to assimilation and propensity towards crime and violence. He was not alone in thinking this, either in Australia or elsewhere. Italians themselves debated the North-South divide in terms of culture and civilization (Verdicchio 1997), and the characterization of the Sicilians as 'inferior types' represented a boundary line between white and less white aliens.

Indeed, while the 1901 Immigration Act had been primarily aimed at keeping out the Chinese, the second- and third-largest groups of 'prohibited' immigrants (i.e. those refused the right to land in Australia) were Southern Europeans: Maltese and Italians. Distinctions within the 'white race' meant that Latins were lower down the racial pecking order than Anglo-Saxons, Alpines and Nordic peoples. Added to this complication was the reclassification of Axis member nationals (from Bulgaria, the Austro-Hungarian Empire, Germany and Turkey) during World War I as hostile aliens. There was even a temporary internment camp in New South Wales, and bans continued until at least 1923. Between 1912 and 1946 (the period when separate figures on the Maltese were kept), the prevailing practice of immigration officers was to question the right of Southern Europeans to land, even if, as in the case of the Maltese, they had British passports. Perceived racial difference here overrode nationality. In the most well-known case, 208 Maltese were kept out of Australia in 1916 (York 1990) by Melbourne immigration officials who gave them the dictation test in Dutch: all failed.

What this reveals about the workings of whiteness is its lack of solidity and stability. Even the taken-for-granted visible signs can be misleading, or be irrelevant to those wielding power in precise situations. Cultural and political factors can override the phenotypical ones. Moreover, the capacity to centre problems around whiteness per se can make other people invisible. Despite First Australians living in Northern Territories and Northern Queensland for millennia, public discourse obliterated them from the picture. The land was read through white eyes as 'empty' because it was neither owned according to private land-ownership laws, nor cultivated in ways that made sense in agrarian norms (planting, cultivation and harvest).

The basis for anxiety about shades of whiteness is expressed again through competition, or at least perceived competition, for work and conditions within international labor markets. It is not feasible to extricate the material from the cultural aspects of whiteness if we seek to understand it in its lived context.

Case Study 3: The Racialization of Working-Class Cultures
'Abject Whites' in the UK

Ethnographic writing on white racialized identities in the UK has focused disproportionately, as has much of the academic work on class, on working-class men. This can be seen as a reflection of the academy's middle-class composition and of ethnography's colonial heritage. Since Victorian times, middle-class academics and philanthropists have conducted surveys of the poor, the work of Friedrich Engels (1969[1844]), Henry Mayhew (1967[1861]) and Charles Booth (1902) being the best-known examples. The objective of such projects may have been to reform, politicize or evangelize the working classes, but the common strands were the revelation of their failings, and the creation of an inventory of what they did not have. In describing them, researchers drew parallels between them and colonized peoples. Anthony Wohl, on the web resource 'Victorian Web' (5) notes that a number of characteristics were applied by British commentators to the nineteenth-century working classes, Irish immigrants and colonial subjects. They were: unreasonable, ir-rational, and easily excited, childlike, superstitious (not religious), criminal (with neither respect for private property, nor notions of property), excessively sexual, filthy, inhabited unknown dark lands or territories and shared physical qualities. Wohl has clearly identified an overlap between the language of 'race' and that of class, locating both as being fixed on the body and culture.

The key point to grasp in the discourse on whiteness is that behavior, appearance and culture are linked. There has to be an explanation for why some of the 'race' placed at the top of the hierarchy clearly do not match the criteria established for superiority: bad genes and dysfunctional culture. From this viewpoint, the language and frames used in order to discursively distinguish (or make) classes, class fractions and 'races', are very similar.

This process of negatively evaluating working-class habitus and behavior has become so dominant a dis-course that in the post-industrial era of structural un- and underemployment, studies demonstrate that such values have to some extent become internalized. Bev Skeggs (1997) observes that the working-class women she interviews themselves often dis-identify from the working class. They define 'working class' by reference to values they personally do not or no longer have, or to economic predicaments they do not face. Indeed, the age of readily-sanctioned reference to a working-class 'us' appears, outside particular work milieux, to have disappeared from their social world. The anxiety around owning white working-class subject positions can be read as a reflection of white middle- and ruling-class attempts to pathologize and racialize them as an 'underclass'. Although the 'underclass' is rarely used as a sociological term in twenty-first century British scholarship (after intensive use in the late 80s and 90s), parts of the underclass debate map onto groups within the working class who are perceived as lacking in respectability: in the contemporary period these are 'Chavs' (Haywood and Yar, 2005; Nayak, 2003), or more abstractly, in Chris Haylett's (2001) argument, 'abject whites'.

She contends that sections of a white 'underclass' are constructed in turn-of-the-century Britain as 'people who are outside/beyond/beneath the nation' (2001: 358). This process involves devaluing social actions carried out by them. The protagonists in the Autumn 1993 'white' riots (in Oxford, Cardiff and Newcastle) 'were not hailed as class revolutionaries or even righteously angered disenfranchised minorities, rather they were an embarrassing sign of what the white working-class poor had become—a disorganized, racist and sexist detritus' (ibid.: 358). Indeed, in the de-unionized post-Fordist landscape, blame for this 'decline' in the working class, is placed on the working class themselves, or at least the poorest sections of it. Over time, argues Haylett, explanations of decline have become increasingly less structural, and more individual, and fixed around pathological working-class masculinities, and backwardness. In short the poor emerge as the exact opposite of the expanding multicultural, cosmopolitan middle classes. Indeed, Haylett stresses that the identity work accomplished in this discourse is relational, that is the multicultural modern group (the British middle classes) depend on the 'abject unmodern' white working class (ibid.: 365) for their own identity.

This 'power-evasive discourse' (Frankenberg, 1994) is picked up in specific relation to 'race', in for example the work on 'color-blind racism' (Bonilla-Silva, 2002) in the USA. Like minorities, with whom they are often compared, working-class Whites in these narratives are culturally disposed to degeneracy, crime, over-fecundity, fecklessness, etc.

'White Trash' in the USA

Similar themes resonate throughout the new studies and problematization of 'white trash' in the USA (Wray and Newitz 1997, Hartigan 2005, 1999, 1997a, b, Wray 2006). In these accounts, whiteness is significantly mediated by class (Bettie 2000, Gibbons 2004, Morris 2005). The polarized pairing of productiveness-unproductiveness is also central. Hartigan's tracing of the development of the phenomenon of 'white trash' in the USA (2005) demonstrates some interesting points of comparison between 'race' and class on one hand, and the UK and the USA on the other. Using the conclusion of nineteenth-century travel writer James Gilmore (6) he distinguishes between elements of the working class: 'The poor white man labors, the mean white man does not labor: and labor makes the distinction between them'.

Again, echoes of the underclass debate resonate loudly, with a moral categorization of the working class into productive and unproductive groups: the deserving and undeserving poor. Writing from the 1860s, says Hartigan, evidenced the struggle between those for whom such 'meanness' was in the blood and those who recognized a degree of environmental input. These competing logics developed into the twentieth century. Racial theorist Madison Grant, for example, understood 'white trash' as a combination of natural habitat and bloodlines: to do with sexuality, urbanization and crime, rather than just immigration (Grant 1916). Eugenics discourse stressed the perils of mixing good with bad genes, and responsibility for policing the genetic border. It argued that a host of antisocial and expensive behavior derived from poor family etiquette and practices. The result of this discourse in popular outlets, contends Hartigan, was heightened middle-class awareness of their racial selves, and of threat from below. In the scenarios popularized in the press, the idea of 'racial poisons' dominated discourse, with the weaker blood multiplying faster than the stronger. Gertrude Davenport (the wife of leading eugenicist Charles Davenport) wrote in a popular magazine in April 1914 that 'the greatest menace of imbecility is not that the imbecile may break into our house and steal our silver, or that he might set fire to our barn, but that he may be born of our flesh' (Hartigan 2005: 95).

Similarly, in Winthrop Stoddard's (1922) Freudian fight for civilization taking place within the Self, class status coincides with racial value:

> Let us understand once and for all [he warns] that we have among us a rebel army—the vast host of the inadaptable, the incapable, the envious, the discontented, filled with instinctive hatred of civilization and progress, and ready on the instant to rise in revolt. Here are foes that need watching. Let us watch them (1922: 87).

The overlap with contemporaneous American eugenics discourse on immigrants from Southern and Eastern Europe is very similar to Stoddard's comments here, and underscores the idea that 'race' and class are intimately connected in discourse of hierarchisation. People's culture and behavior is in the blood, these theories argue, and within the dominant 'race' there are those whose culture and behavior is more like those of subordinate races than those of the dominant. The struggle is for the dominant to remain pure and unpolluted, a theme pivotal to discourse on 'race'. The white trash figure then is marked as an excessive body that pollutes others. It displays the innate behavior that both confirms the depths to which the working class has collapsed (so far from work, so far from respectability), and at the same time emphasizes the industriousness and respectability of the middle-class subjects that fill the signifier 'white trash', with meaning.

Plural Trajectories of Whiteness

I began this chapter by floating the idea that there are a set of internal borders within the ostensibly homogenous 'white' group, and that these borders are contingent on political, economic and social factors that make them more or less relevant. In this final section, I want to draw out some of the complexity involved in the social relations that white working-class people maintain with minorities in Britain, as illustrated through empirical fieldwork.

Ethnographic fieldwork has illuminated what we could call the 'plural trajectories' of whiteness. In other words, how white people in broadly similar class positions make sense of the social material used to understand 'race' in differing ways. We are going to look briefly at two pieces of British ethnographic fieldwork to demonstrate some aspects of these 'plural trajectories': Katherine Tyler's discussions with residents of a former mining town in the English Midlands (2004), and Les Back's study of young people on the 'Riverview' estate in South London (1996).

Tyler's (2004) inter-generational dialogue among small-town Leicestershire inhabitants shows how personal biographies profoundly shape the ways in which people perceive 'Others'. Among the interviewees, no homogenous representative voice is expressed: white superiority is contested by some, just as it is accepted unthinkingly by more. Identification can take the form of empathy. 'Sarah's' experience of growing up working in her Czech immigrant father's shop gives her empathy with the people working in family-run Asian businesses when she hears criticisms of Asian corner shops, for example (Tyler 2004: 304). Moreover, a person may develop a critical angle through mobility and return. Another of Tyler's respondents, 'Jim', returns to the town after three years at university in a small, more multicultural city. He reports that his recognition and awareness of racism increased dramatically after he was reabsorbed into family circles and heard the types of discourse that he previously listened to uncritically. He can now reflect on the older generation's assumptions and dissect them. When his grandmother died, the house she had lived in was bought by an Asian family, something that his uncles were unhappy about. 'The presence of Asians in the home where they were brought up', paraphrases Tyler (2004: 299), 'signifies an intolerable and unacceptable transformation'. Here we see a crucial element of the mechanism of enacting whiteness. A perceived negative change (in this case the retrospective tainting of the family) is attached to an effect (the Asian buyer) rather than a cause (the grandmother's death, the psychological toll of memories of childhood in that home, the broader global changes that brought the family in question from Asia to Britain).

Inter-generational and gendered differences are also revealed by this study. The older people are generally less reflexive about whiteness and quicker to deploy racialized discourse, as are men as compared to women, many of whom see more positives where the men see only negatives.

There are clearly a number of places to be located ideologically in the racialization process, which becomes even more evident in the London housing estates where Les Back worked in the early 1990s. Back's (1996) ethnography of youth culture on South London estates suggests that values determine the salient borders of identity, and that culture becomes the 'modality' (following Stuart Hall) through which they are racialized. Black and white youths there put aside sporadic but real differences in order to ally against Vietnamese and Bangladeshi newcomers (1996: 240–241) in what Back terms 'neighborhood nationalism'. This alliance assumes the form of verbal and occasionally physical attacks. While the black youths are well aware that in other circumstances they could, and indeed have been, the victims of such aggression from their white counterparts, in the context of defining membership of the estate, their secular, linguistic and music-based coalition with white youth in 'Riverview' estate appears to predominate. They thus become what Back terms 'contingent insiders' (1996: 240), while their counterparts in 'Southgate' estate seemed to enjoy a qualitatively different relationship with their white peers, who had 'vacated concepts of whiteness and Englishness ... in favor of a mixed ethnicity that was shared' (ibid.: 241). So while there is frequently tension, there is also often alliance, through personal relationships drawing on shared knowledge and experiences.

Indeed, a recurrent topic in British ethnographic studies is the heterogeneity and elasticity of the category 'white' in its members' affiliations with black and Asian cultures, to the point where, in some specific contexts, terms such as 'black' or 'white' culture become almost ideal-types (7)

These groups of young people illustrate a paradox that resurfaces elsewhere in British fieldwork. In their survey of shopkeepers in a London borough, Wells and Watson (2005) find that not all those championing 'white values' are white, while some champions of white rights include their black neighbors in their embattled and beleaguered 'we'. In these cases the 'Other' is usually Muslim. Clearly, the power relationships at a personal and local level allow for whiteness to be expanded to incorporate those not phenotypically white beneath its cultural canopy for the enactment of both rhetorical and physical violence. People who are not white can be absorbed into honorary whiteness in particular circumstances, yet this invariably involves othering different groups. In fact this othering appears constitutive of the process of redrawing the boundary of whiteness in terms of values, so that it embraces British black or Asian people, depending on the context. In confirming shared values, the groups that share and do not share them are defined.

Conclusions: Overlapping Hierarchies of Class and Whiteness

In previous chapters, I focused on the borders between white and non-white. Here, the concentration has been on the other end of whiteness, between the constituent groups of the white whole. I want to emphasize that these latter borders are contingent, that is, open to political and social change. A group might be considered unproblematically white at one stage in one place, but not in another place at another time. Or, this might change for a specific group in the same place over different periods. Changing economic and social conditions led to different appraisals of who was allowed into Australia and why: what were the criteria? The design and application of the White Australia strategy, as well as the example of the 'inbetween peoples' thesis, are clearly about the parallel boundaries of whiteness; the one separating white from its non-white Other, and those separating the really white from the less so.

While groups such as Jews, Gypsies and immigrants frequently find themselves marginalized within the social relations of 'race', I want to encourage you to think of how the process works in relation to class. We have already noted that for a long time, the way in which membership of classes and 'races' was conceptualized was very similar. One function of the internal borders of whiteness is to isolate a group of Whites as being the sole agents of negative and un-modern behaviors and attitudes, thus removing responsibility for discrimination from the others. As Hartigan concludes:

'Part of what the epithet white trash expresses is the general view held by whites that there are only a few extreme, dangerous whites who are really racist or violently misguided, as opposed to recognizing that racism is an institutional problem pervading the nation and implicating all whites in its operation' (Hartigan 2005: 118–119).

I am tempted here to paraphrase Orwell, and suggest that in the process of racialization, all Whites are nominally equal, but some are more equal than others. This is true not only of how people express racism, but in the representations of how racism is expressed. The idea of portraying, or representing some groups as not-quite-white is part of the same power imbalance as the one that enables racism to function at a collective level. The discourse of 'race' and class are intimately connected.

Indeed, while racist ideas do abound in the working-class communities studied— although this label is contested in Chicago's Midtown (Kefalas 2003), and Detroit's Corktown and Warrendale (Hartigan 1999)— academics and media professionals play a significant role in creating a selective picture in which only the working class express such ideas and live in segregated neighborhoods. This is not borne out, even by the often questionable opinion poll results. Studies of whiteness in middle-class circles, residential areas or workplaces, or at all, are unfortunately few and far between (8). Whiteness is neither just for the wealthy, nor just the poor. Yet the people who have engaged in defining the desirability of including particular segments of their compatriots in the civilized, right-thinking mainstream have been middle- and upper-class British and Americans.

Moreover, under certain conditions, whiteness (as a dominant set of values and assumptions that make various groups problematic) is not even always only for white people. It is clear from survey research that minorities generally have more sympathy for immigrants and asylum seekers, and more of them tend to understand racism as structural rather than individually generated (Lamont 2000, Weis and Fine 1996), yet from the examples of Back (1996), Wells and Watson (2005) and Hoggett et al. (1992, 1996) there is enough to suggest that there might occasionally be a strategic overlap of values between white and black people that coalesce around defending neighborhoods, and possibly jobs. Moreover, minorities do engage to a degree with power-evasive discourse such as color-blind racism (Bonilla-Silva, 2002), just as many of Skeggs' respondents defined 'working class' as not them, but somebody else. There is a great deal of complexity on view in the fieldwork done on white working-class communities, and a number of individual biographical pathways that lead people also to be anti-racist. If this work teaches us anything, it is that attitudes cannot be read off simplistically from class positions.

We should recognize throughout that hierarchies are always in the process of construction, deconstruction and reconstruction: nothing is fixed, not even racialized boundaries. The hierarchies I refer to are expressed in terms of patterns of power relations; that is, the power to name, the power to control and distribute resources. While the group defined as 'white' has historically monopolized this sort of power, who counts as 'white' at a given moment and at a given time is far less certain. This requires us to understand political, social, cultural and economic factors as a messy whole, rather than as easily distinguishable and analyzable components: a challenge, but a worthwhile one.

Discussion Questions

1. What do class and racial identities have in common and what distinguishes them?
2. What role does a specific national context play in the way class and race get linked and unlinked?
3. When we define our own group, we define another implicitly. What evidence of this emerges from the discussion of class and 'race' here?

4. What does the author mean by '... in the process of racialization, all Whites are nominally equal, but some are more equal than others' in this context?

Notes

1. Indenture was a form of labor whereby the worker generally signed up to work for a specified period without pay on the basis that s(he) would receive a lump sum or a parcel of land at the expiry of the contract. However, political and other types of prisoner were also made into indentured laborers in the British Empire, particularly in the seventeenth century.

2. Scottish surgeon Robert Knox's *The Races of Men* (1850), and French aristocrat de Gobineau's *Essai sur l'inegalite des races humaines* (1853–55) are key works in this regard.

3. W.E.B Du Bois' much referred to passage in *Black Reconstruction* (1998: 700), his history of class and race relations in post-bellum America, attempts to find a reason why otherwise poor and oppressed white Southerners sided with the landed elite against the freed slave population in the 1870s. His answer is that it was not merely a question of economics, but of psychology. The status effect of feeling racially superior was equivalent to a 'public and psychological wage' (of whiteness) that they were paid in excess of their meager financial rewards. Barrett and Roediger are not alone in positing whiteness as an overarching mainstream value of Americanness; Horsman (1981), Saxton (1990), Bernstein (1990), Almaguer (1994), Allen (1994), Ignatiev (1996) and Jacobson (1998) all suggest this.

4. 'Social Darwinism' was a framework for understanding the social world, developed from Darwin's research into plants and animals and particularly popular during the last quarter of the nineteenth century. Evolution is cast in social Darwinism as an ongoing struggle for survival with the best-adapted and powerful species surviving at the cost of the weaker ones. It was used to justify imperialism, the class order of society and gender inequalities among other things.

5. 'Victorian Web' is accessible at: http://www.victorianweb.org/history/race/rcov. html. On the overlap of 'race' and class, see also Lorimer (1978).

6. Gilmore, J. *Down in Tennessee*, 1864: 188–89.

7. In their study of the East End of London, Paul Hoggett *et al.* (1996: 113) remark on a similar set of provisional allegiances, noting the large Afro-Caribbean presence in a demonstration following the fatal stabbing of a white schoolboy by a Bangladeshi boy:

    'The paradox is that whilst Afro-Caribbean soccer players can still be the object of crude racial abuse at nearby Millwall Football Club, Afro-Caribbeans can nevertheless also be included in an imaginary community of English-speaking Christian Eastenders which stands opposed to the alien Muslim threat'.

8. Hall 1992; Ware 1992; Pierce 2003; Johnson and Shapiro 2003; Hartigan (1999); Forman and Lewis, 2006); Reay *et al.*, 2007; Clarke and Garner (forthcoming).

References

Allen, T. (1994) *The Invention of the White Race (Vol. 2)*. New York: Verso.

Almaguer, T. (1994) *Racial Fault Lines: the origins of white supremacy in California*. Berkeley: University of California Press.

Anderson, W. (2006) *Cultivating Whiteness: Science, Health and Racial Destiny in Australia*. Cambridge: Cambridge University Press.

Arnesen, E. (2001) 'Whiteness and the Historians' Imagination'. *International Labor and Working Class History* 60:3–32.

Back, L. (1996) *New Ethnicities and Urban Culture: Social Identity and Racism in the Lives of Young People.* London: UCL Press.

Barrett, J. and Roediger, D. (2005) 'The Irish and the "Americanization" of the "New Immigrants" in the Streets and in the Churches of the Urban United States, 1900–1930'. *Journal of American Ethnic History.* 24(4): 4–33.

    (2004) 'Making new immigrants inbetween: Irish hosts and white pan-ethnicity, 1890–1930' in Foner, N. and Frederickson, G. (eds). *Not Just Black and White: Immigration and Race, Then and Now.* New York: Russell Sage Foundation Press, pp. 167–196.

    (1997) 'Inbetween Peoples: Race, Nationality and the "New Immigrant" Working Class.' *Journal of American Ethnic History.* Spring, 1997:3–44.

Bashford, A. (2000) 'Is White Australia possible'? Race, colonialism and tropical medicine. *Ethnic and Racial Studies.* 23(2): 248–71.

Bernstein, I. (1990). *The New York Draft Riots of 1863: their Significance for American Society in the Civil War Period.* New York: Oxford University Press.

Bettie, J. (2000) 'Women without Class: Chicas, Cholas, Trash, and the Presence/Absence of Class Identity.' *Signs.* 26(1): 1–35.

Bonilla-Silva, 2002.

Booth, C. (1902). *Labour and life of the people of London.* London: MacMillan

Brodkin, K. (1994) "How Did Jews Become White Folks?" in Gregory, S. and Sanjck, R. (eds) *Race,* New Brunswick, NJ: Rutgers University Press.

    (1998) How Jews became White Folks: and What That Says About Race in America New Brunswick, NJ: Rutgers University Press.

Clarke, S. and Garner, S. (forthcoming) White Identities. London: Pluto.

Daniels, J. (1997). *White Lies: race, class, gender, and sexuality in white supremacist discourse.* New York, Routledge.

Du Bois, W.E.B. (1998 [1935]). B*lack Reconstruction in the United States, 1860–1880.* New York: Free Press.

Engels, F. (1969 [1844]). *The Condition of the Working Class in England: From Personal Observation and Authentic Sources.* St.Albans: Panther.

Eze, E (1997). *Race and the Enlightenment: a Reader.* Boston: Blackwell.

Forman, T. and Lewis, A. (2006) 'Racial Apathy and Hurricane Katrina: the Social Anatomy of Prejudice in the Post-Civil Rights Era', *Du Bois Review: Social Science Research on Race,* 3: 175–202.

Frankenberg, R. (1994). *White Women, Race Matters.* Madison: University of Wisconsin Press.

Frederickson, G. (1988). *The Arrogance of Race: historical perspectives on slavery, racism and social inequality.* Hanover NH: Wesleyan University Press.

Garner, S. (2003). *Racism in the Irish Experience.* London: Pluto

Gibbons, M. (2004). 'White Trash: A Class Relevant Scapegoat for the Cultural Elite.' *Journal of Mundane Behaviour* 5(1). Online http://www.mundanebehavior.org/issues/v5n1/gibbons.htm Accessed on 25 June 2008.

Grant, M. (1916). *The Passing of The Great Race; or, The racial basis of European history.* New York: Charles Scribner and Sons.

Guglielmo, T. (2003). 'Rethinking Whiteness Historiography: the Case of Italians in Chicago, 1890–1945' in Doane and Bonilla-Silva (eds), pp. 49–61.

Guglielmo, J. and Salerno, S. (2003). *Are Italians white? How race is made in America.* New York: Routledge.

Hall, C. (1992). *White, Male and Middle Class: explorations in feminism and history.* Cambridge: Cambridge University Press.

Haney-Lopez, I. (1996). *White by Law: The Legal Construction of Race.* New York: New York University Press.

Harris, C. (1993). 'Whiteness as Property.' *Harvard Law Review* 106(8): 1707–93.

Hartigan, J. (2005). *Odd Tribes: toward a cultural analysis of white people.* Durham, NC: Duke University Press.

(1999) *Racial Situations: class predicaments of whiteness in Detroit*. Princeton NJ: Princeton University Press.

(1997a) 'Locating White Detroit' in Frankenberg (ed) pp.180–213.

(1997b) 'Name Calling: Objectifying "Poor Whites" and "White Trash" in Detroit' in Wray and Newitz (eds), pp.41–56.

Haylett C. (2001) 'Illegitimate Subjects?: Abject Whites, Neo-Liberal Modernisation and Middle Class Multiculturalism.' *Environment and Planning D: Society and Space*. 19 (3): 351–70.

Hayward, K. and Yar, M. (2005) 'The 'chav' phenomenon: consumption, media and the construction of a new underclass', *Crime, Media and Society* 2(1): 9–28.

Hoggett, P. (1992) 'A place for experience: a psychoanalytic perspective on boundary, identity and culture.' *Environment and Planning D: Society and Space*. 10:345–356.

Hoggett, P., Jeffers, S., and Harrison, L. (1996) 'Race, ethnicity and community in three localities', *New Community* 22(10):111–125.

Horsman, R. (1981) Race and Manifest Destiny: the Origins of American Anglo-Saxonism Cambridge: CUP.

Ignatiev, N. (1996) *How the Irish Became White*. New York: Routledge.

Jacobson, M. (1998). *Whiteness of a Different Colour: European Immigrants and the Alchemy of Race*. Cambridge, MA: Harvard University Press.

Johnson, H., and Shapiro, T. (2003). 'Good Neighborhoods, Good Schools: Race and the "Good Choices" of White Families' in Doane and Bonilla-Silva (eds), *White Out: the continuing significance of racism*. New York: Routledge, pp.173–88.

Jordan, W. (1968). *White over Black: American Attitudes Toward the Negro*, 1550–1812. Chapel Hill: University of North Carolina Press.

Kefalas, M. (2003). *Working-class Heroes: Protecting Home, Community and Nation in a Chicago Neighborhood*. Berkeley: UCLA Press.

Lamont, M. (2000). *The Dignity of Working Men*. Cambridge, MA: Harvard University Press.

Lorimer, D. (1978). *Color, Class, and the Victorians: English Attitudes to the Negro in the Mid-Nineteenth Century*. Leicester: Leicester University Press.

Mayhew, H. (1967 [1861]). *London Labour and the London Poor: A Cyclopaedia of the Condition and Earnings of Those That Will Work, Those That Cannot Work, and Those That Will Not Work*. New York: A.M. Kelley.

Morris, E. (2005) 'From "Middle Class" to "Trailer Trash": Teachers' Perceptions of White Students in a Predominantly Minority School.' *Sociology of Education* 78: 99–121.

Naipaul, V.S. (1969) *The Middle Passage*. London: Penguin.

Nayak, A. (2003) 'Ivory Lives: Economic Restructuring and the Making of Whiteness in a Post-industrial Youth Community'. *European Journal of Cultural Studies* 6(3): 305–25.

Pierce, J. (2003) "Racing for Innocence': Whiteness, Corporate Culture and the Backlash against Affirmative Action' in Doane and Bonilla-Silva (eds), pp.199–214.

Reay, D., Hollingworth, S., Williams, K., Crozier, G., Jamieson, F., James, D., and Beedell, P. (2007). 'Darker Shade of Pale?' Whiteness, the Middle Classes and Multi-Ethnic Inner City Schooling', *Sociology*, 41(6): 1041–1060.

Roediger, D. (1991). *The Wages of Whiteness: race and the making of the American working class*. London: Verso.

Saxton, A. (1990). *The Rise and Fall of the White Republic: Class Politics and Mass Culture in Nineteenth Century America*. New York: Verso.

Shiells, G. (2006) 'A Different Shade of White'. National Library of Australia News, August. Online: http://www.nla.gov.au/pub/nlanews/2006/aug06/article4.html (Accessed on 25 June 2008).

Skeggs, B. (1997). *Formations of Class and Gender: Becoming Respectable*. London: Routledge.

Stoddard, W. (1922). *Revolt Against Civilization*. New York: Scribner.

Tavan, G. (2005). *The Long Slow Death of White Australia*. Carlton, VA: Scribe.

Tyler, K. (2004). 'Reflexivity, tradition and racism in a former mining town.' *Ethnic and Racial Studies* 27(2): 290–302.

Verdicchio, P. (1997). *Bound by Distance: Rethinking Nationalism Through the Italian Diaspora.* Madison, NJ: Fairleigh Dickinson University Press.

Ware, V. (1992). *Beyond the Pale: White Women, Racism and History.* Verso: London.

Weis, L. and Fine, M. (1996) 'Narrating the 1980s and 1990s: Voices of Poor and Working-Class White and African-American Men'. *Anthropology and Education Quarterly,* 27(4): 493–516.

Wells, K. and Watson, S. (2005), 'A Politics of Resentment: Shopkeepers in a London Neighbourhood' *Ethnic and Racial Studies,* 28(2): 261–77.

Wohl, A. (187) 'Race and Class Overview: Parallels in Racism and Class Prejudice', http://www.victorianweb.org/history/race/rcov.html.

Wray, M. (2006). *Not Quite White: White Trash and the Boundaries of Whiteness.* Durham, NC: Duke University Press.

Wray, M. and Newitz, A. (1997) (eds) *White Trash: Race and class in America.* New York: Routledge.

York, B. (1990). *Empire and Race: the Maltese in Australia, 1881–1949.* Kensington, NSW: University of New South Wales Press.

SECTION IV

Key Issues in Racial and Ethnic Inequality

The readings in this section have two goals. The first is for you to consider how different social institutions function to maintain and support racial and ethnic inequality. This occurs through social policies and institutions such as the media, religious institutions, sports, and schools. The second goal is to provide examples of how institutions work to maintain and support racial and ethnic inequality.

Continuing Isolation

Segregation in America Today

By Ingrid Gould Ellen

Editor's Introduction

In this reading, Ellen discusses the persistence of racial-ethnic segregation in housing and some of its causes. She considers several possible explanations: discrimination, income differences, and preferences of neighborhoods by minorities. She then investigates housing segregation for Asian and Hispanic households. A key point raised in the reading is that federal nondiscrimination policies may not be enough to change residential segregation. This reading highlights how social policies may shape, maintain, or lessen segregation and racial-ethnic disadvantage.

Racial segregation remains a stubborn reality in U.S. metropolitan areas. While residential segregation between blacks and whites has declined over the past few . decades, it has changed only slowly, and levels of segregation remain extremely high, especially in the northeastern and midwestern regions of the country. Less segregated than blacks, Hispanics and Asians have experienced levels of segregation that are undiminished since 1980 (in fact, Asians have become slightly more segregated).

The goal of this chapter is to summarize what we know about the possible causes of racial and ethnic segregation in the present-day United States. While focusing largely on black-white segregation, this chapter also explores how the bundle of causes of segregation may differ for other racial and ethnic groups.

The chapter concludes that there is no single explanation for the persistence of segregation. Patterns of settlement tend to change slowly, and thus the legacy of blockbusting, redlining, and the many other blatant acts of discrimination that occurred before the passage of the Fair Housing Act lives on. Yet contemporary

Ingrid Gould Ellen, "Continuing Isolation: Segregation in America Today," *Segregation: The Rising Costs for America*, ed. Pawan Dhingra. Copyright © 2008 by Taylor & Francis Group LLC. Reprinted with permission.

segregation is not simply a relic of the past; it is also the result of ongoing, present-day residential moves that are restricted by ongoing discrimination and racial tensions. Perhaps most central are the everyday decisions of white households to avoid moving to racially integrated and largely minority communities.

The chapter is organized as follows: the first section provides an overview of trends in segregation over the past century. The second section outlines the various possible causes of segregation. The third section summarizes the evidence of the relative importance of these factors in explaining the contemporary segregation of blacks, and the fourth section considers the roots of segregation for Asians and Hispanics. The final section explores policy implications.

Background on Segregation

Some historical perspective on segregation is useful, since segregation levels have changed considerably over the course of the twentieth century. In the early decades of the century, large numbers of blacks migrated from the rural South to the industrial cities of the North. As black households moved into northern cities, segregation in those cities rose dramatically (Cutler *et al.* 1999; Taueber and Taueber 1965). Segregation in southern cities increased as well, as the patterns of residence that developed during slavery continued to break down (Taueber and Taueber 1965). After World War II, a second wave of black migration to northern cities occurred, and again it was accompanied by an increase in segregation. The increases were particularly large in the industrial cities of the Northeast and Midwest. By 1970, nearly 80 percent of the black population in the average metropolitan area would have had to move to a different census tract to achieve racial integration (Cutler *et al.* 1999).

Since 1970, black-white segregation has steadily declined (Lewis Mumford Center 2001; Glaeser and Vigdor 2001; Iceland *et al.* 2002), and, as Table 12.1 shows, the number of racially integrated neighborhoods in U.S. metropolitan areas has grown. Table 12.1 also makes it clear that much of the increase in integration has been driven by the decline in all-white neighborhoods—a shift of census tracts from all-white to moderately integrated. While more than half of all metropolitan census tracts were less than 1 percent black in 1970, just one in five were less than 1 percent black in 2000. Meanwhile, the proportion of census tracts that had a majority of black residents actually increased during this time period. In other words, the declines in segregation between 1970 and 2000 were achieved largely through the integration of predominantly white neighborhoods, not through the integration of predominantly black communities.

While they have not experienced the same declines in segregation (Iceland *et al.* 2002; Lewis Mumford Center 2002), Hispanic and especially Asian households remain considerably less segregated than blacks.

Table 12.1 Distribution of Census Tracts by Percentage Black, 1970–2000 (universe: all metropolitan areas, as defined in 2000)

Racial Composition	1970	1980	1990	2000
<1% black	55.1	41.3	31.8	20.7
1-10% black	22.3	32.5	38.6	46.1
10-50% black	12.4	15.2	17.9	21.8
>50% Black	10.1	11.0	11.7	11.4
Number of census tracts	34,128	42,524	44,159	50,956

Source: Ellen (2007).

Black-white segregation levels remain uniquely high, especially in large cities and in northeastern and midwestern metropolitan areas.

Potential Causes of Segregation

Students of segregation generally divide the explanations for segregation into those that suggest market failures in the housing market and those that imply the housing market is operating just as markets should—sorting people according to their preferences and ability to pay.

Typically, two sorts of market failures are offered. The first is an information failure: households fail to learn about housing opportunities in neighborhoods and jurisdictions in which they are racially underrepresented. For example, white households tend to learn almost exclusively about housing opportunities in white communities, while minority households mostly get information about opportunities in minority neighborhoods. These information failures may be rooted in differences in housing search patterns or in racially segmented information networks.

The second and more disturbing failure is housing market discrimination—the specific acts of sellers, landlords, realtors, and lenders to restrict the choices of minority households and keep them out of white neighborhoods. Also included are more subtle acts of steering, by which realtors steer households to consider homes and apartments in neighborhoods that match their race and ethnicity. These explanations clearly call for policies, such as increased enforcement of fair housing laws, to address the market failures.

The other categories of explanations for segregation, which are typically viewed as more benign, are differences in income and preferences. The argument regarding income differences is obvious: housing tends to be distributed across different neighborhoods according to price and rent levels. Since minority households on average have lower incomes than white households, the two groups end up in different neighborhoods. While such differences in income between racial groups are troubling in themselves, they suggest nothing particularly troubling about the operation of housing markets.

The role of preferences demands more discussion. While researchers tend to group preferences into a single category, there are at least four distinct types of preferences that might explain the observed patterns and that call for distinct responses. First, minority and white households may simply have different preferences for the nonracial attributes of communities, such as the characteristics of the local housing stock and the nature of local public services. These preferences lead them to choose different neighborhoods and jurisdictions. Second, households may desire to live among others of the same race who share the same customs and way of life. Third, households may not care so much about living with others just like them, but they may dislike living among particular racial groups because of individually based racial prejudice. Finally, race-based neighborhood stereotyping may explain the reluctance of whites to share neighborhoods with blacks (Ellen 2000a). Specifically, whites avoid integrated neighborhoods because they assume that such neighborhoods will inevitably become all-black and experience the decline in public services and neighborhood conditions that they associate with largely black areas.

Evidence on Causes of Black-White Segregation

Over the past few decades, many researchers have studied the high levels of residential segregation between blacks and whites and have hotly debated the underlying causes. This section reviews this literature to assess the relative importance of each of the factors outlined above in explaining present-day black-white segregation.

Information Gaps: Evidence

There is surprisingly little research examining the role of information in sustaining segregation. The few studies that have examined and compared how homes in largely minority and largely white neighborhoods are marketed find significant differences (Galster *et al.* 1987; Newburger 1981; Turner and Wienk 1993). For instance, Turner and Wienk (1993) provide intriguing evidence from Washington, DC, that homes for sale in predominantly black or integrated neighborhoods are marketed quite differently than similar homes in predominantly white neighborhoods. In particular, they find that homes in black or integrated neighborhoods are much less likely to be advertised in citywide newspapers and much less likely to be marketed through open houses. These differences in marketing could lead to significant disparities in the housing information available to different racial groups. More recent research investigating whether these patterns hold true today would be welcome.

Researchers also tend to find that blacks and whites rely on somewhat distinctive methods to search for housing, but these differences appear to be modest and the results are not consistent across studies (Turner and Wienk 1993; Farley 1996; Newburger 1999). For example, using 1992 data from Detroit, Farley (1996) finds that black households are less likely to rely on real estate brokers and more likely to rely on informal methods of housing search that include word of mouth and driving through neighborhoods, methods that suggest a more geographically restricted search. Turner and Wienk (1993) find that blacks are more likely to rely on real estate agents in the Washington, DC metropolitan area, while Newburger (1999) reports that low-income black homebuyers in Philadelphia search a wider set of neighborhoods than do their white counterparts. Clearly, more research is needed to understand the role of search practices in explaining segregation.

Discrimination

It is undeniable that housing market discrimination played a forceful role in restricting the mobility of black households in the past. In the public sector, public housing was explicitly segregated by race, and the Federal Housing Administration recommended the use of private, restrictive covenants that prohibited black occupancy and taught its underwriters to avoid integrated areas. Evidence exists that until the passage of the Fair Housing Act, discrimination in the private housing market was widespread, with realtors and lenders commonly refusing to serve blacks moving into white neighborhoods (Massey and Denton 1993).

It is also undeniable that discrimination by sales and rental agents persists (Turner and Ross 2004; Yinger 1995). The best evidence on housing discrimination comes from three national audit studies conducted by the Urban Institute in 1977, 1989, and 2000 (Turner *et al.* 2002). The most recent national audit study of paired testers reveals that while the blatant blockbusting techniques and outright door-slamming behavior that were pervasive in the 1950s and 1960s have faded away, housing market discrimination persists in more subtle forms and continues to be a barrier for black and Hispanic households in both rental and sales markets (Turner and Ross 2004). For example, the study also reports strong evidence that black homebuyers are steered away from white neighborhoods. These forms of housing discrimination are illegal, but they persist nonetheless, which suggests that enforcement of fair housing laws is inadequate.

The most recent national audit study also provides some evidence of a decline in discrimination. The study's authors compared the incidence of discrimination in 1989 and 2000, and reported significant declines in most areas (Turner *et al.* 2002). One exception was discrimination against Hispanic renters, for whom there was little change evident during the 1990s. In addition, the incidence of steering black homebuyers appears to have increased over the decade. Other, less direct evidence of a decline in discrimination comes from

Cutler *et al.* (1999), who analyze racial differentials in house prices to examine the roots of segregation. In particular, they argue that if segregation is largely due to discriminatory barriers keeping black households in predominantly black areas or choices by black households to live in such areas, we would observe blacks paying more than whites for housing in more segregated cities. If segregation is primarily due to the desires of whites to live among other whites, then we would observe whites paying more than blacks for housing in more segregated cities. Using this price differential approach, they find evidence that in 1940 segregation was largely caused by housing market discrimination, restrictive covenants, and other practices that kept blacks out of largely white neighborhoods. However, they conclude that by 1990 the balance had shifted and that segregation had become more a function of the decentralized decisions of whites to avoid black neighborhoods.

The dramatic decline shown in Table 12.1 in the number of neighborhoods with little or no black presence offers some additional, albeit suggestive, evidence that black households attempting to move to all-white areas face fewer barriers today than they have in the past. Table 12.2 provides further support, suggesting that between 1990 and 2000, homogeneous white neighborhoods were ten times more likely to become integrated than were homogeneous black neighborhoods. To the extent that neighborhoods become integrated, they become integrated through the entry of minority households into predominantly white neighborhoods. It is far less likely that neighborhoods become integrated through the entry of white households into predominantly minority areas. Indeed, more than 97 percent of the neighborhoods that became newly integrated in 2000 (i.e., neighborhoods that were integrated in 2000 but not in 1990) were predominantly white in 1990. Strikingly, across all metropolitan areas in the United States, there were only 67 census tracts (out of a total of nearly 50,000) that were predominantly black in 1990 and became integrated in 2000.

It is worth underscoring that none of these studies or stylized facts suggests that discrimination does not exist; rather, they suggest that the nature of discrimination has shifted and that the discriminatory barriers blocking black households from moving into predominantly white neighborhoods have declined in recent decades. Given sufficient effort, black households are now able to find rental and ownership housing in communities that were previously closed to them. Yet discrimination persists, and its continued presence may shape residential patterns. Indeed, the mere presence of discrimination may lead many black households to avoid even seeking homes in predominantly white areas.

Income Differences

Significant differences remain between the economic status of minority and white households. Table 12.3 shows that in 1999 the median income among non-Hispanic whites was nearly 60 percent higher than that for blacks and 44 percent higher than that for Hispanics. On average, Asian households actually had

Table 12.2 Proportion of Census Tracts That Became Integrated in 2000, by 1990 Neighborhood Type

Neighborhood Type in 1990	Percent Integrated in 2000
Homogeneous white	22.8
Homogeneous black	2.0
Homogeneous Hispanic	2.1
Homogeneous other	2.4

Source: Adapted from Ellen (2007).

Table 12.3 Median Household Income and Poverty Rates by Race/ Ethnicity, 1999

Race of Household Head	Median Household Income	Poverty Rate
Non-Hispanic white	$44,157	8.1%
Black	$27,910	24.9%
Hispanic	$30,746	22.6%
Asian	$50,960	12.6%

Source: Poverty rates from Bishaw and Iceland (2003). Income figures from Historical Income Tables, U.S. Census Bureau.

incomes that were 15 percent higher than those of non-Hispanic whites. Large differences in poverty are evident as well, with poverty rates among black and Hispanic households roughly triple the rate for whites and double the rate for Asians. In addition, studies typically find that on average the asset holdings of black households are only about one-fourth or one-fifth of those of white households (Altonji *et al.* 2000; Altonji and Doraszelski 2001). Several studies find that these differences in wealth persist, even after differences in income and other factors have been controlled for (Altonji and Doraszelski 2001).

Despite these significant differences, virtually every study that has examined the role of income differences in driving segregation has found that income differences between blacks and whites account for only a modest share of segregation patterns (Farley 1986; Kain 1986; Gabriel and Rosenthal 1989; Ihlanfeldt and Scafidi 2002).An analysis focused on the San Francisco metropolitan area (Bayer *et al.* 2004) included a broad set of sociodemographic variables—income, education, occupation, household composition, immigration status, years in the United States, and language spoken at home—and found that they play a somewhat greater role in segregation. Even so, this broad set of factors collectively explains only 30 percent of black segregation. (Income, education, occupation, and household composition together account for just 20 percent of black segregation.) Moreover, it is important to stress that this study analyzed residential patterns in a single western metropolitan area, with moderate levels of segregation. Sociodemographic characteristics might explain a smaller fraction of black segregation in more highly segregated areas.

None of these studies considers differences in wealth, and it seems likely that a greater share of segregation could be explained if differences in wealth were also taken into account. Yet one recent study found that racial differences in asset holdings explain very little of the lower rate of black entry into predominantly white areas (South *et al.* 2004).

Preferences

As was noted earlier, it is possible that racial differences in preferences for housing types and local public services help explain black-white segregation levels. There are very few systematic studies that explore the extent of these differences. Galster (1979) finds only minor variations in tastes between blacks and whites, once income and other household characteristics are taken into account. Bajari and Kahn (2005) report that white households have a greater demand for large, single-family detached dwellings, but the authors have limited controls for socioeconomic status. Thus, while the authors control for income and education of the household head, race may still capture differences in permanent income and wealth in their models. In the end, there is too little evidence to conclude that there are meaningful differences in taste for housing and local public services across racial groups.

Several authors have suggested that a key factor driving segregation is a desire for self-segregation or ethnic clustering on the part of blacks (Clark 1986; Patterson 1997). While it is certainly plausible that affirmative desires for clustering on the part of blacks plays a role in segregation, surveys of residential preferences provide little support for the self-segregation hypothesis. Such surveys generally find that black households prefer not to live in largely black neighborhoods and suggest that black households are willing to move into neighborhoods of almost any racial mix, as long as they are not the very first black household in the community (Farley *et al.* 1978, 1993; Bobo and Zubrinsky 1996; Charles 2000). Meanwhile, studies examining housing prices find no evidence that black households pay a premium to live in more segregated areas (Galster 1982; Cutler *et al.* 1999).Cutler *et al.* (1999) also find no relationship between stated desires for segregation among blacks living in a metropolitan area and the actual level of segregation in that area. Moreover, as John Kain (1976) pointed out, given that segregation levels of blacks are so much higher than those of other ethnic groups, we would have to assume that blacks have an unusually strong desire for segregation, far beyond that even of recent immigrants, whose foreign language and customs would seem to make such clustering natural.

This is not to say that black preferences do not contribute to some degree to current segregation. Ihlanfeldt and Scafidi (2002) find that while most blacks prefer integrated neighborhoods, a sizable minority identify all or mostly black neighborhoods as their preferred location. Blacks with stronger tastes for black neighbors tend to live in neighborhoods with a higher percentage of black residents, suggesting that they are acting on those preferences in making their residential choices. Still, the effects are small, and the authors acknowledge that continuing housing segregation cannot be attributed solely to these preferences.

Moreover, the authors ultimately cannot divorce a desire for living among black families from a fear of the hostility one might encounter when entering white areas. Consider that roughly 90 percent of the black respondents to the 1992 Detroit Area Survey who said they would not move into an all-white area reported that their reason was that the whites living there would be hostile and unfriendly (Farley *et al.* 1994). Similarly, analyzing data from Atlanta, Boston, Detroit, and Los Angeles in the mid-1990s, Krysan and Farley (2002) find that a large majority of the black respondents who said that they would not move into an all-white area gave discomfort and fear of hostility from whites as their reason. Only 4 percent of blacks avoiding all-white neighborhoods said they were doing so for cultural reasons. The expressed reluctance among many blacks to move into predominantly white neighborhoods appears to be driven less by benign desires on the part of blacks for self-segregation than by a fear of white hostility. The residential preferences of white households appear to play a more significant role in maintaining segregation. For one thing, survey evidence consistently shows that whites simply care a great deal more about neighborhood racial composition than blacks (Farley *et al.* 1993; Bobo and Zubrinsky 1996). For another, evidence shown in Table 12.2 suggests that neighborhoods are far more likely to become integrated through blacks moving into predominantly white neighborhoods than through whites moving into predominantly black neighborhoods. Recall that just sixty-seven neighborhoods in the entire United States shifted from being predominantly black to being racially integrated between 1990 and 2000. White avoidance of predominantly black neighborhoods appears to be a more significant barrier to integration than the hesitancy of blacks to move into predominantly white areas.

Cutler *et al.* (1999) also find evidence to suggest that white preferences are more critical. As has been noted already, they find that whites pay more than blacks for equivalent housing in more segregated cities, suggesting that whites are willing to pay a premium to live in segregated white neighborhoods. In sum, there is considerable evidence that white household decisions, particularly the decision not to move into predominantly black and integrated neighborhoods, contribute to segregation.

The next question is the dominant motivation underlying this avoidance. There is little evidence to suggest that this white avoidance is motivated by a benign desire on the part of whites to live among other whites. For one thing, surveys of residential preferences suggest that whites are far less resistant to living among nonblack minority groups, such as Asians, than to living among blacks (Emerson *et al.* 2001; Bobo and Zubrinsky 1996; Charles 2000). More fundamentally, it is hard to understand why whites, as the dominant group in U.S. society, would feel any need to cluster in order to enjoy special traditions and customs (Ellen 2000a).

A more plausible explanation for white avoidance is that it is motivated by racial prejudice against blacks; whites avoid mixed neighborhoods because they simply do not want to live near black households. While surely some white households harbor such views, evidence from surveys of racial preference suggests a decline in such prejudice over time (Schuman *et al.* 1997). Of course, since this evidence comes from self-reported surveys, the observed decline may simply be due to greater social stigma attached to expressions of racial prejudice.

A third possibility is that white avoidance behavior is explained by race-based neighborhood stereotyping—the negative views that white households, as well as some black households, hold on the social, economic, and physical characteristics of largely black neighborhoods. White households may not dislike living next to a black household per se; rather, many white households may associate predominantly black neighborhoods with diminished neighborhood quality and resilience. With this viewpoint, race clearly matters but chiefly as a signal of the structural strength of a community. White households, and some minority households too, assume that racially integrated neighborhoods will inevitably become all black and that neighborhood quality will deteriorate (Ellen 2000a). It is naturally difficult to distinguish empirically between individually based racial animus and race-based neighborhood stereotyping, but past research provides considerable support for the notion of race-based neighborhood stereotyping. (Certainly there is no evidence that race-based neighborhood stereotyping is declining, as there is for racial prejudice.) Sampson and Raudenbush (2004) find strong evidence that households use racial composition, particularly percentage black, as a signal of a neighborhood's quality and social cohesion. In addition, several studies find that residents who are more invested in a community's quality and therefore have more to lose from the changes that they believe to be correlated with minority population growth (e.g., homeowners, and households with children) are more resistant to black neighbors than other households, even after differences in socioeconomic status have been controlled for (Charles 2000; Ellen 2000a).

Further support for race-based neighborhood stereotyping comes from the fact that racial composition factors in the decisions of white households to move into a neighborhood to a greater degree than it does in the decision as to whether or not to leave. People already living in a community are likely to have considerable information about its quality and future prospects, and thus will tend to be less concerned about racial composition. By contrast, when choosing among many alternative communities, outsiders may find it easier to rely simply on racial composition as a presumed signal of neighborhood quality and conditions.

Finally, Ellen (2000a) finds that integrated neighborhoods are more likely to remain stable over time if residents and outsiders have reason to believe that they will remain racially stable over time and/or if neighborhood conditions and housing demand are believed to be particularly secure. This may be because of the presence of a stabilizing institutional presence such as a university.

Evidence on Causes of Segregation for Asian and Hispanic Households

There is far less research investigating the bundle of factors responsible for the segregation of Asian and Hispanic households. However, the evidence that exists suggests that the causes differ from those driving black-white segregation and that white avoidance generally plays a lesser role.

First, differences in socioeconomic status appear to explain a much greater share of the segregation experienced by Asians and Hispanics. In their 2004 study of segregation in the San Francisco metropolitan area, Bayer *et al.* find that income, education, occupation, and household composition collectively explained over 60 percent of Hispanic segregation as compared to just 20 percent of black segregation. Earlier studies relying on 1970, 1980, and 1990 census data report similar results: class differences consistently explain a greater share of Hispanic segregation than of black segregation (Massey 1979; Denton and Massey 1988; Alba and Logan 1993; Alba *et al.* 2000). Fewer studies investigate the roots of Asian segregation, but those that do generally find that class differences make a significant contribution; Asians who are college educated, own their homes, and have higher incomes live in communities with much higher proportions of whites (Alba and Logan 1993; Alba *et al.* 2000).

There is also evidence that desire for ethnic clustering on the part of minorities plays a greater role in the segregation of nonblack minorities, especially Asians. To some extent, this clustering is driven by the fact that so many Asians and Latinos are immigrants. In 2000, 69 percent of the Asian population and 40 percent of the Hispanic population in the United States were foreign born (Malone *et al.* 2003).Not surprisingly, immigrant groups tend to cluster when they first arrive in the United States; by settling in communities populated by other immigrants who share their language and customs, immigrants ease the transition to their new environment.

As their time in the United States increases, both Asian and Hispanic households appear to become less segregated (Alba *et al.* 2000). Similarly, in their study of residential patterns in the San Francisco Bay area published in 2004, Bayer *et al.* find that Asians and Hispanics who have stronger English language skills and who are U.S. citizens are less segregated. Specifically, they find that the language spoken at home, English language ability, citizenship status, and years in the United States together account for 40 percent of Asian segregation and 30 percent of Hispanic segregation. Segregated neighborhoods appear to be a stepping stone for foreign-born Latinos and, especially, foreign-born Asians when they arrive in the United States.

Research also suggests that white avoidance generally plays a lesser role in the segregation of Asians and Latinos than it does in the segregation of blacks. Surveys of racial preferences, for example, consistently show that white households are far more comfortable living in neighborhoods with high percentages of Asians and Hispanics than they are in areas with high percentages of blacks (Charles 2000; Bobo and Zubrinsky 1996). Furthermore, Ellen (2000b) finds that the ethnic change that occurs in Hispanic-white and Asian-white areas is driven more by minority demand and demographic realities than by white avoidance behavior. This is in contrast to the change occurring in black-white areas. Class differences between minorities and whites appear to be especially relevant in predicting racial transition in the case of Asian-white communities; Asian-white neighborhoods with poorer Asians are far more likely to lose whites than those with wealthier Asians. By contrast, class differences appear largely irrelevant to subsequent ethnic change in neighborhoods shared by whites and Hispanics, and those shared by whites and blacks. In sum, the causes of segregation appear to vary across minority groups. Although the research is limited, the evidence generally suggests that causes are more benign and transitory in the case of Asians. As their incomes and educations rise, their English skills improve, and their time in the United States increases, their segregation levels tend to diminish. For

Hispanic segregation, the evidence is somewhat more mixed, but again the causes appear more benign and the segregation itself more transitory as compared to the segregation of blacks.

This is not to say that Hispanics and Asians do not face discrimination and prejudice. Indeed, the latest national audit study of discrimination suggests that Hispanic renters continue to face discrimination from rental agents at levels comparable to blacks (Turner and Ross 2004), and that Asians and Pacific Islanders face discrimination in the market for owner-occupied housing (Turner and Ross 2003). The point is simply that, on average, discrimination and white avoidance may not be as central in driving segregation for Asians and Hispanics as they are in the case of blacks.

It is worth underscoring that considering Asians and Hispanics as single, monolithic groups is overly simplistic. Research that explores the segregation levels of different Asian and Hispanic subpopulations typically finds significant variation (Massey and Bitterman 1985; Ellen 2000b; Alba *et al.* 2000). For instance, researchers have typically found that the residential patterns of Puerto Ricans more closely resemble those of blacks than those of other Hispanics (Denton and Massey 1989; Massey and Denton 1993; Massey and Bitterman 1985).

There are good reasons to suspect that the explanations for segregation vary across subgroups as well. For certain subgroups, recent immigrants or groups from particular regions, discrimination and white avoidance may be more central in explaining segregation. Massey and Bitterman (1985) argue that the higher levels of segregation among Puerto Ricans result from their African ancestry and the fact that whites are more likely to perceive them as black. Unfortunately, the national audit studies did not have sufficient sample sizes to explore such subgroups. However, the results do suggest significant discrimination against Hispanic renters but not against Hispanic homebuyers. Turner and Ross (2003) posit that this may be because of the differences between Hispanic renters and homebuyers—that is, renters are far more likely to be lower-income, first-generation immigrants. Native-born white households may be quite open to sharing neighborhoods with higher-income, assimilated Hispanic households but not with more recent, lower-income arrivals. This is consistent with the above-noted evidence suggesting that higher-income, native-born Hispanics experience very low levels of segregation.

Conclusion and Policy Implications

This chapter strives to demonstrate that a multiplicity of factors help to explain the persistence of segregation in U.S. metropolitan areas. In the past, much work on segregation has debated the extent to which discrimination was the key cause of the segregation of blacks. This argument took on a fair degree of urgency because the implication seemed to be that if, and only if, segregation was caused by discrimination, then segregation was something to worry about. If discrimination was not the key cause, then the assumption seemed to be that segregation was driven by benign individual preferences, and we should remain largely unconcerned. Such a dichotomy is false.

The race-based preferences that undergird segregation are simply not so benign. Much of current black-white segregation is caused by the ongoing refusal of whites to move into integrated and largely black neighborhoods because of negative racial attitudes—particularly race-based stereotypes about the quality of life in these communities. While these decisions may not be legally actionable, they are surely more troubling than decisions to cluster voluntarily with other members of one's own ethnic group. Moreover, these decisions are driven by negative attitudes and stereotypes that are themselves shaped by segregation and encourage the continuing discrimination by landlords, real estate agents, and lenders.

Finally, whatever the precise mix of causes, there is a growing body of evidence that suggests that segregation imposes significant social costs. Segregation may fuel prejudice, and there is increasing evidence to suggest that it can have detrimental effects on the life chances of blacks (Cutler and Glaeser 1997; Ellen 2000c; O'Regan and Quigley 1996).

White avoidance appears to play a lesser role in the segregation of Hispanics and Asians than it does in the segregation of blacks. Segregation is driven to a greater extent by differences in socioeconomic status, levels of proficiency with the English language, and minority preferences for ethnic clustering. This is not to say that discrimination and white avoidance do not play a role, but that these factors play a less dominant role than they do in the case of blacks. Put simply, Hispanic households and, particularly, Asian households are better able to translate gains in education and income into greater residential choices.

It is important to reiterate that although they have remained relatively steady over the past few decades, the segregation levels of Hispanics and especially Asians are far less severe than those of blacks. Moreover, in contrast to the growing body of work suggesting that segregation undermines the life chances of blacks, there has been little research on the effects of segregation on Hispanics and Asians. For all these reasons, it remains unclear whether we should think about segregation of these groups in the same light as we think about the segregation of blacks. More research is needed to understand the underlying causes and consequences, and how they vary for particular subgroups.

Finally, what kinds of policies are advisable in light of the findings in this chapter? First and foremost, continued efforts to combat discrimination in housing and mortgage markets are critical. Discrimination continues to restrict housing choices of minority households and discourages them from seeking out housing opportunities in largely white areas. In addition, racial steering by real estate agents preserves existing patterns of segregation and artificially limits demand in largely minority and integrated communities. Finally, housing market discrimination helps to maintain predominantly white areas as an option to which whites can escape, and in this way fuels white avoidance (Yinger 1995).

Fair housing policies should not end with antidiscrimination efforts, however. First, the findings here suggest that government at all levels should be encouraged to provide information that can expose what is false or exaggerated in the stereotypes many households hold about minority groups and their communities. Second, government should ensure that information about available housing opportunities reaches a broad and diverse set of groups. It should consider affirmative efforts to encourage white households to look at homes in minority neighborhoods and to encourage minority households to consider homes in predominantly white areas. Finally, efforts to bolster the quality of schools, neighborhood safety, and the general physical appearance of integrated and changing neighborhoods are also likely to promote the stability of integration (in addition to their obvious direct benefits); visible signs of decline and worries about public services can significantly undermine faith in a neighborhood's strength.

Discussion Questions

1. Why are policies such as the Fair Housing Act inadequate in eliminating race-based housing market segregation entirely? What other factors, outside of market discrimination, explain the ongoing residential segregation?

2. What does the author mean by "information failure" in describing the causes of market segregation? What, in your opinion, can be done to help curb this particular cause?

3. What role does language play in the racial segregation of minorities? Why, according to the author, are non–English speaking minorities more likely to experience housing market segregation?

References

Alba, Richard, and John R. Logan. 1993. "Minority Proximity to Whites in Suburbs: An Individual-Level Analysis of Segregation." *American Journal of Sociology* 98: 1388–1427.

Alba, Richard, John R. Logan, and Brian Stults. 2000. "The Changing Neighborhood Contexts of the Immigrant Metropolis." *Social Forces* 79: 587–621.

Altonji, Joseph, and Ulrich Doraszelski. 2001. "The Role of Permanent Income and Demographics in Black-White Differences in Wealth." NBER Working Paper 8473.

Altonji, Joseph, Ulrich Doraszelski, and Lewis Segal. 2000. "Black/White Differences in Wealth." *Economic Perspectives* 4(1): 38–50.

Bajari, Patrick, and Matthew E. Kahn. 2005. "Estimating Housing Demand with an Application to Explaining Racial Segregation in Cities." *Journal of Business and Economic Statistics* 23: 20–33.

Bayer, Patrick, Robert McMillan, and Kim Rueben. 2004. "What Drives Racial Segregation? New Evidence Using Census Microdata." *Journal of Urban Economics* 56(3): 514–535.

Bishaw, Ale, and John Iceland. 2003. *Poverty: 1999.* U.S. Census Bureau, Census 2000 Brief Series, C2KBR-19.

Bobo, Lawrence, and Camille Zubrinsky. 1996. "Attitudes on Residential Integration: Perceived Status Differences, Mere In-Group Preference, or Racial Prejudice?" *Social Forces* 74(3): 883–909.

Charles, Camille Zubrinsky. 2000. "Neighborhood Racial Composition Preferences: Evidence from a Multiethnic Metropolis." *Social Problems* 47: 379–407.

Clark, William A. V. 1986. "Residential Segregation in American Cities: A Review and Interpretation." *Population Research and Policy Review* 5(2): 95–127.

Cutler, David M., and Edward L. Glaeser. 1997. "Are Ghettos Good or Bad?" *Quarterly Journal of Economics* 112(3): 827.

Cutler, David, Edward Glaeser, and Jacob Vigdor. 1999. "The Rise and Decline of the American Ghetto," *Journal of Political Economy* 107: 455–506.

Denton, Nancy, and Douglas Massey. 1988. "The Dimensions of Residential Segregation." *Social Forces* 67: 281–315.

Denton, Nancy, and Douglas Massey. 1989. "Racial Identity among Caribbean Hispanics: The Effect of Double Minority Status on Residential Segregation." *American Sociological Review* 54: 790–808.

Ellen, Ingrid Gould. 2000a. "A New White Flight? The Dynamics of Neighborhood Change in the 1980s." In Nancy Foner, Ruben G. Rumbaut, and Steven J. Gold, eds., *Immigration Research for a New Century: Multidisciplinary Perspectives.* New York City: Russell Sage Foundation, pp. 423–441.

Ellen, Ingrid Gould. 2000b. *Sharing America's Neighborhoods: The Prospects for Stable Racial Integration.* Cambridge, MA: Harvard University Press.

Ellen, Ingrid Gould. 2000c. "Is Segregation Bad for Your Health? The Case of Low Birthweight." *Brookings-Wharton Papers on Urban Affairs*: 203–238.

Ellen, Ingrid Gould. 2007. "How Integrated Did We Become during the 1990s?" In John M. Goering, ed., *Fragile Rights in Cities.* Lanham, MD: Rowman and Littlefield, pp. 123–142.

Emerson, Michael O., Karen J. Chai, and George Yancey. 2001. "Does Race Matter in Racial Segregation? Exploring the Preferences of White Americans." *American Sociological Review* 66: 922–935.

Farley, John E. 1986. "Segregated City, Segregated Suburbs: To What Extent Are They Products of Black-White Socioeconomic Differentials?" *Urban Geography* 2: 180–187.

Farley, Reynolds. 1996. "Racial Differences in the Search for Housing: Do Whites and Blacks Use the Same Techniques to Find Housing?" *Housing Policy Debate* 7(2): 367–385.

Farley, Reynolds, Howard Schuman, Suzanne Bianchi, Diane Colasanto, and Shirley Hatchett. 1978. "Chocolate Cities, Vanilla Suburbs: Will the Trend toward Racially Separate Communities Continue?" *Social Science Research* 7: 319–344.

Farley, Reynolds, Charlotte Steeh, Tara Jackson, Maria Krysan, and Keith Reeves. 1993. "Continued Residential Segregation in Detroit: 'Chocolate City, Vanilla Suburbs' Revisited." *Journal of Housing Research* 4 (1993).

Farley, Reynolds, Charlotte Steeh, Tara Jackson, Maria Krysan, and Keith Reeves. 1994. "Stereotypes and Segregation: Neighborhoods in the Detroit Area." *American Journal of Sociology* 100: 750–780.

Gabriel, Stuart A., and Stuart S. Rosenthal. 1989. "Household Location and Race: Estimates of a Multinomial Logit Model." *Review of Economics and Statistics* 71: 240–249.

Galster, George. 1979. "Interracial Differences in Housing Preferences." *Regional Science Perspectives* 9(1): 1–17.

Galster, George. 1982. "Black and White Preferences for Neighborhood Racial Composition." *AREUEA Journal* 10: 39–66.

Galster, George. 1988. "Residential Segregation in American Cities: A Contrary Review." *Population Research and Policy Review* 7: 93–112.

Galster, George, Fred Freiberg, and Diane Houk. 1987. "Racial Differences in Real Estate Advertising Practices: An Exploratory Case Study." *Journal of Urban Affairs* 9: 199–215.

Glaeser, Edward, and Jacob Vigdor. 2001. *Racial Segregation in the 2000 Census: Promising News.* Washington, DC: Brookings Institution Center on Urban and Metropolitan Policy.

Iceland, John, and Daniel Weinberg with Erica Steinmetz. 2002. *Racial and Ethnic Residential Segregation in the United States: 1980–2000.* U.S. Census Bureau Special Reports, Washington, DC.

Ihlanfeldt, Keith, and Benjamin Scafidi. 2002. "Black Self-Segregation as a Cause of Housing Segregation: Evidence from the Multi-City Study of Urban Inequality." *Journal of Urban Economics* 51: 366–390.

Kain, John F. 1976. "Race, Ethnicity, and Residential Location." In Ronald Grieson, ed., *Public and Urban Economics*, Lexington, MA: Lexington Books, pp. 267–292.

Kain, John F. 1986. "The Influence of Race and Income on Racial Segregation and Housing Policy." In John M. Goering, ed., *Housing Desegregation and Federal Policy.* Chapel Hill, NC: University of North Carolina Press, pp. 99–118.

Kain, John F., and John M. Quigley. 1975. *Housing Markets and Racial Discrimination: A Microeconomic Analysis.* New York: Columbia University Press.

Krysan, Maria, and Reynolds Farley. 2002. "The Residential Preferences of Blacks: Do They Explain Persistent Segregation?" *Social Forces* 80(3): 937–980.

Lewis Mumford Center. 2001. "Ethnic Diversity Grows, Neighborhood Integration Lags Behind." Available at http://mumford.albany.edu/census/report.html.

Malone, Nolan, Kaari F. Baluja, Joseph M. Costanzo, and Cynthia J. Davis. 2003. "The Foreign-Born Population: 2000." U.S. Census Bureau: Census 2000 Brief.

Massey, Douglas S. 1979. "Effects of Socioeconomic Factors on the Residential Segregation of Blacks and Spanish Americans in United States Urbanized Areas." *American Sociological Review* 44: 1015–1022.

Massey, Douglas S., and B. Bitterman. 1985. "Explaining the Paradox of Puerto Rican Segregation." *Social Forces* 64(2): 306–331.

Massey, Douglas S., and Nancy Denton. 1993. *American Apartheid.* Cambridge, MA: Harvard University Press.

Newburger, Harriet. 1981. "The Nature and Extent of Racial Steering Practices in U.S. Housing Markets." Unpublished manuscript.

Newburger, Harriet. 1999. "Mobility Patterns of Lower Income First-Time Homebuyers in Philadelphia." *Cityscape* 4: 201–220.

O'Regan, Katherine, and John Quigley. 1996. "Teenage Employment and the Spatial Isolation of Minority and Poverty Households." *Journal of Human Resources* 31: 692–702.

Patterson, Orlando. 1997. The Ordeal of Integration: Progress and Resentment in America's "Racial" Crisis. Cambridge, MA: Harvard University Press.

Sampson, Robert, and Stephen W. Raudenbush. 2004. "Seeing Disorder: Neighborhood Stigma and the Social Construction of 'Broken Windows.'" Social Psychology Quarterly 67(4): 319–342.

Schuman, Howard, Charlotte Steeh, Lawrence Bobo, and Maria Krysan. 1997. Racial Attitudes in America: Trends and Interpretations. Cambridge, MA: Harvard University Press.

South, Scott, Kyle Crowder, and Erick Chavez. 2006. "Wealth, Race, and Inter-Neighbourhood Migration." American Sociological Review 71 (February): 72–94.

Taeuber, Karl E., and Alma F. Taeuber. 1965. Negroes in Cities: Residential Segregation and Neighborhood Change. New York: Atheneum.

Turner, Margery Austin, and Stephen L. Ross. 2003. Discrimination in Metropolitan Housing Markets: Phase 2—Asians and Pacific Islanders. Final Report Submitted to U.S. Department of Housing and Urban Development, Washington, DC.

Turner, Margery Austin, and Stephen L. Ross. 2004. "Housing Discrimination in Metropolitan America: Findings from the Latest National Paired Testing Study." University of Connecticut Working Paper.

Turner, Margery Austin, and Ron Wienk. 1993. "The Persistence of Segregation in Urban Areas: Contributing Causes." In G. Thomas Kingsley and Margery Austin Turner, eds., Housing Markets and Residential Mobility. Washington, DC: Urban Institute Press, pp. 193–216.

Turner, Margery Austin, Stephen L. Ross, George C. Galster, and John Yinger. 2002. Discrimination in Metropolitan Housing Markets: National Results from Phase 1 HDS 2000. Final Report Submitted to U.S. Department of Housing and Urban Development, Washington, DC.

Yinger, John. 1995. Closed Doors, Opportunities Lost: The Continuing Cost of Housing Discrimination. New York: Russell Sage Foundation Press.

The News Media and the Racialization of Poverty

By Martin Gilens

Editor's Introduction

Many Americans do not understand the dimensions of poverty in the United States. As Gilens notes in this reading, most Americans associate poverty with African Americans, but it was not always thus. He discusses the racialization of poverty—that is, how poverty came to be, and is, associated with African Americans. The news media have played an influential role in this process, while also generating opposition to poverty programs in general. This reading illustrates how the media are an important force in shaping views of issues related to race and ethnicity in our society.

A s we have seen, racial attitudes play a central role in generating opposition to welfare spending among white Americans and in shaping whites' views on many aspects of poverty and welfare. In this chapter I investigate the historical process by which race has come to dominate the public's thinking about the poor.

It might seem that this question is barely worth asking. After all, it is a simple fact that poor people in this country are disproportionately black. Yet African Americans constitute a small percentage of all Americans, and even though they are more likely to be poor than are whites, they nevertheless constitute a minority of both poor people (of whom 27 percent are black) and welfare recipients (of whom 36 percent are black).[1] As we saw in chapter 3, however, the public exaggerates the extent to which African Americans compose the poor. On average, Americans believe that blacks make up not 27 percent, but 50 percent of all poor people. In the following pages I explore the shifting images of the poor that have held sway during different periods of American history. I argue that the exaggerated link between blacks and the poor that now exists in the public's imagination developed only in the 1960s, and that it developed in response to a series of rather dramatic social changes and events. But I also argue that the racialization of poverty images in this period reflected a preexisting stereotype of blacks as lazy. As media discourse on poverty and welfare became more negative in the mid-1960s, the complexion of the poor grew darker.

African Americans: The Once Invisible Poor

The American public now associates poverty and welfare with blacks. But this was not always the case. Although African Americans have always been disproportionately poor, black poverty was ignored by white society throughout most of American history. The "scientific" study of poverty in America began around the end of the nineteenth century. During this period social reformers and poverty experts made the first systematic efforts to describe and analyze America's poor.[2] Racial distinctions were common in these works, but such distinctions usually referred to the various white European "races" such as the Irish, Italians, and Poles; this early poverty literature had little or nothing to say about blacks. The classic work from this era is Robert Hunter's book *Poverty,* published in 1904.[3] Hunter drew from the existing statistical and ethnographic accounts of poverty to paint a picture of the American poor at the turn of the century. Although Hunter spent considerable time discussing the work habits, nutritional needs, and intelligence of the Italians, Irish, Poles, Hungarians, Germans, and Jews, African Americans escaped his attention altogether.[4]

During the 1920s, African American migration from the rural South to northern cities began to accelerate. These growing black communities, and especially the emergence of Harlem as a highly visible urban black neighborhood, brought some attention to African American poverty. According to one study, white America's "revolutionary recognition" of black life and culture in the 1920s was evident in the popular white-oriented periodicals of the day. During this period popular mass-circulation magazines printed numerous stories on Negro life and culture.[5] But this increased attention focused more on blacks as symbols of the Jazz Age and on Harlem as a place of "laughing, swaying, and dancing."[6] White Americans remained profoundly uninformed and unconcerned about black poverty.

The Great Depression, of course, brought the topic of poverty to the forefront of public attention. But as the American economy faltered, and poverty and unemployment increased, white writers and commentators remained oblivious to the sufferings of the black poor. For example, I. M. Rubinow's *Quest for Security*, published in the middle of the depression and often cited in subsequent literature on poverty, made no mention of blacks.[7] Although poverty remained a pressing concern during the 1940s, the bombing of Pearl Harbor and America's subsequent entrance into World War II naturally focused public concern elsewhere.

During the postwar period, the country's attention turned to rebuilding the domestic economy and fighting communism both at home and abroad. Poverty seemed like a distant problem during the postwar years. The economy grew dramatically after the war, and living standards rose quickly. By one estimate, poverty in the United States declined from 48 percent in 1935, to 27 percent in 1950, to 21 percent in 1960.[8] Along with economic growth came lifestyle changes. By 1960, 86 percent of American homes had televisions, automobile ownership had increased as the population shifted toward suburbs, and middle-class Americans had become homeowners on a scale never seen before.[9] Few people worried about those being left behind during America's postwar growth. In the 1950s Americans—and American journalists—were busy celebrating

"The American Century"; *Time, Newsweek* and *U.S. News and World Report* each published an average of just sixteen stories about poverty *for the entire decade.*[10]

Poverty was "rediscovered," however, in the 1960s. Stimulated first by the publication of John Kenneth Galbraith's *The Affluent Society* (in 1958) and then by Michael Harrington's *The Other America* (in 1962), the American public and policy makers alike began once more to notice the poor. John Kennedy is said to have been shaken by the grinding poverty he saw in West Virginia during the 1960 presidential campaign, where a lack of both education and job opportunities had trapped generations of poor whites in the primitive conditions of rural poverty.[11] And early in his presidency Kennedy launched a number of antipoverty programs focusing on juvenile delinquency, education and training programs, and federal assistance for depressed regions of the country. But the poverty programs of the early 1960s, and the popular images of the poor that went along with them, were just as pale in complexion as those of the turn of the century. Attention to poor blacks was still quite limited both in the mass media and, apparently, among Kennedy administration staffers.[12] If there was a dominant image of poverty at this time, it was the white rural poor of the Appalachian coal fields.

Background Conditions for the Racialization of Poverty

Popular images of poverty changed dramatically, however, in the mid-1960s. After centuries of obscurity, at least as far as white America was concerned, poor blacks came to dominate public thinking about poverty. Two social changes set the stage for the "racialization" of popular images of the poor. The first was the widespread migration of rural southern blacks to northern cities. At the turn of the twentieth century, over 90 percent of African Americans lived in the South, and three-quarters of all blacks resided in rural areas.[13] Blacks had been leaving the South at a slow rate for decades, but black migration from the South grew tremendously during the 1940s and 1950s. The average black out-migration from the South between 1910 and 1939 was only 55,000 people per year. But during the 1940s it increased to 160,000 per year, during the 1950s it declined slightly (to 146,000 per year), and between 1960 and 1966 it fell to 102,000 per year.[14] As a consequence of this migration, African Americans, who accounted for only 2 percent of all northerners in 1910, comprised 7 percent by 1960, and, perhaps more importantly, made up 12 percent of the population in urban areas.[15]

As a result of migration, the population of northern, urban blacks grew steadily during the 1940s and 1950s and continued to grow, though at a slower rate, in the 1960s. But as we will see below, the racialization of public images of the poor occurred fairly suddenly and dramatically between 1965 and 1967. Clearly there is no simple connection between the growth of African American communities in northern cities and public perceptions of the poor as black. Nevertheless, the growth of the black population in the North was one link in a chain of events that led to the dramatic changes in how Americans thought about poverty.

A second change that paved the way for the racialization of poverty images was the changing racial composition of AFDC, the nation's most conspicuous program to aid the poor. As established in the Social Security Act of 1935, the ADC program (as it was then called) was structured in such a way as to permit states to limit the number of black recipients. Individual states were allowed considerable discretion to determine both the formal rules governing ADC eligibility and the application of those rules. At the insistence of southern legislators, the clause mandating that ADC provide "a reasonable subsistence compatible with health and decency" was removed from the Social Security Act, thereby allowing states with large black populations to provide extremely low benefits.[16] In 1940 the national average ADC payment was about $13.00 per month per child; in contrast, black children in Arkansas were receiving only $3.52 per month while those in South

Carolina were getting just over $4 per month.[17] Other southern states also established very low benefit levels, with payments for black children averaging between five and eight dollars per month.[18]

In addition to imposing low benefit levels for black families, states excluded many black mothers from ADC by the discretionary application of "suitable home" policies.[19] These policies gave caseworkers wide latitude to deny ADC benefits to families with children born out of wedlock or to mothers thought to be engaged in illicit relationships. Furthermore, despite the fact that ADC was envisioned as a program to assist single mothers so that they could devote their time to raising their children rather than working for a wage, some southern states provided only seasonal benefits to blacks, eliminating assistance when additional labor was needed in the fields during harvest time.[20]

As a result of these various policies, African Americans were disproportionately excluded from ADC. In 1936 only 13.5 percent of ADC recipients were African American, despite blacks' much higher representation among poor single mothers.[21] Over the next three decades, however, the proportion of blacks among ADC recipients rose steadily (figure 13.1). This increase resulted from a variety of influences, both legislative and economic. For example, the establishment of Social Security survivors' benefits in 1939 removed proportionately more white than black widows from the ADC rolls, thereby increasing the percentage of blacks among those remaining.[22] In addition, an increase in the federal matching-grant contribution to the ADC program from one-third to one-half of total state ADC expenditures encouraged some states to expand their coverage or to begin participating in the ADC program for the first time.[23]

As figure 13.1 shows, the percentage of African Americans among ADC/AFDC recipients increased steadily from about 14 percent in 1936 to about 46 percent in 1973; thereafter the proportion of blacks declines slowly until it reached about 36 percent in 1995. Between the mid-1960s and early 1970s, then, African Americans made up a very substantial minority of AFDC recipients. Consequently as the welfare rolls began to expand in the late 1960s (figure 13.2), the public's attention was drawn disproportionately to poor blacks. Yet the pattern of growth in the proportion of African American welfare recipients shown in figure 13.1 also makes clear that the sudden shift in images of poverty during the 1960s cannot be attributed to any sudden change in the makeup of the welfare population. The proportion of blacks among AFDC participants had been growing steadily for decades. Like black migration to the North, the changing racial composition of the welfare rolls constituted a background condition that contributed to the changes in public perceptions of the poor, but it did not serve as a precipitating cause of those changes. After all, the proportion of blacks among welfare recipients was almost as high in 1960 as it was in 1967, yet public concern in 1960 was still focused on poor whites, in particular, the poor rural whites of Appalachia.

Precipitating Events in the Racialization of Poverty

Gradual demographic changes in residential patterns and welfare receipt by African Americans laid the groundwork for the changes to come in how Americans viewed the poor. But the more immediate precipitating events were the shift in focus within the civil rights movement from the fight for legal equality to the battle for economic equality and the urban riots that rocked the country during the summers of 1964 through 1968.

In the 1950s, African Americans living in the South attended segregated schools, rode segregated buses, and used segregated bathrooms. Blacks could not drink from "white" water fountains, eat in "white" restaurants, or sleep in "white" hotels. African Americans had little voice in government and little hope for fair treatment from the white police or the white judiciary. In the North, legal segregation of the races was less common, but racial discrimination by individuals, governments, and other institutions maintained high levels of both residential and school segregation.[24]

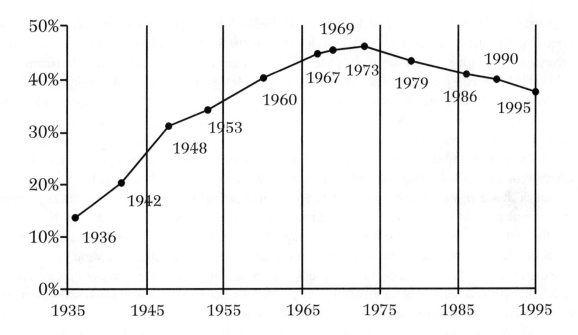

Figure 13.1 Percentage African American among ADC/AFDC Recipients, 1936–1995

Sources: For 1936–53 and 1967–79, Turner, *Federal/State Aid to Dependent Children;* for 1960, Piven and Cloward, *Regulating the Poor;* for 1986–95, U.S. House of Representatives, 1998 Green Book.

Some progress toward racial equality did occur in the immediate postwar years. Fair-employment laws were adopted in twelve states and thirty cities by 1953; median black family income rose from 41 percent of white family income in 1940 to 57 percent by 1952; and school enrollment among blacks increased from 68 percent in 1940 to 75 percent by 1950, only four percentage points lower than white school enrollment.[25] But the South in particular remained steadfast in its resistance to racial equality and its commitment to the *de jure* separatism of Jim Crow. Black protests against racial injustice had been sporadic in the early decades of the twentieth century and had largely died out during World War II. But in the mid-1950s, the modern civil rights movement began a concerted and sustained effort to force an end to the injustice and indignities of racial segregation. In December 1955, Rosa Parks, a black seamstress, was jailed for refusing to vacate her seat on a segregated bus. Ms. Parks' quiet protest began the Montgomery Bus Boycott, led by a previously unknown young black minister named Martin Luther King Jr. The eventual success of the year-long bus boycott led to a decade of demonstrations, protests, and sit-ins throughout the South, all pressing the demand for legal equality and an end to racial segregation.

The struggles of the early civil rights movement were for equal rights, black enfranchisement, and an end to legal segregation. These efforts produced their most significant successes with the passage of the Civil Rights Act of 1964 and the Voting Rights Act of 1965. The Civil Rights Act prohibited segregation in public accommodations and banned discrimination by trade unions and schools, and by employers involved in interstate commerce or doing business with the federal government. It also called for the desegregation of public schools and outlawed some of the voting procedures used to impede African Americans. The Voting Rights Act, passed the following year, banned literacy tests and established federal government oversight of registration and voting in jurisdictions with low voter turnout (primarily southern counties with high proportions of blacks). As a consequence of these and other legal measures, nationwide voter registration rates among African Americans increased from only 29 percent in 1962 to 67 percent in 1970.[26]

In the second half of the 1960s, civil rights leaders shifted their attention from legal inequality to economic inequality. Although the battle for black enfranchisement in the South had a long way to go, the first large urban uprisings during the summer of 1964 and the greater number of ghetto riots during the summers to follow shifted both the geographical and programmatic focus of the struggle for racial equality.

Of course, racial economic inequality was hardly a new concern to civil rights leaders. In 1963 the National Urban League had called for a "crash program of special effort to close the gap between the conditions of Negro and white citizens" and released a ten-point "Marshall Plan for the American Negro." In the same year, Martin Luther King issued a similarly conceived "G.I. Bill of Rights for the Disadvantaged."[27] But these early efforts were almost wholly overshadowed by the struggle for basic civil rights in the South.

In 1966, however, Martin Luther King and the Southern Christian Leadership Conference (SCLC) focused their attention on the plight of the black urban poor of the northern ghettos. With help from the AFL-CIO and the United Auto Workers, King and the SCLC organized demonstrations and rent strikes in Chicago to dramatize the dire economic conditions facing so many urban blacks. King called for a variety of measures aimed at improving the lot of Chicago's black population: integrating the *de facto* segregated public schools, reallocating public services to better serve minority populations, building low-rent public housing units, and removing public funds from banks that refused to make loans to blacks.[28]

For all his efforts, King achieved little in Chicago. Mayor Richard Daley claimed his administration was already making the necessary efforts to improve life for low-income blacks; the more moderate local civil rights organizations resented King's intrusion and the attention he received; and black militants called King a sell-out for compromising with the white political powers. But the concern with northern urban blacks' economic problems exemplified by the Chicago Freedom Movement and the 1968 Poor People's March on Washington (led, after King's assassination, by Ralph Abernathy) helped to focus public attention on the problem of black poverty.[29]

At least as important as the shifting focus of civil rights leaders were the ghetto riots themselves. Poor blacks, for so long invisible to most of white America, made their presence known in the most dramatic way possible. During the summer of 1964 riots broke out in Harlem, Rochester, Chicago, Philadelphia, and New Jersey. Five lives were lost and property damage was estimated at $6 million.[30] Civil rights leaders tried to respond to these disturbances, but much of their attention, and the rest of the country's as well, was still focused on the South. The Voting Rights Act had been passed, but much work remained in actually registering black voters. Mississippi, in particular, had been staunchly resisting blacks' efforts to vote.

To press for voting rights in Mississippi, the leading civil rights organizations united to mobilize local blacks and out-of-state volunteers for the Freedom Summer of 1964. Nine hundred volunteers, many of them white college students from the country's elite universities, joined the effort to register Mississippi's blacks. White Mississippi responded with violence. Twenty-seven black churches were burned that summer in Mississippi, and thirty blacks were murdered between January and August of 1964. But the nation's attention was grabbed by the murder of three young civil rights workers—James Chaney, Andrew Goodman, and Michael Schwerner—the first a black Mississippian, the other two white New Yorkers. The three disappeared while returning from an investigation of the burned-out Mt. Zion Methodist Church in Neshoba County, Mississippi. Only after a six-week search by the FBI were their bodies found, buried in an earthen dam.[31]

Despite the riots, news coverage of race relations during the summer of 1964 was dominated by the events in Mississippi. But in the next few years, ghetto uprisings and the militant voices of Malcolm X, Stokeley Carmichael, and the Black Panthers would become increasingly central fixtures in the struggle for racial equality. In August 1965, the Los Angeles neighborhood of Watts exploded. A six-day riot left 34 people dead (all but three of them black), 900 injured, and nearly 4,000 arrested, and caused $30 million in property damage.[32] The Watts riots were followed that summer by more disturbances in Chicago and in Springfield, Massachusetts. The summers of 1966 and 1967 saw even more rioting, as blacks took to the streets in dozens of American cities. In 1967 alone, rioting led to at least 90 deaths, more than 4,000 injuries, and nearly 17,000 arrests.[33]

There is no doubt that the rioting of the mid-1960s marked a dramatic chapter in American race relations. But the impact of the riots on white Americans' attitudes toward blacks remains subject to debate. Some see the urban riots of the 1960s as ushering in a new era of antiblack racism. Donald Kinder and Lynn Sanders, for example, point out that blacks and whites reacted very differently to the riots, which blacks tended to see as expressions of legitimate grievances, and whites, as senseless violence.[34] Yet survey-based studies reveal little that could be interpreted as a negative shift in whites' racial attitudes during this period. On the contrary, the many survey questions on racial attitudes that span the period of the mid-1960s show either no change or a liberal shift in whites' attitudes.[35] As one in-depth study of the Watts riots concluded, "The very sharp polarization that did occur immediately over blacks' tactics, and particularly over the rioting, apparently did not generalize into more negative or resistant white attitudes toward blacks and their progress. Indeed, if anything, whites' support for blacks' progress seemed, in the long run, to have increased somewhat."[36]

The ghetto riots of the mid-1960s were played out before a rapt television audience, and blacks and whites often drew different conclusions from the upheavals they witnessed. But even if the riots had little lasting impact on white Americans' racial views, there is no question that the ghetto revolts of 1964–67 helped bring the black urban poor to the forefront of American social problems.

Portrayals of Poverty in the News Media

It is clear that the black poor were ignored by white Americans throughout most of our history, including the first two-thirds of the twentieth century, and it is equally clear that blacks now figure prominently in public perceptions of the poor. But did Americans' images of the poor really change dramatically between the early and late 1960s as the historical narrative I have outlined would suggest? Unfortunately, pollsters did not think to ask about perceptions of the racial composition of the poor until recently. But we can examine changes in the way the poor have been portrayed in the mass media. While we cannot assume that media portrayals necessarily reflect popular beliefs, changing images of the poor in the news can tell us how news professionals thought about the poor at different times, as well as what sorts of images of poverty the public was being exposed to through the mass media. Since we have good reason to think that media portrayals have a strong impact on public perceptions (see chapter 6), news images provide at least some evidence of how the American public viewed the poor. At the very least, media coverage will tell us something about the aspects of poverty (or the subgroups of the poor) that played a prominent role in public discussion of these issues during different periods.

To assess changes in news media portrayals of poverty over the past forty-five years, I examined three weekly newsmagazines, *Time, Newsweek,* and *U.S. News and World Report.* I chose these magazines because they are widely read, are national in coverage and distribution, and have been published continuously for many decades. They also contain large numbers of pictures, an especially important consideration in studying the racial portrayal of the poor. To the extent that our interest lies in the perceptions of the racial composition of the poor that magazine readers are likely to form, the pictures of poor people are more influential than the textual information these magazines contain. First, the typical reader of these magazines looks at most, if not all, of the pictures but reads far fewer of the stories. Thus, even a subscriber who does not bother to read a particular story on poverty is quite likely to see the pictures of poor people that it contains.[37] Second, while specific information about the racial makeup of the poor is found periodically in these newsmagazines, such information is quite rare. Between 1960 and 1990, fewer than 5 percent of poverty-related stories had any concrete information on the racial composition of the poor or any subgroups of the poor, such as AFDC recipients or public housing tenants.[38] Finally, research on the impact of news stories and the process by which readers (or TV viewers) assimilate information suggests that people are more likely to remember pictures than words and more likely to form impressions based on examples of specific individuals than on abstract statistical information.[39]

To assess media portrayals of poverty, I first identified every poverty-related story in these three magazines published from 1950 through 1992. Using the *Readers' Guide to Periodical Literature*, I developed a set of core topics, including "poor," "poverty," "welfare," and "relief." For each year, stories indexed under these topics as well as cross-references to related topics were collected. In all, 1,256 stories were found under 73 different index topics.[40] Note that the stories selected for this analysis were only those that focused directly on poverty or related topics. Many stories with a primary focus on race relations, civil rights, urban riots, or other racial topics also included discussions of poverty, but in these contexts readers would expect to find coverage of black poverty in particular and might not draw conclusions about the nature of American poverty in general. By excluding race-related stories, however, this analysis provides a conservative estimate of the extent to which African Americans populate media images of the poor.

Newsmagazine coverage of poverty varied dramatically across this time period. The thick line in figure 13.2 shows the average number of stories on poverty for these newsmagazines for each year from 1950 through 1992. The lack of interest in poverty during the 1950s is apparent; in five of these ten years only a single story on poverty appeared in each magazine, and in no year did more than three stories on poverty appear. Equally clear from figure 5.2 is the first brief spike in media coverage of poverty in response to the Kennedy administration's efforts in 1961 and the much more dramatic growth in media attention to poverty beginning in 1964. The increase in poverty stories in the 1960s was clearly a response to the political initiatives of the Kennedy and Johnson administrations rather than a reaction to any growth in the severity of poverty in America. Indeed, as the thin line in figure 13.2 shows, the poverty rate was declining during this period and continued to decline, more or less steadily, until 1973.

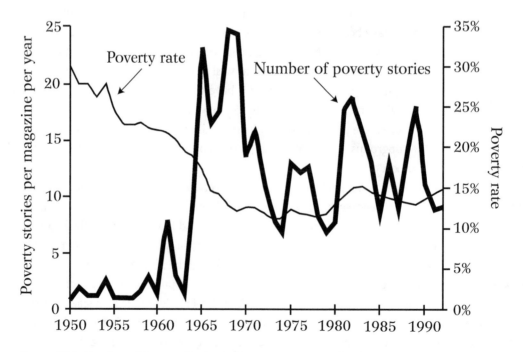

Figure 13.2 Number of Poverty Stories in Newsmagazines and U.S. Poverty Rate, 1950–1992.

Sources: Poverty rate—Murray, *Losing Ground*, p. 245; U.S. Bureau of the Census, *Statistical Abstract: 1995*, p. 480. Poverty stories—*Time, Newsweek,* and *U.S. News and World Report.*

To determine the racial content of newsmagazine coverage of poverty, I identified each poor person pictured in each of these stories as black, nonblack, or undeterminable. In all, 6,117 poor individuals were depicted in the 1,256 poverty stories, and of these race could be determined for 4,388, or 72 percent (poor people for whom race could not be determined are excluded from the results reported below).[41] The three magazines differed in the number of poverty stories published during this period, with *U.S. News and World Report* running 549 stories, *Newsweek*, 391, and *Time*, 316. The percentage of blacks among pictures of the poor was similar at each magazine, however, ranging from 52 percent in *U.S. News and World Report* to 57 percent in *Time*.[42] Combining the coverage of poverty from the three magazines, over half (53.4 percent) of all poor people pictured during these four and a half decades were African American. In reality, the average percentage of African Americans among the poor during this period was 29.3 percent.[43]

Magazine portrayals overrepresent African Americans in pictures of the poor, but the degree of over-representation of blacks has not been constant throughout this period. The thick line in figure 13.3 shows the variation in the percentage of African Americans pictured in poverty stories in *Time*, *Newsweek*, and *U.S. News and World Report* from 1950 through 1992. (Adjacent years with small numbers of poverty stories are combined to smooth out the random fluctuations that result when the percentage of blacks is calculated from a small number of pictures.) Images of poverty in these magazines did change quite dramatically in he mid-1960s. From the beginning of this study through 1964, poor people were portrayed as predominately white. But starting in 1965 the complexion of the poor turned decidedly darker. From only 27 percent in 1964, the proportion of African Americans in pictures of the poor increased to 49 percent and 53 percent in 1965 and 1966, and then to 72 percent in 1967. Nor has the portrayal of the poor returned to its previous predominately white orientation. Although there have been important declines and fluctuations in the extent

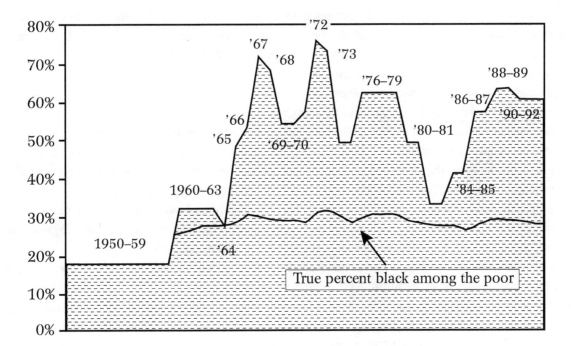

Figure 13.3 Percent African American in Newsmagazine Pictures of the Poor, 1950–1992 (compared with true percent black)

Sources: True percent black—Baugher and Lamison-White, *Poverty in the United States: 1995*, pp. C2–C4. Magazine pictures—*Time, Newsweek*, and *U.S. News and World Report*.

to which blacks have been overrepresented in pictures of poverty (which we will explore shortly), African Americans have generally dominated news media images of the poor since the late 1960s. From 1967 through 1992, blacks averaged 57 percent of the poor people pictured in these three magazines—about twice the true proportion of blacks among the nation's poor.

Early Newsmagazine Coverage of Poverty: 1950–1964

Newsmagazines in the 1950s contained few stories on poverty and few pictures of blacks in the stories that were published. Between 1950 and 1959, only 18 percent of the poor people pictured in these magazines were African American. The increased attention to poverty in the early 1960s was accompanied by some increase in the proportion of blacks depicted among the poor, but this racialization of poverty images was quite modest compared with what was to come.Newsmagazine coverage of poverty was generally rather sparse between 1960 and 1963. The exception was 1961, when a total of twenty-four poverty-related stories appeared in the three magazines (more than in 1960, 1962, and 1963 combined). Much of the press attention to poverty in 1961 was in response to the Kennedy administration's anti-poverty initiatives, with coverage focusing on a new housing bill, the revival of the depression-era food stamp program, and federal aid for distressed areas. These policy-focused stories were illustrated almost exclusively with pictures of poor whites.

A second theme in media coverage of poverty during 1960–63 was welfare abuse and efforts to reduce it. Some of these stories focused on Senator Robert Byrd's 1962 investigation into welfare fraud in Washington D.C., which uncovered welfare recipients who spent their benefits on alcohol or who were secretly living with boyfriends that welfare investigators found hiding in closets or bathrooms. Pictures of poor blacks and poor whites were both found in these strongly antiwelfare stories.

Finally, five of the forty-one stories published from 1960 through 1963 focused on the controversial "crackdown" on welfare by Joseph Mitchell, the city manager of Newburgh, New York. Mitchell claimed that recent black migrants from the South were swelling Newburgh's public assistance rolls. In response he instituted a thirteen-point program aimed at removing as many people from welfare as possible. Not surprisingly, coverage of Newburgh was illustrated with pictures of blacks (although *Newsweek* did point out that in fact 60 percent of relief recipients in Newburgh were white).

Newsmagazine coverage of poverty in the early 1960s presaged later coverage in two ways. First, stories on new policy initiatives tended to be both neutral in tone and dominated by images of whites. This was the case with the Kennedy administration's programs during 1961, and it was repeated in coverage of the Johnson administration's War on Poverty three years later. In contrast, the more critical stories about existing programs, such as reports on the Byrd committee's investigation of welfare abuse, were more likely to contain pictures of blacks. Once again, this pattern is repeated in the later 1960s, as largely negative "field reports" from the War on Poverty programs start to appear in the media.

News coverage of poverty expanded dramatically beginning in 1964 and reached its height between 1965 and 1969. Without question the impetus for this growth in coverage was the Johnson administration's War on Poverty, announced in January 1964. Almost four-fifths of all poverty-related stories published in 1964 dealt explicitly with the War on Poverty, as did a majority of the poverty-related articles appearing in 1965 and 1966. By 1967, stories about urban problems and urban redevelopment had become an important component of poverty coverage, but stories on welfare, jobs programs, and other aspects of the War on Poverty continued to account for most of the poverty-related news coverage.

For our purposes, the most significant aspects of news stories on poverty in 1964 were the strong focus on the War on Poverty and the continued portrayal of the poor as predominantly white. A good example of this overall tendency is the most substantial poverty story of the year, a twelve-page cover story called "Poverty, U.S.A." that *Newsweek* ran on February 17.[44] The cover of the magazine showed a white girl, perhaps eight or ten years old, looking out at the reader from a rustic shack, her hair disheveled and her face covered with dirt. As this picture suggests, the story had a strong focus on Appalachia, but it profiled a variety of poor people from around the country. Yet of the fifty-four poor people pictured in this story, only fourteen were black.[45] Significantly, the poor white people who appeared in this story resided in both urban and rural areas; there were, for example, six photos of poor whites from Appalachia as well as photos of a thirty-seven-year-old "Main Street wino" from Los Angeles, an unemployed father of five from Detroit, and an "old lady alone with poverty" in San Francisco.

This story was typical of War on Poverty coverage during 1964 in its substantial focus on rural poverty, its emphasis on images of poor whites, and its generally neutral tone toward the Johnson administration's antipoverty efforts. Like this story, most of the early coverage of the War on Poverty consisted of descriptions of antipoverty programs, profiles of Johnson's "poverty warriors," and accounts of poverty in America, most often illustrated with examples of individual poor people. Clearly, the expansion of news coverage that accompanied the War on Poverty did not coincide with the racialization of poverty images. At its inception at least, the War on Poverty was not portrayed by the news media as a program for blacks.

The Racialization of Poverty in the News: 1965–1967

The year 1965 saw another large jump in media attention to poverty and a clear turning point in the racialization of poverty images in the news. The percentage of blacks among pictures of the poor jumped from 27 percent in 1964 to 49 percent in 1965. One factor that clearly does *not* explain the larger number of poor African Americans in the news during this period is true change in the proportion of blacks among the poor. As the thin line in figure 13.3 shows, the true percentage of blacks among the poor increased only marginally between the early and late 1960s (from 27 percent to 30 percent), while the percentage of blacks found in news magazine portrayals of the poor more than doubled during this period.

The most conspicuous change in the coverage of poverty between 1964 and 1965 is the tone of stories covering welfare and the War on Poverty. Whereas coverage in 1964 focused on the initiation of the War on Poverty and general descriptions of the American poor, stories in 1965 were much more critical examinations of the government's anti-poverty efforts. Three lines of criticism were prominent: First, many stories questioned Sargent Shriver's leadership of the antipoverty effort, focusing on mismanagement, confusion, and waste in the Office of Economic Opportunity. Second, considerable attention was devoted to local disputes between city government and community groups over control of War on Poverty resources. Finally, substantial coverage focused on difficulties within the Job Corps program, one of the first War on Poverty programs to get off the ground. General stories on the War on Poverty and stories about problems in the Job Corps accounted for most of the poor people pictured in early 1965. Fifty percent of the poor pictured in War on Poverty stories during this period were black, as were 55 percent of those in stories on the Job Corps.

We saw above that media coverage from the early 1960s tended to use pictures of poor blacks to illustrate stories about waste, inefficiency, or abuse of welfare, and pictures of poor whites in stories with more neutral descriptions of antipoverty programs. This pattern is repeated in 1964 and 1965 as coverage of the War on Poverty becomes more critical and portrayals of the poor become "more black." This association of African Americans with negative stories on poverty is clearest in coverage of the Job Corps. The most visible of the War on Poverty's numerous job training programs, the Job Corps consisted of dozens of residential centers in both urban and rural locations at which young men (and less often, young women) were to learn discipline along with basic job skills.

News coverage of the Job Corps program focused on problems such as poor screening of participants, inadequate facilities, and high dropout rates. But the most sensational objections concerned the behavior of Job Corps members and the aversion to Job Corps centers by nearby towns. For example, a long story in *U.S. News and World Report* published in July 1965 (and illustrated with about equal numbers of blacks and nonblacks) reported charges of "rowdyism" at Job Corps centers, including a dormitory riot in Tongue Point, Oregon, "in which lead pipes were hurled" and the alcohol-related expulsion of eight girls from a St. Petersburg, Florida, center. "Another worry," the story indicated, was the "antagonism between Corpsmen and nearby townsmen." People in Astoria, Oregon, for example, "complained about hearing obscene language at the movie theater," while residents of Marion, Illinois, were upset about a disturbance at a roller skating rink that occurred when some Job Corps members showed up with liquor. Although these incidents were not explicitly linked to black Job Corps participants, the pictures of blacks in Job Corps stories (comprising 55 percent of all Job Corps members pictured) was much higher than the proportion of African Americans pictured in the more neutral stories about the War on Poverty from the previous year.[46]

As we will see, the pattern of associating negative poverty coverage with pictures of blacks persists over the years and is too widespread and consistent to be explained as the product of any particular anti poverty program or subgroup of the poor. But the sharp increase in the percentage of African Americans pictured in poverty stories in 1965 can also be attributed to the increasing involvement of civil rights leaders in the antipoverty effort. Neither the civil rights movement nor civil rights leaders were mentioned in any of the thirty-two poverty stories published in 1964, but during the first half of 1965 almost one-quarter (23 percent) of the poverty-related stories made some mention of black leaders. Most of these stories dealt with the battles for control over War on Poverty funds, especially, but not only, those channeled through the community action programs. Although the involvement of black community leaders was a minor element in news coverage of poverty from this period, it undoubtedly helped to shift the media's attention away from the previous years' focus on poor whites.

Coverage of poverty during the second half of 1965 was similar to that of early 1965 with two exceptions. First, the Watts riots, which began on August 11, intensified the growing awareness of black poverty in this country. Perhaps surprisingly, neither the Watts riots themselves nor the problems of inner-city blacks figured prominently in poverty coverage during the second half of 1965. Nevertheless, 26 percent of poverty stories from the latter half of 1965 did make at least a brief mention of the riots. The most common focus of poverty coverage during this period continued to be the War on Poverty. In addition, a number of stories covered the establishment of the Department of Housing and Urban Development (HUD) (but none of the eight stories on HUD and housing programs during this period contained pictures of poor people).

To more fully delineate changes in media coverage of poverty during the crucial years of 1964 through 1967, figure 13.4 shows the main subjects of newsmagazine poverty stories (with 1965 broken into two periods to compare pre-Watts and post-Watts coverage). In every year during the mid-1960s, the War on Poverty was the single most common poverty subject in these magazines, accounting for 45 percent of all poverty stories over these four years. As figure 13.4 shows, coverage of urban poverty did increase in 1966 and 1967 to the point where almost as many stories in 1967 were written on problems of the urban poor as on the War on Poverty. Thus part of the racialization of poverty during this period clearly concerns the growing focus on America's cities.

There is little evidence of an immediate change in media coverage of poverty after Watts. But coverage did change in response to the greater number of riots in the summers of 1966 and 1967. At least as important as the riots themselves were the reactions to those riots, particularly civil rights leaders' greater focus on urban poverty and the government's efforts to address the problems of the black ghettos, or at least to placate their

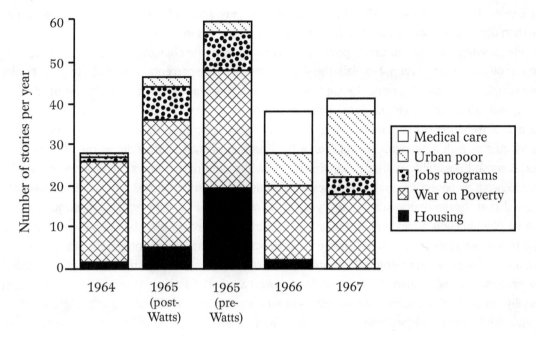

Figure 13.4 Subject Matter of Newsmagazine Poverty Stories, 1964–1967

Source: *Time, Newsweek,* and *U.S. News and World Report.*

residents. As table 13.1 indicates, the percentage of poverty stories that mentioned ghetto riots or civil rights leaders increased from 26 percent in 1965, to 31 percent in 1966, and 38 percent in 1967. (As table 13.1 also shows, the changing pictorial representation of the poor was paralleled by a growing tendency to mention African Americans within the text of poverty-related stories.)

How are we to understand the changing focus of poverty coverage over this four-year period and the concomitant racialization of poverty images? One possibility is that a series of events (e.g., riots, new government programs) led news organizations to focus on new aspects of poverty or new subgroups of the poor and that these subgroups happened to be disproportionately black. This explanation is almost surely true to some degree. For example, pictures of the poor in stories on urban poverty from 1964 through 1967 were 95 percent black. Consequently, the increase in urban poverty stories accounts for some part of the racialization of poverty coverage during this period. On the other hand, even if we exclude urban poverty stories, the percentage of blacks in pictures of the poor grew dramatically over these four years; as table 13.1 shows, of

Table 13.1 Racial Content of Newsmagazine Stories on Poverty, 1964–1967

	1964	1965	1966	1967
Percentage black in pictures of poor people	27	49	53	72
Percentage black in pictures of poor people, excluding stories on urban poverty	27	48	54	58
Percentage of stories mentioning blacks	29	51	55	64
Percentage of stories mentioning riots or civil rights	0	26	31	38

Note: Based on an analysis of all poverty-related stories in *Time, Newsweek,* and *U.S. News and World Report* published between January 1, 1964, and December 31, 1967.

those stories that were not focused on urban poverty, the percentage of blacks among pictures of the poor more than doubled, growing from 27 percent in 1964 to 58 percent in 1967.

While growing attention to urban poverty did contribute to the changing racial portrayal of the poor between 1965 and 1967, it cannot explain the sharp increase in the percentage of blacks in poverty pictures between 1964 and 1965. Coverage during both of these years was dominated by stories on the War on Poverty, with no particular emphasis on urban problems in either year. Furthermore, the jump in percent black had already occurred before the Watts riots in August 1965; indeed, newsmagazine poverty stories included just as high a percentage of blacks in the first half of 1965 as they did in the months following Watts. A second possibility is that the mainstream (white-dominated) news media were more likely to associate negative poverty stories with blacks and neutral or positive stories with whites. I have already suggested that this tendency can be observed in the coverage of poverty from 1960 through 1963, and the same phenomenon might explain the sharp increase in pictures of poor blacks between 1964 and the earlier (pre-Watts) months of 1965. Negative views of blacks were more common in the 1960s than they are today, and it would be surprising if these attitudes were not shared, at least to some degree, by the white news professionals who shaped the coverage of poverty.[47] Notions about blacks' "cultural foreignness," especially with regard to the mainstream values of individual initiative and hard work, might well have led newsmagazine writers, editors, and photographers to associate African Americans with negative coverage of poverty.

Of course, the racial patterns within poverty coverage in 1960-63 and 1964-65 are slender threads on which to hang so important a claim. A wealth of other evidence, however, points in the same direction. In particular, we can make use of the full breadth of newsmagazine coverage between 1950 and 1992 to examine both the differences in the racial portrayals of different subgroups of the poor, and changes over time in racial images of the poor as media coverage responds to changing social conditions. In both cases, we find that positive coverage of poverty—coverage that focuses on either more sympathetic subgroups of the poor or periods in which the poor as a whole were viewed more sympathetically—was more likely to include pictures of poor whites than was the negative coverage of poverty associated with less sympathetic groups and less sympathetic times.

Changing Racial Portrayals of the Poor: 1968-1992

Poverty took on a black face in newsmagazines during the tumultuous years of the mid-1960s. But as urban riots subsided and the country's attention turned toward Vietnam, Watergate, and the economic problems of the 1970s, the racial portrayal of the poor in news coverage did not return to the predominantly white images of the 1950s and early 1960s. Instead, as figure 13.3 indicates, the racial representation of the poor in media images of poverty fluctuated considerably, with very high proportions of African Americans in 1972 and 1973 and dramatic "whitening" of poverty images during the economic recessions of 1974-75 and 1982-83. To understand variations over time in the racial portrayal of poverty, I examine next these three extremes in the racial images of the poor.

Images of Blacks and the "Welfare Mess": 1972–1973

Coverage of poverty during 1972 and 1973 focused primarily on perceived problems with welfare and efforts at welfare reform. Almost half of the poverty coverage in these two years focused directly on welfare or related antipoverty programs, while the next most frequent poverty topic (housing) accounted for only

20 percent of newsmagazine reporting on poverty. As we saw in chapter 1, the percentage of all Americans receiving welfare increased dramatically from about 2 percent in the mid-1960s to about 6 percent in the mid-1970s, while aggregate spending on welfare more than doubled, from .24 percent of GNP in 1965 to .60 percent in 1975.[48] The growth of welfare spending during this period resulted from a number of factors, including higher benefit levels in many states and the court-mandated elimination of residency requirements and "man in the house" rules. The most important components of welfare growth, however, were the jump in the percentage of eligible families that applied for aid and the rise in the percentage of families that were enrolled from among those who did apply.[49]

By the early 1970s, the expansion of welfare had come to be viewed as an urgent national problem that demanded action. Newsmagazine stories during 1972 and 1973 almost invariably referred to this situation as the "welfare mess" and published story after story focusing on mismanagement in state welfare bureaucracies or abuse of welfare by people who could be supporting themselves (or welfare cheating by people who in fact were supporting themselves and collecting welfare at the same time). Of course, newsmagazines did not simply take it upon themselves to turn a critical eye toward welfare; they were reporting on the political events of the time. Numerous welfare reform proposals were debated in Congress during this period; welfare was an important issue in the 1972 presidential election, with both Richard Nixon and George McGovern offering plans to fix the "welfare mess"; and in 1973 President Nixon closed down the Office of Economic Opportunity, the central administrative arm of President Johnson's War on Poverty.

The racial composition of the welfare population hardly changed between the late 1960s and the early 1970s (figure 13.1), but the images of the poor in newsmagazine stories changed dramatically. Fifty-two percent of poor people pictured in poverty and welfare stories from 1969 and 1970 were African American, but in 1972 and 1973 blacks comprised 70 percent of the poor people pictured in stories indexed under poverty and 75 percent of those pictured in stories on welfare. Nor was the heavy representation of blacks limited to stories on poverty and welfare per se. Virtually all poverty-related coverage during these two years—whatever the topic—was illustrated with pictures of blacks. During 1972 and 1973, African Americans composed 76 percent of the poor people pictured in stories on all other poverty-related topics, including housing, urban problems, employment programs, old age, unemployment, and legal aid. Overall, the sustained negative coverage of welfare during 1972–73 was accompanied by the highest proportions of blacks in newsmagazine images of the poor of any point during the entire forty-three-year period examined.

Blacks and Whites in Poverty: 1974–1975

The mid-1970s marked the first severe economic downturn since the tremendous period of sustained growth that began in the early 1960s. Of particular concern during 1974 and 1975 was unemployment, which had risen from under 5 percent in 1970 to 8.5 percent in 1975.[50] In contrast to the very heavily black coverage of poverty in 1972–73, only 49 percent of the poor people pictured in stories published during 1974 and 1975 were black (slightly below average for the entire 1968–1992 period). General stories on poverty and welfare were still common during these years, accounting for 27 percent of all poverty coverage. Not surprisingly, however, given the economic conditions of the time, unemployment and government efforts to combat it emerged as an important focus of poverty-related news coverage, accounting for 24 percent of all poverty stories in 1974–75 (compared with only 3 percent in 1972–73). In addition, 14 percent of poverty stories focused on hunger (also up from 3 percent in 1972–73).

Unlike stories about poverty published in 1972 and 1973, poverty coverage in 1974–75 varied dramatically in racial complexion depending on the topic of the story. General stories on poverty and welfare continued to contain primarily pictures of blacks. Sixty-nine percent of poor people in these stories were African American, a figure hardly changed from the 73 percent black in such stories from 1972 and 1973. But poverty stories that focused on unemployment policy were illustrated predominantly with whites. The poverty-related coverage of unemployment in 1974 and 1975 dealt largely with government jobs programs and other efforts to "put America back to work" and only 37 percent of poor people pictured in these stories were black. Stories on hunger pictured somewhat larger numbers of blacks (50 percent), while the few stories on homelessness from 1974 and 1975 pictured no African Americans at all.

As the focus of media coverage of poverty shifts in response to changing conditions and events, we would expect to find changes in the racial portrayals of the poor. In this case, the negative stories on welfare from 1972 and 1973 contained many more pictures of blacks than the sympathetic stories on unemployment published during 1974 and 1975. To some extent this shift is warranted, since the percentage of blacks among welfare recipients in the early 1970s was higher than the percentage of blacks in jobs programs during the mid-1970s. In other words, African Americans may be associated with the less sympathetic topics of poverty coverage simply because they are more likely to be found among subgroups of the poor that arouse less sympathy. During the 1970s, blacks did in fact compose a larger percentage of welfare recipients than of government jobs programs participants or of the poor in general. Nevertheless, the size of these differences is not sufficient to account for the dramatically larger differences in the racial *portrayals* of these different groups.

In the early 1970s, African Americans comprised about 32 percent of all poor Americans and about 43 percent of AFDC recipients (figs. 13.3 and 13.1, respectively). In contrast, during the mid-1970s, blacks accounted for about 30 percent of the participants in the Comprehensive Employment and Training Act (or CETA) program, which was the largest and most politically prominent jobs program during this period.[51] Since blacks comprised 37 percent of the poor people pictured in unemployment-related coverage during 1974–75, they were actually overrepresented in these sympathetic news stories. Nevertheless, these stories were much more accurate in their racial portrayals than were the unsympathetic stories on welfare from the previous years. That is, African Americans comprised a minority of both welfare recipients and CETA participants, but newsmagazines only slightly exaggerated their representation in jobs programs (37 percent in magazine pictures versus 30 percent in reality during 1974–75) and dramatically exaggerated their numbers among those on welfare (75 percent in magazine pictures versus 43 percent in reality during 1972–73).

While sympathy was extended to unemployed Americans and support was broad for jobs programs such as CETA, welfare continued to be attacked during the mid-1970s, as it had been in the 1972–73 period. *Time* magazine declared in 1975 that "practically everyone feels that welfare has become a hydra—sustaining many who do not deserve help, breeding incredible bureaucracy and inefficiency, and entangling the nation in ideological clashes over just how much aid should go to whom."[52] There were a few sympathetic stories during 1974–75 that drew a connection between national economic difficulties (principally unemployment) and the conditions facing welfare recipients. But most coverage of welfare continued to stress its spiraling costs and the burden of caring for the poor when government was being squeezed for funds due to the state of the economy. Welfare stories continued to stress abuse by welfare recipients who could be supporting themselves and the supposed resentment of the middle class toward paying for "welfare loafers." And unlike the unemployment-related stories, stories on welfare were filled primarily with black faces: during 1974–75, fully 76 percent of the poor people pictured in welfare stories were African American.

In sum, the newsmagazine coverage of poverty and welfare from the affluent period of the early 1970s was overwhelmingly negative in tone and dominated by pictures of African Americans. The economy faltered during 1974 and 1975, however, and in these years news coverage of poverty was decidedly more mixed in tone. Negative stories about welfare were still plentiful, and these stories still tended to be illustrated with pictures of blacks. But more positive coverage of the problems of the unemployed were also common, and in these stories the faces of the poor were predominantly white. These patterns of news coverage from the 1970s are consistent with the patterns we observed in the 1960s: negative coverage of poverty tends to be associated with African Americans while positive coverage is illustrated with pictures of whites. As we will see next, this pattern also extends to the unusually sympathetic stories on poverty published during the "Reagan recession" of the early 1980s.

Sympathetic Coverage of White Poverty: 1982–1983

The recession of the early 1980s brought America's worst economic performance in decades. Per capita gross domestic product fell over 3 percent between 1981 and 1982, unemployment rose to almost 11 percent, and the poverty rate Increased from about 11 percent in 1979 to over 15 percent in 1983.[53] Coincident with this economic downturn were the Reagan administration's domestic spending cutbacks and rhetorical attacks on government antipoverty programs.

The rather dire conditions of America's poor, and the political controversy that erupted in response to President Reagan's efforts to "trim the safety net," led to a substantial increase in the amount of news coverage of poverty. After publishing only 43 stories on poverty in 1979 and 1980, the three weekly newsmagazines published 103 poverty stories in 1982 and 1983. Reflecting the nature of the times, news coverage of poverty during the early 1980s was concentrated on the growing problems of poverty and unemployment and on debates over the proper response of government to these conditions. About 39 percent of poverty-related newsmagazine stories in 1982–83 focused on poverty or government antipoverty programs, with another 28 percent on unemployment or efforts to combat it. In addition, smaller numbers of stories concerned homelessness, housing programs, and legal aid (each constituting 6 percent to 8 percent of poverty coverage).

This period of widespread public concern with poverty also saw the lowest percentage of blacks in magazine portrayals of the poor of any time since the early 1960s. Overall, only 33 percent of poor people pictured in poverty-related stories during 1982 and 1983 were black. But unlike coverage during the recession of 1974–75, news coverage in 1982–83 often drew a connection between national economic conditions and the problems of the poor. Moreover, poor whites in news coverage during the early 1980s were more likely to be found in general stories on poverty and welfare than in stories on unemployment.

The two most common themes of poverty stories during this period concerned the growth of poverty and the debates over government cutbacks. Although a few of these stories sought to convince readers that "The Safety Net Remains" (as a *Time* magazine story from February 1982 was titled), most of this coverage was highly critical of the Reagan administration's efforts to trim government programs for the poor. A good example is *Newsweek*'s prominent story titled "The Hard-Luck Christmas of '82," which proclaimed, "With 12 million unemployed and 2 million homeless, private charity cannot make up for federal cutbacks."[54] This story went on to describe the desperate condition of poor families living in camp tents or in automobiles, portraying them as the noble victims "who are paying the price of America's failure of nerve in the war on poverty." Reflecting the general lack of black faces in these sympathetic poverty stories, "The Hard-Luck Christmas of '82" included only 17 African Americans among the 90 poor people pictured.[55] As a whole, blacks made up only 30 percent of the poor people pictured in general stories on poverty and antipoverty programs in 1982–83.

A less common, but important, theme in poverty stories from this period concerned the "newly poor," that is, formerly middle-class Americans who fell into poverty during the recession of the early 1980s. Typical of this coverage is a (white) family of four profiled in a *U.S. News and World Report* story from August 1982.[56] This story describes how the Telehowski family was "plunged into the ranks of the newly poor" when the father lost his job as a machinist with an auto-parts company. No longer able to afford a car or even an apartment, the Telehowskis reluctantly applied for welfare and became squatters in an abandoned house in inner-city Detroit. The story about the Telehowskis, with their two small children and their determined struggle to support themselves, indicates the extraordinary sympathy that the "newly poor" received in news coverage from the early 1980s. *Newsweek* went even farther in proclaiming the virtues of the newly poor, writing, "The only aspect of American life that has been uplifted by the continuing recession: a much better class of poor person, better educated, accustomed to working, with strong family ties."[57]

It is not surprising, of course, that poverty is portrayed in a more sympathetic light during economic hard times. What is noteworthy, however, is that along with shifts in the tone of news reporting on the poor come shifts in the racial mix of the poor people in news stories. As figure 13.3 shows, the true proportion of blacks among America's poor did not change appreciably between the early 1970s and the early 1980s (or indeed, at any time during the past thirty-five years). But the racial portrayals of the poor in newsmagazines did shift dramatically as media attention turned from highly critical coverage of welfare during 1972–73 to highly sympathetic stories on poverty during the recession of the early 1980s. Some of the racial shift in poverty images is attributable to the different proportions of blacks among different subgroups of the poor. But the fairly small demographic differences can neither explain nor justify the much larger differences between the racial images associated with the sympathetic portrayals of the "deserving poor" in the early 1980s and the unsympathetic portraits of the "undeserving poor" in the early 1970s.

Racial Portrayals of Subgroups of the Poor

The news media's tendency to use pictures of poor blacks in unsympathetic poverty stories and pictures of poor whites in sympathetic stories can also be observed among the various topics in poverty coverage over the entire 1950–1992 period. Table 13.2 shows the percentage of African Americans in pictures of poor people for thirteen different aggregated subject categories.[58] The story topics shown in table 13.2 relate to members of the poverty population that receive varying levels of public support or censure. For example, surveys show greater sympathy for the poor in general than for welfare recipients, and a stronger desire to help poor children or the elderly than poor working-age adults.[59] And despite the negative coverage that the Job Corps

Table 13.2 Percentage African American in Newsmagazine Pictures of the Poor, 1950–1992

Topic	Number of Stories	Number of Poor People Pictures	Percentage African American
Underclass	6	36	100
Urban problems, urban renewal	91	97	84
Poor people, poverty	182	707	59
Unemployment	102	268	59
Legal aid	30	22	56
Welfare, antipoverty programs	399	965	54
Housing, homeless	272	508	52
Children	45	121	51
Employment programs	45	181	50
Education	22	95	43
Medical care	43	36	28
Hunger	52	176	25
Old-age assistance	28	12	0

Notes: An additional 79 stories (not shown above) were indexed under miscellaneous other topics; 133 stories (11% of all poverty stories) were indexed under more than one topic. The database includes all stories on poverty and related topics published in *Time, Newsweek,* and *U.S. News and World Report* between January 1, 1950, and December 31, 1992. A breakdown of detailed subject categories can be obtained from the author.

received in stories from the mid-1960s, we would generally expect more sympathetic responses to stories about poor people in employment programs than to stories about nonworking poor adults.

Of the thirteen topics shown in table 13.2, seven fall into a fairly narrow range in which African Americans comprise between 50 percent and 60 percent of all poor people pictured. These include "sympathetic" topics, such as poor children (51 percent black) and employment programs (50 percent), and "unsympathetic" topics, such as public welfare (54 percent). Of those topics that do differ substantially in percent African American, however, fewer blacks are shown in stories on the more sympathetic topics of education (43 percent black), medical care (28 percent), and hunger (25 percent), while stories about the elderly poor—one of the most sympathetic subgroups of poor people—are illustrated exclusively with pictures of poor whites. In contrast, only African Americans are found in stories on the underclass, perhaps the least sympathetic topic in table 13.2. Although the underclass lacks any consistent definition in either popular or academic discourse,[60] it is most often associated with intergenerational poverty, chronic unemployment, out-of-wedlock births, crime, drugs, and "welfare dependency as a way of life."[61] In fact, blacks do compose a large proportion of the American underclass, the exact proportion depending on how the underclass is defined. But even those definitions that result in the highest percentages of African Americans consider the underclass to include at least 40 percent nonblacks, in contrast to the magazine portrait of the underclass as 100 percent black.[62]

With regard to topic of story, then, we find the same tendency that we found in examining changes in media coverage of poverty over time. In both cases, pictures of African Americans are disproportionately used to illustrate the most negative aspects of poverty and the least sympathetic subgroups of the poor.

TV News Coverage of Poverty

The three newsmagazines examined here have a combined circulation of over ten million copies, and 20 percent of American adults claim to be regular readers of "newsmagazines such as *Time, U.S. News and World Report,* or *Newsweek.*"[63] In addition, these magazines influence how other journalists see the world. In one study, for example, magazine and newspaper journalists were asked what news sources they read most regularly.[64] Among these journalists, *Time* and *Newsweek* were the first- and second-most frequently cited news sources and were far more popular than the *New York Times,* the *Wall Street Journal,* or the *Washington Post.*

Despite the broad reach of these weekly magazines, and their role as "background material" for other journalists, there can be little doubt that television is the dominant news source for most Americans. In recent surveys, about 70 percent of the American public identifies television as the source of "most of your news about what's going on in the world today."[65] If the racial content of TV news coverage of poverty were to differ substantially from that found in newsmagazines, our confidence in the analysis of newsmagazines would be severely limited.

Unfortunately, the analyses of newsmagazine coverage reported above cannot be replicated with television news. First, tapes of television news broadcasts are unavailable for shows aired before the middle of 1968. This alone would preclude the use of television news to examine the critical period of the mid-1960s. In addition, television news stories on poverty typically picture far larger numbers of poor people but provide much less information about the poor individuals pictured than do newsmagazine stories. Still, we can to some degree determine whether newsmagazine coverage of poverty is unique to that medium by comparing patterns of news coverage on television with those found in newsmagazines for the period in which both sources are available.

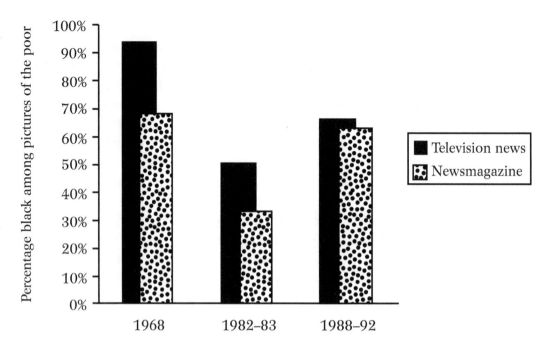

Figure 13.5 Racial Portrayal of Poverty in Newsmagazines and Television News

Source: *Time, Newsweek*, and *U.S. News and World Report*, and ABC, NBC, and CBS nightly news shows. *NS* for the magazines are 275, 226, and 556 poor people, and *Ns* for television are 84, 669, and 1,100 poor people, for the three time periods respectively.

The first question we might ask is simply whether the ups and downs of news attention to poverty found in newsmagazines is repeated in television news coverage. To examine this relationship, I searched the *Vanderbilt Television News Index and Abstracts* for all stories on poverty and related topics broadcast on the ABC, NBC, and CBS nightly news between 1969 and 1992.[66] In all, there were 3,387 such stories during this twenty-four-year period, ranging from a high of 570 stories in 1969 to a low of only 14 stories in 1980. Similarly, during the same period the three newsmagazines published the largest number of poverty stories in 1969 (73 stories) and the fewest in 1979 (20 stories) (the second-smallest number of poverty stories in newsmagazines was found in 1980). Over the entire period, there is a clear correspondence between the number of stories on poverty appearing in any year in television news and newsmagazines: the correlation between the number of stories per year in TV and newsmagazines is .57. Some of the poverty coverage in newsmagazines and on network television is a product of a news organization's decision to draw attention to some specific aspect of poverty. However, the substantial correlation between the ebbs and flows of stories about the poor in these two media suggest that the quantity of poverty coverage in any time period is largely determined by "real world" events such as economic conditions and political initiatives.

The second, and more important, question concerning the similarities between television and newsmagazine coverage of poverty concerns the racial representation of the poor. Measuring the racial representation of poverty in television news requires the painstaking examination of hours of television news stories. Because it was impossible to code the full twenty-four years of television news, I chose three historical periods: 1968, the earliest year for which TV news shows are available and a year in which magazines portrayed the poor as predominantly black; 1982–83, a time when magazine images of poverty contained the lowest proportion of blacks for the entire period studied; and 1988–92, a more recent period that also contained a high proportion of blacks in newsmagazine stories on poverty.

Figure 13.5 shows the percentage of blacks among pictures of the poor for these three periods. We see first that the overrepresentation of African Americans in poverty stories that generally characterized newsmagazine coverage after 1964 was also true for television news. In fact, in each of the three periods examined, television news exaggerated the percentage of blacks among the poor to an even greater extent than did the newsmagazines. Equally important, the changing patterns of racial representation found in the newsmagazines is reflected in television news as well. In both media, 1968 contained extremely high proportions of blacks among pictures of the poor; 1982-83, the smallest proportions; and 1988-92, proportions somewhere in the middle. Of course, a more complete analysis of poverty coverage in these two media might reveal some important differences. But the data examined suggest that the patterns of coverage found in newsmagazines are not idiosyncratic to that particular medium. Television news also substantially exaggerates the extent to which blacks compose the poor, and as with newsmagazine coverage, the complexion of poverty in TV news shifts over time as events draw attention to more sympathetic and less sympathetic subgroups of the poor. In short, it appears that the distorted coverage of poverty found in newsmagazines reflects a broader set of dynamics that also shape images of the poor in the even more important medium of television news.

Conclusions

Perhaps it is unreasonable to expect a "sociologically accurate" depiction of poverty in news stories. Certainly some aspects of poverty and some subgroups of the poor are more newsworthy than others. And news departments, after all, are in the business of selling news. If news photographers seek out the most sensational images of poverty to attract readers or viewers we should hardly be surprised. For most Americans, the most powerful images of poverty are undoubtedly the black urban ghettos. These concentrations of poverty represent the worst failures of our economic, educational, and social welfare systems. Yet they also represent a minuscule portion of all the American poor. Only 6 percent of all poor Americans are blacks living in urban ghettos.[67]

Furthermore, and most significantly, racial distortions in the portrayal of poverty are not limited to stories on the urban underclass. The overrepresentation of blacks among the poor is found in coverage of most poverty topics and appears during most of the past three decades. Yet just as importantly, black faces are *unlikely* to be found in media stories on the most sympathetic subgroups of the poor, just as they are comparatively absent from media coverage of poverty during times of heightened sympathy for the poor.

Journalists are professional observers and chroniclers of our social world. But they are also residents of that world and are exposed to the same stereotypes and misperceptions that characterize society at large. As we will see in chapter 6, the stereotype of the lazy black has been a staple of our culture for centuries and its reflection in contemporary news coverage of poverty is only one current manifestation of this long-held belief.

Discussion Questions

1. Racialization concerning poverty is discussed in this reading. Can you think of other social policies that are racialized in our society?
2. How do the media function to shape views of an issue?

Affirmative Action

By Stephen Caliendo

Editor's Introduction

Affirmative Action has been one of the most politicized social issues in the recent history and modern discourse of the United States. In this reading, the author discusses the history of Affirmative Action, the politics of Affirmative Action, and recent court cases involving the use of Affirmative Action as social policy.

I n the preceding chapters, we explored the depth, persistence, and complexity of racial and economic inequality in the United States, as well as ways that government officials within the context of a representative democracy are able and willing to address it. The cycle of advantage and disadvantage that appears in Figure 2.2 is at once simple and complex. It is simple in the sense that it involves three major elements: housing, education (both K–12 and postsecondary), and employment. It is complex because of the interrelationship among these elements, as well as additional considerations that affect those relationships (such as the criminal justice system and health disparities). Along the way, we have wrestled with some difficult normative questions. This chapter is no different in that respect. The most difficult questions reside here because rather than merely describing inequality, we are now forced to think about ways to reduce inequality and eliminate injustice. As noted in the Introduction, there is an assumption that inequality in America needs to be addressed. Otherwise, this chapter would be irrelevant. Those who believe that inequality is not problematic or that any existing inequality is the result of individuals making poor choices (as opposed to being systemic) need not wrestle with the issues that we consider here.

In this chapter, we explore steps that have been taken to address inequality in the twentieth century, tracing the successes and failures over the past 50 years. While there has been a spattering of ad hoc attempts at progress, the most persistent and systematic programs fall under the umbrella term "affirmative action."[1] The term has been heavily stigmatized, however, largely because it is misrepresented as a quota system that offers awards (jobs, admission to college and professional schools, etc.) to racial minorities at the expense of whites. While quota programs have existed in the past, they are illegal in most respects today. Still, there are legitimate concerns over how affirmative action affects both whites and members of racial minority groups, so it is important to explore a brief history of these programs, their current practice, and the extent to which programs operating with this philosophical undercurrent are the answer to systemic inequality in the United States.

Though affirmative action programs have been codified in legislation, the most important movement on this issue has come from the courts. The US Supreme Court has issued a number of decisions that give guidance (and constraint) to institutions that wish to take race into consideration for the purposes of increasing diversity or acknowledging that historical injustices place additional burdens on persons of color. Consequently we will give disproportionate attention to the judicial branch of the US government in this chapter and focus on the potential for it to serve as a countermajoritarian force in a representative democracy. Recall James Madison's concerns about majority tyranny and the fact that nonelected judges who serve life terms are uniquely positioned to represent those to whom the majority of citizens might deny rights. As we will see, members of racial minority groups have needed protection at times; at other times, it is whites who have claimed to be disadvantaged and have sought protection from infringement of their rights.

History of Affirmative Action in America

The legal rights of persons of color—specifically those of African descent—to avoid discrimination emanate from the Fourteenth Amendment to the US Constitution. Passed as one of the three Civil War amendments, it includes a constitutional provision that guarantees citizens' rights be upheld and protected by the state governments, as well as the federal government. This amendment is at the center of many legal and theoretical conflicts relating to civil rights and civil liberties in the United States. Whereas the first ten amendments to the Constitution (the Bill of Rights) were believed to apply only to the federal government for much of our nation's history, a gradual incorporation of those constitutional provisions by the courts to apply to the states through the Fourteenth Amendment has resulted in more widespread protections for citizens. With respect to racial nondiscrimination, a series of Supreme Court cases has helped to clarify these protections, including the *Brown v. Board of Education* case that halted legally mandated racial segregation of public schools. Recall from Chapter 4, however, that the Court's decision in *Brown* pivoted on the psychological harm that was done to students of color as a result of being segregated from whites. It left open the question of what rights whites had with respect to actions by government and private institutions to increase diversity and/or account for historical injustice when making decisions that involved the selection of individuals for various positions.

A series of executive and legislative measures have also been enacted, beginning with New Deal–era requirements for avoidance of racial discrimination by employers and in public works programs[2] in the early part of the twentieth century. As we have seen, the most meaningful and sweeping antidiscrimination legislation has been the Civil Rights Act of 1964. Title VI of that law prohibits discrimination on the basis of race, color, or national origin by any entity that receives federal financial assistance; Title VII has clear language indicating that discrimination on the basis of sex is similarly prohibited.[3]

It is important to keep in mind the substantive difference between having a policy of nondiscrimination, which can only be enforced through legal proceedings in which someone complains of and proves that discrimination occurred, and policies of preferential treatment, which are designed to proactively address systemic inequality. The latter category of policies fall under the umbrella of affirmative action. In the 1960s, during the height of the civil rights movement, President Lyndon Johnson instigated an affirmative action policy through an executive order to force federal agencies to be attentive to their practices in hiring and awarding contracts with an eye toward avoiding discrimination.[4] Similar policies were adopted at the state level, and institutions of higher education began to use a variety of mechanisms to diversify the student body and to recognize that colorblind merit admission policies were by their nature disadvantageous to students who faced barriers to achieving those ostensibly objective markers (e.g., grade point average, board exam scores, ability to write a strong essay) that other applicants did not face (see Chapter 4).[5]

The friction generated by affirmative action policies stems from the reality that positions, whether in colleges or for employment, often reflect a zero-sum game—there are a set number of openings, with more applicants than opportunities. Traditional notions of meritocracy that are key aspects of American cultural identity suggest that individuals should compete based on their abilities and hard work and that factors that lie beyond the individual's control should never be taken into consideration.[6] The assumption of meritocracy, however, requires a relatively level playing field (or equal starting line, depending on the metaphor applied), which does not reflect the reality of American racial history. As the cartoon in Figure 14.1 suggests, whites were willing to deny access and opportunity to African Americans for centuries, and though now all Americans generally agree that racial discrimination (let alone slavery) is inappropriate, we are not nearly as willing to consider the consequences of persistent disadvantage that have arisen from those centuries of exclusion.

It is not difficult to understand why there is resistance. The limitation of the cartoon, of course, is that the same two characters appear in each of the six panes. Although the cartoonist needed to use this technique to be concise and convey a powerful message, he is unable to capture the important temporal dynamic that arises from current generations of whites claiming that they "never owned a slave." In the cartoon, the white racist in the first four panes is the same as the person who recognizes in the last two that racial prejudice and discrimination are wrong. Because the character equates racism (which is systemic) and prejudice (which is interpersonal), however, he refuses to take actions that would help to rectify past wrongs. He also feels that doing so would be equally improper because it relies on considerations of race. The notion that any consideration of race is racist has helped to perpetuate systems of disadvantage. Whites, who still overwhelmingly control the levers of power in the United States, have been led to believe that the real racists are those who advocate a sophisticated consideration of systemic racism in public policymaking and public discourse.

On the other hand, affirmative action programs should not be viewed as the solution to America's racist past. We have had various forms of affirmative action policies in place for half a century, and as we have discovered, we are far from having a society where all races and ethnicities have the same opportunities for success. We have, however, made great progress in that time on a number of fronts, and while it would be improper to assume that affirmative action policies were solely responsible for that, dismissing them out of hand is also unwise. Instead, in order to appreciate the nuance and complexities of this controversial issue, we consider three Supreme Court cases that have given shape to affirmative action policy in the United States.

From Davis to Ann Arbor to Austin

The first meaningful test of affirmative action policy in the United States came when Allan Bakke, who is white, complained about being denied admission to the University of California–Davis medical school in 1973 and again in 1974. The program, he claimed, was unconstitutional because it denied him the opportunity to compete for all of the available seats in the incoming class. Each year, the school admitted one hundred applicants but had two separate admission programs. One program, which had eighty-four seats, was open to applicants of any race, ethnicity, or educational background. The other program was reserved for applicants who identified themselves as "economically and/or educationally disadvantaged" or members of a racial minority group. The benefit of being considered under the set-aside program was that one would not be compared to applicants in the other program and that the grade point average cutoff that applied to applicants in the other program was not in effect. Bakke's scores were higher than several of the students who were admitted under the second program, which meant that if he would have been permitted to compete for those seats, he would have been admitted. Though whites who were economically or educationally disadvantaged were eligible for consideration (Bakke was neither), none had been admitted in the four years that the program was in place. On this basis, Bakke argued that he was being denied equal protection under the Fourteenth Amendment by the state of California because of his race.

In *Regents of the University of California v. Bakke*,[7] the Supreme Court agreed with Bakke and ruled that such quota programs were unfair to whites (and unconstitutional), but the Court was clear that other types of programs that took race or other systemic disadvantage (including gender) into consideration were permissible. Specifically, the Court pointed to the plan that Harvard University used in admission, which considered racial minority status as a plus factor as part of a formula that contains a number of criteria for consideration. Justice Powell, who wrote the opinion for the Court, noted that race, as well as other characteristics, was part of the diversity that is valued in higher education. This established race as a factor standard that many institutions of higher education still use in admissions decisions.[8] It was precisely this type of plan that was challenged twenty-five years later when the Court heard the next case dealing with affirmative action in higher education.

In 2003 the Court considered two cases simultaneously, both relating to the University of Michigan. In *Gratz v. Bollinger*,[9] the Court struck down the policy that the university used for undergraduate admissions, but in *Grutter v. Bollinger*,[10] the Court upheld the policy being used by the law school. In essence, the Court felt that awarding twenty points to underrepresented racial and ethnic groups in the undergraduate program was disproportionate[11] and that institutions should take a more holistic approach to admissions decisions with respect to diversity. In the law school case, however, the Court found that the policy invoked a narrowly tailored approach to consider race in admissions decisions in a way that was consistent with its desire to have a diverse incoming class in order to enrich the educational experience. Because the law school did not define diversity solely in terms of race or ethnicity and could award weight to an applicant's rating based on other factors that would enhance diversity, the Court, in a 5–4 decision, upheld the program. Justice Sandra Day O'Connor, who wrote the opinion, indicated that she hoped and expected that such policies would not be necessary in another twenty-five years (see Box 14.2). It is difficult to look into the future to determine the degree to which such policies will be necessary. Though rates of college graduation for African Americans are slowly increasing,[12] the gap between white student graduation rates and those of African Americans and Latinos[13] still exist. More relevant to this issue, however, is the degree to which students of color would be granted admission to colleges if affirmative action plans were not in place.

It did not take twenty-five years for the Court to come back to the issue this time. On October 10, 2012, the Supreme Court heard oral arguments in *Fisher v. University of Texas at Austin*.[14] Abigail Fisher, a white woman who was rejected by the University of Texas at Austin, complained that she had been denied equal treatment under the law as a result of the university's affirmative action policy. The Obama administration, as well as fourteen states, urged the Court to uphold racial preferences in college admissions.[15] At central issue in *Fisher* was whether colleges and universities had taken the Court's advice from *Grutter*, narrowing their use of racial preferences, or whether, as one scholar speculated, they have taken the *Grutter* decision "as a

BOX 14.1 Representing: JUSTICE CLARENCE THOMAS

Only the second African American to be appointed to the US Supreme Court, Clarence Thomas has opposed racial preferences and affirmative action throughout his career. While critics argue that he benefited from affirmative action policies, Thomas has consistently claimed that he was harmed by the policy because he felt that it placed a stigma on him when he graduated from Yale University.

Thomas was born in rural Georgia in 1948 and grew up in the sort of abject poverty described in Chapter 3. There was no sewage system or paved roads. Thomas's mother worked as a housekeeper and accepted church charity to make ends meet. He learned to value education from his grandfather, with whom he lived during his formative years. Thomas was not insulated from racism; he dropped out of seminary in Missouri and even supported work of the Black Panthers while an undergraduate at Holy Cross. President Reagan appointed Thomas to a position in the Department of Education and later at the Equal Employment Opportunity Commission. After serving on the US Court of Appeals for a year, he was appointed by President George H. W. Bush to replace Justice Thurgood Marshall, who successfully argued the *Brown v. Board of Education* school desegregation case before the Supreme Court as a lawyer and who was the first African American to serve on the Court.

While Thomas clearly benefited from racial preferences on a number of occasions throughout his career, the humiliation he felt when he applied for jobs after graduating from Yale Law School stuck with him. That experience has affected his attitudes about affirmative action generally, as well as his ruling on racial preferences cases such as *Grutter v. Bollinger* and *Gratz v. Bollinger* (see below). Besides the stigmatization argument, Thomas believes that affirmative action programs in education are not effective because they do not guarantee assistance for minority students who may not be pre- pared to compete. Further, he agrees with those who argue that racial integration may not necessarily be beneficial to students of color. In fact, he has noted that forced integration suggests an underlying racism that "anything that is predominantly black must be inferior."

Opponents of racial preferences celebrate Thomas as a champion with credibility on the subject, while proponents dismiss him as a hypocrite and an opportunist. What is clear, however, is that Thomas's ideas about affirmative action have been shaped by his life experiences, and his justifications do not fall neatly in line with most of the people who agree with him on the issue. In many ways, Thomas embodies the complexity of an issue that has been oversimplified in American public discourse.[a]

---

a   "Clarence Thomas," The Oyez Project, http://www.oyez.org/justices/clarence_thomas; Ariane de Vogue, "'Silent' Justice Outspoken on Affirmative Action," ABC News, September 30, 2007, http://abcnews.go.com/TheLaw/story?id=3667079; Maureen Dowd, "Could Thomas Be Right?" *New York Times*, June 25, 2003, http://www.nytimes.com/2003/06/25/opin- ion/could-thomas-be-right.html?src=pm.

signal that court supervision of preferences would be lax."[16] Before the case was decided, some suspected that the Court would be more clear about how "disadvantage" must be defined so that economically challenged whites are not discriminated against and affluent applicants of color are not advantaged in such programs.[17] In the end, the Court vacated (set aside) the lower court's decision that the University of Texas's policy was constitutional. Justice Anthony Kennedy argued in his majority opinion that the 5th Circuit Court of Appeals did not apply strict scrutiny in its analysis of the program and ordered it to do so. He noted that for the policy to withstand constitutional muster, the burden was on the university to show that attempts to attain a diverse student body were "narrowly tailored to that goal." Opponents of affirmative action viewed the ruling as a victory (because it failed to uphold the existing policy), but so did supporters (because the Court did not rule that considering race in admission was unconstitutional).[18] Irrespective of how the Supreme Court eventually rules on this issue, we are left with two important and interrelated considerations.

First, affirmative action in college (or graduate/professional school) admissions is not a guarantee of a degree or a job. Once a student is admitted, he or she needs to do the same work as any other student to be successful. Given the tremendous disparities in K–12 education, many students of color who are admitted under affirmative action programs are not as well prepared for college as their white counterparts. In this way, such programs are not an effective interruption of the cycle of disadvantage, as they are essentially setting up those students for failure. Second, white students who attend underfunded schools are at a disadvantage

BOX 14.2 Representing: JUSTICE SANDRA DAY O'CONNOR

Three years before she retired from the US Supreme Court, Sandra Day O'Connor wrote one of the most relevant opinions regarding affirmative action in a generation. A Republican state legislator from Arizona, O'Connor was the first woman in the United States to be minority leader of a state senate and the first woman to serve on the Court.

O'Connor was born to rancher parents in southeastern Arizona during the Great Depression. The ranch had no electricity or running water until she was seven years old. O'Connor was sent to boarding school so that she had a chance for a quality education. She attended Stanford for her undergraduate degree and law school. She was appointed to the Arizona Court of Appeals for two years prior to taking her seat on the Supreme Court in 1981.

In *Grutter v. Bollinger*, O'Connor wrote for a 5–4 majority that the University of Michigan's law school admissions program, which takes racial minority status into account when making decisions, was constitutional and advanced the cause of providing for a better education through a diverse student body. She added that in twenty-five years, hopefully, racial preferences in higher education would be unnecessary. Seven years after that ruling, O'Connor wrote an essay clarifying that her "twenty-five years" remark was not meant to be a deadline, as many opponents of affirmative action inferred (and promised to hold the Court to that mark). What she meant was that social scientists should reexamine the educational benefits of diverse student bodies at that time.

While the Court has the opportunity to be counter-majoritarian (and thus protect minority rights), research has demonstrated that it rarely makes decisions that run contrary to public opinion on salient issues. George Washington University law professor Jeffrey Rosen notes that when the Court decided the *Bakke* case in 1978, public opinion was against affirmative action, so it was not surprising that the decision constrained efforts to increase racial minority enrollments in higher education. By 2003, however, when the University of Michigan cases were decided, the public was much more divided on the issue, which is consistent with the 5–4 decision in *Grutter*, as well as the decision in the companion case, *Gratz*, that limited affirmative action programs. We may never know the degree to which O'Connor or the other justices took public opinion into consideration as they reviewed the cases (and they may not know themselves), but such nuance in decisions reminds us that judges and justices, though they are not directly accountable to the people, are important aspects of representation in the United States.[a]

a   Thomas R. Marshall, *Public Opinion and the Supreme Court* (Boston: Unwin Hyman, 1989); Jeffrey Rosen, "Affirmative Action and Public Opinion," *New York Times*, May 23, 2011, http://www.nytimes.com/roomfordebate/2011/05/22/is-anti-white-bias-a-problem/affirmative -action-and-public-opinion; "Sandra Day O'Connor," Oyez Project, http://www.oyez.org/justices/sandra_day_oconnor; Peter Schmidt, "Sandra Day O'Connor Revisits and Revives Affirmative-Action Controversy," *Chronicle of Higher Education*, January 14, 2010, http://chronicle.com/article/Sandra-Day-OConnor-Revisit/63523/.

if colleges do not consider economic or educational disadvantage in their admission process.[19] It has been argued that middle-class students of color who attend strong high schools also gain entrance under affirmative action programs, and while that is not the intent of such programs (because those students can compete in a colorblind system), we must be careful not to extrapolate these few cases too broadly. As we have seen, race and poverty are still closely related in the United States, and even minority students from financially secure families face subconscious prejudice in schools in the form of tracking.[20] One study estimated that admission of racial minority students to the most selective colleges would be reduced by more than half without racially conscious affirmative action programs.[21]

Affirmative Action Beyond the Classroom

Affirmative action receives the most attention as it pertains to college and graduate/professional school admission, but it is important to consider its effect on employment and housing separately. Neither of these areas presupposes that individuals have a college education, so even if affirmative action programs are effective in higher education, they do not always lead to equality in housing opportunities or employment (the other two primary elements of the cycle of disadvantage). Further, even if a person who faced systemic disadvantage early in life obtains a college degree, subconscious (if not overt) racial prejudice is still a relevant factor in housing, as well as in hiring (see Chapters 3 and 5, respectively).

Affirmative action policies in employment work a bit differently than they do in higher education. Employers do not necessarily have a battery of comparable items to judge applicants by, as college admissions officials do, nor do employers usually have a set number of openings with all applicants submitting by a deadline. Consequently the sort of rankings and comparisons that are part of college admissions are not appropriate or possible for employers. Instead, employers monitor diversity in terms of hiring and promotion and, where necessary, develop policies to address deficiencies.[22] Most of the time such policies are voluntary, but occasionally a court orders a business to use affirmative action as a result of a lawsuit.[23] Hiring quotas based on race are illegal, yet many Americans (particularly whites) are suspicious about their use and have a personal story about someone in their family who was denied employment (or perceived that he or she was denied employment) for being white.

This disconnect is partially psychological in the sense that whites often have a nagging suspicion that they are being discriminated against in favor of persons of color, but it is also warranted in the sense that many companies have aggressive targets or goals in terms of diversity that tread dangerously close to the quota line (or at least feel that way to white applicants). Title VII of the Civil Rights Act of 1964[24] was designed to prohibit discrimination against persons of color in the workforce. The bill, as well as subsequent Court decisions (such as *Griggs v. Duke Power Company* 1971),[25] is clear that it is not enough for employers not to *intend* to discriminate (which would be a difficult measure to prove); they must proactively avoid discrimination. Proactively avoiding discrimination, however, is not the same as affirmative action. That standard merely represents a call for equal opportunity that is intentionally protected. Affirmative action programs, such as that which was at issue in the Court's 2009 *Ricci v. DeStefano*[26] decision, go farther by instituting procedures that actively seek racial and ethnic (or gender) diversity.[27]

With respect to housing, there are no formal affirmative action policies. Most of the effort in housing has been to ensure that persons of color are not discriminated against, but with respect to sales and rentals, there is no governmental mandate or widespread practice of ensuring diversity in neighborhoods. As noted in Chapter 3, there were efforts to increase homeownership among African Americans and Latinos through the mortgage agencies Fannie Mae and Freddie Mac (these nicknames refer to the Federal National Mortgage Association and the Federal Home Loan Mortgage Corporation, respectively), but those agencies were placed into conservatorship due to the housing crisis in 2008, meaning that the federal government took control of them. As a result, there is uncertainty as to the effect on minority borrowers if they must rely on private banks to lend without the backing of the US government.[28]

Affirmative Action Ballot Initiatives and Referendums

Measuring public opinion about affirmative action can be difficult, as is capturing public sentiment on any issue relating to race. Americans are sensitive to accusations of being racially prejudiced, and white Americans in particular tend to be concerned with being accused of being racist when they are not conscious of harboring any racial animosity. Most Americans favor affirmative action programs when asked directly and in the abstract, but when asked whether it is worth paying a price of disadvantaging whites to help minorities, a majority respond that it is not. Further, when asked specifically about "programs that give preferences in hiring, promotions and college admission," only preferences for the handicapped have a majority of support.[29] Further, some analysis has found that support for women receiving preferential treatment for affirmative action is greater than that for racial and ethnic minorities[30] and that white women have benefited most from affirmative action programs.[31] There can also be an interest effect such that women[32] and racial minorities[33] are more likely than men and whites, respectively, to prefer affirmative action programs. Further, whites who oppose affirmative action with respect to racial minorities often support it when it is alternately framed as a benefit to women. As might be expected, attitudes toward both types of affirmative action are related to prejudices toward women and racial minorities.[34, 35]

When voters have had the opportunity to weigh in on affirmative action through ballot initiative or referendum, they have mostly supported bans on race-conscious policies in hiring and school admission. The first state to adopt such a ban was California, which won approval of Proposition 209 in 1996. Prop 209, as it is known, is an amendment to Article I of the California constitution and reads as follows: "The state shall not discriminate against, or grant preferential treatment to, any individual or group on the basis of race, sex, color, ethnicity, or national origin in the operation of public employment, public education, or public contracting."[36] On its face, of course, the language is entirely race neutral and protects persons of all races and ethnicities from discrimination. The measure, though, was explicitly a response to California's affirmative action policies, and it ignores historical, systemic disadvantage for women and persons of color, assuming that each Californian starts at roughly the same point and therefore can be assured fair, unbiased competition for open positions.

As expected, Prop 209 started a trend. In 1997, Washington State passed Initiative 200; in 2006, the Michigan Civil Rights Initiative passed; in 2008, Nebraska voters passed Initiative 424; and in 2010, the Arizona Civil Rights Initiative was approved by voters. All of these measures were pushed and supported by California businessman Ward Connerly, who is multiracial (see Box 14.3). While three of his anti-affirmative action initiatives failed to be approved for ballots in 2008, the only one to fail that year was in Colorado (in an extremely close vote).[37]

To more clearly understand the dynamic of increased support for affirmative action programs that benefit women versus those that benefit persons of color, it is useful to consider some of the difference between legal challenges to affirmative action policies and ballot-based efforts to eliminate the practice. The plebiscite language almost always includes gender, as well as race, color, ethnicity, and national origin, but legal challenges are almost always narrowly targeted at advantages to persons of color (even though, as noted above, white women have benefited disproportionately from these programs). For example, the language for the Michigan measure in 2006 banned "affirmative action programs that give preferential treatment to groups or individuals based on their race, gender, color, ethnicity or national origin for public employment, education or contradicting purposes."[38] In the landmark University of Michigan cases that went before the US Supreme Court, though, whites brought the suits, alleging that the policies were unfairly beneficial to persons of color.[39] In cases that involve alleged discrimination, courts have different standards in determining whether a law relating to sex is constitutional as compared with a law relating to race. Sex-related issues are subjected to intermediate scrutiny, while race-related issues must pass strict scrutiny. This means that government policies that result in preferences or discrimination based on race are very difficult to sustain because the government must demonstrate that it has a compelling interest in having a law that on its face (i.e., without taking historical factors into consideration) discriminates and that the policy in place is narrowly tailored to achieve that interest. With respect to sex, however, government must only show that the law "further[s] an important government interest by means that are substantially related to that interest."[40] Accordingly, affirmative action policies that benefit women specifically are more likely to withstand legal scrutiny than those that specifically aim to address racial discrimination.[41]

Perhaps this is not surprising. Americans want to live in a race-neutral meritocracy and believe that we do. Many of us have friends (or at least friendly acquaintances) of different races and ethnicities. Most of us do not recognize racial resentment in ourselves, we celebrate Martin Luther King Day, and we do not use racial epithets, even when we are angry. Absent a purposeful recognition and consideration of the complexities described in this book, the language of these ballot proposals fits neatly with our core values and beliefs about what America *should* be.

The primary difference between proponents of bans on affirmative action policies and supporters of affirmative action is the degree to which they are willing to acknowledge the systemic effects of historical discrimination and prejudice. Neither Ward Connerly nor Jesse Jackson[42] hates America or is trying to leverage personal gain from the policies they champion. They may disagree about the degree to which discrimination persists, the potential stigmatizing effect on minorities as a result of the programs, the value of racial diversity in the workplace and schools, and the degree to which whites are harmed by racially conscious policies, but it would be difficult to argue that either man does not have the best interest of the country at heart.

Reasonable people can (and do) disagree about the ability of affirmative action programs to appropriately rectify systemic disadvantages or lead to more racial equality. To be considered to be reasonable, however, each of us must seriously and honestly reflect on the various ways that we may be advantaged or disadvantaged by a system that is rooted in fundamental inequality. Most Americans would agree that a colorblind—or at least color neutral—society would be preferable, but we are unable to wish away the realities of the lingering racism that continues to characterize American society.

BOX 14.3 Representing: WARD CONNERLY

As founder and president of the American Civil Rights Institute,[a] Ward Connerly advocates for equal treatment of American citizens irrespective of race or ethnicity. He is the author of two books: *Creating Equal: My Fight Against Race Preferences*[b] and *Lessons from My Uncle James: Beyond Skin Color to the Content of Our Character.*[c]

Connerly is most widely known for supporting affirmative action bans in a number of states since the mid-1990s. Rather than lobbying representatives to sponsor legislation and advocate for passage, he used the plebiscite option that is available in twenty-four states. In some states, ballot measures must be passed by state legislatures before they can be presented to the public for a vote, but in other states, signatures can be collected for presentation, thus bypassing elected officials altogether. Ballot initiatives or referendums are not permissible at the federal level under the US Constitution.

After a high-profile victory in his home state, California, he helped usher in similar bans in Michigan, Washington, Arizona, and Nebraska. Several other attempts failed to win ballot placement, and one (in Colorado) failed. In 2003, Connerly backed California Proposition 54, which would have amended the state constitution to prohibit using racial classifications at all. It was soundly defeated, garnering only about 36 percent of the vote. Connerly claimed that classifying people by race or ethnicity is antiquated and divisive, but opponents persuasively argued that the measure would have hindered medical treatment that sometimes is more effective when tailored to specific ethnic or racial groups.

Though his record of success is mixed, Connerly has been a vocal champion of the vision of American society that Martin Luther King imagined. Critics claim that his vision of a colorblind society, while laudable, is premature and that America has yet to do the hard work to get us to a place where we can be judged not on the color of our skin but on the content of our character. Connerly is of mixed racial descent, and he has said that the continual race mixing in the United States is making racial classifications irrelevant. Such a view challenges the reality of racism in the United States today, but it is consistent with the fact that race is a social, not a biological, construct. While we cannot know for sure how long it will take for America to truly be majority-minority (in terms of number of citizens, as well as power balance), it seems inevitable that sooner or later, the United States will be characterized by a numerical minority of whites. When that happens, we can expect another shift in the way we talk about race and racism in America.[d]

a   http://www.acri.org.
b   Ward Connerly, *Creating Equal: My Fight Against Race Preferences* (San Francisco, CA: Encounter).
c   Ward Connerly, *Lessons from My Uncle James: Beyond Skin Color to the Content of Our Character* (San Francisco: Encounter).
d   National Conference of State Legislatures, "Initiative, Referendum and Recall," 2011, http://www.ncsl.org/default.aspx?tabid=16600; Tanya Schevitz, "Prop. 54 Defeated Soundly/State Initiative on Racial Privacy Raised Issues about Health, Education," *San Francisco Chronicle*, October 8, 2003, http://www.sfgate.com/politics/article/Prop-54-defeated-soundly-State-initiative-on-2583626.php; "Ward Connerly," American Civil Rights Institute, 2007, http://www.acri.org/ward_bio.html; Zevloff, "After Colorado Loss, Ward Connerly May Pull the Plug on Affirmative-Action Bans."

Summary

Legal rights aside, most Americans (not just whites) do not really understand how affirmative action programs are designed, what they are intended to do, or whether they are effective. An honest, holistic appraisal reveals that the evidence of the effectiveness of such programs is inconclusive. Anecdotally, we can point to individuals who were provided opportunities (and were able to capitalize on them). It is more difficult to measure the long-term psychological effects on whites, many of whom feel as if they are at a disadvantage for college admission and employment, and minorities, some of whom might interpret acceptance under these programs as a tacit indicator of their unworthiness[43] (see Boxes 14.1 and 14.3). Under these circumstances, we

BOX 14.4 *What Can I Do?:* OWN YOUR PRIVILEGE

"Privilege" is a confusing term. Often it is used as an absolute: "Bill Gates is privileged." However, privilege is a relative construct. While it is difficult to identify ways in which Bill Gates does not have privilege, most of us have characteristics that, in our cultural context, confer privilege on us, as well as others that do not. If we embrace the absolute construction, we lose the ability to understand privilege as a meaningful concept—if there is always someone who is more privileged in one way or another, privilege does not mean anything at all.

Whites, on the whole, have privilege compared to persons of color, all other things being equal. Of course, all other things are rarely equal, so white women may have some advantages over women of color, but are relatively disadvantaged compared to white men. Heterosexuals are privileged compared to those who are gay, lesbian, or bisexual, but a heterosexual Latina can hardly be considered privileged in any absolute sense. Accordingly, it is useful for us to be mindful of the ways in which we are privileged and the ways we may be disadvantaged. Owning our privilege is one way of coming to terms with the complicated realities of living in a pluralistic society with a history of discrimination based on a number of characteristics. That puts us in a much better position to evaluate policy options or select candidates who will represent our interests with respect to our views on diversity and equality.

Are you able-bodied? If so, you have privilege with respect to physical ability. Even if disabled persons are not overtly discriminated against due to conscious hostility, fear, or discomfort, the world is designed and mostly inhabited by able-bodied persons. This leads to a host of disadvantages that most able-bodied people do not even notice. Are you handsome or pretty (by some commonly accepted standards, however problematic they may be)? While there are some disadvantages to being perceived as conventionally attractive (particularly for women, as our sexist culture often reduces women to their appearance), being conventionally attractive often comes with some privilege. Are you right-handed? Of average height and weight? Do you have full vision and hearing? What other privileges can you identify? Take a day or even a couple of hours and, as you move about, try to be attentive to the ways that these characteristics give you an advantage over someone who does not possess them.

Far from being a count-your-blessings exercise, the point of reflecting on and owning privilege is to become aware of how advantages and disadvantages are perpetuated on a daily basis. It reminds us that if we limit our critique of inequality to the intent of persons or groups of persons who are racist, sexist, homophobic, and so on, we are overlooking most of the inequality and disadvantage that exists.

need to decide whether affirmative action programs do more harm than good or, put another way, whether America would be a more just and equitable nation if we did not have them.

Ultimately, affirmative action programs serve more as a bandage than a cure, with most proponents believing that removing such programs would exacerbate the inequality that still exists.[44] Others believe that affirmative action programs will lead to a colorblind, gender-neutral society.[45] Opponents, however, believe that the bandage is keeping the wound from healing properly. From any perspective, it is clear that a permanent solution to America's persistent racial and economic inequality must be found elsewhere.

Discussion Questions

1. Identify your privileges. What are some of the ways in which you can "own" your privilege?
2. What are some important distinctions between how Affirmative Action operates in the classroom vs. the workplace?
3. Do you feel that Affirmative Action is more or less justified in the classroom or the workplace, or do you see no difference? Explain your answer.

Religion, Race, and Poverty

By Charles H. Lippy and Eric Tranby

Editor's Introduction

This reading discusses the segregation of religious institutions in the United States, along with the role of religious attendance in shaping attitudes and opinions about race and poverty. The authors further discuss how religious institutions foster racial and ethnic inequality, and what might change that fact.

In This Chapter

Racial inequality and separation are pervasive issues in American life, extending even to American religious life. In this chapter, we explore the causes and consequences of the racial segregation of congregations in American life. In particular, we show how racial segregation leads to increased stereotyping of others, creates distinct religious subcultures, and shapes attitudes about other races in ways that perpetuate racial inequality. We next discuss the literature on racially integrated congregations, including their promise and the difficulties associated with creating them. We then describe the sociological research on issues raised in the previous chapter, focusing on the African American church. Finally, we explore the role of religion in providing services to the poor or needy.

Main Topics Covered

- Racial segregation
  - is a persistent feature of American religious life, with roots in the racial split of Protestant churches caused by slavery.
  - shapes perceptions of racial and religious "others" in predictable ways.
  - of religion shapes attitudes towards other racial groups and explanations for racial inequality in ways that perpetuate racial inequality.
- Racially integrated congregations may help reduce racial inequality by bringing people of different races into close contact with each other. There are significant barriers to creating racially integrated congregations.
- The contemporary role of the African American church is influenced by both racial inequality and racial segregation.
- Some religious groups are engaged in providing services for the poor and needy, but many are not.

Racial Inequality in American Religious Life

Racial inequality is a fact of American life. On average, African Americans and (to a lesser extent) Latinos in America, as shown in Table 15.1, have less wealth and less income than white Americans and are thus more likely to live in poverty. They also have higher unemployment rates and are more likely to be uninsured. Moreover, whites and Asian Americans are 20 per cent more likely to complete high school and twice as likely to receive a college degree as are African Americans and Latinos. In addition, African Americans are more likely than whites to die of heart disease, stroke, liver disease, diabetes, AIDS, accidental injury, homicide, and all kinds of cancers. These inequalities have numerous causes, but are not related to biological differences in intelligence, physical ability, or economic behavior between racial groups. Instead, racial inequality in the American experience can be traced to the needs of colonial economic structures and the development of racist explanations to justify ongoing economic and political inequality.

Racial groups are also separated and segregated from each other in American life. This divide reinforces patterns of racial inequality. If you randomly selected two people from the same neighborhood or school, they would be of the same race 80 per cent and 60 per cent of the time, respectively. Seven out of ten Americans have same-race social circles (defined as the five people they talk to most often). Ninety-five per cent of married Americans are married to someone of the same race, although interracial relationships and marriages are increasing.

Table 15.1 Racial inequality in American life

Race	Median household net worth (2008)	Median household income (2008)	Poverty rate (2010)	Unemployment rate (2010)	Medical uninsurance rate (2009)	Incarceration rates (2006, men)
White Americans	$90,000	$65,000	13.0%	8.2%	12.0%	0.07%
Asian Americans	$92,000	$73,578	12.1%	7.0%	17.2%	0.04%
Latino Americans	$8,000	$40,466	26.6%	10.8%	32.4%	1.9%
African Americans	$6,000	$39,879	27.4%	15.5%	21.0%	4.8%

Source: Current Population Survey 2010, US Census Bureau 2009, Federal Bureau of Investigation 2007

Does this racial segregation persist in American religious life? Martin Luther King, Jr., repeatedly said that "eleven o'clock Sunday morning is the most segregated hour and Sunday school is still the most segregated school of the week." This is still true today. Research from the ongoing National Congregations Study found that if you randomly selected two people from the same congregation, they would be of the same race 98 per cent of the time. Ninety-three per cent of American congregations can be considered racially homogeneous (meaning that more than 80 per cent of the members of that congregation are of the same race). This segregation is most prominent among Protestant denominations, with 95 per cent of Protestant congregations being racially homogeneous. Other denominations and families are more integrated, with 14 per cent of Catholic congregations being racially mixed and 27.5 per cent of mosques, temples, and synagogues being racially mixed. Thus, the larger the religious tradition, the more segregated it is. In addition, the more choices people have of places to worship, the more they choose to be with people who are racially similar.

Causes of the Racial Segregation in Religion

There are two major sources of the racial segregation of religion: the historical division of American Protestant congregations into African American and white churches and the development of immigrant churches and religions. Chapter 11 described the history of the African American church, particularly how the split between African American and white churches is rooted in the American heritage of slavery and racism. Although there have been extensive efforts on the part of some churches to foster racial integration and unity and although racially based organizational structures within white denominations have largely broken down, there has been remarkably little progress towards racial integration between African American and white churches at the congregational level. For example, white churches, on average, have only 2 to 3 per cent African American membership. This historical division of religion is self-reinforcing, with white and African American churches developing distinct cultures and concerns (described below and in Chapter 11) that make it difficult to integrate the two religious expressions.

As described in Chapter 18, immigrants bring their religions with them when they come to the US. Although these churches quickly adapt to US congregational forms, as described in Chapter 19, those who practice non-Christian religions or Christian congregations that hold services in a foreign language are likely to be highly racially segregated. In fact, ethnic ties and consciousness of national origins are pervasive in such congregations, with little overlap between worshippers of different ethnic backgrounds.

Consequences of the Racial Segregation in Religion

Sociologists have focused extensive research on the consequences of racial segregation for how Americans understand racial inequality, particularly unequal outcomes for African Americans. They have found that racial isolation shapes our perceptions of racial others, creates distinct religious cultures, and shapes racial attitudes in ways that perpetuate racial inequality.

Classic research in social cognition demonstrates that the isolation of groups from each other in everyday life has predictable consequences for our understanding of others. This research distinguishes "in-groups" or those who are in an individual's group and with whom one interacts frequently and "out-groups" or those who are not in the group and therefore with whom one does not regularly interact. Racial isolation creates biased perceptions of racial in-groups and out-groups. In isolated environments, similarities among in-group members are exaggerated and differences with out-group members are exaggerated. This results in a mini-mizing of differences among out-group members so they are more easily stereotyped. Further, exaggerated similarity and difference result in differential attribution of positive and negative behaviors, such that people are more likely to evaluate in-group members positively and believe that positive actions are attributed to an individual's "goodness" or "moral character," while negative actions are attributed to structural forces outside the person's control. On the other hand, out-group members are evaluated more negatively and those negative actions are attributed to failure of the individual, while positive actions are attributed to structural forces such as government hand-outs or reverse racism. Moreover, we are more likely to remember positive experiences with in-group members and negative experiences with out-group members, dismissing contradictory experi-ences as exceptions to the "rules" we cognitively develop about in-groups and out-groups.

Social cognition research suggests that these biases result from any form of racial segregation. Racial isolation in religious life, however, magnifies these biases because, as discussed in Chapters 1 and 11, religion strengthens the social bonds within the religious group by, in part, heightening the group's distinctions from other groups. In other words, due to racial segregation, religious in-groups and out-groups are nearly identical to racial in-groups and out-groups.

Religion also creates separation between the races by developing distinct explanatory cultures. Research demonstrates that religion provides individuals with what Ann Swidler calls a cultural "toolkit" that helps people organize experiences and evaluate reality. For believers, these tools are often explicitly based in faith and are central to the ways in which they interpret and organize other situations and experiences, including how they make sense of issues of racial inequality. The white evangelical Protestant toolkit has been the subject of the most scholarly attention. Michael Emerson and Christian Smith argue that it consists of ac-countable freewill individualism, relationalism, and antistructuralism. Accountable freewill individualism is the theological understanding that one is accountable to other people, but most importantly to God, for their freely made choices. Relationalism is a strong emphasis on interpersonal relationships, rooted in the theologi-cal understanding that salvation can come only from a personal relationship with Christ. Antistructuralism is the inability or unwillingness to accept explanations based on social structural influences, such as prejudice, discrimination, or high levels of unemployment.

In contrast, the African American Protestant toolkit is built on community action to change systems of inequality, collective responsibility for social inequality, and structuralist explanations for racial inequality in American society. The African American church, then, uses these tools in order to establish places for promoting collective social action. The Catholic toolkit is built on communalism, or a rejection of individu-alistic explanations for, and responsibility toward, social inequality, which favors structural and institutional approaches to social problems. This toolkit is connected with the Catholic history, described in Chapter 6, of helping poor immigrant groups, and with the labor movement and its critique of capitalist structures and the government that supports them.

Sociological research demonstrates that the social cognition biases and the distinct explanatory cultures and toolkits that result from the racial segregation of churches combine to shape attitudes towards other racial groups and to provide explanations for racial inequality. Emerson and Smith, along with others, using data from 1996, find that white evangelical Protestants are more likely to favor individualistic explanations for African American inequality, such as a lack of motivation and ability, and less likely to favor structural explanations, like discrimination or a lack of access to education. These racial attitudes, combined with social isolation from African Americans, lead white evangelicals to resist structural and group-based understandings of inequality.

Eric Tranby and Penny Edgell have also done research that focuses on these issues. An overview of their findings is reported in Table 15.2. In addition to confirming Emerson and Smith's findings, Tranby and Edgell found that regardless of religious tradition, whites who are highly involved in religious activities are less sympathetic to explanations for racial inequality that point to white privilege and domination, such as

Table 15.2 *Attitudes towards African American inequality among religious groups*

	Which of the following are important explanations for African American inequality?				
	Prejudice and discrimination	Discriminatory laws and institutions	Lack of access to good schools and social connections	Lack of effort and hard work	Poor family upbringing
Population	80.7%	53.8%	54.2%	70.9%	86.2%
White Evangelical Protestants	72.1%	34.1%	32.8%	71.5%	85.9%
White Mainline Protestants	76.6%	34.7%	41.0%	60.8%	81.3%
White Catholics	78.8%	39.2%	50.8%	63.8%	85.8%
African American Protestants	91.7%	87.7%	78.4%	83.3%	88.1%
Hispanic Catholics	85.2%	60.2%	62.3%	80.3%	84.4%
Attends church monthly or more frequently	78.7%	53.2%	52.5%	74.0%	86.7%
Attends church less than monthly	82.9%	54.5%	56.0%	67.4%	85.7%

Source: 2003 American Mosaic Survey

discrimination or bias in laws and institutions, and are also less likely to favor structuralist accounts, such as a lack of access to good schools and jobs. On the other hand, they found that white Catholics are more sympathetic to explanations for African American inequality that place the responsibility on whites, such as prejudice and discrimination, and are less likely to blame poor upbringing for inequality. These results are mediated in part by education and gender, with less educated, but religiously involved, whites and non-religious women being more sympathetic to the structural explanation of African American disadvantage, while the more educated religiously involved and evangelical women are less likely to believe that racial inequality stems from biased laws and institutions and are more likely to blame African American inequality on poor upbringing in African American families.

Tranby and Edgell also investigated how religion shaped explanations for racial inequality among African Americans and Hispanics. African Americans who hold orthodox religious beliefs are more sympathetic to explanations for racial inequality focused on bias in laws and social institutions, and to structural causes, such as a lack of access to good schools and social connections. This finding represents a toolkit built on discourse about the lack of access to good schools, good jobs, and good education, and a discourse about the crisis in the African American family. Hispanic Catholics are especially likely to think that biased laws and social institutions are important explanations for explaining African American inequality. This finding reflects that Catholicism provides a set of religious cultural tools that favor structural and communal understandings of racial inequality and foster institutional solutions.

Sociological research demonstrates that the social cognition biases, distinct explanatory cultures and tool-kits, and fully separate explanations for racial inequality that result from the racial segregation of churches combine to perpetuate racial inequality in the US. First, people place in-group needs and priorities above those outside of the group. Because of this and because of racial segregation, resources and social networks are more likely to be shared within, rather than across, racial groups.

Table 15.3 Preferred solutions for African American inequality

	African Americans should not receive special help with jobs and schools	African Americans should not get more economic help from the government	Charities should do more to help African Americans
Population	43.5%	45.8%	44.7%
White Evangelical Protestants	59.7%	65.1%	29.4%
White Mainline Protestants	49.7%	49.4%	43.1%
White Catholics	48.9%	50.9%	50.1%
African American Protestants	19.0%	20.7%	59.4%
Hispanic Catholics	41.5%	40.1%	42.9%
Attends church monthly or more frequently	44.5%	46.8%	47.0%
Attends church less than monthly	43.7%	45.7%	45.4%

Source: 2003 American Mosaic Survey

Second, distinct toolkits and racial attitudes combine to favor different solutions to racial inequality. As shown in Table 15.3, white evangelical Protestants and whites who are more religiously involved tend to oppose both government and private charitable solutions for inequality, such as affirmative action programs or economic help. Instead, reflecting their emphasis on relationalism, white evangelical Protestants emphasize interpersonal and faith-based solutions to racial inequality; in particular, they seek to convert people to Christianity as a way to develop strong cross-racial relationships. White Catholics favor private charitable solutions over government ones, while African American Protestants and Hispanic Catholics favor both government and private charitable solutions for racial inequality. These preferences are more than symbolically important. A long line of sociological research demonstrates that government programs, such as affirmative actions, poverty alleviation, and anti-discrimination laws are the most effective in reducing societal levels of racial inequality. Neither private charities nor cross-racial relationships strongly affect societal levels of racial inequality, although they can make a difference in the lives of individuals. Thus, the racial segregation of churches has a profound impact on perpetuating ongoing racial inequality in the US.

Racially Integrated Congregations

If the segregation of American religious life is partially responsible for racial inequality, might more racially integrated congregations help alleviate or reduce racial inequality? Recent research by Brad Christerson, Korie L. Edwards, and Michael Emerson suggests that this may be the case. They find that racially integrated congregations promote social ties across groups, with 83 per cent of individuals who attend a racially mixed congregation reporting having one or more opposite race friends in their social circles. These social ties serve to reduce the social cognition biases and stereotypes about race described in the previous section because members of racially integrated congregations have more positive attitudes about people of different races. These congregations also appear to reduce racial inequalities between members, such that members of

Box 15.1 Evangelical Protestant Solutions to Racial Inequality

Michael Emerson and Christian Smith (2000) argue that the evangelical toolkit helps explain white evangelical approaches to solving the race problem as well. Evangelical solutions emphasize the need to get to know people of other races, to "love thy neighbor," and for everybody to become a Christian. Evangelicals are, in turn, extremely mistrustful of, and often vehemently opposed to, structural and state-based solutions to racial problems because they do not address what they believe to be the true roots of the problem. Second, evangelical solutions to race problems do not "advocate for or support changes that might cause extensive discomfort or change their economic and cultural lives" (2000:130). Thus, Emerson and Smith argue that while many evangelicals may want to see an end to race problems, they are constrained by their "toolkit" to call only for voluntaristic, faith-based solutions that would achieve the desired effects gradually and incrementally, such as converting people to Christianity and forming strong cross-racial relationships.

these churches are, on average and regardless of race, economically better off than members of non-racially mixed congregations. This effect appears to be caused by membership in the church, but the causal effect is particularly hard to unravel. Additional research finds that members of racially integrated congregations develop racial attitudes that reflect structural understandings of racial inequality. Members also emphasize interpersonal relationships as one of many ways to reduce racial segregation and inequality in American life.

These congregations achieve more racial equality between members by focusing on what Marti calls "religious racial integration," or the process by which members gain an identity in, and commitment to, the congregation, in order successfully to attract and retain members. This occurs in three stages in the lived experiences of members. First, members must begin by establishing a connection with the congregation through similar interests or beliefs. Second, persons must reorient their religious identity away from bases that exist outside the congregation and become rooted in the interests, values, and preferences of the congregation. Third, members must integrate their ethnic and racial heritage into a single religious organization. Separate research by Penny Edgell finds that having religious leaders of multiple racial backgrounds and a religious symbolism that is rooted in religious text and tradition promotes this integration.

However, there are significant barriers to the establishment of more racially integrated churches. As described in Chapter 4, most people attend a church close to them. Therefore, racially integrated congregations are more likely to occur in relatively racially diverse neighborhoods or areas. As described above, the races tend to be segregated into different neighborhoods in the US. This residential racial segregation limits the number and location of racially integrated churches.

There are other barriers to achieving this integration, even if the congregation is in a fairly racially diverse area. First, existing congregations often have a tradition, and reputation, of being racially segregated. Therefore, most racially integrated congregations are newly formed. Second, different theological understandings and worship styles across racial groups can create conflict in a congregation. In particular, research by Korie L. Edwards demonstrates that most racially integrated churches do not assemble their own distinctive style of congregational life or balance religious cultures. Instead, they continue to reflect the worship practices, organizational structure, and cultural style of white churches with only symbolic elements representing African American, Latino, and Asian cultures. This dominance can leave many nonwhite members of the church feeling disconnected from the church or upset that tightly controlled services that dominate in the white tradition do not allow for the Holy Spirit to move within the congregation. Third, the sustained focus on religious racial integration that is necessary to maintain these congregations can be hard to maintain in the long term, particularly for whites who do not have to deal with racial inequality in their everyday lives.

Figure 15.1 Racially integrated congregations help promote social ties and reduce inequality across racial groups. However, there are significant challenges to establishing and creating these congregations

© Najlah Feanny/Corbis

African American Religion Revisited

Contemporary sociological research has brought other insights into the African American church and mosque. As described previously, African American churches in general are more likely to engage in community and social justice than white churches because of African Americans' historic inability to participate fully in economic, social, and political life. This is particularly true of inner city churches. The African American toolkit, described above, is used to motivate social actions by church members. For example, Mary Pattillo-McCoy, in her ethnographic study of two African American churches, finds that community meetings targeted at curbing youth delinquency, working to close a neighborhood drug house, or inspiring individuals to vote used rhetorical, interactional, and material tools that emphasized the collective responsibility of church members towards an issue.

African American mosques play a similar role in the African American community, especially mosques located in the inner city. In a study of an African American Sunni mosque, Victoria Lee finds that the mosque provides the driving force for change within the community, establishing a multifaceted development program to assist Muslims as well as the community. Importantly, Islam provides African Americans with an opportunity to shape a new identity distinct from an African American Protestant one that is rooted in the history of slavery. Islam also provides religious tools built on highly structured codes, norms, and rituals that address issues important to the inner-city African American community, such as the dissolution of family values, the sexualized stereotype of African American women, and the prevalence of drugs and violence.

However, African American religion is not a monolithic entity that emphasizes uniform issues or concerns. There are substantial class differences in African American religion. The African American church does, in general, bring poor and middle class African Americans together by providing a cultural blueprint for activities with the community. However, upper-class and upwardly mobile African Americans are more likely to become members of churches in white denominations, partly in an effort to conform to their new social status and disaffiliate from an inner-city lifestyle. This helps to perpetuate resource disparities between white and African American churches.

In addition, the African American religious experience, especially in the inner city, is dominated by multiple small "niche" churches. Omar McRoberts finds important consequences of this particularism in his study of the twenty-nine African American churches within a half-mile radius of the Four Corners neighborhood of Boston. These churches do allow people to find a church that aligns with their personal beliefs. However, because many of these churches are located in storefronts, they crowd out small businesses that rely on those spaces to provide a home for their products and services. This contributes to the lack of economic growth in inner city neighborhoods. Additionally, many of these small, storefront churches are run and attended by commuters who do not live in the neighborhood. Thus, religious leaders and members of these churches may have little attachment to the neighborhood, making them less inclined to respond to the needs of the community.

Box 15.2 The Role of the African American Mosque in the Community

Victoria Lee (2010: 154–55) discusses the role that the Mosque she studied played in the broader community:

The Masjid [Mosque] has emerged as a driving force for change within the local community. A decade ago, the mosque established a multifaceted development program to assist Muslims and the larger community. Its mission statement promotes the development of spiritual, intellectual, and physical resources, the fostering of family stability, and communal and societal advancement. Concretely, it has set up a block watch that meets every month to encourage positive community development, fight crime, and remove trash and blight. It works with the police to prevent drug trafficking as well. The mosque's charismatic leaders have forged a close working relationship with their neighborhood, the nearby hospital, and the mayor of Northeastern City to rehabilitate abandoned houses and revitalize the surrounding area. The Masjid alone has invested in more than a half-million dollar's worth of property to help stabilize the community. Their daily congregational prayers, educational programs, and watchful presence reduce crime and negative activities in the neighborhood. The Masjid also plans to open a high school for Muslim students not only to instill Islamic moral values but also to get young people off the street and to provide them with vocational skills as a way to move forward in a community with limited economic opportunity.

Northeastern City has recognized the Masjid as a positive force in community stabilization. A plaque honoring the Masjid for its community contributions stands at a nearby intersection for visitors to see. However, gaining the city's and neighborhood's trust has not been immediate. Sister Makarim noted that residents were skeptical when the Muslims first arrived in the neighborhood. Neighborhood opinion changed when Muslims, decidedly fed up with the blatant crime surrounding the mosque, lined up on the street, side by side, to keep vigil through numerous nights to fend off the drug trade. Their actions angered the drug dealers, but the residents came to appreciate and welcome the Muslims' presence and contributions to the quality of local life.

Figure 15.2 Many congregations provide for the short-term needs of the poor and needy. Here, homeless men prepare to sleep at a night shelter held at a church in Glendora, CA

© Marmaduke St. John/Alamy

Religion and Social Services

To help alleviate poverty and reduce inequality, many congregations provide social services to the poor and the needy. Social services provided by congregations include homeless shelters, food shelves/pantries, job training, drug and alcohol rehabilitation, family planning, and other services, especially those in urban areas and African American congregations.

Some people argue that religious groups and congregations are uniquely suited to deliver social services and can replace the state in providing these services. In this argument, religious organizations specialize in a more holistic kind of social service activity that focuses on personal transformation to provide long-term solutions to people's problems. This holistic approach is thought to be an important alternative to social services delivered by nonreligious organizations, like government agencies, that focus on the short-term needs of clients.

These ideas culminated in the Charitable Choice provision of the 1996 welfare reform law. This provision directs government funding to religious organizations to provide social services through various block grants to state agencies. Funds received through the Charitable Choice initiative must be used to fulfill public social service goals and cannot be used for religious activities, but the government cannot require the providers to remove religious materials from the site. Much controversy surrounds this provision, especially concerns about whether faith-based organizations would be willing to serve anyone without proselytizing and whether there would be religious tests for persons who delivered the services; however, it remains in force today.

Research by Mark Chaves and William Tsitsos from 2001 reveals that the assumptions behind the Charitable Choice provision are flawed, at best. Social services provided by religious groups are most likely to be aimed at meeting short-term emergency needs and require limited contact with needy people. Moreover, government social service programs and collaborative programs are the most likely to engage in holistic service delivery.

Finally, as of 2007, according to the National Congregations Study, only 36 per cent of congregations had expressed any interest in using Charitable Choice funds and only 10 per cent had applied for funds.

More broadly, the assumption that religious groups and congregations do a lot to combat poverty or provide social services is flawed. Mark Chaves, using the 1998 National Congregations Study, found that 12 per cent of congregations ran food shelves or other food programs and 4 per cent ran or participated in housing or homeless programs. Overall, 40 per cent did some kind of social service work on an occasional basis, and, on average, only 2 to 4 per cent of a congregation's budget goes toward social service projects. This work is commonly done by a core group of individuals within the congregation, with only 15 per cent of weekly service attenders reporting that they regularly participate in their congregations' social service activities. On a national scale, the volunteerism of religious individuals and groups is laudable and certainly makes a difference in people's lives, but federal, state, and local governments still spend a hundred times more on social services than all congregations in the US combined.

Key Points You Need to Know

- Racial segregation is a persistent feature of American religious life.
- The larger the religious tradition, the more segregated it is.
- The more choices people have of places to worship, the more they choose to be with people who are racially similar.
- There are two major sources of the racial segregation of religion: the legacy of the historical division of African American Protestant and white Protestant churches, and the development of immigrant churches and religions.
- Racial segregation shapes our perceptions of racial others by generating biased ideas of members of racial and religious out-groups.
- Racial segregation creates distinct religious cultures that people use to organize experiences and evaluate reality.
- Racial segregation shapes attitudes towards other racial groups and explanations for racial inequality.
- The effects of the racial segregation of America combine to perpetuate racial inequality by reinforcing disparate social and resource networks, and leading people to favor different solutions for racial inequality.
- Racially integrated congregations may help reduce racial inequality in American life by promoting social ties and the sharing of resources between people of different racial groups.
- There are significant organizational and structural barriers to the success of racially integrated congregations.
- African American religion is not a monolithic entity that emphasizes the same issues or concerns.
- Although religious groups provide many social services in the US, assumptions about their effectiveness and ability to replace the role of the government in social service provisions are flawed.

Discussion Questions

1. What are the causes and consequences of the racial segregation of American religion?
2. In what ways does religion provide explanations for, and solutions to, racial inequality?

3. Should religious congregations work to reduce racial inequality? Why or why not?
4. If you had one, was the congregation you grew up in mostly racially homogeneous or racially mixed? Did you ever talk about race issues? What effects do you think the racial composition of your church had on you?
5. Would you go out of your way to attend a racially mixed congregation? Why or why not?
6. What is the role of the African American church and mosque in the community?
7. How does class mobility affect the African American church?
8. Should religious organizations do more to provide social services? Why or why not?

Further Reading

Becker, P.E. (1998) "Making Inclusive Communities: Congregations and the 'Problem' of Race," *Social Problems*, 45: 451–72.

Chaves, M. and Tsitsos, W. (2001) "Congregations and Social Services: What They Do, How They Do It, and With Whom," *Nonprofit and Voluntary Sector Quarterly* 30: 660–83.

——— (2001) "Religious Congregations and Welfare Reform," *Society* 38: 21–27.

Christerson, B., Edwards K.L., and Emerson M.O. (2005) *Against All Odds: The Struggle for Racial Integration in Religious Organizations*, New York: New York University Press.

Edgell, P. and Tranby, E. (2007) "Religious Influences on Understandings of Racial Inequality in the United States," *Social Problems*, 54: 263–88.

Edwards K.L. (2008) "Bring Race to the Center: The Importance of Race in Racially Diverse Religious Organizations," *Journal for the Scientific Study of Religion*, 47: 5–9.

Emerson, M.O. and Sikkink, D. (1999) "Equal in Christ, but Not in the World: White Conservative Protestants and Explanations of Black-White Inequality," *Social Problems* 46: 398–412.

Emerson, M.O. and Smith, C. (2000) *Divided by Faith: Evangelical Religion and the Problem of Race*, Oxford: Oxford University Press.

Lee, V.J. (2010) "The Mosque and Black Islam Towards an Ethnographic Study of Islam in the Inner City," *Ethnic and Racial Studies*, 11: 145–63.

Lincoln, E.C. and Mamiya L.H. (1990) *The Black Church in the African American Experience.* Durham, NC: Duke University Press.

McRoberts, O. (2003) *Streets of Glory: Church and Community in a Black Urban Neighborhood*, Chicago: University of Chicago Press.

Marti G. (2009) "Affinity, Identity, and Transcendence: The Experience of Religious Racial Integration in Diverse Congregations," *Journal for the Scientific Study of Religion*, 48: 53–68.

Nelson, T.J. (2004) *Every Time I Feel the Spirit: Religious Experience and Ritual in an African American Church*, New York: New York University Press.

Pattillo-McCoy, M. (1998) "Church Culture as a Strategy of Action," *American Sociological Review* 63: 767–84.

Roof, W.C. and McKinney, W. (1987) *American Mainline Religion: Its Changing Shape and Future*, Camden, NJ: Rutgers University Press.

Tranby, E.P. and Hartmann, D. (2008) "Critical Whiteness Theories and the Evangelical Race Problem: Extending Emerson and Smith's *Divided by Faith*," *Journal for the Scientific Study of Religion*, 47: 341–59.

Wood, R. (2002) *Faith in Action: Religion, Race, and Democratic Organizing in America,* Chicago: University of Chicago Press.

Race in Sports

The Continuing Dilemma

By Leonard J. Elmore

Editor's Introduction

Sports are a great passion around the world and in the United States. Race and ethnicity are important aspects of sports, in terms of the athletes who compete and the public that watches the competitions. In this reading, the author discusses the many issues concerning race and ethnicity in sports.

Introduction

The relationship between race and sports has unfortunately not changed a great deal over the years. An emotionally demonstrated national obsession with sports naturally and rationally must include a discussion of sports' impact on race and society, and equally, any discussion of race and society must include sports. Today, race continues to be a polarizing factor in our society. It is simply a bit more muted than it was twenty, thirty, or fifty years ago.

It is well known that sports have the potential to obliterate racial barriers and create more meaningful understanding and empathy among our body politic. Sports can continue to create and generate educational and financial opportunities for many individuals of every hue who are underserved or simply shut out of the mainstream of opportunity. Sports can also affirm a much-needed individual accountability that is required when striving for the American dream. As a true meritocracy in theory, sports in America represents the power of dreams, work ethic, and perseverance, just as Horatio Alger said.[1] Because of its noble intentions and outcomes and the diversity of participation, sports should be the place where it is easy to discuss differences without the emotional references to race that touch off dividing controversy. Sports should be the arena devoid of racial politics since success ought simply to be about ability and outcome. But, no such luck. Like the complexities and prejudices of modern American society, race and racial politics are used as weapons and excuses. Like society, ignorance, fear, and anger involving race distort the promise of sports and alter the American dream of equality.

Historical Racism in Sports

Historically, sports have felt the impact of society and have reflected social values of the times. For example, at the turn of the century, horse racing presented a great opportunity for blacks to compete in sports, among and against whites. The most prolific jockey of his time was a gentleman by the name of Isaac Murphy, a black man who won three Kentucky Derby crowns.[2] But too much success probably led to the ruling right around 1900 that barred black jockeys from competing.[3] Now, obviously, the vehicle was probably *Plessy v. Ferguson*, separate-but-equal, a ruling that essentially legalized segregation once again.[4] The social backdrop was the post-Civil Rights social and economic gains made by blacks, and these economic gains fueled white anger and envy. Murphy died at an early age from stresses symptomatic of the victims of racism, alcoholism, and poor health care. Murphy's experience symbolized how society could use sports to control and, in this case, block symbolic yet highly visible avenues of achievement for blacks.

Who can forget Jack Johnson and his *Unforgivable Blackness?*[5] The heavyweight championship was a definition of manhood in the twentieth century. The fact that a black man not only destroyed all comers, including whites, but also had the temerity to date and marry white women rocked America.[6] Johnson was brought down by an openly racist judicial system in Chicago that misused the law designed to stop interstate prostitution.[7] Johnson's conviction was designed to send two messages: black Americans shouldn't get too giddy or uppity with Johnson's dominance and symbol of masculinity, and race mixing was still forbidden.

Similarly, Fritz Pollard, a pro football star quarterback who doubled as coach, was also victimized by a combination of old-fashioned racism and by the white majority's fear of competing against and losing to black athletes.[8] And sure, against Max Schmeling, Joe Louis served a purpose during the ideological and physical fight against Nazi propaganda.[9] Joe Louis was everybody's All-American.[10] With Joe Louis, sports once again presented symbols used to benefit American society, but once again, as any Pullman car porter or housemaid in 1930s Harlem could tell you, racism was still prominent. Post-World War II presented a complexity to American social norms that changed the course of United States history. Black men fought for their country against Nazism and Japanese imperialism, but they were ruled by Jim Crow at home.[11] Through their patriotism, a compelling case was made for eradicating discrimination. But in baseball, America's pastime, segregation was still the rule of the day.

However, the prowess of black players could not be denied. It took a combination of events and the shrewd exploitation of opportunities, including the passing of New York state antidiscrimination legislation that led to Jackie Robinson's debut in Brooklyn.[12] The aftermath of World War II tested social acceptance of segregation in the North and sent shivers down the spines of folks in the South. After all, baseball's segregation was as much about job security as it was about white superiority. Pre-Robinson white players knew black players were their equal. However, they also knew that acceptance of integration meant back to the farm, back to the factories, and otherwise losing jobs in a depression period marked by widespread poverty that affected all of working-class America, regardless of ethnicity. Their lack of education, skills, and opportunity made many white players vulnerable if forced to compete in an integrated real-world workforce. The other irony was that Negro League baseball was a cottage industry owned by and predominately patronized by blacks.[13] The black entrepreneur, Rube Foster, did very well.[14] However, baseball's integration experiment and the subsequent invitation to black players to play in the major leagues ended the Negro Leagues as a viable business.[15] Therefore, Jackie Robinson was the emblem of social change albeit grudgingly. Slowly, but surely, Robinson's success and the success of those African American players who followed ultimately sent the most obvious racial stereotypes underground in a way that the values of the Tuskegee airmen and other World War II fighting men of color could not.

In post-World War II America, it was sports that elicited the loudest calls for equality. It was sports that appeared before society to take another look at racial policy. To be sure, *Brown v. Board of Education*[16] in 1955 and civil rights legislation to follow tried to assure de jure equality, but de facto equality was a question of winning minds and breaking down barriers. It was a role that could be uniquely filled by sports.

The historical view of race and sports in America is instructive in tracing America's progress towards a society where race is not supposed to matter. The opportunities for equality and true understanding among diverse people presented by sports after the Civil Rights movement haven't always paralleled opportunity in minority communities. After the Great Society, black and now Latino communities continue to struggle with inferior education, with crime, with poverty, and with higher unemployment rates than their white counterparts.[17] But there can be no denying that for the athletes able to break through to prominence since Jackie, there have been opportunities for economic and financial gain as well as a gain in influencing society one way or another. It's the path to those opportunities and the intersection with social change and controversy that is discussed within this chapter. In doing so, the point has to be made that the discussion must be held in the context of a society striving to be colorblind, but that is all too often blinded by color.

Athletic Superiority Versus Intellectual Inferiority

Probably the greatest controversy regarding race and sport in our social fabric is the debate over athletic superiority and the ever-present, but now probably underground, discussion of intellectual inferiority.[18] Some argue that genetic makeup is a valid discussion when trying to find out why athletes of African descent are so dominant in a number of sports.[19] Some also argue that genetic makeup is fair game in determining discrepancies among the races when measuring intelligence quotient.[20] Let's consider this. People of Sub-Saharan African descent number approximately 800 million in Africa.[21] Another 169 million are found in the Americas and Europe.[22] However, this makes up roughly only 14 percent of the global population. Yet black athletes hold nearly every major running world record from 100 meters to the marathon, and these are athletes of African descent.[23] In the United States, 80 percent of the professional basketball players, 70 percent of the NFL players, and about 30 percent of Major League Baseball players are of African descent (arguably 30 percent of Major League Baseball because even though they aren't called "black," Latin Americans with dark skin are of African descent).[24] Now around the world, even in sports like soccer, rugby, and cricket, blacks are represented and have taken up residence at the star level in numbers far greater than they are represented in their countries' populations. The question is, "Why?" We know that social and economic barriers to participation in the so-called major sports are low. But environment and choice do not offer enough of an explanation in this sports-crazed world where so many are entering competitive sports for the potential rewards.

Malcolm Gladwell has openly lamented the fact that society is afraid to have this discussion.[25] In one article, he states:

> Few object when medical scientists talk about the significant epidemiological differences between blacks and whites and the fact that blacks have a higher incidence of hypertension than whites and twice as many black males die of diabetes and prostate cancer as white males, that breast tumors

appear to grow faster in black women than in white women. ... So why aren't we allowed to say that there might be athletically significant differences between blacks and whites?[26]

Now the most prominent reason we fear unvarnished discussion of this controversial subject is because of the history of misusing so-called "scientific differences." Genetic findings have been perverted by Jensen and Shockley to support theories of intellectual inferiority.[27] The Bell Curve used statistics to support the same.[28] It is a well-known fact that if you squeeze the numbers hard enough, pretty soon they'll scream what you want them to scream.[29] The fear among most right-thinking people is rooted in the history of science's preoccupation with black physiology and mentality in ways designed to confirm theories of inferiority and to rationalize slavery and other subjugation.

Historically, racial politics often compared people of African descent to animals rather than to other races.[30] The fear in using genetic rationalization to support theories of black sports dominance is possibly, as Dr. Harry Edwards observed, an underhanded way to say that "blacks are closer to beasts and animals in terms of their genetic and physical and anatomical make up than they are to the rest of humanity."[31] The fear among all of us is that whatever society gives to African descendents in terms of an acknowledgment of domination in sports, it deducts from recognition of mental and intellectual capabilities.

So, regardless of where anybody stands on the questions of racial athletic dominance and why this dominance occurs, these are legitimate questions to ask and subjects to discuss. Generalizations about black and white intelligence usually sneak sports prowess into the mix anyway. Only when discussed candidly will American society finally lay to rest the unspoken but very prevalent notion that extraordinary athleticism and intellectual capacity are mutually exclusive. But before the definitive statement can be made, we have to explore the images that give rise to and buttress the mistaken assumptions about black and white athletes.

Media Racism

Media portrayal of athletes both black and white sometimes reflects but often determines perception and shapes versions of reality. Fair coverage remains available, but one has to look past the sensationalism, particularly in this burgeoning age of athlete criminal accusations and lawbreaking. The treatment of these types of stories is in stark contrast depending upon whether the accused is black or white. Without pronouncing on guilt or innocence, it is instructive to recall the imagery of O. J.,[32] Kobe,[33] and most recently Michael Vick,[34] as presented by the media prior to adjudication. In contrast, let's examine the treatment of Mark Chmura, a former Green Bay Packer tight end who was accused of sexually assaulting a seventeen-year-old girl.[35] Or Jeff Reardon, the former Major League Baseball pitcher found not guilty by reason of insanity for armed robbery.[36] In the O. J., Kobe, and Michael Vick cases, the public was polled by the media, often revealing a disheartening polarization across racial lines. There was no proliferation of public polling in the Chmura case or the Reardon case, and the reason is most likely that the results would not have been as sensational or as incendiary as those involving race. The polls reflect two different views based on different experiences with and perceptions of the system. The Duke lacrosse case where the charged athletes were ultimately vindicated is another example of a media-feeding frenzy that spurred polarization and conclusion jumping.[37] Besides the justice that had been served, the other positive result was a remark by one of the accused young men to the effect that he now knows how the system can be perverted and how the powerless can get ground up in a runaway process.

Is it the obvious—that black players in the hallmark sports of football and basketball are the majority and making on average millions of dollars, living lives that most American males can only dream about and that envy unleashes the thinly veiled revulsion and stereotyping manifest in much of the unbalanced media reporting and portrayals that occur today? As the esteemed president and CEO of the National Consortium for Academics in Sports and the founder of the respected Center for the Study of Sports in Society, Richard Lapchick, wrote, "Those types of imbalances and stereotypes are both persistent and consistent. In fact the damage done by this persistence and consistency may for now be irreversible even among educated people who ought to know better."[38]

Richard Lapchick, in an article entitled *Crime and Athletes: The New Racial Stereotypes of the 1990s*, describes asking a group of distinguished academics and international fellows at an elite meeting to write down five words that these fellows would use to describe American athletes.[39] There were positive adjectives, no doubt about it, but invariably, not one of these highly educated people missed listing at least one of the following words: "dumb," "violent," "rapist," and "drug user."[40] The result of the imbalanced portrayal of today's athletes, especially black athletes, provides an undue influence on how society perceives them, even among those who should know better. A question to ask is this: If transgressions committed by black athletes suddenly disappeared and society and the media were left simply with the same accusations and transgressions committed by white athletes, how would society view those athletes? What words would be used to describe those athletes? Simply put, the numbers of black athlete offenders as compared against offenders in any category overall do not support the stereotypes believed by too many and advanced by media and spread throughout our digital nation.

Media imagery is also focused on portraying sports and entertainment as prime avenues of success for African Americans rather than keeping sports in perspective and highlighting accomplishments of prominent black community leaders and captains of industry.[41] The media paints perceptions in a way that has impact much the same as symbols work outside of sports. In the general media, the impact of seeing whiteness associated subtly and obviously with intellectual, economic, political, and moral superiority, while blackness is associated with sexuality, misogyny, laziness, and community pathology is dangerous and damaging.[42] This no doubt colors how we feel about ourselves and how we feel about others. Make no mistake, some athletes, particularly black athletes and other athletes of color, actually buy into the skewed media images and even exacerbate situations by acting as caricatures. Their apparent lack of respect for themselves, others, and the sport in which they participate only serves as fodder for those who would feed the extreme images rather than portray truthfulness. The responsibility of image rests as much with the athletes as it does with the purveyors of the image. The players are the caretakers of their own image. They've got to be responsible. They must be accountable. Still, social debate and open candid discourse will continue to help determine perception.

Education

With regard to another important aspect of race and sports, education, there exists a real need for educator accountability in closing the achievement gap between minority students and their white counterparts. Unless the gap closes, kids of color continue to lose ground in developing the skills required to compete in the global marketplace. Consequently, national production potential in global market leadership will be jeopardized. Today we are witness to a shrinking number of open seats in colleges and the rising cost of a college education.[43] Families of all persuasions are searching for financial aid. Poor graduation rates for minority male student-athletes, particularly in basketball, have sparked discussions tinged with racial politics. Even though many of us might have believed that collegiate athletics were somewhat immune to racial politics, the stark examples of a lack of academic success befallen a particular group of athletes have given rise to more innuendo and more code words. Scarce resources always prompt conservative outcry among those who are accustomed to advantage. Even moderate voices rise in opposition to programs that smack of preferential treatment for those who are not like them. This is all about whose ox is being gored. But given the prospects of opportunity for a number of our nation's athletes of color, it must sadly be recognized that many of them have dropped the ball. Many of our athletes of color are missing an opportunity for themselves and for their communities. Notwithstanding a free education and access to academic support systems that are, fairly or not, of better quality than those available to many of their non-athletic counterparts, too many of our kids are wasting away potential.

The talented athlete of any color possesses virtues coveted by corporate America: leadership qualities, work ethic, perseverance, the ability to remain poised under pressure, and innate intelligence. Each of these skills is required to compete in sports at the highest levels. These skills need only be refined and cultivated. That is what colleges and universities are supposed to do—create leaders. That is their responsibility. The student-athlete's job is to have vision, to be assertive, to be an advocate, and to be responsible for his or her education. Yes, our national education system has problems, from the beginning to the end. Many high schools under-prepare student-athletes. College athletic programs recruit the best athletes, not necessarily the best students. There exists a subtle built-in prejudice against student-athletes at many institutions that is manifest in patronizing attitudes, dummy courses, or, on the other end of the spectrum, overt hostility with little or no empathy for the pressures of the student-athlete.

Notwithstanding the hurdles, success stories are common where young men and women of color do overcome the obstacles, and they do achieve.[44] The common denominators in those people are desire, discipline, assertiveness, and the acceptance of responsibility for one's education rather than the abdication of that responsibility. Yet, it all begins with opportunity.

The nineteen-year-old age rule in college basketball is an example of leading with opportunity. When the NBA instituted the rule requiring draftees to be nineteen years old and one year removed from high school, many people complained that it was unfair to deny these high school stars a chance to play in the league.[45] The lawyers were lining up looking for players to test the rule in court. Yet, if you look at the 2007 college basketball season, with the exception of Kevin Durant and Greg Oden, few other freshmen really proved themselves ready to play at the next level.[46] Yes, some of them were drafted, but in my view, very few of them proved that they could play immediately at the professional level. In fact, the weaknesses of many who believed that they were first-round material coming out of high school have been exposed in college competition, and this has forced these athletes to return for at least another year of college to try and fix their athletic shortcomings. If these athletes enjoy the college experience or see that their games must improve to play professionally, then a sizable number of those young people will stay a third year to realize their potential. Because of the NCAA academic rules that demand progress towards a degree, pretty soon somebody is going to get an education![47] By spending time on a campus and understanding what a university community expects of them, these young men might avoid the social and psychological pitfalls experienced by their failed predecessors. In turn, they might help change perceptions, and the educational experience will change the athletes for the better and positively alter images. Even "can't miss" basketball athletes like Durant and Oden actually went to class and enjoyed school. This confirms that the rule promotes personal growth beyond basketball skill development.

The argument against age limits in pro sports, particularly the argument that eighteen- to nineteen-year-olds should be able to become pro athletes, again smacks of racial politics in a peculiar way. To declare unfairness and then unfavorably compare the plight of the overwhelming number of young black men seeking to use basketball as a stepping-stone to a miniscule shot at the pros, against the number of white athletes who leave high school to pursue a career in baseball, hockey, or tennis, is an argument that misses the point. The failure of a young black athlete to make it in the NBA is a failure felt by the entire minority community. These communities feel the failures of the majority of these kids who think that they're going to get there and ultimately do not. The problem is that pain of failure is unique to that community. For the African American community where there remain more males behind bars than college-age men in college,[48] we ought to be building superhighways towards colleges rather than erecting barriers of hoop dreams. Narrow is the entryway to the NBA, and repercussions are felt all the way down to grade school where young men so often forsake school under the pretext of "getting ready for the league."[49] One should not worry about the one in 10 million guys like LeBron James, Kobe Bryant, Kevin Garnett, Amar'e Stoudemire, and now, Kevin Durant and Greg Oden. Instead one should worry about the other 9,999,999 who never make it and foreclose educational opportunities for development as individuals. What becomes of these young men when thrown back to the mean streets once basketball does not work out?

The arguments that compare white athletes in baseball, hockey, and tennis don't factor in this community and personal failure issue. Again, it's a question of experience. Although the NBA would have been happier with a twenty-year-old rule, the NBA knows that even with the nineteen-year-old restriction, it is better served by more mature and potentially better-educated players.[50] Promulgating the age restriction was a business decision; there is no question about it. The extra year prompts young men to enter college, if nothing else, to capture and remain in the limelight. The kids now know that it takes an extra year, and recognize that they have to get into college. Most young men will not go play in Europe as an alternative, because teams in Europe will not generally want them at that age. European teams have enough of their own eighteen-year-olds playing over there. So now college becomes the crucible, and pretty soon people will start to aim towards that. Ultimately, that is what we should want to do, to get athletes of color into college. Let's get them in and then see if we can impact and change minds. College is where the weaknesses of many will be uncovered, and that may encourage some guys to stay another year. The age limit represents goals that are correct and proper. Arguments against the age restriction do not factor in the impact in the minority community.

Hiring

Image and perception are also important factors in hiring decisions in sports. Hiring issues on the coaching and executive levels of college and pro sports are influenced by perception as much as they are in corporate America's boardrooms. The dearth of black Division I head coaches in college, black head coaches in the NFL, and minority managers in Major League Baseball is well documented.[51] While we've seen progress, the numbers of minority general managers in the NFL and MLB, as well as the number of minority collegiate athletic directors are disturbing.[52] It is far easier to make the case for disparate treatment of minority groups in these instances as opposed to a disparate impact. Most specifically, team owners, university presidents, and search committees make hires based in large part on who they know.[53] When they review lists of new hires, many minority candidates are not on those lists.[54] The solution is greater personal exposure to capable minority candidates.[55] If decision-makers, social or professional, don't include minority candidates in their social circles, these candidates will not come to the front of anyone's mind when an important hire needs to be made.

Jim Delany, the commissioner of the Big Ten Athletic Conference, had a great idea: mandatory social networking sessions between athletic directors and minority coaches to get better acquainted, to know who's out there, and to increase the comfort level of interaction. Progress on the minority hiring front has occurred recently and is due in part to the Black Coaches Association and their programs aimed at greater exposure, the Fritz Pollard Alliance and its role in instituting the NFL's Rooney Rule, and the NCAA and its coaching academy. These organizations have been beacons in increasing the number of black coaches on the field and the number of candidates in the pipeline.

Retention of minority coaches is an important issue in equivalence to their scarcity.[56] Studies have shown that minority football and basketball head coaches have to be better to be perceived just as good.[57] In the NBA, believe it or not, black head coaches have shorter tenures by almost a season against comparable records of their counterparts.[58] Now, is race the causal factor? Maybe. On its face, the numbers are compelling. Just like in a real-world workplace with law firms that struggle with retention rates of minority, particularly black, attorneys,[59] these attorneys become disillusioned with partner associate relationships where black associates don't feel the same commitment to their mentoring as their white counterparts. Black associates leave without ever qualifying for partner. The rationale is the same in sports. Unfortunately, people tend to gravitate and feel comfort towards those who share common ground and common interests. Focus should shift toward further effectuating Jim Delany's networking idea, the NCAA's coaching academy, Fritz Pollard Alliance's and BCA's programs—these organizations offer viable parts of resolving this continuing problem.

Personal Responsibility

Not all of the blame for distorted perceptions and polarized viewpoints can be laid at the feet of the media or our educational system, or even the vocal minority of haters among us. Athletes of color must accept and assume some responsibility. They must bear the burden of accountability for their situation as well. Among the best-paid individuals in the world for what they do, pro athletes of color attain a lofty position as a direct result of a legacy of suffering, of sacrifice, of activism, and of triumph.[60] Far too many of today's star athletes are ignorant or blind to the struggles of those who preceded them. Far too many of our star athletes, with a few exceptions, exist in a vacuum where their special treatment is the thing that sets them apart, particularly by those people who tell them, "You're not like everybody else." That special treatment is due to their world-class status as athletes. But this otherworldly status seems to bring on a kind of amnesia as to the racial and social realities in which star athletes of color live. A superstar athlete of color has real influence over so many aspects of society, including young people, and so many times this influence is wasted or diverted from doing good, focusing rather on doing well. Instead of choosing commercialism over social activism, today's athlete must stand up, grab the reins, and do what he can do to lead us to change. William Rhoden's book, Forty Million Dollar Slaves: The Rise, Fall, and Redemption of the Black Athlete, decries the neutrality of black athletes in the struggle for change.[61] There is a quote in Rhoden's book that describes minority athletes claiming an abdication of their social responsibility because they are labeled as "a slave."[62] Given the resources and the attendant power that these young men and some women have, if they are slaves, they choose to be.[63] They have become slaves to the special treatment that is given to them. That special treatment amounts to a divide and conquer strategy that may not be applied intentionally, but it operates by effect.

Accountability? That comes in resisting the extreme trappings of the celebrity life that renders these athletes as caricatures. The NBA Dress Code is a great example of misunderstanding the message.[64] Yes, it has served the NBA's purposes of moderating its product's appearance for corporate sponsors and others, but it has also served the players well in softening their images.[65] The NBA athletes whining and crying about being told what to wear and not wanting to look like somebody else is really funny to me, because it is all about appropriateness.[66] How many people watch the NBA draft? When was the last time a player walked up on that stage not wearing a suit and tie? Now when your employer tells you to go business casual at minimum, how can you fight about that?

In terms of accountability, our community, the black community, has to shoulder some of the load as well. Our athletes, for better or worse, are our most visible products and some of our most shining examples. As parents, as community leaders, we continue to push our kids towards sports to the detriment of education—where becoming a pro carries more social weight than becoming a professional in something other than sports. You've seen the commercials. Even with examples of those of us who have done both, we still push our kids towards sports. Why?

John Hoberman wrote a book in 1997 called Darwin's Athletes: How Sports Has Damaged Black America and Preserved the Myth of Race. Dr. Hoberman opines that black overinvestment in sports is the consequence of racist limitations on black achievement in other areas.[67] He urges black intellectuals to do more to counteract sports and entertainment, especially hip-hop, a fixation among black youth which he believes, and I believe, has stunted intellectual development and created, in my mind, a kind of mutant culture beyond anything Jackie Robinson could've imagined when he integrated America's pastime.[68] For the record, Dr. Hoberman, who is white, has been castigated by a number of black scholars for being an outsider writing about things of which he has no experience or frame of reference. It is difficult to see the relevance of his race in what could be considered a wake-up call to all of America. The concept of race and sport and the impact of sport on society and vice versa will require closer scrutiny at a time when you look to the highest court in the land, the United States Supreme Court.[69] The makeup on the Supreme Court, even with the addition of Justice Sonia Sotomayor, has radically shifted to what can be considered a hostile right.

Coaches have tremendous influence on the people who come through their athletic programs. When a parent or caregiver turns a son or daughter over to the coaches, a parent is essentially expecting those coaches to become a surrogate parent. When you're talking about a coach providing mentorship, guidance, and leadership, the coach plays a prominent role because of the amount of time spent with student-athletes. This does not mean that a professor or a counselor cannot play a role in that light, but many times it's the coach who touches the motivational buttons of young athletes spurring self-discipline, assertiveness, and those things that an individual needs to grow as an athlete but also to grow as a person. When looking at a college coach's contract, in many instances whether inferred or expressed, the number of games the coach wins takes precedence over the number of people who graduate from the program or what players become when their playing careers are over. Coaches are the ones responsible for the recruiting of these athletes, and nowadays, character absolutely has to count.

A commonly expressed lament is that colleges are recruiting the best athletes instead of the best student-athletes. That lament is not to say that we do not want to provide educational opportunities to some athletes who might be on a borderline because success stories exist in that vein. There are ways other than SAT scores to measure capability and aptitude. Schools should recruit holistically to discover who is capable of doing collegiate work and provide that opportunity to those students. The idea of providing more scholarships is a terrific one that is going to become a question again of dollars and cents.[70] In many major programs, the dollars may be there for additional scholarships, but accomplishing that goal takes moving people so that they are comfortable walking in that direction. Scholarships and providing educational opportunities for a child (and an eighteen-year-old can be considered a child) place a great responsibility on the coach who brings him into a particular athletic program. A coach's responsibility is for the whole person, not just winning or losing. A lot of coaches would debate that,[71] perhaps arguing "that's not what I get paid for." I disagree.

Conclusion

Just as post-World War II desegregation and civil rights struggles were influenced by and had influence on sports in society, the same potential exists for the future. Affirmative action, privacy rights, and education issues in sports and society might serve as a compass directing our nation towards new territory, or backward, depending on how you look at it. Sports are the American way of life. There is no escaping the impact and the influence of sports on our culture and society. It is ironic that Chief Justice John Roberts used a multitude of sports analogies in his exchanges with the U.S. Senate committee during his Supreme Court confirmation hearings.[72] Perhaps it is the conceptual simplicity of sports that is perceived as justice or its impartiality that elicits sports references from all walks of life. Justice Roberts's use of the baseball umpire metaphor may be an insight from where America's leadership from the right and the left might find a reasonable rationale and inspiration going forward.[73]

Recollecting the Supreme Court rulings on Seattle and Jefferson County that appear to open the door to the resegregation of those school districts by overturning the last resort consideration of race as a factor in maintaining racially balanced schools, one must be struck by Chief Justice Roberts's rationalization stating that "the way to stop discrimination on the basis of race is to stop discriminating on the basis of race."[74] If one had his ear, one could chide the Chief Justice on this inane pronouncement and say, "If you persist in using sports analogies, you need to start reasoning like someone who truly wants to end racial polarization and stop reasoning like Yogi Berra." If sports are the American way of life and race is also an American way of life, both will remain intertwined in our society and will result in an unavoidable but necessary ongoing discussion. This discussion will continue until such time that we as a nation have reached that lofty perch where color does not matter anymore.

Discussion Questions

1. What might be some of the ways in which sports in the United States break down or maintain stereotypes of athletes of color?
2. Do you think that similar stereotypes apply to female athletes? Why or why not?
3. Are there examples from the media that you can think of that influence how we think about race and sports? What are some examples from your own experience?

Notes

* Attorney and analyst for ESPN, ABC, and CBS. Len Elmore is a 1987 graduate of Harvard Law School. He was a college All American basketball player at the University of Maryland and played professionally in both the American Basketball Association and the National Basketball Association. This chapter is based on a speech delivered by Mr. Elmore on October 4, 2007, at the West Virginia University College of Law as part of the West Virginia University College of Law Sports and Entertainment Law Society Symposium, "Reversing Field: Examining Commercialization, Labor & Race in 21st Century Sports Law," available at http://www.law.wvu.edu/reversingfield.
1. Horatio Alger, Jr., Ragged Dick or Street Life in New York With the Boot-Blacks (1868).
2. National Museum of Racing Hall of Fame, Hall of Fame Jockeys: Isaac B. Murphy, http://www.racingmuseum.org/hall/jockey.asp?ID=205 (last visited July 19, 2009).
3. Dr. Leroy Vaughn, Black People and Their Place in World History, ComputerHealth.org, http://www.com-puterhealth.org/ebook/1865post.htm (last visited July 14, 2009).
4. Plessy v. Ferguson, 163 U.S. 537 (1896).
5. Unforgivable Blackness: The Rise and Fall of Jack Johnson (PBS television broadcast Jan. 17–18, 2005).
6. Id.
7. Id.

8. *See* Bob Dolgan, *Hearts And Pro Football's Hall Of Fame Finally Open For Fritz Pollard, Sports Pioneer And NFL Player*, Black Athlete Sports Network, Mar. 6, 2005, *available at* http://blackathlete.net/artman2/publish/Football_7/Hearts_And_Pro_Football_s_Hall_Of_Fame_Finally_Ope_485.shtml.

9. *The Fight: American Experience* (PBS television broadcast Sept. 2004).

10. Donald Spivey, *The Black Athlete in Big-Time Intercollegiate Sports, 1941–1968*, 44 Phylon Quarterly 116, 125 (1983).

11. Ronald Takaki, Double Victory: A Multicultural History of America in World War II (2000).

12. Michael A. Bamberger & Nathan Lewin, *The Right to Equal Treatment: Administrative Enforcement of Antidiscrimination Legislation*, 74 Harv. L. Rev. 526, 589 (1961).

13. Warren Goldstein, *Before You Could Say Jackie Robinson*, N.Y. Times, May 16, 2004, at 7.

14. Rube Foster, *Negro Baseball Leagues*, BlackBaseball.com, http://www.blackbaseball.com/rube-foster.html (last visited July 14, 2009).

15. Joel Maxcy, *The Demise of African American Baseball Leagues: A Rival League Explanation*, 2 J. Sports Econ. 35, 49 (2001).

16. 394 U.S. 294 (1955).

17. Michael K. Brown, Whitewashing Race: The Myth of a Color-Blind Society 69 (2003).

18. Jon Entine, Taboo: Why Black Athletes Dominate Sports and Why We're Afraid to Talk About It (2001).

19. *Id.*

20. Richard E. Nisbett, *Race, Genetics, and IQ, in* The Black-White Test Score Gap 86 (1998).

21. The World Bank Group Sub-Saharan Africa, *Data Profile*, http://ddp-ext.worldbank.org/ext/ddpreports/ViewSharedReport?&CF=&REPORT_ID=9147&REQUEST_TYPE=VIEWADVANCED&HF=N/CPProfile.asp&WSP=N (last visited July 19, 2009).

22. The African Diaspora Medical Project, http://www.admproject.org/admproject/news-nov07.html (last visited May 20, 2009).

23. *See* Entine, *supra* note 18.

24. *See* Richard Lapchick, *The 2006–07 Season Racial and Gender Report Card: National Basketball Association*, University of Central Florida, May 9, 2007, *available at* http://web.bus.ucf.edu/documents/sport/2006_racial_gender_report_card_nba.pdf; *see also* Richard Lapchick, *The 2006 Racial and Gender Report Card: National Football League*, University of Central Florida, Sept.26, 2007, *available at* http://web.bus.ucf.edu/documents/sport/2006_racial_and_gender_report_card_national_football_league.pdf; Richard Lapchick, *The 2006 Racial and Gender Report Card: Major League Baseball*, University of Central Florida, *available at* http://web.bus.ucf.edu/documents/sport/2006_racial_gender_report_card_mlb.pdf (last visited July 14, 2009).

25. Malcolm Gladwell, The Tipping Point: How Little Things Can Make a Big Difference (2000).

26. Malcolm Gladwell, *The Sports Taboo*, The New Yorker, May 19, 1997, *available at* http://www.gladwell.com/1997/1997_05_19_a_sports.htm.

27. Arthur R. Jensen, *How Much Can We Boost IQ and Scholastic Achievement?*, 39 Harv. Educ. L. Rev. 1, 123 (1969).

28. Richard J. Herrnstein & Charles Murray, The Bell Curve: Intelligence and Class Structure in American Life (1994).

29. Nicholas Lemann, *The Bell Curve Flattened*, Slate, Jan. 18, 1997, http://www.slate.com/id/2416/.

30. *See Brief on Race and Genetic Determinism*, CRG: Council for Responsible Genetics, *available at* http://www.councilfor-responsiblegenetics.org/ViewPage.aspx?pageId=71 (last visited July 19, 2009).

31. Entine *supra* note 18, at 3.

32. *See O.J. Simpson Profile*, N.Y. Times, Oct. 4, 2008, *available at* http://topics.nytimes.com/top/reference/timestop-ics/people/s/o_j_simpson/index.html/.

33. *See* Mike Wise & Alex Markels, *Lakers' Star Bryant Is Charged With Sex Assault at Colorado Spa*, N.Y. Times, July 19, 2003, *available at* http://www.nytimes.com/2003/07/19/sports/pro-basketball-lakers-star-bryant-is-charged-with-sex-assault-at-colorado-spa.html.

34. *See Vick Faces Prison Time After Agreeing to Plead Guilty*, ESPN.com, Aug. 21, 2007, http://sports.espn.go.com/nfl/news/story?id=2983121.

35. *See* Carrie Antlfinger, *Jury Selected in Chmura Sexual Assault Trial*, ABC News, *available at* http://abcnews.go.com/Sports/story?id=99913&page=1 (last visited July 19, 2009).

36. *See Reardon Charged With Armed Robbery*, ESPN.com, Dec. 28, 2005, http://sports.espn.go.com/mlb/news/story?id=2272046.

37. *See* Rachel Smolkin, *Justice Delayed*, American journalismReview.com, Aug./Sept. 2007, http://www.ajr.org/Article.asp?id=4379.

38. Richard Lapchick, *Crime and Athletes: The New Racial Stereotypes of the 1990s*, *available at* http://web.bus.ucf.edu/sport-business/articles.aspx?y=2000 (last visited July 19, 2009).

39. *Id.*

40. *Id.*

41. Arthur A. Raney and Jennings Bryant, Handbook of Sports and Media 451 (2006).

42. Reynard Blake Jr., *Dismantling the 'Bling' Another Look at Hip-Hop*, The Black Commentator, July 15, 2004, *available at* http://www.blackcommentator.com/99/99_hip_hop.html (last visited July 14, 2009).

43. Eric Kelderman, *Public Colleges Face Rising Demand, Reduced Support*, Stateline.org, Jan. 7, 2005, http://www.stateline.org/live/ViewPage.action?siteNodeId=136&languageId=1&contentId=15900.

44. Mavis G. Sanders, *Overcoming obstacles: Academic achievement as a response to racism and discrimination*, Journal of Negro Education, Winter 1997, *available at* http://findarticles.com/p/articles/mi_qa3626/is_199701/ai_n8740048.

45. Dick Vitale, *Don't Keep Best High Schoolers out of NBA*, ESPN.com, Apr. 26, 2005, http://espn.go.com/dickvitale/vcolumn050425_ageplan.html.

46. Jeff Shelman, *Butch Slips Into Redshirt Comfortably*, ESPN.com, Nov. 20, 2003, http://sports.espn.go.com/ncb/columns/story?columnist=shelman_jeff&id=1666499.

47. NCAA By-law 14.4.3.1(b).

48. Vincent Schiraldi & Jason Ziedenberg, *Cellblocks or Classrooms?: The Funding of Higher Education and Corrections and Its Impact on African American Men*, Justice Policy Inst., *available at* http://www.eric.ed.gov/ERICDocs/data/ericdocs2sql/content_storage_01/0000019b/80/1a/e7/8f.pdf (last visited July 14, 2009).

49. Preston Williams, *A New Meaning For Playground Basketball*, Wash. Post, Feb. 24, 2003, at A1.

50. Ian O'Connor, *NBA Age Limit Plan Ought To Be Stuffed*, USA Today, Apr. 18, 2005, at 11C. *But see* Andre Smith, *Describing Racism as Asymmetrical Market Imperfections, or How to Determine Whether the NBA Dress Code is Racist, supra* p. 46 (describing that little evidence exists that "straight to the NBA" from high school athletes were less mature or less prepared than college attending athletes); *see also* Michael McCann, *The Reckless Pursuit of Dominion: A Situational Analysis of the NBA and Diminishing Player Autonomy*, 8 U. Pa. J. Lab. & Emp. L. 819, 828 (2006) (detailing the maturity and success of many NBA players that eschewed college for the NBA).

51. Yoji Cole, *Despite Black Super Bowl Coaches, Sports Aren't Level Playing Field*, DiversityInc, Feb. 2, 2007, http://www.diversityinc.com/public/1226.cfm; Chris Elsberry, *Dungy Continues Fight For Minority Hiring*, Connecticut Post, Feb. 19, 2008, http://www.connpost.com/sports/ci_8309075.

52. Gerald Eskenazi, *Study Faults Teams' Efforts on Hiring Minority Coaches*, N.Y. Times, Feb. 25, 1998, at C2.

53. Michael Smith, *Race an Issue, But Networking Still The Key*, ESPN.com, Feb. 10, 2006, http://sports.espn.go.com/nfl/columns/story?columnist=smith_michael&id=2304091.

54. *Id.*

55. *See Professional Equality: The Rooney Rule, infra* pp. 350–418.

56. Ronald B. Woods, Social Issues In Sport 207 (2007).

57. George B. Cunningham, *Already Aware of the Glass Ceiling: Race-Related Effects of Perceived Opportunity on the Career Choices of College Athletes*, 7 Afr.-Am. J. 57, 71 (2003).

58. David Leonhardt and Ford Fessenden, *Black Coaches in NBA Have Shorter Tenures*, N.Y. Times, Mar. 22, 2005, at A1.

59. Kimberly Atkins, *Women and Minorities Struggle to Advance in Top Law Firms*, Daily Record of Rochester, Apr. 24, 2007, http://findarticles.com/p/articles/mi_qn4180/is_20070424/ai_n19034317.

60. Arthur Ashe, A Hard Road to Glory: A History of the African American Athlete (1993).

61. David J. Leonard, *Golden Shackles: A Veteran Journalist Finds Little Racial Progress in the World of Pro Sports*, Wash. Post, Aug. 13, 2006, at BW08.

62. William C. Rhoden, 40 Million Dollar Slave: The Rise, Fall and Redemption of the Black Athlete 207 (2006).

63. *Id.*

64. Mike Wise, *Opinions on the NBA's Dress Code Are Far From Uniform*, Wash. Post, Oct. 23, 2005, at A1.

65. John Eligon, *NBA Dress Code Decrees: Clothes Make the Image*, N.Y. Times, Oct. 19, 2005, at D5.

66. *But see* Andre Smith, *Describing Racism as Asymmetrical Market Imperfections, or How to Determine Whether the NBA Dress Code is Racist, supra* p. 46 (describing the NCAA Dress Code as racist and destructive of black entrepreneurial opportunity).

67. John Hoberman, Darwin's Athletes: How Sport Has Damaged Black America and Preserved the Myth of Race 6 (1996).

68. *Id.* at 8.

69. Kenneth L. Shropshire, In Black and White: Race and Sports in America 103 (1996).

70. *See* Alfred Dennis Mathewson, *Exploring the Commercialized Arms Race Metaphor, supra* p. 34 (proposing a significant increase in scholarships for athletics, rather than reductions, for NCAA imposed penalties).

71. Ben Adler, *Infighting: Hate the Player, Not the Game—A discussion on the Role of Athletes in Academia*, CampusProgress.org, Apr. 3, 2006, http://www.campusprogress.org/features/827/infighting-hate-the-player-not-the-game.

72. Associated Press, *Text of John Roberts' Opening Statement*, USA Today, Sept. 13, 2005, at A1 (Chief Justice Roberts' opening statement reads in part "Judges are like umpires. Umpires don't make the rules; they apply them. The role of an umpire and a judge is critical. They make sure everybody plays by the rules").

73. *Id.*

74. Parents Involved in Cmty. Sch. v. Seattle Sch. Dist. No. 1, 551 U.S. 701, 127 S. Ct. 2738, 2768 (2007).

How Couples Manage Interracial and Intercultural Differences

Implications for Clinical Practice

By Gita Seshadri and Carmen Knudson-Martin

Editor's Introduction

This reading discusses the ways in which couples who are either interracial or intercultural manage some of the differences that exist between them. While this is the focus of the article, the discussion has importance for all long-term relationships. The authors examine strategies couples use to cope with differences and conflicts and how they move toward forging a satisfying couple relationship.

This study focused on how couples managed their interracial and intercultural differences. To understand their experiences, a qualitative grounded theory analysis was used (n = 17). Analysis revealed that couples experienced most issues as cultural issues; race only occurred during their interactions with "others." They appeared to organize their responses according to four relationship structures: Integrated, Singularly Assimilated, Coexisting, and Unresolved. Couples in each of these structures managed daily process through four sets of relationship strategies: (a) creating a "we," (b) framing differences, (c) emotional maintenance, and (d) positioning in relationship to familial and societal context. These findings are a step toward a strength-based and research-informed education and clinical interventions for this population.

Therapists are increasingly likely to be working with couples who come from different racial and cultural backgrounds (Rastogi & Thomas, 2009). It is therefore important to understand how these couples successfully manage their differences. Unfortunately, most of the previous literature has approached the issues of interracial and intercultural marriages from a problem perspective (e.g., Bratter &

King, 2008; Fu, Tora, & Kendall, 2001; Solsberry, 1994). While it is true that interracial/intercultural couples may face a number of hurdles and negative stereotypes, there is an emerging trend to approach the topic from a more positive stance and focus instead on the relational processes that make these relationships successful (e.g., Gaines & Agnew, 2003; Thomas, Karis, & Wetchler, 2003; Yancey & Lewis, 2009). However, research that draws directly on the lived experience of interracial and intercultural couples remains limited and has been conducted primarily with Black-White couples (e.g., Foeman & Nance, 2002; Karis, 2003; Killian, 2001a).

The purpose of this study was to discover how interracial couples from a range of backgrounds create strong, meaningful relationships despite potential problems. Our goal was to develop grounded theory regarding how couples manage racial and cultural differences, negative societal stereotypes, and social and interpersonal contexts to construct relationships that work for them. Because of our interest in the relational processes involved, we approached the study from a social constructionist perspective and used an ecological systems lens to help focus our analysis.

Social Construction of Interracial/Intercultural Relationships

From a social constructionist perspective, marriage is a major site of reality construction as partners integrate and redefine past and present experience to create new relational meaning, structure, and processes (Berger & Kellner, 1994). What it means to live within an intercultural/interracial marriage is created as partners interact with each other within larger family, community, and societal contexts. Thus, marital partners are not two distinct individual selves; they continuously shape and co-create each other and their social worlds (Gergen, 2009). Race and culture are also socially constructed categories that hold no intrinsic meaning, but whose meanings evolve through social interaction. Thus, we begin with the assumption that dealing with racial and cultural differences is a complex and fluid process that is negotiated across time, geography, and fluctuating interpersonal and societal contexts.

Race and Culture

In this study, we use the term race to describe social identification attached to physical traits such as skin and hair color, despite huge variations among people that are considered a part of a particular racial group (DeFrancisco & Palczewski, 2007). Race becomes meaningful to the people involved and to the larger society through processes of categorization and identification (Rodkin, 1993). Prejudice and discrimination result when racial differences are used hierarchically to promote the interests of the majority (Kottak & Kozaitis, 2007). We are thus interested in how participants personalize, make meaning of, and respond to racial categorizations and discrimination within their relationships.

We use culture to refer to shared meanings, beliefs, and traditions that arise as a group shares common history and experiences that give "particular interpretations of the world" (Paré, 1996, p. 25). A social constructionist view of culture makes room for multiple ways of understanding and performing one's culture (Laird, 2000). When two or more cultures intermix through marriage or a significant relationship, questions surface as to how stories and traditions "should be" followed and how differences will be addressed. We focus on understanding how couples utilize these differences to create tradition, meaning, and strength in their relationships.

The meanings attached to race and culture are fluid and can be difficult to separate. It is therefore not surprising that much of the research on interracial and/or intercultural couples conflates these concepts (Henderson, 2000; Reiter & Gee, 2008). The term "interracial" is often used interchangeably with intercultural and interethnic and is sometimes referred to as "intermarried," "intermixing," or "heterogamy" by researchers and in popular culture (Henderson, 2000; Reiter & Gee, 2008). In this study we attempted to distinguish between the interracial and intercultural experiences of the participants, with primary interest in how participants themselves viewed and responded to these issues.

Ecological Systems Theory

To further organize and focus study of couple meaning and interaction within larger social context, we integrated Bronfenbrenner's (1986) five systemic levels of interaction, using the couple rather than the individual as the developmental unit of focus. Interview questions and analysis thus focused on the processes of interaction between the microsystem (the couple—creating the "we"), mesosystem (the family—"we and us"), exosystem (the community—"we and them"), macrosystem (society—"we and the world"), and chronosystem (time—"we and life"). Although we conceptualize bi-directional influence across systemic levels, Bronfen- brenner's ecological systems theory helped us focus this study on the part the individual couples play in negotiating the influence of context (Tudge, Mokrova, Hatfield, & Karnik, 2009).

How Can Interracial Couples Create Positive Working Marital Relationships?

There is considerable interest in the clinical literature regarding how to address multicultural issues and incorporate attention to cultural and racial differences as part of couple therapy (Greenman, Young, & Johnson, 2009; McGoldrick & Hardy, 2008; Rastogi & Thomas, 2009; Thomas et al., 2003). Several authors have developed assessment guides to help couple therapists in working with these issues (Henrikenson, Watts, & Bustamante, 2007; Laszloffy, 2008). Yet research to guide this work is limited (Murray, 2004). Most have quantitatively explored attitudes toward interracial marriages and the factors involved in predicting divorce, happiness, satisfaction, and stability (e.g., Bischoff, 2005; Bratter & King, 2008; Bratter & Eschbach, 2006; Dirlic, Miyahara, & Johartchi, 2006; Levin, Taylor, & Caudle, 2007). There is a need for more study of the process issues involved as interracial couples construct a life together (Cheng, 2005; Karis & Killian, 2009; Troy, Lewis-Smith, & Laurenceau, 2006).

Because society accepts racially homogeneous couples, how to deal with the "outside" is a greater focus for interracial couples (Henderson, 2000, p. 422). Killian (2001b) reported increased resistance to the relationship by family and friends when couples announce their engagement. Even though couples themselves may not view racial differences as important (Karis, 2009; Leslie & Letiecq, 2004), what couples do in response to situations of prejudice and discrimination is an important area for study (Henderson, 2000; Hill & Thomas, 2000).

Nonetheless, or perhaps in response to these issues, previous research suggests a number of potential strengths among interracial/intercultural couples. Such couples tend to report awareness of differences and curiosity about possible differences (Ham, 2003; Ting-Toomey, 2009). Directly dealing with these issues may actually enhance intimacy (Gaines et al., 1999; Troy et al., 2006). How couples communicate about difference within the relationship and with others seems to be of prime importance (Llerena-Quinn & Bacigalupe, 2009). The processes involved may require and/or promote commitment, intentionality, and secure attachment (Gaines & Agnew, 2003; Ting-Toomey, 2009; Troy et al., 2006). Similar interests and egalitarianism may also help promote successful interracial marriages (Yancey & Lewis R. (2009)).

The above research provides some interesting clues to the processes involved in creating strong interracial/intercultural marriages. However, nearly all of this research has focused on Black-White couples. As Jacobs and Labov (2002) pointed out, interracial couples also include variations of Hispanic, Asian, and Caucasian relationship and combinations where neither partner is Caucasian. In the study reported here, we sought to deepen understanding of the relational processes involved in successful interracial/intercultural marriages by extending study to a much wider range of diversity and by exploring how partners respond to various levels of contextual influences. Understanding these processes is particularly important so that clinical practice does not reinforce experiences of social isolation and marginalization that interracial/intercultural couples may experience. Social stigmatization also puts them at a higher risk of divorce and emotional isolation (Bratter & King, 2008).

Method

To understand the lived experiences of interracial/intercultural couples, we conducted a grounded theory analysis of interviews with seventeen couples. This study was part of the Contemporary Couples Study, which explores how diverse couples are responding to a changing social environment. Questions from the larger study were used in this study; however, various probes based on the literature, ecological systems theory and social constructionism were included to specifically understand the interracial/intercultural couple experience.

We approach the study of interracial/intercultural marriage from a strength-based perspective because we live in Southern California where there is considerable intermixing of races and cultures, and we are committed to expanding acceptance of these relationships. Each of us has experienced interracial/intercultural relationships personally or in our family and we often see clients with this background. Our working relationship is also interracial/intercultural, with first author being of East Indian-American background and the second author Scandinavian-American. We engaged regularly in conversations about our different perspectives on the data, always keeping in mind our basic concern: what works for these couples?

Sample

To participate in the study, couples had to (a) define themselves as an interracial couple who grew up with different customs, traditions, and expectations, (b) be heterosexual, and (c) be married for at least 2 years. This allowed us to study couples who had achieved a measure of stability and who were not confounded with the additional experiences raised by same-sex relationships.

Seventeen participant couples in California were identified through snowball sampling and word of mouth. We used categorizations from the US Census in 2000 to describe the couples' racial backgrounds: (Caucasian, Asian, African American, and Native Hawaiian/Pacific Islander). Multiracial individuals were included as well. Nine of the seventeen couples had at least one partner that was foreign born. Cultural categories included (in no particular order): Filipino, Mexican, Anglo, Chinese, American, German, Scottish,

East Indian, Puerto Rican, Black, Nigerian, Colombian, and Vietnamese. Ages ranged from 26 to 59 (mean, 38.1) and years married ranged from 2 to 29 (mean, 9.4 years). Twelve of the couples had children; 29 children total, ranging from 9 months to 42 years old. Participants included a range of educational backgrounds and occupations, but as Rosenfeld (2005) noted, interracial couples tend to have higher levels of education, which was reflected in this study, with 53% having at least some graduate education.

Interviews

Couples were interviewed together in their homes or another location convenient to them. Each partner was also briefly interviewed separately. Together, the interviews lasted approximately 1–1/2 hr. Interviews were tape recorded and then transcribed.

The semi-structured interviews followed a common interview guide focusing on couple processes in relation to each level of contextual influence. Questions were designed to access the interaction of varying levels of systemic experience, including how partners deal with each other, with family members, and with the larger community and societal expectations. Sample questions include, How do you categorize your racial background? What do these categories mean to you? How do people react to your visible racial differences? Where is it a problem? How do you deal with this? What to you constitutes a good relationship? Think of a time when there was conflict between the two of you. How did you resolve it? How do you negotiate culture within your relationship?

The individual interview consisted of one question: "Is there anything you would like to add about your relationship and being in an interracial couple to our discussion, without the presence of your partner?" with several probes to access multiple realities (Killian, 2003). The couples' experiences were taken at face value; the purpose of including individual interviews was to gain a richer perspective; to include multiple realities, rather than a search for the "truth" (Gergen, 2009).

Grounded Theory Analysis

Grounded theory analysis began during the interviews as we attempted to understand the couples' experience. It was based on Charmaz's (2006) constructivist approach in which the interviews and analysis are not viewed as separate from the researcher. Historically, Glaser and Strauss (1967) took qualitative analysis to a new level when they offered an approach to building theory that was not based on hypotheses and preconceived ideas, and acknowledged the role of the researcher in the research process. Glaser and Strauss deepened qualitative analysis to address "interaction as interpretive," which emphasized action and process (Charmaz, 2006, p. 7). Charmaz (2006) takes their work further in that these analytic processes are considered a part of "reality construction" of the participant experience (p. 10) rather than rigid rules and instructions.

Initial/Open Coding

In initial coding/open coding, codes are constructed based upon what is known. We used line-by-line coding during initial coding to identify the emerging categories related to strength, meaning, and strategies of what works for the couples, which yielded 29 codes. For example, when a wife said "I thought I was pretty westernized until I married my husband. Then I realized that I was actually pretty Asian in a lot of ways. I think

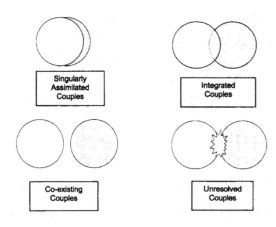

Figure 17.1 Intercultural/Interracial relationship structures.

it's relative to who I'm with," this initially was coded as "shifting lenses depending on context" and "differences are noticed when with others."

Focused Coding

In focused coding, initial codes were grouped or refined to create larger conceptual categories based upon how they fit with the data. To use the previous code as an example, shifting lenses became part of a theme of "ways of framing differences" which was an overall strategy of how the couples made their relationship work. We also used the codes as a comparative check list across all of the couples and found that there were common themes of structure around difference, integration, co-existing singularly assimilated, and unresolved. We conceptualized these as "relationship structures." (See Figure 17.1).

Analytic Coding

Analytic coding took focused coding one step further, making the coding more analytical to create theory and explanations reflective of the participants' experience. Our goal was to determine how the various categories we discovered were linked together to explain what works to create relationship success for the couples in this study and also how this fit within ecological systems theory and social constructionism. We identified four key relational strategies: creating a we, framing differences, emotional maintenance, and how the couple positioned themselves with others which were used by all the couples except those categorized as "unresolved." We explored what was involved in implementing each of these strategies and how these may work differently depending on how the couple structures around difference. For example, we explored how framing differences would present differently in each ecological level, i.e., this would have to be addressed in how couples created a "we" (microsystem) as well as how they explained this to their families (mesosystem) and how each type of relationship structure might deal with this differently (insecurities would conflate this for unresolved couples).

According to Charmaz (2006), trustworthiness "begins with the intent to learn and understand" as well as asking substantial and relevant questions that can be challenging (p. 19). To address trustworthiness, constant comparison of checking and rechecking was performed throughout the coding process, in addition to the use of memos and journals. Checking and rechecking helps to look for differences and challenge researcher bias (Corbin & Strauss, 2008). Memos and journals served to create conversation between the authors regarding the concepts and codes that were created. Triangulation of multiple perspectives of the participants through individual and couple interviews and multiple researcher perspectives also enhanced trustworthiness.

Results: What Works? Relationship Structures and Strategies

Couples in this study experienced their differences primarily as cultural rather than racial. Racial issues were only identified when describing their initial attraction to each other and in explaining incidences involving others, such as when the couple encountered prejudice and discrimination in their families, communities, and society. Further, racial issues in the context of familial interactions appeared to become mostly invisible for most couples after their partners "got to know" the rest of the family.

Four Structures of Organization

Couples organized around their cultural differences according to four distinctive relationship structures: integrated, co-existing, singularly assimilated, and unresolved. Couples in each of these, except the unresolved group, described developing relationships that appeared to work for them and in which they appeared happy. Although couples may not fit neatly into only one structure across all circumstances, these categories were very helpful to us in recognizing and appreciating diversity in "what works."

Integrated (Four Couples)

The "Integrated" couples organized their cultural differences in a way that melds both cultures together by celebrating each. When these couples communicate, both partners voices appear validated, and each seems willing to engage in the other's culture. Mark and Selma, a German and Venezuelan couple, discussed the integration of food:

> So having him tell me how his mom used to cook this or that dish, and then me knowing how I do it, or how my mom used to do it, and then learning from both, kind of like merging them, or picking one (Selma).

Rather than not cooking the dish, or having Mark make the dish himself, Selma integrates through cooking, by attempting to learn about how the dish is made. Both partners regularly integrate in this way.

Coexisting (Three Couples)

In the "Coexisting" structure, partners appear to retain their separate cultures, but they are rarely integrated. For these couples, differences are seen as positive and even attractive. Thus, they retain two ways of doing many aspects of their lives (i.e., religion, parenting, spending styles, childcare and/or household responsibilities, etc.) and appear to have an "agree to disagree mentality." Agreeing to disagree can be more difficult when the couple has children. For example, Andrew and Elena, an African American-Mexican couple who each have children from previous relationships, noted that if they had a child together religion might become more contentious. Andrew points out: "I think it's just we respect each others' opinion ... we don't have any children in common ... if we did, I think that would been a point of ... [wife interjects] conflict ... [husband interjects] discussion" (Andrew/Elena).

Singularly Assimilated (Seven Couples)

In this relationship structure, one partner is more assimilated to the partner's culture than the other partner. Cultural differences are not highlighted in the discussion, as one culture appears to have taken a nearly invisible back seat. Partners that have assimilated do not seem to feel resentful about the lack of their cultures' presence in the various aspects of their relationship. In fact, the assimilated partner often sees the partner's culture as the "right" way. Thus, their assimilation does not seem to be as a compromise as a "conversion." When there is conflict, singularly assimilated couples will attempt to resolve the issue.

For example, Marcus [White] sees his assimilation to his wife Deborah (Mexican-Japanese) as making things easier in their relationship around going to her side of the family's events and family parties during the holidays:

> (sigh) It made it easier! [laughs] Because I could join you for whatever! And if we had something going on, we were a flexible family that could get together whenever, I guess it was easier on us because of that (Marcus).

Unresolved (Three Couples)

The "Unresolved" relationship structure describes the couples who do not seem to know what to do with difference, or have conflict around difference that is creating a rift in their relationship, which they ignore. These unaddressed conflicts and tension around culture appear related to insecurities in the relationship. For example, James (Black) describes how Molly, who is White, appears insecure around Black women: "She starts feeling out of place, and when she sees Black women, she says, 'oh you like her,' and then she wants to kiss me, and all that insecurity" (James).

Relational Strategies for Managing Differences

Regardless of the kind of the relationship structure, couples used four major strategies to manage their cultural and racial differences on a day-by-day basis: (a) Creating a We, (b) Framing Differences, (c) Emotional Maintenance, and (d) Positioning themselves with family and societal contexts. Each of the strategies involved multiple tasks.

Creating a "We"

Couples in this study create a "we" that becomes a new co-constructed narrative reality of their relationship that transcends difference. This reality gives birth to shared meaning within the couple relationship. Elements of creating a "we" include friendship, common ground, similar goals, working together over time, and commitment.

Friendship. Many of the couples discussed friendship as an initial source of connection in their relationship. Maria: "We would laugh a lot together. That was the thing ... Even though we get mad at each other, even to this day, we can still laugh at each other over stupid stuff" (Maria, Coexisting). Thus, although Maria and David agree to co-exist around their cultural differences, they have a shared sense of "we." Friendship was also cited by the unresolved couples as a strategy that brought the couple together; however, the unresolved couples did not report the other components of the creating a "we," such as similar goals and working together over time.

Common ground. Couples report on common ground despite their differences. Even coexisting couples describe holding similar core values. Elena (Mexican): "You have a different way of doing, I have a different way ... the expectations are the same, and we have kind of the same value system but, different" (Elena, Coexisting).

Similar goals. Using common ground as a source of strength allows the couple to create similar goals around culture. Mary (Filipino) regards her own upbringing as well as Jim's (Mexican) upbringing as similar.

"He is from here and I was born and raised in the Philippines. But the upbringing. We are almost similar as well. That made it easy, definitely" (Mary, Singularly Assimilated).

Working together over time and commitment. As couples experience common ground and goals over time, the sense of "we" is supported. Maria points out the importance of this commitment to "we": "David has been extremely loyal, committed, and his family comes first, and that is the reason why I have hung on" (Maria, Coexisting).

Framing Differences

In addition to creating a "we," couples needed a way to frame differences. They did this in a variety of ways, including making racial and cultural issues not central, sharing differences as attractive, flexibility and respect about culture, differences as something to learn about, and celebration of differences.

Making racial and cultural differences not central. Couples in this study saw their racial and cultural differences not as important as others made them to be. Some described looking beyond racial lines within themselves and others. Ashley (Caucasian woman married to a Nigerian man) also frames cultural differences in relationships with friends as not important, "We have very similar beliefs, it's not about the cultural background, it's about the person, and what that person can bring to the relationship, more than anything else" (Ashley, Integrated).

Sharing racial differences as an attraction. Even when couples said racial and cultural differences not central, many referenced having a racial attraction to their partner. Mary (Filipino): "I noticed that he wasn't Filipino, he was REALLY dark and REALLY buffed" (Mary, Singularly Assimilated). Her husband Jim noted, "I had a preference for Asian women" (Jim, Singularly Assimilated).

Flexibility, respect, and understanding around cultural rules. Couples in this study needed to be willing to be flexible enough to engage in practices that are different than they are used to understand their partners. Laurie (Vietnamese/Chinese) discusses her mother-in-law not originally accepting her marriage to Asheesh (East Indian). However, Laurie was willing to indulge her mother-in-law and be respectful and flexible with the practices in her husband's culture: "She wanted to know everything. My stars were looked at, she needed to know the day I was born, the time I was born, so she could submit that information" (Laurie/Asheesh, Integrated).

This respect, understanding, and openness in relationships make room for two cultural voices. Two cultural voices can be present in the coexisting and integrated styles only. In the co-existing style there is little integration; each voice is present as a different way of doing things, whereas within the integrated structure both voices are interwoven.

Differences are something to learn about. Having an openness to learn about their partner's culture extends to incorporating this in their relationship, as well as communicating about it to their partner:

> Laurie is very cool about just, making, and going the extra mile just to fit in ... all my mom's friends love her. They always say positive things about her, and partly because Laurie is amiable, non-threatening, she assimilates to the right degree. (Asheesh, Integrated).

Celebration and appreciation of the partner's culture. Part of being open includes a willingness to celebrate and appreciate the other partner's culture. Daniel notes that making attempts to learn Chinese impressed his mother-in-law's friends: "And I was speaking Chinese to them. They were saying I'm a good looking Caucasian guy. They called me the ghost, "guayje," anyways, they kind of liked the good looking white guy" (Daniel, Singularly Assimilated).

For the integrated couples, this celebration of cultures appears as give and take with both backgrounds present. With the singularly assimilated couples, this celebration and appreciation appears one sided, or there is little presence of one background in comparison with the other. This celebration is not present for the unresolved couples. For the coexisting couples, this celebration and appreciation is performed from afar (e.g., a couple visiting one partner's homeland after 20 + years of marriage) if at all. Instead, they allow each other to celebrate their own cultures to the extent that they wish.

Emotional Maintenance

Couples in this study report dealing with emotions and insecurities that are triggered from various difficult encounters and events within their various social contexts, such as dealing with a family member's disapproval. They do this by communicating emotions and insecurities, making adjustments around culture, and finding support as a couple.

Communicating emotions/insecurities. As a part of emotional maintenance, couples noted communicating emotions and insecurities to their partner as a source of strength. Dylan talks about his mother who initially held racial and cultural prejudice toward his wife Arlene. He describes how he validated Arlene's intuition regarding this: "Yeah Arlene, you are right. You know, we had to actually be there with her face to face, to really tell, … But when we were physically there … then I started to see it" (Dylan, Coexisting).

Making adjustments around culture. Even the singularly assimilated and co-existing couples described willingness to make some adjustments in response to cultural differences. This sets these couples apart from the unresolved couples. However, making these adjustments does not always come easily. For example, Deborah described adjusting her cultural style of conflict: "I think the … hot Latina, comes out, and we [Latinas] do things with passion and fire! And 'you are going to know about it' kind of thing!" (Deborah, Singularly Assimilated). She recalled having to learn to "tone it down" so that her husband was able to hear what she was saying and not shut down based on her approach to him.

Finding support as a couple. When faced with not being accepted by other members of society or with their partners' families, couples reported leaning on those that *do* support them as a way to get through this difficulty. Elena and Andrew utilized therapy to move through the roadblock of her family not accepting Andrew owing to racial and other issues. In addition, Andrew reported drawing on the support of friends: "Talking to friends. I have a friend that is married to a Mexican American woman. And you know, he has been through some similar things but not to the same magnitude" (Andrew, Coexisting).

Positioning in Relation to Societal and Familial Context

This strategy describes how the couple deals with various social contexts, as described in Bronfenbrenner's (1986) ecological systems theory and includes their response to discrimination and negative judgments by others. It is also how these interracial/intercultural couples form protection and communicate their relationship to family members, communities, society, and the law. Tasks include communicating the "we" to family members and society, nonreactivity to others, speaking up constructively, appropriate use of humor, and giving others time and space to accept partner.

Communicating the "we" to family members, community, and society. A majority of the couples interviewed discussed having to set boundaries with family members and society around cultural prejudice and racial discrimination. Dylan discussed how he shuts out these feelings at church: "You can just feel people … they are not saying anything, but you can read body language. They are not saying anything but you can see them glaring at us." To which he says: "because I don't pay attention [to the looks] … I am there for one reason" (Dylan, Coexisting). Even when one partner assimilated, couples described the importance of drawing the line on the expected changes, especially with other family members. For example, Samantha converted to Juan's religion. Nonetheless, Juan defended Samantha's childhood baptism in a different church when his mother did not think it was valid.

> And I had to draw the line with her and say, this is a personal choice, not your choice, and she feels
> that she has been baptized in the eyes of God. And it doesn't have to be made a display in our church.
> Just for your benefit. She doesn't like that, but she is respectful (Juan, Singularly Assimilated).

Nonreactivity to others. Couples also described finding ways to resist reactive responses such as anger, impulsivity, and pushing another's buttons when others did not seem accepting. For example, Deborah recalls messages that it was okay to be friends across races, but not when it came to intimate relationships: "We thought, so what? Who cares? I mean because if we are all friends ... then why can't you be with that person?" (Deborah, Singularly Assimilated).

Speaking up constructively. Couples also challenge cultural prejudice and discrimination by speaking up. Maria mentioned working with a White man who openly expressed his prejudice to her: "He said he could never marry a woman like me, because he could never have children with a woman like me ... yeah, [softly]. And I said 'I feel sorry for you.' And I don't know what else to say." (Maria, Coexisting).

Use of humor appropriately. Couples also use humor to address cultural prejudice and racial discrimination and decrease their intensity. For example, Maria discusses interactions when others questioned her connection to her children:

> But when they were babies, people would ask me, "Are those your children? ... I mean ... people
> say the stupidest things. You know? And don't even realize what they are saying. But, I just laugh
> it off, you can't get mad at it" (Maria, Coexisting).

Giving family members/others time and space to accept partner. Often times, couples reported encountering difficulties with family members and their partner owing to racial issues. Most of the couples cited that giving family members' time to accept their partners at their own timeline was what helped and worked. Giving space to others did not mean physical space and/or cutting off, rather emotional space, to give the person time to come around on their own terms. Elena remembers: "for my parents, it took them awhile ... to get to know him, and surpass the racial ... process their own racism, and see him as a person" (Elena, Coexisting). Couples also suggested that once family members start to relate to their partners as persons, cultural prejudice and racial discrimination diminish.

Discussion: Moving Toward Strength

This study responds to the call for interracial/intercultural couple research that addresses process-oriented issues and "how to" questions (Cheng, 2005; Troy et al., 2006). Unlike previous research, this study included a wide range of cultural and racial combinations. Analysis captured two major aspects of relational maintenance, (a) the structures through which couples organize around difference and (b) the on-going relational strategies utilized. Thus, although utilizing similar processes to maintain their relationships, the structure of "working" relationships may look quite different. Some couples integrate each culture across most aspects of their lives, while others co-exist side-by-side without expecting that partners incorporate each others' cultures. In a third group, one partner primarily assimilates to the other culture and seems quite happy with that. It is less important what the relationship structure is than that a couple have a relationship structure that works for both of them.

For example, previous research has suggested that successful interracial marriages must include the needs of both spouses, and thus are egalitarian (Yancey & Lewis, 2009). This conclusion most closely fits the integrated relationship structure in this study; however, the co-existing couples also took care to retain and value both cultural voices. Even when one partner generally assimilated to the other's culture, the other partner was willing to accommodate when it was important to the other. On the other hand, unresolved couples do not take these steps to respect and validate each other's cultural backgrounds and seem unable to find a way to organize around differences that works for them.

Level of commitment was an important factor found by Gaines and Agnew (2003) to mediate stability of interracial marriages. The relational strategies demonstrated by the "working" couples in this study appear to be ways that commitment to each other and the relationship is demonstrated. They were interested and curious about their partners' cultures. Although this was most clearly demonstrated by the integrated couples through their deliberate sharing in each other's worlds, even when partners did not adapt substantially to the other's culture, these couples demonstrated cultural respect and interest. Ting-Toomey (2009) termed this mindfulness, which was a conscious way of thinking and asking about one's behavior and background rather than unconsciously reacting.

Like Henderson's (2000) work noting external influences on interracial couple interaction, this study points to a number of strategies that a couple can use to better manage the external issues and social pressures of "others and outsiders" (p. 428). Although some research has suggested that interracial couples may isolate in response to prejudice and discrimination (Hibbler & Shinew, 2002), this study offers a more nuanced view. Couples created boundaries and were selective with whom they associate. Finding sources of social support appeared to be strength for the couples studied.

It is also important to note as suggested previously (i.e., Childs, 2009) that it was not just Black-White couples who experienced discrimination and prejudice; these experiences appeared across all racial and cultural backgrounds. Participants discussed the importance of a couple identity, of creating a "we" that included being comfortable with conversations around cultural integration and becoming racially and culturally sensitive and aware. They were then also able to intentionally position themselves in relation to the larger society and "stand together" in the face of instances of discrimination and negativity.

Couples tended to blur (what we considered) cultural issues and at times termed them personality issues, interchanged them with race categories, or minimized the impact of culture in their relationship. We see this confusion in a playful way as David and Maria discuss his attraction to her, David first refers to liking her personality because she was always happy and then adds: "and she had that hot blooded Puerto Rican personality. Maria engages in this cultural characterization: "and I had wild long hair." David found this cultural image appealing and personalizes it back to her: "sexiest woman on the island (laughing)" (David/Maria). As with David and Maria, couples seemed not to want to focus too much on issues experienced as cultural or racial, and seemed to prefer to think of them as personality, perhaps because of the already stigmatized view from society that cultural and racial differences are problematic or because culture has become deeply ingrained and experienced as personal.

The interviews were also designed to help clarify distinctions between cultural and racial experiences. It is interesting to note that the participants in this study did not necessarily frame *either* as central to their lives and often linked definitions of personality, race, and culture in their descriptions of their relationships. Nonetheless, cultural issues appeared most salient to them within the internal working of their marriages, while racial issues became more relevant when they interacted with others and the larger community. The results offer a framework that can be used to inform future research and as a guide for interracial/intercultural couple education, premarital counseling, and relationship therapy.

Table 17.1 A Clinical Guide to Relational Strategies for Interracial and Intercultural Couples: An Ecological Perspective

Microsystem: the couple
    Creating a "we" as a couple
        How is your relationship like a friendship? How is it not?
        What are the similarities between your cultural beliefs and values?
        How do you show your commitment and loyalty to each other?
        What are your relationship goals? As a couple? As a family?
    Framing differences between partners
        Is one person's race or culture more important in your relationship?
        In what ways do you find your racial or cultural differences attractive?
        How do you show flexibility, respect, and interest in each other's culture and race?
        How do you attempt to learn about and participate in your partner's culture?
        Are there times that race or cultural differences divide you?
    Emotional support for each other
        How do you acknowledge each other's feelings regarding issues of culture and discrimination?
        What cultural adjustments have you made to support your partner? What made you willing to do this?
Mesosystem—friends and family—we and us
    Framing Differences with Families and Friends
        How do you demonstrate curiosity with your partner's family members regarding their culture?
        What messages about culture do you receive from family and friends?
        How do you celebrate and accommodate your partner's culture when with family or friends?
        How do you respond if friends or family need space to accept your relationship?
    Emotional support in family context
        How do you support each other in front of your families?
        How do you support each other with situations of prejudice/discrimination with family members?
        Whom do you rely on for support as a couple or individually? How is this support helpful to you?
    Positioning Relationship in Family Context
        How do you want to represent your couple relationship with your families?
        How do you stand together to deal with negativity from family members?
        What helps you respond constructively to discrimination or negativity by friends or family?
Exosystem—the community: we and them
    What messages regarding race and culture do you receive from the larger community?
    How do you communicate your identity as a couple in the larger community?
    Have you experienced instances of prejudice or discrimination in the larger community?
    How do you validate of each other's emotions in these circumstances?
    Where do you find support in the larger community?
    How do you respond to disapproval or discrimination in the larger community?
Macrosystem—society: we and the world
    Explore how partners support each other in having coherent stories about how they fit within the larger society, especially around issues of prejudice/discrimination
    Explore with the couple how they want to position themselves with society. Is this different from how they do this with family and community?
Chronosystem—time: we and life
    How have couple processes for friendship, working together, commitment, continual united priorities changed over time?
    How are the couple's interracial experiences influenced by historical time and location?
    What is required to promote continued commitment and connection over time?

Implications for Practice

The results of this study suggest that it will be useful to first help interracial/intercultural couples identify the relationship structures through which they organize around their differences. Figure 17.1 provides a useful tool that can stimulate this discussion. Couples can consider how their current relationship patterns honor each culture in ways that support both partners. They can also compare their current patterns with their ideals and explore whether partners agree about this and how their organization around differences has changed over time or may vary depending on the circumstances or issues.

We assume that unresolved couples are the most likely to seek therapy, but each relationship structure may need different areas of assistance. Identifying the couple's general structure for dealing with differences thus provides a foundation from which to explore their day-to-day strategies for creating a working relationship. These occur not only within the couple unit, but across each contextual level of systemic interaction. Table 17.1 provides a set of questions developed from our study results and organized around Bronfenbrenner's (1986) ecological framework that can guide education and clinical work.

The analysis pointed to four areas that are particularly important: (a) creating a "we," (b) framing differences, (c) emotional maintenance, and (d) positioning themselves with family and societal contexts.

Creating a "We"

Couples in this study transcended racial and cultural differences to create a coherent "we." It is thus important to help the couple find their common ground and to focus on their commitment and how they work together. The results suggest that issues regarding how well the "we" is working may vary. For example, partners seeking integration may either experience power struggles or feel compelled to sacrificed valued parts of themselves to maintain the integration. There may be little room for separateness. Co-existing couples may need to define those places where they do integrate and consider how they demonstrate a "we" while preserving space for what is uniquely important to each. Singularly assimilated couples may need to explore how their structure works to create a sense of inclusion for the more accommodating partner. It may be necessary to consider whether the accommodating partners grieve loss of cultural traditions or expectations, particularly around significant life transitions and to engage the other partner in identifying how they adapt to their partners in ways that are not necessarily cultural or know when something cultural remains important to their partners.

Framing Differences

The "working" couples in this study frame differences in positive ways. Discussions about how partners learn about, participate in, and celebrate their partners' cultures and racial context are likely to help deepen this appreciation. Unresolved partners are especially likely to need help learning how to demonstrate their initial attraction to difference in more tangible ways. As nearly all couples in this study tend not to make racial and cultural difference central, discussion about these may open new awareness and help couples to address issues they may have avoided. In the study, both partners, including the co-existing and singularly assimilated couples, demonstrated flexibility and were willing to go out of their way to demonstrate respect for racial and cultural differences. Clinical couples may benefit from openly revisiting this issue and, as suggested by Ting-Toomey (2009), consider how to be more aware and mindful of the influences of each person's background and how to respect them.

Emotional Maintenance

The "working" relationships in this study described skills in emotionally supporting each other around racial and cultural differences, both at the intracouple level and as they interacted with family, friends, community, and in the larger society. Partners may need help communicating their own insecurities and responding positively to their partners'. We suggest that therapists make visible these kinds of issues and explore how partners respond to each other. Identifying examples of *mutual* support may be an important foundation from which to improve relational functioning regardless of relationship structure (Knudson-Martin & Huenergardt, 2010). It is possible that integrated couples have ignored or neglected hurt feelings or doubts to promote "peace" in the relationship. This may be especially true for persons from collectivist cultures (Moghadam & Knudson-Martin, 2009). Co-existing "live-and-let-live" approach could also become a basis for not emotionally attuning to each other. Singularly assimilated structures could invite one person to provide more emotional support than the other. All couples may benefit from identifying others who support them and taking steps to use this support to shore up their relationships.

Positioning Themselves with Family and Societal Contexts

The interracial/intercultural couples in the study had to take active steps to communicate their "we" with family and societal contexts, even in the face of disapproval. It will be important to raise these larger context issues and help couples stand together in these instances. Partners may have different expectations regarding how to represent their relationship to others depending on their own structure for dealing with differences and the level of systemic interaction. For example, co-existing couples may not expect partners to engage in cultural events with family members, but need to know when it is important to support their partners in drawing a line and when to accommodate. However, when dealing with the larger context it may be enough to avoid reactivity and maintain good humor.

Limitations and Directions for Future Research

This study captures a snapshot in time of a small sample of couple experience with interracial and intercultural issues. Although this study identifies processes that appear to be important in helping couples maintain their relationships, the interviews were not designed to specifically access marital success or measure marital quality, satisfaction, or happiness. Longitudinal research and studies examining possible links between the relationship structures and strategies identified in this study and these outcome measures would be useful.

This study was conducted in California where there is considerable mixing of cultures and races. It is not clear how the results transfer to other social contexts. Like previous studies (e.g., Rosenfeld, 2005), this sample reported relatively high levels of education. Study of couples with less education and income is needed. In addition, the issues of gender and power in this study appeared to be complex and are likely to intersect with other determinants of social privilege such as race and class (Garcia & McDowell, 2010). However, an in-depth analysis of these variables was beyond the scope of this study and is an important area for further research.

Although the interview questions in this study were comprehensive, they did not include all the issues relevant to interracial/intercultural couples. For example, issues relating to sexual relationships were not explored in depth, even though a number of participants in this study described being sexually attracted by their racial differences. This analysis also focused on couple dynamics. Future research should be more specifically directed toward how to effectively parent multi-racial and cultural children. Family of origin issues would also be an interesting area for future study, as many of the participants in this study reported mixed cultural or racial heritages.

This study provided an important step toward the evolution of research-informed practice that takes a less problem-focused view of interracial and intercultural differences. The lessons from this study suggest that many couples find their lives enhanced by their differences demonstrate relational strategies that enrich their lives. We hope that future studies and practice will continue to develop these important themes.

Discussion Questions

1. What are some results from the study of intercultural and interracial couples that have implications for couples of the same race and/or culture?
2. What are some differences in the ways in which the couples in the study have to address intercultural and interracial as opposed to people who are not in intercultural and interracial relationships?

References

Berger, P., & Kellner, H. (1994). Marriage and the construction of reality: An exercise in the microsociology of knowledge. In G. Handel & G. G. Whitchurch (Eds.), *The psychosocial interior of the family* (4th ed., pp. 19–36). New York: Aldine de Gruyter.

Bischoff, R. (2005). Inter-cultural and inter-racial couples: The implications of the research on practice. *Journal of Couple and Relationship Therapy, 4*(4), 79–83.

Bratter, J. L., & Eschbach, K. (2006). What about the couple? Interracial marriage and psychological distress. *Social Science Research, 55*(4), 1025–1047.

Bratter, J. L., & King, R. B. (2008). "But will it last?": Marital instability among interracial and same-race-couples. *Family Relations, 57*(2), 160–171.

Bronfenbrenner, U. (1986). Ecology of the family as a context for human development: Research perspectives. *Developmental Psychology, 22*, 723–742.

Charmaz, K. (2006). *Constructing grounded theory: a practical guide through qualitative analysis.* Thousand Oaks: Sage Publications.

Cheng, S. (2005). *The differences and similarities between biracial and monoracial couples: a sociodemographic sketch based on the census 2000.* Paper presented at the meeting of the American Sociological Association, annual meeting, Philadelphia, PA.

Childs, E. C. (2009). *Fade to black and white: interracial images in popular culture.* Lanham: Rowman and Littlefield Publishers.

Corbin, J., & Strauss, A. (2008). *Basics of qualitative research* (3rd ed.). Thousand Oaks: Sage Publications.

DeFrancisco, V. P., & Palczewski, C. H. (2007). *Communicating gender diversity: a critical approach.* Los Angeles: Sage Publications.

Dirlic, I., Miyahara, R., & Johartchi, T. (2006). *Affiliation to one's culture of origin and attitudes towards interracial couples.* Tacoma, WA, USA: Western Psychological Association.

Foeman, A., & Nance, T. (2002). Building new cultures, reframing old images: Success strategies of interracial couples. *Howard Journal of Communications. 13*(3), 237–249.

Fu, X., Tora, J., & Kendall, H. (2001). Marital happiness and inter-racial marriage: A study in a multi-ethnic community in Hawaii. *Journal of Comparative Family Studies, 32*(1), 47–60.

Gaines, S. O., & Agnew, C. R. (2003). Relationship maintenance in intercultural couples: An interdependence analysis. In D. J. Canary & M. Dainton (Eds.), *Maintaining relationships through communication: relational, contextual, and cultural variations* (pp. 231–253). New Jersey: Lawrence Erlbaum Associates.

Gaines, S. O., Granrose, C. S., Rios, D. I., Garcia, B. F., Page Youn, M. S., Farris, K. R., et al. (1999). Patterns of attachment and responses to accommodative dilemmas among interethnic/interracial couples. *Journal of Social and Personal Relationships, 16*(2), 275–286.

Garcia, M., & McDowell, T. (2010). Mapping social capital: A critical contextual approach for working with low-status families. *Journal of Marital and Family Therapy, 36,* 96–107.

Gergen, K. (2009). *An invitation to social construction* (2nd ed.). Los Angeles: Sage Publications.

Glaser, B. G., & Strauss, A. (1967). *The discovery of grounded theory: strategies for qualitative research.* New York: Aldine Transactions.

Greenman, P. S., Young, M. Y., & Johnson, S. M. (2009). Emotionally focused couple therapy with intercultural couples. In M. Rastogi & V. Thomas (Eds.), *Multicultural couple therapy* (pp. 143–165). Los Angeles: Sage Publications.

Ham, M. D. (2003). Asian American intermarriage: A socio-political construction and a treatment dilemma. *Journal of Couple and Relationship Therapy, 2*(2/3), 151–162.

Henderson, D. (2000). Racial/ethnic intermarried couples and marital interaction: Marital issues and problem solving. *Sociological Focus, 33*(4), 421–438.

Henrikenson, R. C. Jr, Watts, R. E., & Bustamante, R. (2007). The multiple heritage questionnaire. *The Family Journal, 15,* 405–408.

Hibbler, D., & Shinew, K. J. (2002). Interracial couples' experience of leisure: A social network approach. *Journal of Leisure Research, 34*(2), 135–157.

Hill, M. R., & Thomas, V. (2000). Strategies for racial identity development: Narratives of black and white women in interracial partner relationships. *Family Relations, 49*(2), 193–200.

Jacobs, J. A., & Labov, T. G. (2002). Gender differentials in intermarriage among sixteen race and ethnic groups: Special issue on race and ethnicity. *Sociological Forum, 17*(4), 621–646.

Karis, T. (2003). How race matters and does not matter for white women in relationships with black men. In V. Thomas, T. A. Karis & J. L. Wetchler (Eds.), *Clinical issues with interracial couples: theories and research* (pp. 23–40). New York: Hawthorne Press.

Karis, T. A. (2009). "We are just a couple of people": An exploration of why some Black-White couples reject the terms cross-cultural and interracial. In T. A. Karis & K. D. Killian (Eds.), *Intercultural couples: exploring diversity in intimate relationships* (pp. 89–110). New York: Routledge Press, a Taylor & Francis Group.

Karis, T. A., & Killian, K. D. (Eds.) (2009). *Intercultural couples: exploring diversity in intimate relationships.* New York: Routledge, Taylor & Francis Group, LLC.

Killian, K. D. (2001a). Crossing borders: Race, gender, and their intersections in interracial couples. *Journal of Feminist Family Therapy, 75*(1), 1–31.

Killian, K. D. (2001b). Reconstituting racial histories and identities: The narratives of interracial couples. *Journal of Marital and Family Therapy, 27*(1), 27–42.

Killian, K. D. (2003). Homogamy outlaws: Interracial couples' strategic responses to racism and to partner differences. In V. Thomas, T. A. Karis & J. L. Wetchler (Eds.), *Clinical issues with interracial couples: Theories and research* (pp. 3–21). New York: Hawthorne Press.

Knudson-Martin, C., & Huenergardt, D. (2010). A socio-emotional approach to couple therapy: linking social context and couple interaction. *Family Process, 49,* 369–384.

Kottak, C., & Kozaitis, K. (2007). *On being different: diversity and multiculturalism in the North American mainstream.* New York: McGraw-Hill.

Laird, J. (2000). Culture and narrative as central metaphors for clinical practice with families. In D. H. Demo, K. R. Allen & M. A. Fine (Eds.), *Handbook of family diversity* (pp. 338–358). New York: Oxford University Press.

Laszloffy, T. A. (2008). Therapy with mixed-race families. In M. McGoldrick & K. V. Hardy (Eds.), *Re-visioning family therapy: race, culture, and gender in clinical practice* (2nd ed. pp. 275–285). New York: Guilford Press.

Levin, S., Taylor, P. & Caudle, E. (2007). Interethnic and interracial dating in college: A longitudinal study. *Journal of Social and Personal Relationships, 24*(3), 323–341.

Leslie, L. A., & Letiecq, B. L. (2004). Marital quality of African American and white partners in interracial couples. *Personal Relationships, 11*(4), 559–574.

Llerena-Quinn, R., & Bacigalupe, G. (2009). Constructions of difference among Latino/Latina immigrant and non-Hispanic White couples. In T. A. Karis & K. D. Killian (Eds.), *Intercultural Couples: Exploring Diversity in Intimate Relationships* (pp. 167–187). New York: Routledge Press, a Taylor & Francis Group.

McGoldrick, M., & Hardy, K. V. (Eds.) (2008). *Re-visioning family therapy: Race, culture, and gender in clinical practice* (2nd ed.). New York: Guilford Press.

Moghadam, S., & Knudson-Martin, C. (2009). Gendered power in cultural contexts part III: Couple relationships in Iran. *Family Process, 48,* 41–54.

Murray, C. (2004). Clinical issues with interracial couples: Theories and research. [Review of the book Clinical issues with interracial couples: Theories and research, by V. Thomas, T. A. Karis, & J. L. Wetchler]. *Family Journal, 12*(3), 329–330.

Paré, D. A. (1996). Culture and meaning: Expanding the metaphorical repertoire of family therapy. *Family Process, 35*(1), 21–42.

Rastogi, M., & Thomas, V. (2009). *Multicultural couple therapy.* Los Angeles: Sage Publications.

Reiter, M. J., & Gee, C. B. (2008). Open communication and partner support in intercultural and interfaith romantic relationships: A relational maintenance approach. *Journal of Social and Personal Relationships, 25*(4), 539–559.

Rodkin, P. C. (1993). The psychological reality of social constructions. *Ethnic and Racial Studies, 16*(4), 633–656.

Rosenfeld, M. J. (2005). A critique of exchange theory in mate selection. *American Journal of Sociology, 110*(5), 1284–1325.

Solsberry, P. W. (1994). Interracial couples in the United States of America: Implications for mental health counseling. *Journal of Mental Health Counseling, 16*(3), 304–318.

Thomas, V., Karis, T. A., & Wetchler, J. L. (Eds.) (2003). *Clinical issues with interracial couples: theories and research.* New York: Hawthorne Press.

Ting-Toomey, S. (2009). A mindful approach to managing conflict in intercultural intimate couples. In T. A. Karis & K. D. Killian (Eds.), *Intercultural couples: exploring diversity in intimate relationships* (pp. 31–49). New York: Routledge, Taylor and Francis Group.

Troy, A. B., Lewis-Smith, J., & Laurenceau, J. (2006). Interracial and intraracial romantic relationships: The search for differences in satisfaction, conflict, and attachment style. *Journal of Social and Personal Relationships, 23*(1), 65–80.

Tudge, J. R. H., Mokrova, I., Hatfield, B. E., & Kamik, R. B. (2009). The uses and misuses of Bronfenbrenner's bioecological theory of human development. *Journal of Family Theory and Review, 1,* 198–210.

Yancey, G., & Lewis, R. (2009). *Interracial families: current concepts and controversies.* New York: Routledge, Taylor and Francis Group.

Collateral Damage in the Classroom

How Race and School Environment Influence Teachers' Attitudes and Behaviors Toward Their Students

By Ivory A. Toldson and Mercedes E. Ebanks

Editor's Introduction

This reading discusses racial disparities in teachers' attitudes and behaviors toward students. It uses data from a nationally representative survey of students to show that there are differences in perceived fairness and safety among students of different racial and ethnic groups.

This study examined how school safety and fairness directly influences teachers' classroom attitudes and behaviors and indirectly shapes student outcomes. Researchers used critical race theory and humanism as heuristic frameworks to conceptualize the process by which children of diverse backgrounds learn and develop in the classroom and how teachers experience the school environment. The study participants included all Black, Latino, and White students who completed the National Crime Victimization Survey: School Crime Supplement of 2009 (NCVS-SCS). Students of all races, who perceived their teachers as more caring, respectful, and empathetic, and less punitive, generally reported higher grades. Black students were less likely than White students to perceive empathy and respect from their teachers, even when they were making good grades. Similarly, Black students perceived their teachers to be significantly more punitive. Implications included suggestions for developing effective teacher education programs.

Racial disparities in discipline, grade retention, placement in special education, and assignment to honors classes suggest that Black students' in the United States have a very tenuous presence within the school system. According to an independent analysis of the National Center for Education Statistics High School Longitudinal Study of 2009 (Ingels et al., 2011), 17.9% of Black males and 13.7% of Black females have repeated a grade, compared to 8.1% for White males and 5.6% for White females. Twenty-five percent of Black males and 14.5% of Black females have been suspended or expelled from a school, when the national average is 9.8%. Twenty-nine percent of the parents of Black students reported receiving a call from the school regarding problem behavior with their son or daughter, compared to 14% of the parents of White students.

The extent to which racial biases in schools and classrooms contribute to racial disparities in academic success is a subject of debate. Today, of the more than 6 million teachers in the United States, nearly 80% are White, 9.6% are Black, 7.4% are Hispanic, 2.3% are Asian, and 1.2% is another race (Toldson, 2011b). Eighty percent of all teachers are female. Relative to the composition of P–12 students in the United States, the current teaching force lacks racial and gender diversity. Black men represent less than 2% of the teaching force, of a student body that is 7% Black male. By comparison, White female teachers comprise 63% of the teaching force, of a student body that is 27% White female (Toldson, 2011b). Some school advocates suspect that teachers who lack cultural proficiency may relate to Black and Hispanic students in a manner that undermines their potential. This study specifically examines how race and school environment influence teachers' attitudes and behaviors toward their students.

Literature Review

Race, School Environment and Student Discipline

Elevated public awareness and perceptions of violence have increased schools' reliance on suspensions, zero tolerance and other exclusionary disciplinary policies (Christle, Nelson, & Jolivette, 2004; Skiba & Peterson, 1999). One study found that Black students with a history of disciplinary referrals were more likely to receive negative perceptions and less deference from teachers (Gregory & Thompson, 2010). There are also general concerns about the reliability and subjectivity in disciplinary referrals (Vavrus & Cole, 2002; Wright & Dusek, 1998). Through ethnographic research, Vavrus and Cole (2002) found that many suspensions resulted from a buildup of nonviolent events, where one student often carries the brunt of many students' misbehaviors. However, some studies suggest that school culture and administrative leaders can mitigate high suspension rates (Mukuria, 2002). For example, regular monitoring and analysis of narrative disciplinary referrals have been recommended to improve precision and application of disciplinary measures that are consistent with the students' infractions (Morrison, Peterson, O'Farrell, & Redding, 2004; Sugai, Sprague, Horner, & Walker, 2000).

With respect to disproportionate suspension rates among Black students, many studies have noted the influence of ecological variables beyond the school (Day-Vines & Day-Hairston, 2005). Eitle and Eitle (2004) found that Black students were more likely to be suspended in majority Black grade schools. Cultural expressions of certain behaviors, such as movement and speech, may be misinterpreted as threatening to teachers who lack cultural awareness (Day-Vines & Day-Hairston, 2005). Another study revealed that natural adaptations to life in some impoverished areas indirectly influence the students' chances of being suspended from school (Kirk, 2009). Few studies have examined suspensions and disciplinary referrals among Hispanic students. One study noted Hispanic students' rates of suspensions and number of referrals were generally greater than Whites, but less than Blacks (Kaushal & Nepomnyaschy, 2009).

Improving teacher efficacy and teacher-student dialogue and aligning their mutual understanding of school rules also demonstrated effectiveness (Pas, Bradshaw, Hershfeldt, & Leaf, 2010; Thompson & Webber, 2010). "Whole-school" and schoolwide interventions that focus on schoolwide improvements in instructional methods, positive reinforcement, such as teacher "praise notes" (Nelson, Young, Young, & Cox, 2010), behavioral modeling, and data-based evaluation, have also demonstrated effectiveness (Bohanon et al., 2006; Lassen, Steele, & Sailor, 2006; Luiselli, Putnam, Handler, & Feinberg, 2005). Resilience and skill building among students also reduced behavioral problems and subsequent disciplinary referrals among students (Wyman et al., 2010). Attention to students' mental health may also reduce suspensions and disciplinary referrals among Black male students (Caldwell, Sewell, Parks, & Toldson, 2009).

Race, School Environment, and Empathy, and Respect

Research evidence suggests that persons of a privileged social group need to make conscious adjustments to develop authentic relationships with less privileged groups (Ullucci, 2011). Standard rubrics of evaluating teachers, such as knowledge, pedagogy and organization, are insufficient because they do not account for the vast diversity in the classroom or the sociocultural context of education (Nieto, 2006). Therefore, the teaching force, which is approximately 80% White, needs to develop mechanisms for teachers to cultivate empathy and respect for students of a different race. Empathy, moral and spiritual values, and self-interest are three factors that motivate people from privileged social groups to promote equity in the classroom (Goodman, 2000).

Exposing teacher educators to different cultures is one strategy to increase their cultural awareness and empathy toward racially different students (Houser, 2008; Marx & Pray, 2011). Multicultural training workshops have also been identified as a strategy to help teachers develop an awareness of their personal biases that may threaten their capacity to empathize with other races (Pickett, 1995). Some pedagogical methods have been evaluated that have demonstrated effectiveness in helping teachers develop and convey empathy toward their students. For example, one approach instructs teachers to allow students to self-reflect and connect classroom lessons to their community environment (Rios, Trent, & Castaneda, 2003). A sense of social justice, insight, and the ability to challenge conventional wisdom help teachers to cultivate an empathetic understanding of their students (Nieto, 2006).

A relationship between respect and academic success for Black males was found through analyzing three national surveys (Toldson, 2008). High-achieving Black male students reported that their teachers were interested in them "as a person," treated them fairly, encouraged them to express their views and gave extra help when needed. Teachers who were effective also routinely let their students know when they did a good job. Overall, Black male students who were successful perceived their teachers to be respectful people who treated them like they matter and nurturing people who builds up their strengths, instead of making them "feel bad" about their weaknesses.

Toldson (2011a) found that schools with more gang activity had lower overall levels of academic achievement among students. Students in schools with gang activity were also more likely to report being distracted from doing schoolwork because of other students misbehaving. These findings collectively suggest that, teachers and administrators in schools with more gang activity are perceived by students to spend more time confronting problematic students, which may compromise the academic priorities of the school.

Students in schools with less gang activity are more likely to report that teachers care about students, treat students with respect, spend less time punishing students, and are less likely to report that teachers do or say things that make students feel bad about themselves (Toldson, 2011a). Black students are significantly more likely to experience disillusionment with their teachers (Lewis, James, Hancock, & Hill-Jackson, 2008). Many teachers, particularly in urban school districts, may become disenchanted because they feel they have little control over the conditions and circumstances that weaken student achievement (Toldson, 2011a).

Theoretical Framework

Researchers used critical race theory and humanism as heuristic frameworks to conceptualize the process by which children of diverse backgrounds learn and develop in the classroom and how teachers experience the school environment. Critical race theory (CRT) examines White privilege and institutional racism. When viewing a racially diverse classroom with the tenants of CRT, a White teacher who takes a "colorblind" approach to teaching Black and Latino students, and ignores social inequalities, inadvertently promotes a racially prejudiced hegemony (Kohli, 2012). In previous studies, critical race theory has been used to demonstrate instructional techniques to develop agency and activism with students (Knaus, 2009), as well as the dynamic that leads to harsher punitive measures at majority minority schools (Zirkel et al., 2011).

This study also used humanistic perspectives to explore interpersonal dynamics between teachers and students that are conducive to a healthy learning environment. Humanistic psychology is based on the principles that in order for a person to grow and mature, they require a nurturing environment that provides them with genuineness, unconditional positive regard, and empathy (Rogers, 1992). Genuineness is defined as an openness and self-disclosure, unconditional positive regard is the feeling of acceptance, and empathy is expressed in the ability to listen to and understand. Humanistic theorists believe that both educators' feelings toward their students and knowledge of culture are important to the learning process (Barr, 2011). Humanistic teachers do not separate the cognitive and affective domains; rather they insist that schools need to provide students with a nonthreatening environment so they will feel secure to learn. Once students feel secure, learning becomes easier and more meaningful (Boyer, 2010).

Research Questions

Studies have found that teachers who lack cultural proficiency may not be able to relate to minority children and therefore may undermine their academic potential. Teachers' level of empathy, feelings of safety, and racial views can influence students' performance, grades, and disciplinary actions (Day-Vines & Day-Hairston, 2005). Toldson's (2011a) findings suggest that schools with more gang activity distract administrators and teachers from academic instruction and refocus priorities to problematic student behaviors. A noticeable void in the literature was research that examined the intersection of race and school environment on teachers' attitudes and behaviors toward their students. Four research questions are proposed for further investigation:

1. Do teachers' attitudes and behaviors toward students influence their academic success?
2. Does students' race influence teachers' attitudes and behavior toward their students?
3. Does the school environment influence teachers' attitudes and behaviors toward students?
4. Does the influence of the school environment depend on the race of the student?

Method

Participants

The study participants included all Black, Latino, and White students who completed the National Crime Victimization Survey: School Crime Supplement of 2009 (NCVS-SCS). The database was selected for this study because it had a clear indicator of academic success; had adequate Black and Latino adolescent representation; was a national survey that included multiple states and geographic areas; and had adequate measures of contributing factors, such as school environment and school safety measures. The database is indexed for public analysis at the *Interuniversity Consortium for Political and Social Research* (United States Department of Justice Bureau of Justice Statistics, 2010).

Procedure

Using data from the Bureau of the Census, the Bureau of Justice gathered data for the SCS as a supplement to the NCVS. The NCVS-SCS used a stratified, multi-stage cluster sample design. The Bureau of Justice described their selection of respondents as a "rotating panel design," in which households were randomly selected and all age-eligible individuals became members of a panel. Those selected in the panel were interviewed every six months for a total of seven interviews over a three-year period. The Bureau of Justice designated the first interview as the incoming rotation and the second through the seventh interview were in the continuing rotations. After the seventh interview, the household leaves the panel and a new household is rotated into the sample.

The NCVS-SCS surveyed 12- to 18-year-old adolescents who attended school in 2009. The survey population responded to questions regarding crime prevention measures employed by their schools, their participation in after-school activities, their perception of school rules, the presence of weapons, drugs, alcohol and gangs in their schools, and their fear of victimization at school. The NCVS-SCS used paper and pencil interviewing and computer-assisted telephone interviewing. Initial interviews were conducted in respondents' households and subsequent computer-assisted interviews were conducted by an interviewer calling from a centralized telephone facility using an automated version of the paper instrument to administer the questions.

The Census Bureau's Disclosure Review Board (DRB) vetted data collected for the NCVS-SCS. For confidentiality and anonymity, recoding procedures and a control number scrambling routine were performed before the file was released for public use. Responses to the NCVS-SCS are confidential by law under BJS Title 42, United States Code, Sections 3735 and 3789g and by the Census Bureau under Title 13, United States Code, Section 9.

[...]

Discussion

On a basic level, this study found that teachers' attitudes and behaviors toward students and the school environment had a relationship with academic success among Black, Latino, and White students. Students of all races, who perceived their teachers to be more caring, respectful, empathetic, and less punitive, generally reported higher grades. These students were also more likely than low achieving students to perceive their school environment to be safe, supportive, and fair.

Black and Latino students were more likely to feel unsafe in their school. Black students were also less likely than White students to perceive empathy and respect from their teachers, even when they were making good grades. Similarly, Black students perceived their teachers to be significantly more punitive. A Black student who reported C's was far more likely to perceive their teachers to be punitive than a White student who reported D's and F's.

The overall safety and fairness of the school influenced teachers' empathy and respect for Black students significantly more than for White students, as reported by the students. Black students at unsafe schools also reported more punitive teacher behaviors. Among students of all races, school safety significantly indirectly affected grades, however for Black and Latino students, safety indirectly affected feelings of support.

When revisiting the theoretical framework, the findings demonstrate that teacher empathy is associated with improved academic outcomes, which is consistent with a humanistic perspective. With respect to CRT, racial dynamics appeared to alter the school environment along racial lines. White students' response patterns demonstrated a structure whereby teacher empathy and respect was central to students' academic success, school safety had no measurable influence on teachers' compassion for their students, and teacher punishment had no measurable impact on students' grades. Contrarily, Black students' response patterns reflected a dynamic, whereby school safety significantly diminished the overall level of empathy and respect that students perceived from teachers and punishment from teachers significantly reduced students' grades.

The results of this study have implications for policymakers, curriculum writers, teacher preparation programs, and professional development and training sessions. Teacher preparation programs should expand multicultural class offerings and incorporate multicultural emersion experiences. Teacher trainees' educational process should allow students to examine their own beliefs, biases, and attitudes toward other races. Courses should include discussions and assignments that encourage students to understand their fears and vulnerabilities which will enable them to be conscious of their decision making process to be fair to all students regardless of race.

Readers should consider several limitations within the context of the findings. First, since data were collected about socially desirable attributes, some participants may have used impression management during self-report procedures. Although all surveys were confidential, it is likely that some respondents may have embellished grades and other desirable attributes, and denied suspensions and other negative attributes. In addition, the survey was lengthy and solicited information beyond this study's scope. The length may have created some fatigue and led to "Yea-Saying" or "Nay-Saying," whereby respondents tend to select only the positive or negative answers on the survey. Finally, this study measures students' perceptions and does not objectively record teachers' attitudes or behaviors.

A special issue of *The Journal of Negro Education* established guidelines for effective teacher education programs (Toldson, 2011b), which are relevant to the study findings. Overall, effective teacher education programs:

- Should prepare teachers of all races, genders, and socioeconomic backgrounds to educate diverse classrooms
- Should contribute to eliminating the achievement and discipline gaps that exist between Black students and students of other races
- Use modern approaches to helping teacher trainees understand diverse classrooms, such as the use of multimedia, documentary film, service learning, and volunteering
- Use effective recruitment strategies to diversify America's teaching force
- Understand the influence of federal- and state-level educational policies on building teacher education programs to accommodate Black students
- Respect the unique role of historically Black colleges and universities in preparing and recruiting Black teachers
- Actively work to combat institutional racism and culturally biased assessments to promote teacher diversity and when training teachers to serve diverse classrooms

Recommendations for Educational Intervention and Future Research

Research on the effects of teachers' attitudes and its effects on Black, Latino, and White students is a vital concern as to develop culturally appropriate strategies to reduce teacher attrition, prevent high school dropout, and mitigate the impact of high stakes testing. School leaders need to understand how the teachers' negative attitudes and behaviors towards students originate and what interventions improve the learning environment. Future research should focus on studying the benefits of teacher preparation programs. Multicultural awareness, teacher philosophy and theory, and classroom management courses should encourage open dialogue about self-awareness, identify their own biases, judgments, and behaviors towards other races.

Local and national measures and educational policies should address students' feeling of safety, fairness, and support by school personnel. A replicate study should address the limitations of the current study and design a more specific survey with fewer questions to prevent fatigue and possible false responses. Future studies should also investigate if there is a significant difference between Black, Latino and White teachers with respect to their attitudes and behaviors toward Latino and Black students and the effects that may have on students and their perception and academic performance.

Conclusions

There are several important findings from this study, which contributes to the current literature base on teachers' attitudes on race, environment, and behavior toward Black, Latino, and White students. The current research addresses a topic that is often ignored because of the discomfort with discussing biases and unfair treatment within the education system. Students' perception of their teachers' attitudes and behaviors affect their learning experiences. This has an accumulating and detrimental effect on the future of children and their education, which affect communities and society, and long-term effects on the lives of these children.

Discussion Questions

1. What strategies do the authors recommend for alleviating the disparities in discipline in schools?
2. How does the environment of the school influence student grades and sense of well-being?
3. How would you change schools in the future so that more equitable treatment of students is accomplished?

References

Barr, J. J. (2011). The relationship between teachers' empathy and perceptions of school culture. *Educational Studies (03055698), 37*(3), 365–369.

Bohanon, H., Fenning, P., Carney, K. L., Minnis-Kim, M. J., Anderson-Harriss, S., Moroz, K. B., et al. (2006). Schoolwide application of positive behavior support in an urban high school. *Journal of Positive Behavior Interventions, 8*(3), 131–145.

Boyer, W. (2010). Empathy development in teacher candidates. *Early Childhood Education Journal, 38*(4), 313–321.

Caldwell, L. D., Sewell, A. A., Parks, N., & Toldson, I. A. (2009). Guest editorial: Before the bell rings: Implementing coordinated school health models to influence the academic achievement of African American Males. *Journal of Negro Education, 78*(3), 204–215.

Christle, C., Nelson, C. M., & Jolivette, K. (2004). School characteristics related to the use of suspension. *Education & Treatment of Children, 27*(4), 509–526.

Day-Vines, N. L., & Day-Hairston, B. O. (2005). Culturally congruent strategies for addressing the behavioral needs of urban, African American male adolescents. *Professional School Counseling, 8*(3), 236–243.

Eitle, T. M. N., & Eitle, D. J. (2004). Inequality, segregation, and the overrepresentation of African Americans in school suspensions. *Sociological Perspectives, 47*, 269–287.

Goodman, D. J. (2000). Motivating people from privileged groups to support social justice. *Teachers College Record, 102*(6), 1061.

Gregory, A., & Thompson, A. R. (2010). African American high school students and variability in behavior across classrooms. *Journal of Community Psychology, 38*(3), 386–402.

Houser, N. O. (2008). Cultural plunge: A critical approach for multicultural development in teacher education. *Race, Ethnicity and Education, 11*(4), 465–482.

Ingels, S. J., Pratt, D. J., Herget, D. R., Burns, L. J., Dever, J. A., Ottem, R., et al. (2011). High school longitudinal study of 2009 (HSLS:09). Base-year data file documentation (NCES 2011–328). Washington, DC: U.S. Department of Education, National Center for Education Statistics.

Kaushal, N., & Nepomnyaschy, L. (2009). Wealth, race/ethnicity, and children's educational outcomes. *Children & Youth Services Review, 31*(9), 963–971.

Kirk, D. S. (2009). Unraveling the contextual effects on student suspension and juvenile arrest: The independent and interdependent influences of school, neighborhood, and family social controls. *Criminology, 47*(2), 479–520.

Knaus, C. B. (2009). Shut up and listen: Applied critical race theory in the classroom. *Race, Ethnicity & Education, 12*(2), 133–154.

Kohli, R. (2012). Racial pedagogy of the oppressed: Critical interracial dialogue for teachers of color. *Equity & Excellence in Education, 45*(1), 181–196.

Lassen, S. R., Steele, M. M., & Sailor, W. (2006). The relationship of school-wide Positive Behavior Support to academic achievement in an urban middle school. *Psychology in the Schools, 43*(6), 701–712.

Lewis, C. W., James, M., Hancock, S., & Hill-Jackson, V. (2008). Framing African American students' success and failure in urban settings. *Urban Education, 43*(2), 127–153.

Luiselli, J. K., Putnam, R. F., Handler, M. W., & Feinberg, A. B. (2005). Whole-school positive behaviour support: Effects on student discipline problems and academic performance. *Educational Psychology, 25*(2/3), 183–198.

Marx, S., & Pray, L. (2011). Living and learning in Mexico: Developing empathy for English language learners through study abroad. *Race, Ethnicity and Education, 14*(4), 507–535.

Morrison, G. M., Peterson, R., O'Farrell, S., & Redding, M. (2004). Using office referral records in school violence research: Possibilities and limitations. *Journal of School Violence, 3*(2/3), 39–61.

Mukuria, G. (2002). Disciplinary challenges: How do principals address this dilemma? *Urban Education, 37*(3), 432.

Nelson, J. A. P., Young, B. J., Young, E. L., & Cox, G. (2010). Using teacher-written praise notes to promote a positive environment in a middle school. *Preventing School Failure, 54*(2), 119–125.

Nieto, S. (2006). Solidarity, courage and heart: What teacher educators can learn from a new generation of teachers. *Intercultural Education, 17*(5), 457–473.

Pas, E. T., Bradshaw, C. P., Hershfeldt, P. A., & Leaf, P. J. (2010). A multilevel exploration of the influence of teacher efficacy and burnout on response to student problem behavior and school-based service use. *School Psychology Quarterly, 25*(1), 13–27.

Pickett, L. (1995). Multicultural training workshops for teachers. *Transactional Analysis Journal, 25*(3), 250–258.

Rios, F., Trent, A., & Castaneda, L. V. (2003). Social perspective taking: Advancing Empathy and advocating justice. *Equity & Excellence in Education, 36*(1), 5-14.

Rogers, C. R. (1992). The necessary and sufficient conditions of therapeutic personality change. *Journal of Consulting & Clinical Psychology, 60*(6), 827.

Skiba, R., & Peterson, R. (1999). The Dark Side of Zero Tolerance. *Phi Delta Kappan, 80*(5), 372.

Sugai, G., Sprague, J. R., Horner, R. H., & Walker, H. M. (2000). Preventing school violence: The use of office discipline referrals to assess and monitor school-wide discipline interventions. *Journal of Emotional & Behavioral Disorders, 8*(2), 94.

Thompson, A. M., & Webber, K. C. (2010). Realigning student and teacher perceptions of school rules: A behavior management strategy for students with challenging behaviors. *Children & Schools, 32*(2), 71-79.

Toldson, I. A. (2008). Breaking barriers: Plotting the path to academic success for school-age African-American males. Washington, D.C.: Congressional Black Caucus Foundation, Inc.

Toldson, I. A. (2011a). Breaking barriers 2: Plotting the path away from juvenile detention and toward academic success for school-age African American males. Washington, DC: Congressional Black Caucus Foundation, Inc.

Toldson, I. A. (2011b). Diversifying the United States' teaching force: Where are we now? Where do we need to go? How do we get there? *The Journal of Negro Education, 80*(3), 183-186.

Ullucci, K. (2011). Learning to see: The development of race and class consciousness in White teachers. *Race, Ethnicity and Education, 14*(4), 561-577.

United States Department of Justice Bureau of Justice Statistics. (2010). National Crime Victimization Survey: School Crime Supplement, 2009. In Inter-university Consortium for Political and Social Research (Ed.). Ann Arbor, MI.

Vavrus, F., & Cole, K. (2002). "I didn't do nothin'": The discursive construction of school suspension. *Urban Review, 34*(2), 87.

Wright, J. A., & Dusek, J. B. (1998). Compiling school base-rates for disruptive behavior from student disciplinary referral data. *School Psychology Review, 27*(1), 138.

Wyman, P. A., Cross, W., Brown, C. H., Qin, Y., Xin, T., & Eberly, S. (2010). Intervention to strengthen emotional self-regulation in children with emerging mental health problems: proximal impact on school behavior. *Journal of Abnormal Child Psychology, 38*(5), 707-720.

Zirkel, S., Bailey, F., Bathey, S., Hawley, R., Lewis, U., Long, D., et al. (2011). 'Isn't that what 'those kids' need?' Urban schools and the master narrative of the 'tough, urban principal.' *Race, Ethnicity & Education, 14*(2), 137-158.

SECTION V

Future Issues: Immigration and a Changing United States

T he lone reading in this section addresses the issue of immigration. Immigration has always been a factor in the United States, as we often refer to ourselves as "a nation of immigrants." However, today, immigration is a critically divisive issue for many Americans. This fact makes the consideration of immigration policy an important topic for the present and future.

Epilogue

Making Race in the Twenty-First Century

By Natalia Molina

Editor's Introduction

In this reading, the author discusses immigration past and present, and the politics of immigration in the contemporary United States. She starts with an overview of this issue and ends with a discussion of how the politicized nature of the immigration issue may play out in the near future.

Throughout this book I have demonstrated that race is not made in just one moment or by just one powerful person or group. Instead race is created across time by various players who attach different (and sometimes contradictory) meanings to both cultural and structural forces. Yet despite the multiplicity of influences that help shape our concept of race, common themes prevail. These themes are often molded and transformed, or even revived and recycled, by those in power to advance explicit and/or implicit agendas. The use of a relational lens deepens this understanding of race as *made* by revealing how easily racial scripts are adopted and adapted to apply to different racialized groups.

This examination of the historical experiences of Mexican immigrants and Mexican Americans also demonstrates that racial regimes do not stay completely intact, nor do they entirely disappear. For example, we saw that, although the 1848 Treaty of Guadalupe Hidalgo conferred citizenship on Mexicans living in the United States, in practice the widespread public perception of Mexicans as nonwhite often rendered them ineligible for citizenship. We saw, as well, that long after the nineteenth century had turned into the twentieth, *Mexican* continued to be imbued with negative meanings. Policies, practices, discourses, and representations portrayed

Mexicans as deportable, diseased, dependent. These depictions contributed to long-lasting representations of Mexicans that persisted far beyond the reach of the immigration regimes that institutionalized such views. These examples demonstrate a powerful reality about race and racism: it succeeds by repetition. Racial scripts work in part because they are not wholly new. Their familiarity itself generates credibility, making ideas about race that might otherwise be considered outrageous or flagrantly racist seem normal. Racial scripts make it both possible and permissible to consider racist ideas as simply common sense.

Just over forty years after its passage, the 1924 Immigration Act was drastically reformed by the Hart-Celler Act, commonly referred to as the 1965 Immigration Act. The 1965 Act's supporters, including President Lyndon Johnson, expressed concern that existing immigration laws did not sufficiently embody American democratic principles. They argued that an overhaul of immigration policy was in order. The broader context of the mid-1960s debate over immigration was defined in important ways by the civil rights movement, which sought to end the country's long history of racial discrimination, and by the cold war, which pressured the United States to strengthen its international image as a champion of a democratic way of life that stood in sharp contrast to communism. These overlapping domestic and foreign policy interests set the stage for a political consensus concerning the need for changes in immigration law.

The 1965 Immigration Act ushered in a new immigration regime, which, like the 1924 Immigration Act, changed the face of U.S. immigration in powerful ways. Most notably the 1965 Act abolished the national quota system. It also established an annual ceiling of 170,000 immigrants from the Eastern Hemisphere and 120,000 from the Western Hemisphere. The Act continued the changes first established by the 1952 McCarran-Walter Act, which included the policy of giving preference to the family members of citizens (particularly parents, spouses, children, and siblings), as well as to immigrants with professional, technical, and other labor market skills deemed valuable to U.S. employers. Two major changes ensued in the years following the passage of the 1965 Act: immigration increased dramatically, and the countries of origin represented in the largest immigrant streams changed considerably. Most surprisingly immigration from Latin America and Asia expanded swiftly.

Along with a major shift in immigration regimes, race relations in the United States were changing significantly at this time. Civil rights movements were reaching their apex, seeking an end to racism, demanding equal opportunity and the realization of the full rights of citizenship promised by the Fourteenth Amendment. The federal government responded in ways that marked a major change in how racial justice and discrimination would be addressed in formal channels. In addition to the passage of such legislative milestones as the 1964 Civil Rights Act and the Voting Rights Act of 1965, during the Johnson administration, the government began to enact affirmative action programs. These were aimed at increasing access to jobs and educational opportunities, with the goal of remedying past discrimination against aggrieved groups, particularly African Americans, but also other minorities, women, and the disabled.[1] Johnson inaugurated many of these programs, and he explained his reasoning on the matter in a now infamous quote: "You do not take a person who for years has been hobbled by chains and liberate him, bring him up to the start of a race and say, 'you're free to compete with all the others,' and still justly believe you have been completely fair."[2]

Americans have long been divided over whether or not the government has a duty, or even a right, to intervene in matters of equality and inequality. In the decades following the 1960s, some argued that anti-discrimination policies had swung too far from the center and were now resulting it what has been termed "reverse discrimination." Such attitudes are evidenced in the *Board of Regents of the University of California v. Bakke* (1978). Allan Bakke sued after the University of California at Davis twice denied him admission to its medical school. He claimed the university had violated his rights by admitting others under a minority quota system, while refusing him entry. The Supreme Court ruled in Bakke's favor, concluding that the university's decision denied Bakke his individual rights guaranteed by the Fourteenth Amendment.[3] By virtue of its being handed down by the highest court in the country, the *Bakke* decision effectively institutionalized the concept of reverse racism. After *Bakke* legal and social efforts aimed at ending affirmative action programs gained traction and continue to this day.[4] This decision is part of a larger logic of color blindness that actively ignores, and thus further entrenches, systematic racial inequalities in the present.

Racial Scripts in a Color-Blind Society

Many people believe that we of the twenty-first century are past the overt racism and racialization that has plagued the United States from its earliest days as individual colonies. Some commentators believe the civil rights movement and affirmative action ameliorated the worst of the country's past wrongs (such as slavery and Jim Crow segregation). Thus, they argue, there is no longer a need for a conversation about righting past wrongs or for initiating and maintaining affirmative action–type programs. Along these same lines, some people argue that mainstream America's racial sensibilities have shifted to the point where, as a group, we have become "color-blind." Since we no longer see "race," we no longer judge others by their race. For this group, the election of President Barack Obama is evidence that we are now "beyond race." In fact, according to this view, we are at the beginning of a new era of race making, or rather, of *not* race making.

I join sociologist Eduardo Bonilla-Silva and others in rejecting these views of the present as a postrace era. In his insightful book, *Racism without Racists: Color-blind Racism and the Persistence of Racial Inequality in the United States,* Bonilla-Silva presents extensive data from interviews that demonstrate how some whites, including those who would consider themselves progressive, and members of racialized groups who have benefited from what the historian George Lipsitz has termed a "possessive investment in whiteness,"[5] can believe they are color-blind but still engage in racist practices. By uncovering collective practices that continue to perpetuate racism, Bonilla-Silva draws our attention to the normally hidden structural aspects of racism, showing us why ceasing to talk about race does not make race disappear.

Even if as individuals we could succeed in willing ourselves to not see race, or at least to not act on our perceptions, the long reach of past racism in areas such as government lending, private real estate practices, zoning regulations, unequal access to health care, and disproportionate exposure to toxic environments is now institutionalized.[6] This kind of structurally embedded racism affects nearly every aspect of our everyday lives, advantaging some of us and disadvantaging others with respect to how and where we live, work, learn, and play, as well as positively or negatively affecting our ability to accrue assets, manage our health, and sustain a good quality of life.

This aspect of racism in America—the extent to which it is both invisible and everywhere—is why even when we think we are not talking about race, we are. Certain terms, such as *inner city* (ghetto) or *preppy* (white, upper-middle class), and certain subjects, such as welfare (government handouts to lazy minorities), are so imbued with racial meaning that they can and do convey racist ideas and attitudes beneath a veneer of neutrality or objectivity. A recent controversy involving the *New York Times* provides an example of this kind of invisibly racist terminology, and one that is directly related to topics examined in this book. In 2012 the *Times* came under criticism for its continued use of the term *illegal immigrant,* and a public debate ensued. Other news organizations, such as CNN, ABC, NBC, and the explicitly conservative Fox News, had ceased referring to undocumented immigrants as illegal in response to both internal and external pressures. Critics, arguing that the term is offensive and that its repeated use dehumanizes immigrants, requested that the *Times* use other terms, such as *unauthorized, immigrants without legal status,* or *undocumented.* The *Times*'s public editor, Margaret Sullivan, who represented the newspaper in many of these debates, defended the term as appropriate because it is "clear and accurate; it gets the job done in two words that are easily understood." Explaining the *Times*'s resistance to dropping the terminology, she said, "It's simply a judgment about clarity and accuracy, which readers hold so dear. . . . Just as 'illegal tenant' in a real estate story (another phrase you could have seen in *Times* articles or headlines) is brief and descriptive, so is 'illegal immigrant.' In neither case is there an implication that those described that way necessarily have committed a crime, although in some cases they may have. The *Times* rightly forbids the expressions 'illegals' and 'illegal aliens.'"[7]

Sullivan's argument divorces the term *illegal immigrant* from its historical production. The racial genealogy of the term can be traced back to its earlier iterations in previous immigration regimes, *peon* and *wetback*. The contention that the term is merely "brief and descriptive" also ignores the fact that in America, *illegal immigrant* is not race-neutral. The term, which once referred specifically to Mexicans, broadened to encompass all Latinos when, following changes in the 1965 Immigration Act, increasing numbers of immigrants from Central American, South American, and Caribbean countries arrived, searching for jobs or seeking refuge from war and political oppression. Likewise Sullivan's argument ignores the fact that having been exempted from the quotas of the 1924 Immigration Act (thanks to the clout of barons of agriculture and railroads who needed the cheap labor), Mexicans were then turned into criminals with new border surveillance. The Border Patrol was created, initiating a new era of policing policies and practices that increasingly linked Mexicans to illegality.[8] The term also fails to consider the decades following the 1920s, when debates, policies, and practices continuously reinscribed Mexicans as immigrants (regardless of the actual length of their residency or the status of their citizenship) or deemed them unworthy of citizenship. By papering over such a complex history, the term *illegal immigrant* does more to erase than to "clarify."

Moreover it is a descriptor that criminalizes immigrants. Prior to the passage of the 1924 Immigration Act, there was a one- to five-year statute of limitations for unlawful entry into the United States. With the Act's removal of this statute, immigrants who lack documentation are suspended permanently in a state of deportability. Although unauthorized residence is a civil violation, it is often portrayed as an aberrant crime. The circulation of criminalization discourse gives rise to another negative stereotype, the immigrant as criminal, in much the same way that the use of *peon* did in the early twentieth century. Then, in midcentury, the LPC label wielded by officials in California's Imperial Valley created a variant—the readily de portable, diseased Mexican—while INS raids throughout the Southwest solidified the notion of the Mexican as *wetback*.

In her earnest, "color-blind" defense of the *Times*'s continued use of a racially charged term, Sullivan is by no means a lone voice. We also see the concept of color blindness at work in the explosion of immigration legislation that has been proposed since 2006, all aimed at overhauling current immigration policy. The first of these efforts, the Sensenbrenner Bill, set the tone for the many legislative proposals to come. In December 2005 Representative James Sensenbrenner (R-Wisconsin) introduced H.R. 4337, a bill designed to dramatically change the consequences of undocumented immigration. Existing laws had already established undocumented immigration as a crime and endorsed the no-statute-of-limitation provision introduced in the 1924 Immigration Act (even though such a provision normally is reserved for a very small number of capital crimes, such as murder and kidnapping). Thus all undocumented immigrants live with the specter of deportation. The legislation Sensenbrenner proposed would have made undocumented immigration, such as overstaying a visa, a *federal* crime, specifically a felony, the highest type of offense in the criminal court system, on par with aggravated assault, arson, and rape. This change would transform the estimated 10 million undocumented immigrants into felons, making them permanently ineligible for citizenship. But H.R. 4337 did not stop there. The proposed legislation also sought to make it a federal crime to knowingly help any undocumented person. In so doing, that provision would place friends and family members in the untenable position of either having to turn in any undocumented person they knew or having to face the possibility that they would themselves be charged with a federal crime.[9] The bill did not specify a particular immigrant group as its target; it was clear, however, from media coverage, political debates, and public reaction to the proposed legislation, that the bill was understood to be aimed at Mexicans living in the United

States, a population of 8.5 million, 3 million of whom are in the United States illegally.[10] Sensenbrenner's Bill passed the House but died in the Senate.

Despite its failure to become law, H.R. 4337 triggered a flood of copycat legislation. From 2010 through the spring of 2012 alone, state legislatures across the nation proposed 164 anti-immigration laws. The bills are similar to each other and reflect both the content and spirit of the Sensenbrenner legislation. This commonality is not surprising, given that some of the proposed laws have been crafted by anti-immigrant groups, most notably the American Legislative Exchange Council (ALEC), or their content has been vetted by attorney Kris Kobach. Kobach helped devise the leviathan bill in the latest round of state legislation, Arizona's anti-immigration Support Our Law Enforcement and Safe Neighborhoods Act. Proposed as S.B. 1070, this legislation passed the Arizona legislature under its carefully crafted, race-neutral title in April 2010. It has since served as a model for laws in other states. Meanwhile Kobach, who is the secretary of state of Kansas, has acted as a consultant on numerous anti-immigration proposals in other states. He also serves as counsel to the Immigration Law Reform Institute, which is the legal arm of the virulently anti-immigrant Federation for American Immigration Reform. The other key source of model anti-immigration legislation, ALEC, is a powerful organization whose members include legislators and corporate leaders. Despite the group's bill-crafting activities, the organization maintains that it is not a lobby.[11] Because some of the immigration bills introduced in state legislatures originally were workshopped at ALEC meetings, the bills are strikingly similar; some even share the same name (gleaned from S.B. 1070). Significant funding for these state-level proposals can be traced to companies that own privately operated prisons. The private prison industry was a particularly strong supporter of S.B. 1070, suggesting economic motives behind that law.[12] Critics of the country's burgeoning prison system call it "the prison industrial complex" because of its rapid growth since the 1980s, an expansion that has far outpaced crime rates, indicating that this system is more likely about profits than about crime and punishment.[13]

Anti-immigration bills have been successfully enacted by legislatures in Arizona, Alabama, Georgia, Indiana, South Carolina, and Utah. Many of these new laws have been stayed when challenged in court by the federal government and/or civil rights groups. Even when they are short-lived, however, these kinds of laws are significant because they signal the emergence of a "new immigration regime," marked, as in the past, by a long era of public and private debate about immigration. Unlike the debates that characterized the 1924 Immigration Act, of which Mexicans were the explicit target, today legislators propose bills that purport to be race-neutral efforts to strengthen law enforcement. That the underlying intent of the latest round of laws is quite different becomes evident when the "wrong" people are snared in this immigration net. Events following the implementation of a new law in Alabama provide a case in point.

Alabama's law, H.B. 56, was passed in 2011 as the Beason-Hammon Alabama Taxpayer and Citizen Protection Act. This law stands out from the other Arizona copycat laws because of its draconian measures. It is regarded as the most severe of the state immigration bills that have passed to date. Among other provisions, it permits police officers to act as immigration agents.[14] If, in the course of routine stops, police officers suspect persons of being undocumented, they are allowed to demand proof of their legal status. The law bars undocumented immigrants from receiving any public funding at the state level, which would include schooling and health care. Anyone who knowingly "aids or abets" an undocumented immigrant (a provision that could mean anything from hiring to living with or coming to the emergency assistance of such a person) is subject to prosecution. Law officers have the right to ask any person to produce identification to prove legal residence, and in situations involving driving, to produce a valid driver's license.[15]

Supporters of the Alabama law (and others like it) argue that this legislation is race-neutral. The questionable nature of that contention was revealed in the aftermath of two traffic stops that occurred in Alabama in November 2011. In the first incident, an Alabama police officer pulled over the driver of a rental car that had improper tags on its license plate. The driver turned out to be a German Mercedes-Benz executive.

(Mercedes-Benz operates a plant in Vance, Alabama.) He presented his German national identification card, but when he was unable to also produce a driver's license, the police officer arrested him. A few weeks later a second foreign national executive was stopped by the police while driving. This time the driver was a Japanese man, Ichiro Yada, a manager from Honda, who was on an assignment at the company's Alabama factory. The police stopped Yada at a checkpoint intended to catch unlicensed and/or undocumented Latino drivers. Even though he produced an international driver's license, a passport, and a work permit, Yada was ticketed for failing to produce a U.S. government–issued license.[16]

These incidents would seem to confirm the race-neutrality of the state's new law. The Alabama police apparently were ready and willing not only to stop non-Latino drivers but to ticket or even arrest them. It is what happened next that explodes the myth of neutrality. These cases caused a media uproar, making headlines nationwide. Why? After all, the ticketing, arrest, and even deportation of working-class and poor Latinos in Alabama (and elsewhere) do not make local news, let alone prompt national-level coverage. The November 2011 traffic stops were big news precisely because the drivers involved were not the type of person the law was meant to snare. In fact the two foreign nationals' corporate connections heightened the outcry. Policing immigrants is considered acceptable, at least by those who support H.B. 56 and comparable legislation, when it catches Latino immigrants; it clearly is not considered acceptable, however, when foreign nationals who are connected to global capitalism become entangled in the immigration net. The key point here is that although the legal language of a law may be scrupulously race-neutral, enforcement is racialized. In practice American anti-immigration laws are applied overwhelmingly to Latinos.

Another way to pursue this issue of racialized law enforcement is to contrast the media reactions to the Alabama incidents involving foreign businessmen with events that did not receive comparable attention. The stories on the former circulated much more widely than have stories involving civil rights violations of citizens of Mexican descent. In Maricopa County, Arizona, for instance, it has been shown that Latino drivers are five to nine times more likely to be pulled over than are non-Latino drivers. (The ratio varies by region within the county.) Officers routinely use "looking disheveled" as grounds for stopping drivers, along with the allegedly suspicious behavior of having passengers in the back seat of a vehicle, which officers claim can be an indication of human smuggling. Once pulled over, drivers and passengers might be arrested for "avoid[ing] eye contact" or for "appear[ing] nervous." In one case, a sheriff stopped a U.S. citizen of Latino descent. He asked her to step out of her vehicle and then told her to sit on the hood of his car. When she refused that directive, he slammed her against his car three times. The woman was five months pregnant. She was cited for failure to provide identification. In another case, officers followed a Latina U.S. citizen as she was driving home, on the grounds that her license plate light was out. But the officers did not turn on their flashing lights or direct the woman to pull over. When the woman tried to enter her home, the officers pushed her to the ground, kneed her in the back, handcuffed her, and cited her for "disorderly conduct." In 2012 the U.S. Department of Justice initiated a lawsuit against the Maricopa County Sheriff's Department and its sheriff, Joe Arpaio, for what the government alleges is a "pattern of unlawful discrimination."[17]

Racial Scripts in a New Immigration Regime Era

What is the role of racial scripts in the new immigration regime? We have seen throughout this book how racial scripts serve to readily communicate and reinforce which immigrants are and are not worthy of inclusion in the nation. A stark contemporary example is Maricopa County's ongoing "battle" against Latinos, citizens and noncitizens alike. County Sheriff Joe Arpaio has adopted a policy of "zero tolerance towards the criminal element." "Fighting illegal immigration" is at the top of this agenda. Arpaio's policies fail to distinguish not only between citizens and noncitizens but also between legal and nonlegal immigrants, those who have no criminal record and are employed but have overstayed their visas, and those who have committed crimes. Arpaio is extreme in his actions, but he is not alone. His actions are in keeping with the ever expanding connections between policing and immigration laws and agencies.[18]

Arpaio, who calls himself "America's toughest sheriff," is somewhat of a poster child for the anti-immigrant cause. His statements on the Maricopa County Sheriff's Department website suggest that he is determined to deserve this title: "The Maricopa Sheriff's Office, headed by Joe Arpaio, is one of the most talked about and nationally recognized Sheriff's Offices in the country today. Why? Because we are innovative. No other detention facility in the country, state or county, has 2,000 convicts living in tents; no other county or state facility can boast of a gleaning program that results in costs of under 15 cents per meal per inmate; few others can say they have women in tents or on chain gangs."[19] Arpaio has ordered the installation of immigrant detention tent camps outside the county's permanent detention facilities. The temperature in Arizona can reach over 110 degrees in the summer, with temperatures soaring much higher inside the temporary tents. The detainees are shackled and forced to wear prison stripes. Male prisoners are also made to wear pink underwear. Arpaio himself calls this makeshift prison a "concentration camp." The tent encampment is fully surrounded by an electrified fence. The conditions within this temporary prison are so inferior that they have been protested by dozens of civil rights and immigrant rights groups and have been the subject of an Amnesty International investigation. As happened with the detainees awaiting deportation in the jerry-rigged camp in Los Angeles's Elysian Park in 1954 during Operation Round-Up (see Chapter Five), these atrocities in Maricopa County did not take place behind the scenes in some hidden location. Arpaio's "concentration camp" stands in plain sight, just outside of Phoenix, the fifth largest city in the country.

Many of Arpaio's tactics rely on racial scripts that readily communicate that those in the camp have not only committed a crime but are deviant in other ways as well.[20] These signs are readily understandable to us because they revisit and revise past scripts, some of which are specific to Mexicans and some of which are not. By ordering Mexicans in the camps to wear wide-striped prison uniforms, Arpaio encourages us to connect them to the Jews forced into Nazi concentration camps and to African Americans incarcerated in the convict leasing camps that were established in the South after the abolishment of slavery to ensure the continuation of a cheap labor supply.[21] We recognize the color pink as female-gendered and thus as intended to emasculate male detainees who are forced to wear pink socks, underwear, and bracelets.[22] The strategy also echoes a practice common in Nazi concentration camps, where gay prisoners were forced to wear a pink triangle on their uniforms. These distinct histories and particular material conditions remind us that racialization is not homogeneous; they are also evidence of the ways racial scripts produced throughout history can be borrowed and tailored for use in other settings and time periods.

Counterscripts for a New Immigration Regime

Just as we see old and new racial scripts circulating during this new immigration regime, we also see resistance. These counterscripts teach us about moments of possibility as longtime activists, first-time protesters, attorneys, religious leaders and church members, and an array of other people pursue common cause across the color line and also across citizenship lines. In a social and legal climate wherein an individual can become an outcast or the target of a public campaign or even be prosecuted for aiding an undocumented immigrant, citizens helping noncitizens draws attention to the humanitarian grounds for these efforts, as well as the civil rights grounds. This important aspect of protesting immigration legislation that criminalizes immigrants marks the work of Lydia Guzman, a Mexican American who lives in Maricopa County. Guzman developed an advocacy organization, Respect-Respeto, to warn the undocumented community about immigration sweeps. She is willing to risk becoming a police target herself for coming to the aid of immigrants because she sees the Respect-Respeto warning systems as a way to protect families. The system helps to ensure that the children of detained or deported adults remain safe and cared for in their parents' or regular caregivers' absence.[23]

Mary Rose Wilcox, who serves on the Maricopa County Board of Supervisors, is a fourth-generation Mexican American, an outspoken advocate for comprehensive immigration reform, and a vocal critic of the Maricopa County Sheriff's Department. Her actions led to her being targeted and falsely accused in a series of corruption charges. The judge who dismissed the case against Wilcox cited a connection between the county attorney, Andrew Thomas, and Sheriff Arpaio as having improperly motivated the charges leveled against her.[24]

These women are not alone in their efforts to expose injustice in Maricopa County. Various immigrant rights and civil rights groups, as well as religious delegations, also have protested the Sheriff's Department's practices, particularly its tent prison. In 2012 a large delegation of Unitarian Universalists wearing shirts that read, "We are standing on the side of love," massed in front of the tent encampment. The delegates chanted "We are with you" in Spanish and English, hoping the detained immigrants would be able to hear that pledge of solidarity.[25] Others, like the punk rock band Desaparacidos, have spotlighted the abusive powers of the Maricopa County Sheriff's Department and linked them to histories of extralegal violence by groups such as the KKK. In 2012 the band released MariKKKopa, a song in which they call out the routine practices of the Sheriff's Department, such as widespread round-ups of immigrants, disregard for warrants when searching immigrants' homes (during raids conducted in the middle of the night), and the physical abuse of immigrants.[26]

These individual actors and groups are following in the antiracist tradition established by many before them who also fought back with counterscripts, reaching across normally divisive barriers. Martin Luther King Jr. is remembered for fighting for racial justice, but one of his last organizing efforts was the Poor People's Campaign, which was designed to prompt the government to meet the needs of the poor in terms of jobs, health care, and housing. Malcolm X, a Nation of Islam leader who later founded the Muslim Mosque,

Figure 19.1 The Rev. Leslie Takahashi Morris and the Rev. Susan Frederick Gray were part of a delegation of religious leaders who visited "Tent City," Maricopa County, Arizona. Photo © 2012 Dea Brayden, Unitarian Universalist Association.

was an avowed black separatist. In the years before he was assassinated, having been influenced by his experiences abroad, he began to embrace Islam's universalism. As a result, his stance shifted toward a Third World movement approach similar to the politics of Che Guevara, the Argentine Marxist revolutionary. At various times unlikely alliances have formed in cities with diverse populations, such as Los Angeles. There, in the conservative climate of the cold war, Mexican Americans, African Americans, Japanese Americans, and Jews came together to protect and advance their communities. More recently, in March 2010, University of California, San Diego students protested increasing budget cuts that threaten to price some students out of an education. Championing social and educational justice and demonstrating a keen awareness of interlocking systems of oppression, the students drew connections between issues of class related to the looming budget cuts and wider struggles, such as the drive to improve the racial climate on campus and better the working conditions of custodial staff made vulnerable under a contract labor system.

Although immigration issues cut across a range of communities and interests, we often fail to perceive these links. When we allow connections to remain hidden, racial scripts are more likely to appear natural, a simple manifestation of "common sense." Understanding the relational nature of race and exposing the links sustained by the use of racial scripts brings us one step closer to denaturalizing these scripts and, in the process, challenging the dominant narratives and power structures they support.

Discussion Questions

1. How would you assess and evaluate claims of "race-neutral" laws? What evidence needs to be considered to make this assertion?
2. How is race "made" in the contemporary United States?
3. How do you see immigrants and immigration as changing the United States?

CPSIA information can be obtained
at www.ICGtesting.com
Printed in the USA
LVHW062115160921
697998LV00004B/21